# Global Mental Health

# Anthropology and Global Public Health: Critical Approaches and Constructive Solutions

This series publishes books at the intersection of medical anthropology and global public health that use robust theoretical and ethnographic insights to develop practical public health solutions. Using accessible language to communicate complex global health problems, they examine concrete failures and successes in global health through an anthropological lens emphasizing historical, ecological, political, and sociocultural contexts. They also showcase leading methodological approaches, both qualitative and quantitative. The series publishes books in two formats: Tightly orchestrated edited volumes consisting of original writing by leading scholars advance major themes and methods and provide instructors with important new tools for integrating medical anthropology and global public health into the curricula of both disciplines. Short, single-authored books focused on a particular global health problem are constructed in three sections: a broad introduction to the problem and literature to date; a case study illustrating key issues and methods; and constructive solutions, including broader implications for application in public health programs.

## Editorial Board

### Series Editors

Emily Mendenhall, Georgetown University
Peter Brown, Emory University

### Series Editorial Board

Peggy Bentley, University of North Carolina, Gillings
Svea Closser, Middlebury College
Clarence C. Gravlee, University of Florida
Craig Hadley, Emory University
Judith Justice, University of California San Francisco
Brandon A. Kohrt, Duke University
Kenneth Maes, Oregon State University
Mark Nichter, University of Arizona
Linda M. Whiteford, University of South Florida
Sarah S. Willen, University of Connecticut
Amber Wutich, Arizona State University

### Volumes in this series

1. *Pesticides and Global Health*, Courtney Marie Dowdall and Ryan J. Klotz
2. *Global Mental Health: Anthropological Perspectives*, Brandon A. Kohrt and Emily Mendenhall, editors

ANTHROPOLOGY AND GLOBAL PUBLIC HEALTH

# Global Mental Health
## Anthropological Perspectives

Edited by

Brandon A. Kohrt and Emily Mendenhall

Routledge
Taylor & Francis Group

LONDON AND NEW YORK

First published 2015 by Left Coast press, Inc.

Published 2016 by Routledge
2 Park Square, Milton Park, Abingdon, Oxon OX14 4RN
711 Third Avenue, New York, NY 10017, USA

*Routledge is an imprint of the Taylor & Francis Group, an informa business*

**Library of Congress Cataloging-in-Publication Data:**
Global mental health (Kohrt)
  Global mental health : anthropological perspectives / edited by Brandon Kohrt and Emily Mendenhall.
     p. ; cm. — (Anthropology and global public health ; 2)
  Includes bibliographical references and index.
  ISBN 978-1-61132-923-0 (hardback : alk. paper) —
  ISBN 978-1-61132-924-7 (pbk. : alk. paper) —
  ISBN 978-1-61132-926-1 (consumer ebook)
     I. Kohrt, Brandon, editor. II. Mendenhall, Emily, 1982- , editor. III. Title. IV. Series: Anthropology and global public health ; v. 2.
  [DNLM: 1. Anthropology, Medical. 2. Mental Health Services. 3. Health Services Accessibility. 4. World Health. WM 30.1]
  RA418
  306.4'61—dc23
                          2014041403

ISBN 978-1-61132-923-0 hardback
ISBN 978-1-61132-924-7 paperback

# Contents

# Foreword

## Vikram Patel

MY FIRST BRUSH WITH MEDICAL ANTHROPOLOGY was a short course at the London School of Hygiene and Tropical Medicine in 1992 (then, one of the few formal learning opportunities in this discipline available in London) and poring through hallowed volumes on anthropological perspectives on mental health in Africa in the library of the School of Oriental and African Studies. My focused reading was in preparation for a two-year fellowship to research depression in Zimbabwe. The concepts, methods, and knowledge I encountered were altogether different from what I had been exposed to thus far: essentially fairly orthodox medical and psychiatric training. And it greatly influenced my somewhat malleable mind: as I boarded my flight to Harare, I felt I was about to set out on a journey that would lead to my discovering that depression was an invention of Western psychiatry, the result of the medicalization of poverty.

Three years later, after an intensive period of mixed-methods research, I returned to India with an altogether different perspective, one that bridged the two poles of cross-cultural psychiatry. It was clear that there was a syndrome of suffering that bore uncanny resemblance to what psychiatry called "depression." But at the same time, there were important differences in how this presented in the primary care and traditional medical practitioner clinics of Harare (for example, few spoke of feeling depressed), how those affected and their care providers understood this condition (for example, few considered this a mental disorder), or what they called it (most often "thinking too much," a label that, as authors contributing to this volume describe, seems to have wider cross-cultural currency than "depression"!). Moreover, the experience of depression was deeply embedded in the person's social world, and factors such as marital conflict and income insecurity were key risk factors, just as they were in London. These experiences profoundly influenced my thinking about mental illness in "non-Western" settings and set the foundation for my program of research in India. Medical anthropology became an indispensable asset in my quest to understand mental illness and ultimately to help alleviate suffering through contextually appropriate interventions. This was my initiation into the then nascent field of global mental health.

Global mental health is a discipline of global health, "the area of study, research and practice that places a priority on improving health and achieving equity in health for all people worldwide" (Koplan et al. 2009). Like its parent, global mental health draws its inspiration from a range of disciplines, among which anthropology takes pride of place. Much of the recent academic and programmatic focus in global mental health has been on the implementation of evidence-based interventions for mental illness, particularly in low-resource settings. Optimizing the acceptability and feasibility of the implementation of these interventions, and enhancing their effectiveness, requires them to be exquisitely sensitive to contextual factors, especially cultural and social influences on mental health. It is crucial to ensure that they can be delivered by available human resources, typically involving task-shifting to community health workers or laypeople. The frameworks and methods rooted in anthropology—in particular, its avatar of medical anthropology—are integral to achieving these objectives. This book serves to document, through an array of original contributions, the now vibrant interface of anthropology and global mental health.

In doing so, this book makes unique contributions to both disciplines. The book traces the anthropological origins of current debates in the field related to psychiatric diagnoses, healing and health systems, and the personal and social experience of mental illness across cultures. The emphasis on ethnography grounds conceptual debates about global mental health in the experience of people around the world suffering from mental illness, as well as the experiences of family members and health care workers dedicated to reducing their suffering. The detailed narratives reveal the alarming fates when contextually sensitive systems of mental health care, which are consistent with the highest principles of human rights and scientific evidence, are not available. The ethnographic approach demonstrates the complex nature of the pathways that connect social determinants, such as poverty and migration, with mental illness. These pathways are influenced by context, and the direct impacts of social disadvantage on mental health—such as lack of access to water or exposure to violence—need to be uncovered and addressed. The contributors engage with the complexity of categorizing and conceptualizing these processes and frame their narratives in a manner useful to public health practitioners, clinical mental health practitioners, and policy makers. The incorporation of critical medical anthropology reveals that crude dichotomies of global versus local oversimplify both problems and solutions: in the end, both perspectives are relevant, to varying degrees in different contexts, to understanding the experience of and recovery from mental illness.

The three sections of the book demonstrate anthropological contributions to key challenges in global mental health. The first section addresses the social and structural origins of mental illness in a global context. The contributors' ethnographic narratives reveal that illness cannot be isolated from the context in which it occurs. Context shapes who is affected, and it sheds light on potential multisectoral interventions ranging from water resources and education policies to community-based psychosocial services. The second section addresses treatment approaches and access to care in both low- and high-resource settings. The contributors reveal that challenges at the intersection of culture and care are not limited to low- and middle-income countries but are aspects of mental health service systems globally. The final section explores the new and prioritized area of task-sharing of mental health care to nonspecialist providers, focusing on the experiences of the providers. These narratives uncover who becomes involved in these processes and their varied motivations, qualifications, and supervision, with illustrative cases from Ethiopia, Haiti, Mozambique, Liberia, and the United States.

This book is truly global in its focus on both high- and low-income countries' mental health services, thus addressing issues that affect all health systems. The contributions range from psychiatric residents in Boston and peer providers in Chicago to nurses in Liberia and community health workers in Haiti. Through the narratives of patients and health-care providers, the chapters taken together demonstrate a range of barriers to accessing care. Even when care is available, it may not reach those who need it. Additionally alarming are the narratives from the United States and Romania demonstrating failure to apply evidence-based practices and the concomitant harm this can do to patients and families. Task-sharing and related approaches in Haiti and Liberia represent potential solutions to both problems of access and evidence-based care. The anthropologists represented in this volume demonstrate an ability to engage with both psychiatric categories and cultural concepts of distress, offering a critically important bridge between the need to provide evidence-based care and the need to respect local knowledge and context. Their works illustrate the importance of idioms of distress such as "thinking too much," whether in Ethiopia, Haiti, or Nicaragua, as a way to express distress and as an avenue to identify those potentially in need of psychosocial and mental health services. Cultural concepts of distress are also crucial for appropriate training and delivery of services in a non-stigmatizing, culturally compelling manner.

The editors build on these ethnographic narratives to outline the role of anthropology for the future of global mental health. The editors highlight key areas for ethnography to inform both broad socioeconomic and targeted clinical interventions. They call for ethnographies of health systems and health system change. They call for growth in cadres of medical anthropologists from low- and middle-income countries. Indeed, building the capacity of medical anthropologists in these settings is critically important for the growth and relevance of the discipline to global health and as a means to influence local practice, and is a central responsibility of anthropologists from high-income countries. The involvement of anthropologists and the use of ethnographic methods should be standard practice to address the challenges faced in achieving the vision of mental health for all, everywhere.

## Reference

Koplan, J. P., Bond, T. C., Merson, M. H., Reddy, K. S., Rodriguez, M. H., Sewankambo, N. K., and Wasserheit, J. N., for the Consortium of Universities for Global Health Executive Board. (2009). Towards a common definition of global health. *Lancet* 373 (9679): 1993–1995.

# Acknowledgments

THIS BOOK IS A COMPILATION OF YEARS OF FIELDWORK and commitment to anthropology and global mental health, summarized in narrative after narrative in the pages to follow. We are grateful for the many people around the world who have participated in our research studies, educating us about the ways of experiencing, coping, and surviving various forms of mental illness. Our work would be impossible without our interlocutors who share their time, cultural knowledge, personal stories, and perceptions on the worlds in which they live.

As opposed to lone anthropologists working in isolation, many of the contributors to this book work in partnership and solidarity with scholars from around the world. Indeed, many of the chapters in the pages to follow come from years of research and collaboration. In some cases, these are stand-alone ethnographic projects that benefited from the guidance of or contacts with other scholars in-country. Others are small ethnographic projects that are part of larger mixed-methods studies. And in some cases, these chapters stem from years of collaboration and dedication of interdisciplinary research teams, on which the contributors served as representative anthropologists. We believe this is a very productive engagement between anthropology and global health dialogues and are grateful for the many people we have worked with through the years. In our own work, we are especially appreciative of Janice Cooper, Mark Jordans, Wietse Tol, and Carol Worthman (BK) and Elizabeth Jacobs, Dorairaj Prabhakaran, Shane Norris, Victoria Mutiso, and David Ndetei (EM) for exemplifying the personal and professional rewards of such collaborations.

We are grateful for the commitment of the contributors, who agreed to write slightly differently than they commonly do, in order to put people's narratives at the fore. Their commitment to sharing people's stories and describing their interlocutors' experiences through these stories makes this book different from other texts about global mental health. We hope the readers agree that the authors have done an incredible job communicating their important work in engaging ways that provide context and personalization of deeply distressing experiences. We believe also that the contributors to this volume have demonstrated successfully that it is possible to survive trauma, cope with severe mental illness, and thrive amid adversity, and that there are many important approaches from global mental health that can make a big difference in people's lives.

Many of the contributors to this book have benefited from the mentorship of Peter J. Brown of Emory University. More than thirty years of educating medical anthropologists has left a legacy of students who carry on his passion and commitment. Peter's fondness for narrative and communicating complex problems through accessible and applicable ways is at the heart of this project. There is no way to sum up our collective gratitude: thank you.

This book is part of a series championed by (former) senior editor at Left Coast Press, Jennifer Collier Jennings. Her unremitting support of this book series at the intersection of anthropology and global health, focused on critical problems and constructive solutions, has been foundational to its success. Thanks to Anvita Bhardwaj for her assistance with the manuscript.

Finally, we are grateful for the people in our lives who make our work possible and each day of our lives better than the last. Thank you to Christina (BK) and Adam (EM), our partners whose love supports us, our loving parents who continue to stand by our sides, and our sweet children, Ceiran (BK) and Fiona (EM), who bring more love and laughter to our lives than we ever thought possible.

Introduction
# Anthropological Perspectives on Global Mental Health
Brandon A. Kohrt and Emily Mendenhall

## Naresh's Story

"We were very relieved when the psychiatrist told us that Naresh did not have a mental illness. There is nothing wrong with his *dimaag* (brain–mind)," Naresh's mother explained a few weeks after she and her son visited the psychiatric outpatient department of a major hospital in Kathmandu, Nepal. Naresh, an 11-year-old boy living in Kathmandu, had been suffering from headaches, nausea, vomiting, sudden episodes of sweating and facial flush, and repeated visions of his neighbor's corpse hanging. The family had pursued multiple forms of treatment from pediatricians, gastroenterologists, psychiatrists, a clinical psychologist, and a traditional healer.

Naresh's father asserted that this was a gland problem because Naresh was nearing puberty. Naresh's mother expressed concern that her son's condition arose from a bodily problem, specifically a bout of typhoid four months prior. She said that typhoid had weakened her son and made his *man* (a Nepali term for the "heart–mind," the organ of emotion and memory) more sensitive. She then added that loss of his *saato* (a Nepali term for "soul" or "spirit," which also reflects a person's vitality) likely had played a major role, as well. He lost his soul when he went to the apartment of the neighbor who had committed suicide by hanging a few months earlier. The loss of his *saato* also made his *man* weak and caused him to have visions of hanging corpses. Naresh was uncertain about the cause of his affliction. Through the diagnostic maze of different health care providers, Naresh had acquired a list of diagnoses that included intestinal parasites, post-traumatic stress disorder, and soul loss. His family, like many others in the globalizing environment of transforming mental health care, was confronted with a variety of affliction labels and healing rituals that had existed for centuries in Nepal as well as diagnoses and treatments even younger than Naresh.[1]

*Global Mental Health: Anthropological Perspectives*, edited by Brandon A. Kohrt and Emily Mendenhall, 13–17. © 2015 Left Coast Press, Inc. All rights reserved.

## ANTHROPOLOGICAL PERSPECTIVES ON GLOBAL MENTAL HEALTH

Naresh's story introduces how mental illness can impact profoundly the well-being of individuals, families, and communities. His family's complex engagement with the mind, body, and spiritual aspects of their lives illustrates the complexity of mental health conditions and underscores the importance of understanding cross-cultural interpretations and treatments of mental illness. Like Naresh's story, the chapters in this book shed light on the experience of mental illness and its treatment through stories of a mother living in a water-scarce region of Bolivia, a teenage survivor of sexual violence in Belize, educated but unemployed young Ethiopian men, a young woman spending her life in a Romanian psychiatric institution, a community advocate living with severe persistent mental illness in Liberia, and an American woman navigating through psychiatric care after enduring military trauma in Afghanistan. Our goal is to explore the challenges in identifying, preventing, and treating mental illness across settings varied by culture and by access to health care and other material resources. Addressing mental health in global context is similar in some ways to dealing with infectious disease such as HIV/AIDS and malaria, maternal and child health problems, and chronic health conditions such as diabetes and cardiovascular disease. However, the influence of culture on mental illness symptoms, causes, and treatment also leads to unique aspects distinct from those of other health problems. Mental health and illness are thus especially suited to methods, theories, and questions in the province of anthropology. This book brings together a range of unique and innovative anthropological studies in the field of global mental health.

Anthropological perspectives are crucial to address the daunting and rapidly growing burden of mental illness worldwide. One metric used to understand this burden is called the global burden of disability-adjusted life years, or DALYs, a calculation of the impact of health problems on productive activity in society. This is an important measure for health conditions, including social trauma and mental illness. For example, interpersonal abuse is measured by the DALYs, and depression is the second leading cause of morbidity according to the DALYs (Murray et al. 2012). Mental and behavioral disorders are one of the largest contributors to DALYs, accounting for 22.5% of the global burden. This proportion has grown rapidly, with a 37.6% increase from 1990 to 2010, and the projected rise in the future is greatest in low- and middle-income countries (LMICs) in Asia, Africa, and South America (Murray et al. 2012). Apart from the DALYs, suicide is the most explicit measure of mortality related to mental illness. The numbers of deaths globally from mental illness are daunting and often underreported and understudied. Suicide accounts for more deaths worldwide than war and homicide combined: more than 800,000 people die by suicide each year (WHO 2011).

With this growing burden of mental illness worldwide, there is a desperate need for prevention and treatment. However, the processes used in other fields of medicine are inadequate to reduce the burden of mental illness. Mental illness cannot be diagnosed with a blood test or chest X-ray. Instead, diagnosis needs to take into account cultural aspects of symptoms and presentation to prevent over- or under-diagnosis. Prevention is not simply averting exposure to specific environments or other persons with an illness. Rather, it is intricately linked to every aspect of experience, ranging from social relationships to economic resources to other health conditions. Furthermore, treatment is more complex than simply delivering medications because mental illness stems not only from biology but also can develop out of social conditions and experiences. Thus, treatment requires culturally adapted psychological treatments and delivery of care that will not worsen mental health problems through stigma and economic burdens within the health care system.

There have been major advances in culturally adapted, evidence-based care in the past decade as well as major national and international movements impacting low- and middle-income countries. Yet, there remains a huge gap among the burden of mental health problems, the detection of those problems, and the availability of culturally and clinically appropriate care. An overall lack of economic resources, a lack of funds devoted to the health sector generally, and weak political will in some settings are common barriers to elevating mental health in low- and middle-income countries. There are also internal conflicts among the fields of public health, cultural psychiatry, and medical anthropology with regard to both the ends and the means of global mental health, which will be discussed in Chapter 1 on the history of anthropology and global mental health.

There is a growing interest in global mental health among scholars and practitioners in anthropology and global health. The purpose of this volume is to take global mental health issues directly into ethnographic accounts. Ethnography provides an opportunity to unpack the complexities of global mental health problems as well as social, cultural, economic, and political variants that may shape how mental illness is experienced and expressed across contexts. The ethnographic accounts in this book explore current studies of the leading global mental health issues in a world that has undergone significantly more globalization, dissemination, and creolization of understanding mental health and illness in the past thirty years. The contemporary anthropological studies bring these critical mental health issues to the fore by detailing the complexities of these issues at the individual, community, and political level. This book is divided into three sections: the sociocultural determinants of mental health and illness, treatment approaches and access across cultural and economic settings, and the current issues regarding a global mental health workforce and the concept of task-sharing.

In this book, we address three foundational issues at the intersection of anthropology and global mental health. First, using examples from Bolivia, Ethiopia, Colombia, and Egypt, we examine how social contexts, ranging from water availability to employment to political turmoil, all can contribute to mental health problems. This work is crucial because it illustrates that prevention of mental illness cannot be limited to psychiatric medication or psychotherapy. Because some mental illness stems from living social inequalities, preventions and treatments must address social problems apart from medical problems in order to elevate mental health. Second, through case studies from the Dominican Republic, Romania, India, and the United States, we discuss the challenges in existing treatment approaches, ranging from discriminatory barriers to care, to lack of access to appropriate psychological treatments, to potential misuse of treatments related to psychotropic medication and institutionalization. Because treatment for mental health is so often underfunded and therefore unavailable, it is important that we understand the potential problems related to poor access to mental health. Appropriate care attends to the whole person, not only the biomedical aspect of physiological and/or neurological problems. In the third section, we take a critical look at innovations in treatment strategies, with a particular focus on task-sharing as a way to employ nonspecialists to deliver mental health services in low-resource settings. Task-sharing has become the *en vogue* approach to mitigating mental illness in low- and middle-income countries because it can contribute to good mental health at relatively low cost. Together these chapters illustrate how, given the often limited funds in the health sector, drawing from existing health systems can be vital for elevating mental health care, despite the many complications of this approach.

The ethnographic accounts running through the pages of these three sections are the heart of this book. We introduce more details on these topical areas and the role of anthropology in them at the beginning of each section to illustrate the ties between the ethnographic accounts and major themes. Before we jump into these ethnographic accounts, however, in the first chapter we provide important information about the history of anthropology and global mental health to orient the reader into the historical debates, intellectual queries, lessons learned, and future of this discipline. Then, in Chapter 2, we introduce the methods utilized in this book, from ethnography to in-depth one-on-one qualitative interviews to standardized psychiatric assessments of depression and anxiety and even biological markers of stress. This methods section discusses how the contributors conducted their studies, thereby illustrating their in-depth approaches; references for further reading also are provided at the end of Chapter 2. Finally, our conclusion (following Chapter 19) is not one that brings together the major themes discussed throughout the book. Instead, it looks beyond the ethnographic chapters to suggest where we can go from here. There is a great deal to be done in global mental health research and practice, and this final chapter lays out eight potential avenues for anthropologists to contribute to improving mental health around the world.

## Note

[1] Excerpt edited from Kohrt and Harper 2008.

## References

Kohrt, B. A., and Harper, I. (2008). Navigating diagnoses: understanding mind–body relations, mental health, and stigma in Nepal. *Culture, Medicine, and Psychiatry,* 32: 462–491.

Murray, C. J. L., Vos, T., Lozano, R., Naghavi, M., Flaxman, A. D., Michaud, C., et al. (2012). Disability-adjusted life years (DALYs) for 291 diseases and injuries in 21 regions, 1990–2010: a systematic analysis for the Global Burden of Disease Study 2010. *The Lancet,* 380 (9859): 2197–2223.

World Health Organization. (2011). Suicide prevention and special programmes. http://www.who.int/mental_health/prevention/suicide/country_reports/en/index.html/.

Chapter 1

# Historical Background: Medical Anthropology and Global Mental Health

Brandon A. Kohrt, Emily Mendenhall, and Peter J. Brown

THERE IS A LONG HISTORY of scholarship and engagement at the intersection of anthropology and global mental health. Historically, mental health problems—in terms of diagnoses, research, and clinical practices—are inextricably linked to sociopolitical issues ranging from colonialization to migration to global markets and other issues (cf. Littlewood and Dein 2000). Prior to the 20th century, most mental health care around the world was provided by family members, and in some areas, asylums have been used for custodial purposes (Shorter 1997). Throughout most of human history, demons, spirits, sorcerers, and spiritual or religious processes have been seen as the cause of behaviors that we now consider mental illness (Clifford 1990; Hunter and Macalpine 1963; Zargaran et al. 2012). As such, religious leaders and traditional ethnomedical healers treated health problems considered mental illness in biomedical nosologies.

Within complex societies, secular understandings of mental illness marked the early development of their medical systems. For example, Galen and others in Greek medicine developed theories for severe depression and psychosis (Reiss 2003). Ayurvedic, Tibetan, and Chinese medicine also promulgated theories of constitutional and humoral balance that were used to understand, diagnose, and treat the symptoms of mental illness (Clifford 1990; Kleinman 1980; Kleinman and Lin 1980; Lad 2002; Wujastyk 1998). Asylums first came into use in ancient Persia and then spread to metropolitan areas of Europe. Such ideas and practices were then spread through colonialism, as the British, Dutch, and French instituted "lunacy laws" and asylum practices. The end of the 19th century was also a period of rapid growth and transformation in the theories and practice of biomedicine, including psychiatry and neurology. This was exemplified by German scientists, including Emil Kraepelin, Alois Alzheimer, Franz Nissl, and others, who searched for biological causes of mental and neurological conditions, which were still commonly considered spiritual afflictions at that time (Shorter 1997).

*Global Mental Health: Anthropological Perspectives*, edited by Brandon A. Kohrt and Emily Mendenhall, 19–35. © 2015 Left Coast Press, Inc. All rights reserved.

## ORIGINS OF MENTAL HEALTH RESEARCH IN ANTHROPOLOGY

Anthropology has been inextricably linked with the origins of global mental health research and intervention. In 1898, anthropologists Charles Seligman and W. H. R. Rivers (also a physician) were part of the Cambridge University expedition to the Torres Strait between Papua New Guinea and Australia (Littlewood and Dein 2000). The pair studied varied native concepts ranging from kinship, to perceptions of color, to modes of healing (Rivers 1924). Later in his career, Rivers influenced mental health care by taking lessons learned from observing healing in the Torres Strait and applying them to British soldiers receiving medical and psychological treatment during World War I (Kleinman 2006). On the other hand, Seligman's research looked for signs of mental illness and concluded that it was largely absent from the Torres Strait islanders. His conclusion, later refuted, is now known as the "Seligman error." This error refers to the assumption that an illness category does not exist in a certain culture if the symptoms known elsewhere are not observable. For example, if a diagnostic criterion for schizophrenia were "delusions of persecution by the CIA" and this were not observed in a specific cultural group, then that cultural group would be assumed not to suffer from schizophrenia. However, if the symptoms are viewed as culturally relative, then schizophrenia may be observable in that culture but in a different form or with a different content.

The Torres Strait expedition exemplified how symptoms of mental illness may vary from one cultural context to the next. Emil Kraepelin, considered the father of current diagnostic frameworks in psychiatry and a contemporary of Rivers and Seligman, also conducted cross-cultural work in mental health (Jilek 1995). Prior to World War I, he visited a Dutch asylum in Jakarta. There he observed Javanese patients to determine if they demonstrated similar symptoms to persons with mental illness whom he studied in Germany.

During the early 20th century, anthropology grew in the same academic and clinical institutions that promoted psychology and medicine. As anthropological fieldwork became more logistically feasible in colonies around the world, anthropological research was often utilized as a tool for colonial management. Much of early anthropology in the 1920s and 1930s supported colonial concepts of cognitive "primitivism" that were used to justify political subjugation (Bock 1999). For example, both Franz Boas (1911), the father of American anthropology, and Lucien Lévy-Bruhl, the father of French anthropology, wrote important volumes on the "primitive mind." These were group-level generalizations (Bock 1999). A remnant of the age of exploration and colonialism, "primitive mind" studies illustrated how the "other" is different, if not deficient, in mentality and pre-logical thought. Boas showed that these mental differences were culturally learned patterns of thought and not a reflection of biological differences in brain size or shape.

Anthropologists also were influenced by the work of Sigmund Freud and the psychoanalysis movement. A school of research that combined psychoanalysis and anthropology, referred to as "Culture and Personality," arose in the United States between the First and Second World Wars (Bock 2000; LeVine 2001). Pioneers such as Irving Hollowell, Ruth Benedict, Margaret Mead, and Gregory Bateson focused on group-level variation in psychology, emotions, sexuality, and child-rearing practices using a psychoanalytic frame of reference (Bock 1999). In a famous volume, *Patterns of Culture*, Benedict (1934) classified the modal personalities of different cultural groups as paranoid, megalomaniacal, Apollonian, and Dionysian. Benedict's discussion of "tradition" resembled Freud's discussion of culture as group neurosis. The "Culture and Personality" approach also spawned "national character studies," in which enemies of the United States in World War II were described and analyzed according to stereotyped group identity. Hallowell (1941) employed Freudian anxiety theories to describe how anxiety motivates behaviors differently across cultures, and his work contributed to the beginning of *ethnopsychology*, advancing the study of self, human nature, and motivation within particular cultural contexts.

After the Second World War, Anthony F. C. Wallace and other psychological anthropologists criticized the Culture and Personality school because of its reliance on descriptions of homogeneous and stereotypical "character" for an entire social group while failing to account for obvious individual variations within that group (Bock 1999; Wallace 1968). The tension between individual and group is important, especially in child development and adolescence. Mead's work on gender and culture (1949) examined how males and females were shaped by their societies and cultural ideals. She showed that incongruence between individual and cultural ideals of masculinity, femininity, and sexuality could be a source of distress and deviance. The fundamental principle of these findings is that culture creates a model of an appropriate "modal" personality and that social institutions (such as coming-of-age rituals or schools) shape how individuals think they should behave. The creation of gendered identities is a case in point, and Mead's book *Sex and Temperament in Three Primitive Societies* (1935) clearly illustrated gender variations. In later iterations of this approach, Beatrice and John Whiting (1974) demonstrated how such institutions became both the progenitors and resolving bodies of cultural conflict for individual development. The Whitings were Harvard anthropologists who developed new approaches to studying and conceptualizing childhood cross-culturally. They demonstrated that culture shapes the parameters for conflict during child development, and culture also provides the mechanisms children learn to resolve these conflicts. The nature and pathways of conflict resolution vary among cultures. In 1972, Francis Hsu suggested that the "Culture and Personality" approach be renamed "psychological anthropology."

## Differentiation of Psychological Anthropology, Medical Anthropology, and Cultural Psychiatry

There are some divergences among psychological anthropology, medical anthropology, and cultural psychiatry, which became relevant in the late 20th century. Psychological anthropology followed the ideas of culture, personality, and child development to focus on so-called "normal"—or culturally appropriate—patterns of thought and behavior (Bock 1980; Levine 1999; Lutz, White, and Schwartz 1992). This included the exploration of the cognitive categorization of the world as experience—that is, *how* people think about and interpret their worlds (Shore 1995). This approach was also linked to the structural anthropological analysis of such cultural materials as mythology, pioneered by Claude Lévi-Strauss (1949), which argued that universal human thought processes were based on binary oppositions (e.g., good/evil) and their transformations.

Medical anthropology and cultural psychiatry have focused on how social phenomena, such as suffering and social-psychological distress, influence the so-called "abnormal" phenomena in thought, emotions, and behavior, as well as the role of social, political, economic, and health institutions in shaping definitions of normality and sickness (Littlewood 1990, 2002). These fields focus more on cultural theories of illness causation and on the techniques of diagnosis and healing that practitioners utilize (Desjarlais 1992; Kleinman 1980; Weiss et al. 1986; Wikan 1990). For example, the ethnologist George Devereux and the Haitian psychiatrist Louis Mars defined the field of *ethnopsychiatry* as the study of local healing systems for mental illness and cultural contributions to psychopathology (Devereux 1980; Gaines 1992). As such, ethnopsychiatry could be considered one component of the medical anthropological field of *ethnomedicine*, which is the study of local medical systems whose medical and religious belief systems can be difficult to differentiate. Devereux's (1980) definition of culture was rooted in psychoanalytic theory in which universal unconscious conflicts were socially resolved. He considered shamans as neurotics and viewed healing ceremonies as producing vicious cycles of psychic conflict. Similarly, Lévi-Strauss described the "shamanistic complex" of ethnopsychiatry as involving three sets of beliefs: (1) the shaman's belief in his power to heal; (2) the patient's belief in the power of the shaman; and (3) the social group's belief both in the power of the shaman and in the likelihood that the patient would be cured (Lévi-Strauss 1963). He considered the climax of shamanistic curing rituals to be a form of *abreaction*, as described in psychoanalytic theory.

Because the modern medical specialty of psychiatry is embedded in the context of contemporary Western cosmopolitan culture, particularly European and North American culture, that field also has been the subject of anthropological investigation. For example, anthropologists such as Howard Stein (1985), Tanya Luhr-mann (2000), and Charles Nuckolls (1996) have examined the unconscious as-pects in both the training of psychiatrists and in the subjective cultural assump-tions built into their patterns of diagnosis and patient interaction. Similarly, the *Diagnostic and Statistical Manual of Mental Disorders*, often referred to simply as *DSM*, published by the American Psychiatric Association, is considered by many to be a cultural construct in which diagnostic categories are formed by consensus and change over time. Because the constructs are inherently malleable and chang-ing, the *DSM* is a text that has been interpreted and contested by anthropologists (Young 1995). One important critique of psychiatry with a long intellectual his-tory is that it remains blind to its own cultural assumptions and therefore is sub-ject to use as an instrument of social control by a hegemonic state apparatus. The "anti-psychiatry movement" has some of its roots in the historical analysis "mad-ness" by Michel Foucault (1964) and also is characterized by the works of Thomas Szasz and others (Nasrallah 2011; Szasz 1961).

The transcultural psychiatry movement began at McGill University in the 1950s with the work of Eric Wittkower, Raymond Prince, Jane and H. B. M. Murphy, and others (Murphy 1976; Murphy, Wittkower, and Chance 1964; Prince 1985; Wittkower 1970). These researchers were concerned with cross-cul-tural differences in causation, risk factors, and representation of psychopathol-ogy. The movement often employed Western psychiatric categories as the start-ing point for making comparisons. The International Pilot Study on Schizophrenia employed a similar framework, reaching the conclusion that schiz-ophrenia generally appears the same across all cultures, with similar findings iden-tified in three successive studies (Craig et al. 1997; Harrison et al. 2001; Leff et al. 1992; Sartorius, Jablensky, and Shapiro 1977; Sartorius et al. 1972). However, others have criticized the study for downplaying cultural differences, particularly the lower prevalence of chronic schizophrenia in non-industrial settings (Klein-man 1988). These cross-national studies have done little to alter conceptualiza-tions or treatment of the disorder; this is in part due to methodological problems in the cross-national studies (Cohen 1992; Edgerton and Cohen 1994; Patel et al. 2006). Early cross-cultural studies of depression have led to statements stereotyp-ing Western depression as more psychological—characterized by guilt and self-blame—whereas non-Western psychiatry is more somatic (Murphy, Wittkower, and Chance 1964). Current endeavors in transcultural psychiatry include the works of Laurence Kirmayer and Cécile Rousseau, whose focus includes aborigi-nal populations and immigrants in Canada from the perspective of symptom presentation, cultural influences on healing, and cultural consultation in clinical care (Kirmayer 2006; Rousseau and Measham 2007; Rousseau, Morales, and Foxen 2001).

## PUBLIC HEALTH AND BIOMEDICAL FRAMING OF MENTAL HEALTH

The intellectual framing of programs such as WHO's Mental Health Gap Action Programme (mhGAP), concepts such as DALYs, and initiatives such as Grand Challenges in Global Mental Health take biomedical psychiatric categories as the starting point for understanding suffering affecting emotions, behavior, cognition, and social relations. These include mood disorders (such as depression and bipolar disorder), anxiety disorder (such as panic and generalized anxiety disorder), stress and trauma disorders (such as post-traumatic stress disorder), psychotic disorders (such as schizophrenia), substance use disorders (such as alcohol use disorder), child development disorders (such as autism and attention deficit hyperactivity disorder), somatoform disorders (such as chronic pain and conversion disorders), cognitive disorders (such as Alzheimer's dementia), personality disorders (such as borderline personality disorders), and neurological disorders (such as epilepsy).

These categories have been codified most recently in the fifth edition of the *Diagnostic and Statistical Manual* (*DSM*) (American Psychiatric Association 2013) and in the tenth edition of the World Health Organization's *International Classification of Disease* (ICD) of mental and behavioral disorders (WHO 2004). The nosological organization, labels, symptom lists, and criteria for psychiatric diagnoses have changed considerably over the history of the *DSM*. As described below, medical anthropologists and others have produced critical analyses of the changing *DSM* as evidence of the "cultural construction" of definitions of normality and abnormality (Alarcon 2009; Kleinman 1991). Questioning the cross-cultural universality of biomedical categories and logic has been a regular and important theme in medical anthropology (Kleinman 1988).

The epidemiological data on global mental health has been problematic because of difficulties in measurement and a general paucity of population-based research. On a cross-national basis, the rates of different mental disorders appear to vary widely, with a large portion of the variance resulting from how measurement is conducted and what tools are used (Steel et al. 2009; Van Ommeren 2003). Yet there is convincing evidence that both the prevalence and incidence of these problems are higher than previously thought and are likely increasing, at least with regard to the percent contribution to disability worldwide (Hicks 2014; Murray et al. 2013).

## GLOBAL INITIATIVES IN MENTAL HEALTH CARE

During initial growth of the fields of anthropology and cultural psychiatry, there was limited application of this research to clinical and public health interventions due to a range of conceptual, economic, and political barriers. The main application of these fields was typically care of refugees from low- and middle-income countries in high-income countries. In the 1970s, the World Health Organization made the first attempts at developing initiatives for primary care delivery of mental health services in low- and middle-income countries (see Part III, this volume). Attention to the scope of the global mental health problem was revived with the publication of *World Mental Health* (Desjarlais et al. 1995) and a major WHO report (2001).

However, when the Millennium Development Goals were established in the United Nations Millennium Declaration (United Nations 2000), mental health was far from the front of the agenda (Miranda and Patel 2005). Almost two decades later, there are dedicated efforts by a select group of researchers, policy makers, and funders advocating for the representation of mental health in the global public health agenda, development goals, and interventions (Collins et al. 2013; Tomlinson 2013), with the rallying call that there can no be "no health without mental health" (Prince et al. 2007). Although mental health was included in the WHO's definition of health in its 1948 charter (1946), in reality the global health community has long ignored mental health issues (Collins et al. 2013; Miranda and Patel 2005).

The attention that global mental health has received in recent years may be linked to the growing use of the epidemiological research metric, the Disability-Adjusted Life Year (DALY), which combines both morbidity and mortality in measuring the global burden of health problems (Murray 1994). While the interpretation and application of the DALY are not without critique (Anand and Hanson 1997; Arnesen and Nord 1999), the use of the DALY metric has benefited research, intervention, and advocacy efforts by demonstrating that mental, neurological, and substance use disorders constitute a large portion of the global burden of disease (Murray et al. 2013). The global study of the DALY burden has also demonstrated that mental health problems are clearly not limited to high-income nations. In fact, they are increasing worldwide, particularly in low- and middle-income countries (Murray et al. 2013). Recognition of these facts was highlighted in 2007 with a *Lancet* volume that launched the Movement for Global Mental Health (MGMH) (Patel et al. 2011; Prince 2008). In terms of on-the-ground community health workers and mental health, the publication of Vikram Patel's lay guide entitled *Where There is No Psychiatrist* is of particular note (Patel 2003). All of this work anticipated the design of the WHO strategic action plan—the current Mental Health Gap Action Programme (mhGAP) approach, which emphasizes task-shifting (WHO 2010).

The mission of the MGMH is to reduce the gap between the burden of mental illness and the availability of effective mental health services throughout the world (Patel et al. 2011). The initial members comprised many of the authors in the 2007 Lancet Global Mental Health series, and it has now expanded to be a worldwide organization with open memberships and an international advisory group. MGMH has been housed at various institutions in low- and middle-income countries and is currently operated from the Public Health Foundation of India. Key advocacy points for the MGMH include (1) increasing funding for mental health services and personnel; (2) expanding research to determine evidence-based mental health treatments; (3) supporting development of government mental health policies; and (4) advancing the human rights of persons with mental illness (Collins et al. 2011; Drew et al. 2011; Patel et al. 2011; WHO 2010). Our goal through the ethnographic accounts in this book is to demonstrate how anthropology offers a crucial lens for global mental health across settings varied by economics, culture, and region. We explore the intersection of anthropology and psychiatry to identify constructive ways to understand and treat mental illness.

The World Health Organization, through mhGAP, has drawn attention to the mismatch between the burden of mental illness and the availability of appropriate treatment, including psychosocial interventions and psychotropic medication. This movement prioritizes task-shifting mental health care from mental health specialists (such as psychiatrists and psychologists) to mid- and low-level health care givers (such as nurses, health auxiliaries, and lay community health workers).

Nevertheless, mental health has been generally neglected in global health programs, both past and present. There is a range of reasons for this. First, its diagnosis and measurement remain problematic because there are no sure biological measures and tests to detect mental illness. This contrasts with other conditions that have biological markers for identification, including infectious diseases, such as malaria and HIV, and non-communicable diseases, such as diabetes, anemia, and chronic lung disease. Second, the stigma of mental illness deters general health workers from participating in mental health trainings and from implementing mental health services. This same stigma is also reflected in the attitudes and actions of policy makers, government officials, and donor organizations. Third, the marginalization of psychiatry and mental health within the field and practice of medicine also transcends to programs and policies in global health. This marginalization refers to the secondary status of mental health services as compared with putative physical health domains. The marginal status is reflected in the lesser competitiveness, lower compensation, and limited funding for mental health careers and services in both HICs and LMICs. These factors contribute to the limited number of randomized trials and other evidence-generating intervention research studies to establish effective standards of mental health care in low- and middle-income countries and other low-resource settings. Traditional notions about a "hierarchy of need" also have implied that mental health should only be addressed after infectious diseases, maternal and child health, and basic living standards. In other words, there is a common perception in global health that mental health treatment is a luxury add-on to be considered only after basic health services are provided.

Many of these "upstream" issues may be considered outside of the bailiwick of biomedicine. There are also cultural myths held by health workers and donors in high-income countries that LMIC populations are "poor but happy" and that mental illness is a disease of "civilization." These are myths that trace their roots to early research suggesting that mental illness did not occur in colonized societies, and to biological tropes of "short but healthy" in the field of global nutrition studies. There is also significant debate about approaches to mental health research within the fields of psychiatry, cultural psychiatry, and global mental health. These critical debates have been about diagnostic approaches, interventions, and health care systems and have included both medical professionals as well as advocacy groups representing mental health service users and their families. Moreover, there is a history of anti-psychiatry that dates back to the 1960s during the period of President Kennedy's Community Mental Health Centers Act. Such debates have highlighted crucial issues that require ongoing attention for the continued development of the field of global mental health, as seen in the recent priorities identified by the Grand Challenges Canada and National Institutes of Health (Collins et al. 2011; Collins et al. 2013; Tomlinson 2013).

## CURRENT DEBATES IN ANTHROPOLOGY, GLOBAL MENTAL HEALTH, AND CULTURAL PSYCHIATRY

This introduction has described how the fields now referred to as medical anthropology and cultural psychiatry have evolved over the past century. These disciplines have informed much of what is central to the mission of global mental health and have developed tools for critique that can be used to examine and advance the field. With the growth of the Movement for Global Mental Health, Grand Challenges in Global Mental Health, and initiatives such as WHO mhGAP, cultural psychiatrists, social scientists, human rights advocates, and others have been invited to contribute to these initiatives and to provide reflections on the direction and methods in the field (Swartz 2012). Patel (2014) identifies four categories of critiques about the global mental health movement: (1) psychiatric diagnostic categories are not valid cross-culturally (Fernando 2011; Summerfield 2008, 2012); (2) biomedical interventions have a limited role for socially determined health problems (Kleinman 2012a, 2012b; Summerfield 1999); (3) pharmaceutical companies drive the agenda and practice for the global mental health movement (Applbaum 2009, 2010; Biehl 2004; Han 2013; Petryna, Lakoff, and Kleinman 2006); and (4) global mental health is a form of medical imperialism (Summerfield 2012).

At a conceptual level, the critiques of global mental health relate to power, knowledge, and practice. For example, who has the authority to generate knowledge and evidence? What forces endow different systems of knowledge with greater power for dissemination and implementation? Who within health care systems and beneficiary communities is culturally authorized to provide feedback and critique in reshaping practice? How is such feedback provided and incorporated into practice? And what medical, social, and economic ends are ultimately served by cross-cultural, international, and global efforts in psychiatry? These debates are not unique to global *mental* health, as global health likewise struggles with similar challenges regarding power relations in diagnostic labeling, practice, policy, and funding (Biehl and Petryna 2013; Farmer et al. 2013).

The debate around "universal" mental health conditions is a heated one at the intersection of anthropology, cultural psychiatry, and global mental health. This complicated issue can be roughly separated into two viewpoints. On the one hand, researchers and clinicians find that using *DSM* definitions of mental health disorders across cultures and nations is useful for identifying, evaluating, and treating mental health problems in global context. This approach accepts that there are some mental illnesses (or collections of symptoms) that are universal. This concept of universality is an important one because it also brings up the issue of biomedical treatment as something that similarly can be applied across contexts. On the other hand, researchers find the notion of universal measures of mental illness to be a difficult one, because they perceive mental distress to be culturally and socially mediated. They believe that the way people experience and express mental distress, then, is rooted in local contexts that shape psychological suffering and therefore cannot be transported to other contexts. Thus, these two notions of global mental health gravitate toward opposite poles, one accepting the notion of universality and the other rejecting it. Exchanges from academics and practitioners at extremes of these positions have brought heated debates to conferences, listservs, and the literature.

Yet, as medical anthropologists engaged in global mental health, we recognize the importance of these debates for both theory and practice, and we are committed to a project of drawing them closer to the center. The chapters in this book, therefore, illustrate how cultural and social contexts shape mental health experiences as well as demonstrate the utility of locally derived *and* internationally standardized diagnostic tools and treatment protocols. We argue that triangulation of multiple methods is an effective way to capture the myriad factors that shape mental health from the individual to the community level. Moreover, we move beyond studies that examine only individual-level experiences of mental health—which has been largely the domain of medical anthropologists to date—in order to examine some of the systemic issues shaping mental health care services in resource-constrained settings.

Nevertheless, a major limitation of this book is that much of our research concentrates on people's experiences with common mental disorders, such as generalized anxiety disorder, unipolar depression, and post-traumatic stress disorder, as opposed to severe mental disorders. While there is some focus on severe mental disorders, such as schizophrenia (and other forms of psychosis) and bipolar disorder, our attention to common mental disorders in this volume reflects the larger unequal focus on common mental disorders within the discipline of anthropology. Within this arena, then, we can assume that local contexts play an important role in how distress manifests and how people manage their distress (by addressing it, ignoring it, or revering it). However, focusing on social and structural determinants of mental health conditions without considering the unique biomedical problems and necessities for treatment and recovery can be limiting. Thus, in this volume, we accept that there are some conditions that are experienced and expressed across cultures and recognize that this fact is extremely important for developing treatment strategies for interventions in resource-poor settings.

Anthropology, through the focus on collection of ethnographic data, is helpful to consider in some of the current debates within and about global mental health. Our goal is to de-essentialize the sides of the debate by examining actual case studies. One of the key issues that carries across all of the chapters here is the medicalization of suffering. The pioneers of critiquing medicalization, Margaret Lock and Nancy Scheper-Hughes, have pointed out that medicalization is a crucial process in terms of identification and treatment; however, the challenge is the "bracket creep," when what is considered an illness and what is offered as treatment are too tightly bracketed or constrained. The chapter by Emily Mendenhall (Chapter 12) demonstrates some of these challenges. A Mexican immigrant mother with numerous psychosocial stressors suffers from a range of mental health problems. However, rather than receive a psychosocial or psychotherapy treatment, she is treated through hospitalization and antipsychotic and antidepressant medication, although the latter may have contributed to her development of diabetes. Her interaction with the health community, then, is focused on diabetes management, and she fails to get wrap-around psychosocial treatment. Throughout the third section of the book, "Task-Sharing and Alternative Care Models," we discuss the concept of task-sharing, which, by allowing a broader range of individuals to become mental health workers (including local laypeople), may assist in addressing many psychosocial issues. Task-sharing has tremendous potential, as illustrated by trials of interpersonal therapy, cognitive therapy, and behavioral activation in various low- and middle-income countries.

Anthropologists have taken on various roles in the movement for global mental health. Applied anthropological studies have focused on reducing stigma in global mental health efforts, aiding identification and referrals of persons with mental disorders through promotion of local idioms of distress in health communication, and cultural adaptation of interventions. This study of mental illness by anthropologists spurred ongoing debate regarding the role of culture in suffering, especially suffering related to cognitive, emotional, and behavioral processes. Ultimately, anthropological perspectives provide insight into the ways larger social and cultural factors impact who is identified with mental illness, the labels and idioms used to describe psychological distress, the types of treatments available, the efficacy of treatment, and the social consequences and stigma for persons labeled with mental illness and their families.

## References

Alarcon, R. D. (2009). Culture, cultural factors and psychiatric diagnosis: review and projections. *World Psychiatry*, 8 (3): 131–139.

American Psychiatric Association. (2013). *Diagnostic and Statistical Manual of Mental Disorders (Fifth Edition): DSM-5*. Washington, DC: American Psychiatric Association.

Anand, S., and Hanson, K. (1997). Disability-adjusted life years: a critical review. *Journal of Health Economics*, 16 (6): 685–702.

Applbaum, K. (2009). Getting to yes: corporate power and the creation of a psychopharmaceutical blockbuster. *Culture, Medicine, and Psychiatry*, 33 (2): 185–215.

——. (2010). Shadow science: Zyprexa, Eli Lilly and the globalization of pharmaceutical damage control. *BioSocieties*, 5 (2): 236–255.

Arnesen, T., and Nord, E. (1999). The value of DALY life: problems with ethics and validity of disability adjusted life years. *BMJ: British Medical Journal*, 319 (7222): 1423.

Benedict, R. (1934). *Patterns of Culture*. Boston: Houghton Mifflin.

Biehl, J. (2004). Life of the mind: the interface of psychopharmaceuticals, domestic economies, and social abandonment. *American Ethnologist*, 31 (4): 475–496.

Biehl, J., and Petryna, A. (2013). *When People Come First: Critical Studies in Global Health*. Princeton, New Jersey: Princeton University Press.

Boas, F. (1911). *The Mind of Primitive Man*. New York: McMillan.

Bock, P. K. (1980). *Continuities in Psychological Anthropology: A Historical Introduction*. San Francisco: W. H. Freeman.

——. (1999). *Rethinking Psychological Anthropology: Continuity and Change in the Study of Human Action*. 2nd ed. Prospect Heights, Illinois: Waveland Press.

——. (2000). Culture and personality revisited. *American Behavioral Scientist*, 44 (1): 32–40.

Clifford, T. (1990). *Tibetan Buddhist Medicine and Psychiatry*. York Beach, Maine: Samuel Weiser, Inc.

Cohen, A. (1992). Prognosis for schizophrenia in the Third World: a reevaluation of cross-cultural research. *Culture, Medicine, and Psychiatry* 16 (1): 53–75.

Collins, P. Y., Insel, T. R., Chockalingam, A., Daar, A., and Maddox, Y. T. (2013). Grand challenges in global mental health: integration in research, policy, and practice. *PLoS Medicine*, 10 (4): e1001434.

Collins, P. Y., Patel, V., Joestl, S. S., March, D., Insel, T. R., Daar, A. S., and Stein, D. J. (2011). Grand challenges in global mental health. *Nature*, 475 (7354): 27–30.

Craig, T. J., Siegel, C., Hopper, K., Lin, S., and Sartorius, N. (1997). Outcome in schizophrenia and related disorders compared between developing and developed countries. A recursive partitioning re-analysis of the WHO DOSMD data. *British Journal of Psychiatry*, 170: 229–233.

Desjarlais, R. R., Eisenberg, L., Good, B., and Kleinman, A. M. (1995). *World Mental Health: Problems and Priorities in Low-Income Countries*. New York: Oxford University Press.

Devereux, G. (1980). *Basic Problems of Ethnopsychiatry*. Chicago: University of Chicago Press.

Drew, N., Funk, M., Tang, S., Lamichhane, J., Chavez, E., Katontoka, S., and Saraceno, B. (2011). Human rights violations of people with mental and psychosocial disabilities: an unresolved global crisis. *The Lancet*, 378 (9803): 1664–1675.

Edgerton, R. B., and Cohen, A. (1994). Culture and schizophrenia: the DOSMD challenge. *British Journal of Psychiatry*, 164 (2): 222–231.

Farmer, P., Kim, J., Kleinman, A., and Basilico, M. (2013). *Reimagining Global Health: An Introduction*. Berkeley: University of California Press.

Fernando, S. (2011). A "global" mental health program or markets for Big Pharma? *Open Mind* (September/October): 22.

Foucault, M. (1964). *Madness and Civilization: A History of Insanity in the Age of Reason*. New York: Vintage.

Gaines, A. D. (1992). Ethnopsychiatry: the cultural construction of psychiatries. In A. D. Gaines (ed.), *Ethnopsychiatry: The Cultural Construction of Professional and Folk Psychiatries*, pp. 3–50. Albany: State University of New York Press.

Hallowell, A. I. (1941). The social function of anxiety in a primitive society. Reprinted in R. Littlewood and S. Dein (eds.), *Cultural Psychiatry and Medical Anthropology: An Introduction and Reader* (2000), pp. 114–128. New Brunswick, New Jersey: Athlone Press.

Han, C. (2013). Labor instability and community mental health: the work of pharmaceuticals in Santiago, Chile. In J. Biehl and A. Petryna (eds.), *When People Come First: Critical Studies in Global Health*, pp. 276–301. Princeton, New Jersey: Princeton University Press.

Harrison, G., Hopper, K., Craig, T., Laska, E., Siegel, C., Wanderling, J., and Wiersma, D. (2001). Recovery from psychotic illness: a 15- and 25-year international follow-up study. *British Journal of Psychiatry*, 178: 506–517.

Hicks, M. (2014). Epidemiology of mental health in conflict-affected populations. *The Lancet Global Health*, 2: 249-e250.

Hsu, F. L. K. (ed.). (1972). *Psychological Anthropology: Approaches to Culture and Personality*. Cambridge, Massachusetts: Schenkman.

Hunter, R. A., and Macalpine, I. (1963). *Three Hundred Years of Psychiatry, 1535–1860: A History Presented in Selected English Texts*. London/New York: Oxford University Press.

Jilek, W. G. (1995). Emil Kraepelin and comparative sociocultural psychiatry. *European Archives of Psychiatry and Clinical Neuroscience*, 245 (4–5): 231–238.

Kirmayer, L. J. (2006). Beyond the new cross-cultural psychiatry: cultural biology, discursive psychology and the ironies of globalization. *Transcultural Psychiatry*, 43/1 (March): 126–144.

Kleinman, A. (1980). *Patients and Healers in the Context of Culture: An Exploration of the Borderland between Anthropology, Medicine, and Psychiatry*. Berkeley: University of California Press.

——. (1988). *Rethinking Psychiatry: From Cultural Category to Personal Experience*. New York: Free Press/Collier Macmillan.

——. (1991). *Rethinking Psychiatry*. New York: New York Free Press.

——. (2006). *What Really Matters: Living a Moral Life amid Uncertainty and Danger*. New York: Oxford University Press.

——. (2012a). Medical anthropology and mental health: five questions for the next fifty years. In M. C. Inhorn and E. A. Wentzell (eds.), *Medical Anthropology at the Intersections: Histories, Activisms, and Futures*, pp. 116–128. Durham, North Carolina: Duke University Press.

——. (2012b). Rebalancing academic psychiatry: why it needs to happen—and soon. *British Journal of Psychiatry*, 201 (6): 421–422.

Kleinman, A., and Lin, T.-Y. (1980). *Normal and Abnormal Behavior in Chinese Culture*. Dordrecht: D. Reidel.

Lad, V. D. (2002). *Textbook of Ayurveda*. Albuquerque, New Mexico: The Ayurvedic Press.

Leff, J., Sartorius, N., Jablensky, A., Korten, A., and Ernberg, G. (1992). The International Pilot Study of Schizophrenia: five-year follow-up findings. *Psychological Medicine*, 22 (1): 131–145.

Lévi-Strauss, C. (1949). The effectiveness of symbols. In R. Littlewood and S. Dein (eds.), *Cultural Psychiatry and Medical Anthropology: An Introduction and Reader* (2000), pp. 162–178. New Brunswick, New Jersey: Athlone Press.

——. (1963). *The Sorcerer and His Magic*. New York: Basic Books.

LeVine, R. A. (1999). An agenda for psychological anthropology. *Ethos*, 27 (1): 15–24.

——. (2001). Culture and personality studies, 1918–1960: myth and history. *Journal of Personality*, 69 (6): 803–818.

Littlewood, R. (1990). From categories to contexts: a decade of the "new cross-cultural psychiatry." *British Journal of Psychiatry,* 159: 308–327.

——. (2002). *Pathologies of the West: An Anthropology of Mental Illness in Europe and America.* Ithaca, New York: Cornell University Press.

Littlewood, R., and Dein, S. (2000). Introduction. In R. Littlewood and S. Dein (eds.), *Cultural Psychiatry and Medical Anthropology: An Introduction and Reader,* pp. 1–34. New Brunswick, New Jersey: Athlone Press

Luhrmann, T. M. (2000). *Of Two Minds: The Growing Disorder in American Psychiatry.* New York: Knopf.

Lutz, C., White, G. M., and Schwartz, T. (1992). *New Directions in Psychological Anthropology.* Cambridge/New York: Cambridge University Press.

Mead, M. (1935). *Sex and Temperament in Three Primitive Societies.* Republished, New York: Harper Perennial, 2001.

——. (1949). *Male and Female: A Study of the Sexes in a Changing World.* New York: W. Morrow.

Miranda, J. J., and Patel, V. (2005). Achieving the Millennium Development Goals: does mental health play a role? *PLoS Medicine,* 2 (10): e291.

Murphy, H. B., Wittkower, E. D., and Chance, N. A. (1964). Cross-cultural inquiry into the symptomatology of depression. *Transcultural Psychiatric Research Review,* 1: 5–21.

Murphy, J. M. (1976). Psychiatric labeling in cross-cultural perspective. *Science,* 191: 1019–1028.

Murray, C. J. (1994). Quantifying the burden of disease: the technical basis for disability-adjusted life years. *Bulletin of the World Health Organization,* 72 (3): 429.

Murray, C. J., Vos, T., Lozano, R., Naghavi, M., Flaxman, A. D., Michaud, C. et al. (2013). Disability-adjusted life years (DALYs) for 291 diseases and injuries in 21 regions, 1990–2010: a systematic analysis for the Global Burden of Disease Study 2010. *The Lancet,* 380 (9859): 2197–2223.

Nuckolls, C. W. (1996). *The Cultural Dialectics of Knowledge and Desire.* Madison: University of Wisconsin Press.

Patel, V. (2003). *Where There Is No Psychiatrist: A Mental Health Care Manual.* London: Royal College of Psychiatrists Publications.

Patel, V. (2014). Why mental health matters to global health. *Transcultural Psychiatry,* 51: 777–789.

Patel, V., Cohen, A., Thara, R., and Gureje, O. (2006). Is the outcome of schizophrenia really better in developing countries? *Revista brasileira de psiquiatria,* 28 (2): 149–152.

Patel, V., Collins, P. Y., Copeland, J., Kakuma, R., Katontoka, S., Lamichhane, J., and Skeen, S. (2011). The movement for global mental health. *British Journal of Psychiatry,* 198: 88–90.

Petryna, A., Lakoff, A., and Kleinman, A. (2006). *Global Pharmaceuticals: Ethics, Markets, Practices.* Durham, North Carolina: Duke University Press.

Prince, R. (1985). The concept of culture-bound syndromes: anorexia nervosa and brain-fag. *Social Science and Medicine,* 21 (2): 197–203.

Prince, M. (2008). Introducing the movement for global mental health. *Indian Journal of Medical Research,* 128 (5): 570–573.

Prince, M., Patel, V., Saxena, S., Maj, M., Maselko, J., Phillips, M. R., and Rahman, A. (2007). No health without mental health. *The Lancet,* 370 (9590): 859–877.

Reiss, T. J. (2003). *Mirages of the Selfe: Patterns of Personhood in Ancient and Early Modern Europe.* Stanford, California: Stanford University Press.

Rivers, W. H. R. (1924). *Medicine, Magic, and Religion: The Fitz Patrick Lectures.* New York: Harcourt, Brace, and Company, Inc.

Rousseau, C., and Measham, T. (2007). Posttraumatic suffering as a source of transformation: a clinical perspective. In L. J. Kirmayer, R. Lemelson, and M. Barad (eds.), *Understanding Trauma: Integrating Biological, Clinical, and Cultural Perspectives,* pp. 275–293. Cambridge: Cambridge University Press.

Rousseau, C., Morales, M., and Foxen, P. (2001). Going home: giving voice to memory strategies of young Mayan refugees who returned to Guatemala as a community. *Culture, Medicine, and Psychiatry,* 25 (2): 135–168.

Sartorius, N., Jablensky, A., and Shapiro, R. (1977). Two-year follow-up of the patients included in the WHO International Pilot Study of Schizophrenia. *Psychological Medicine,* 7 (3): 529–541.

Sartorius, N., Shapiro, R., Kimura, M., and Barrett, K. (1972). WHO international pilot study of schizophrenia. *Psychological Medicine,* 2 (4): 422–425.

Shore, B. (1995). *Culture in Mind: Culture, Cognition and the Problem of Meaning.* New York: Oxford University Press.

Shorter, E. (1997). *A History of Psychiatry: From the Era of the Asylum to the Age of Prozac.* New York: John Wiley and Sons.

Steel, Z., Chey, T., Silove, D., Marnane, C., Bryant, R. A., and Van Ommeren, M. (2009). Association of torture and other potentially traumatic events with mental health outcomes among populations exposed to mass conflict and displacement: a systematic review and meta-analysis. *JAMA,* 302 (5): 537–549.

Stein, H. (1985). *The Psychodynamics of Medical Practice: Unconscious Factors in Patient Care.* Berkeley: University of California Press.

Summerfield, D. (1999). A critique of seven assumptions behind psychological trauma programmes in war-affected areas. *Social Science and Medicine,* 48 (10): 1449–1462.

——. (2008). How scientifically valid is the knowledge base of global mental health? *British Medical Journal,* 336 (7651): 992–994.

——. (2012). Afterword: against global mental health. *Transcultural Psychiatry,* 49 (3): 519.

Swartz, L. (2012). An unruly coming of age: the benefits of discomfort for global mental health. *Transcultural Psychiatry,* 49: 531–538.

Szasz, T. S. (1961). *The Myth of Mental Illness: Foundations of a Theory of Personal Conduct.* New York: Dell.

Tomlinson, M. (2013). Global mental health: a sustainable post Millennium Development Goal? *International Health*, 5 (1): 1–3.

United Nations. (2000). 55/2. United Nations Millennium Declaration. Resolution adopted by the General Assembly. New York: United Nations.

Van Ommeren, M. (2003). Validity issues in transcultural epidemiology. *British Journal of Psychiatry*, 182: 376–378.

Wallace, A. F. C. (1968). Psychological preparations for war. In M. Fried, M. Harris, and R. Murphy (eds.), *War: The Anthropology of Aggression and Armed Conflict*, pp. 173–182. Garden City, New York: American Museum of Natural History, Natural History Press.

Weiss, M. G., Sharma, S. D., Gaur, R. K., Sharma, J. S., Desai, A., and Doongaji, D. R. (1986). Traditional concepts of mental disorder among Indian psychiatric patients: preliminary report of work in progress. *Social Science and Medicine*, 23 (4): 379–386.

Whiting, B. B., and Whiting, J. W. M. (1974). *Children of Six Cultures: A Psycho-Cultural Analysis*. Cambridge, Massachusetts: Harvard University Press.

Wikan, U. (1990). *Managing Turbulent Hearts: A Balinese Formula for Living*. Chicago: University of Chicago Press.

Wittkower, E. D. (1970). Transcultural psychiatry in the Caribbean: past, present, and future. *American Journal of Psychiatry*, 127 (2): 162–166.

World Health Organization (WHO). (1946). Preamble to the Constitution of the World Health Organization as adopted by the International Health Conference, New York, 19–22 June, 1946; signed on 22 July 1946 by the Representative of 61 States (Official Records of the World Health Organization, no. 2, p. 100) and entered into force on 7 April 1948.

——. (2001). *The World Health Report 2001: Mental Health: New Understanding, New Hope*. Geneva: World Health Organization.

——. (2004). *The ICD-10 Classification of Mental and Behavioural Disorders: Clinical Descriptions and Diagnostic Guidelines*. Geneva: World Health Organization.

——. (2010). *mhGAP Intervention Guide for Mental, Neurological and Substance-Use Disorders in Non-Specialized Health Settings*. Mental Health Gap Action Programme (mhGAP). Geneva: World Health Organization.

Wujastyk, D. (1998). *The Roots of Ayurveda: Selections from the Ayurvedic Classics*. New Delhi: Penguin Books.

Young, A. (1995). *The Harmony of Illusions: Inventing Post-Traumatic Stress Disorder*. Princeton, New Jersey: Princeton University Press.

Zargaran, A., Mehdizadeh, A., Yarmohammadi, H., and Mohagheghzadeh, A. (2012). Zoroastrian priests: ancient Persian psychiatrists. *American Journal of Psychiatry*, 169 (3): 255.

Chapter 2

# Anthropological Methods in Global Mental Health Research

Emily Mendenhall and Brandon A. Kohrt

HOW RESEARCHERS COME TO KNOW what they know is intrinsic to one's disciplinary bedrock. Anthropologists are known for unconventional methods of exploring phenomena in the world, such as "hanging out." We call this ethnography, or participant observation, which includes spending time with people and learning how they know what they know and why they do what they do. This research method is distinct from other disciplines because it provides freedom for the researcher to explore the world without the disciplinary or methodological boundaries imposed, for example, by a questionnaire that has been developed apart from the people or problem the researcher is trying to understand. Such an approach often allows for a critical and in-depth exploration of how things work in a particular culture or community. Ethnography is a foundational method applied in this book.

In the past few decades, anthropologists have begun to couple ethnographic methods with methods from other disciplines to bolster understanding of certain phenomena and to speak across disciplines to various audiences. The medical and psychological anthropologists who have contributed to this book have drawn on ethnographic methods, life history narratives, and in-depth, open-ended interviews to develop an understanding of how the people in their studies experienced, remembered, and defined their life experiences. Many also used surveys to generate a base understanding of, for example, what people thought or had experienced, such as stress throughout their lives or consistent access to certain types of health care, whether biomedical or traditional. While for some contributors, qualitative methods were fundamental for learning about mental illnesses, many triangulated this approach with psychiatric inventories and even biomarkers to measure stress in the body. Psychiatric inventories can be used to evaluate the number of symptoms someone experiences that relate to mental illness, which then enables researchers and clinicians to determine if an individual might be categorized within a predetermined "mental disorder." While there has been some debate about what

*Global Mental Health*: *Anthropological Perspectives*, edited by Brandon A. Kohrt and Emily Mendenhall, 37–50. © 2015 Left Coast Press, Inc. All rights reserved.

these categories mean, especially from one culture to the next, they can be useful in identifying what symptoms someone experiences and how such symptoms may shape or result from various factors, from biology to life experiences. Finally, some contributors to this book have used biomarkers to evaluate how stress affects biology through samples of blood, saliva, or even hair.

This chapter serves as a guide to the methods utilized in this book. Here we describe the types of methods employed across the chapters, using the research presented in this book to exemplify how anthropologists conduct global mental health research. Details of the specific research methods employed are not presented systematically here but are provided in other publications referenced at the end of this chapter. Please refer to this list for further reading around and clarification of methods utilized for specific research endeavors.

## ETHNOGRAPHIC METHODS

Many authors draw from ethnographic methods—that is, they practice participant observation alongside people living in a community that may well be unlike their own, either culturally or geographically (see, for exemplars, Bourgois 2002; Desjarlais 1997; Nakamura 2013). In many cases, the people who are "researched" also become friends over the many months, and even years, that the anthropologist spends in the community; some ethnographers become part of people's families because they spend so much time conducting research and living side by side with the people they study. Therefore, although objectivity is important to studying behaviors, beliefs, and social interactions, the line between the researcher and the researched can be blurry—anathema to other research methods. Yet this very characteristic of ethnography, this blurred line, can bring forth unique insights into cultural and social processes through which people experience life. For example, Jeffrey Snodgrass's chapter, "Festive Fighting and Forgiving" (Chapter 10), examines the annual Holi festival in rural India, where he observed a group (village) participating in a holiday that maintained a prescribed social order. By living with a family and observing their experiences firsthand, he was able to describe in detail the ways in which the event played out. As an ethnographer, Jeffrey was both a part of the festival and an observer who took extensive fieldnotes about the events of the day, which he later interpreted and situated into his larger research agenda. By observing everyday life over time, we can begin to understand the deeper meanings in how people talk, move, interact, and communicate about certain events in their lives. Indeed, Snodgrass's chapter demonstrates how the cultural practice of Holi can function as a form of social resilience. Thus, ethnography is an extremely useful method for studying mental illnesses in cultures that hold social meanings different from those held by biomedicine, which is the dominant view of mental illness in the United States.

## QUALITATIVE INTERVIEWS: NARRATIVE AND OPEN-ENDED

Another common anthropological research method is the qualitative interview, which can take various forms (see Bernard 1998) but broadly is an interview that asks someone to answer questions in his or her own way. In other words, qualitative questions do not provide "quantitative" or prescribed answers; instead, participants speak from their own experience. This approach might take the form of a life history narrative interview, which explores someone's life story over the course of several hours of conversing (see El-Shaarawi, Chapter 4; Mendenhall, Chapter 12) or over several meetings (see Mains, Chapter 5; Yarris, Chapter 7), or in an in-depth interview that delves deeply into one's beliefs and experiences around a certain topic (see Keys, Chapter 9).

The life history narrative interview, which follows the interviewee's life trajectory through an exploratory, iterative process (Ochs and Capps 1996), is an important anthropological approach to studying mental illness. The life history narrative may be conducted in one meeting but in many cases is collected over a series of meetings, as described by Kristin Yarris in "Grandmothers, Children, and Intergenerational Distress in Nicaraguan Transnational Families" (Chapter 7). Emily Mendenhall's chapter, "The 'Cost' of Health Care" (Chapter 12), demonstrates how intensely a life history narrative can explore social and psychological problems that intersect with health problems throughout a life. Beatriz's story illustrates the depth through which she remembers, organizes, and makes meaning of her life experiences. Importantly, personal narrative accounts are subjective and should be considered in light of the contemporary time and place through which an interlocutor shares her or his story (see also Mendenhall 2012). But the distinct order through which she shares her story provides insight into cultural, social, and psychological factors that may play a fundamental role in the course of one's life. This qualitative approach, therefore, employs an iterative approach to exploring the characteristics of the life of an individual, or group, that may provide unique insight into their past and present mental health.

In contrast, the in-depth open-ended interview, which focuses on a specific topic as opposed to an individual's life story, is a common method applied in public health. However, anthropologists often couple this type of interview with ethnographic research or other methods, such as surveys or psychiatric inventories (see Wutich et al., Chapter 3; Kaiser and McLean, Chapter 16). This is exemplified in Kenneth Maes's article, "Task-Shifting in Global Health" (Chapter 17), which integrates participant observation in an event involving volunteer community health workers with in-depth interviews of those workers that investigate their roles and experiences as community health workers. These interviews are meant to be an iterative process of information gathering, built around an interview guide that allows the study participant (that is, the interviewee) to guide the anthropologist in learning about their beliefs and experiences. In many cases, the anthropologist has his or her own objectives for the interview and may gently guide the respondent back to the core research questions; however, the anthropologist provides space for the respondent to share as much as she or he wishes on a certain topic and to open up the discussion to other topics that the study participant finds relevant. This approach enables the anthropologist to learn more about the perspective of the person being interviewed in order to uncover what she or he deems meaningful in everyday life.

## SEMI-STRUCTURED AND STRUCTURED SURVEYS

Many researchers combine qualitative research methods, such as ethnography, life history narrative, and in-depth, open-ended interviews, with more direct questions through surveys (see Kohrt et al. 2009; Kohrt and Hruschka 2010). These questions might be semi-structured to allow for study participants to provide short answers relevant to their personal life experiences; these provide some subjective insight on the part of study participants. Others use structured surveys to determine how people respond to a prescribed list of research questions. For example, if the researcher wishes to know the religion of a participant, she might ask: "What is the religion you practice?" In a semi-structured interview, the study participant would answer freely to define what that question means personally and what religion he or she practices (if any). To this, someone might respond, "Shamanism" or "I'm a Catholic." In a structured survey, by contrast, the respondent would have to select an answer from a prescribed list of responses. Therefore, "What is the religion you practice?" might be followed by a list, such as: (a) Judaism; (b) Islam; (c) Catholicism; (d) Protestantism; (e) Buddhism; (f) Hinduism; (g) None.

While this list might appear to be extensive at first glance, in some contexts it can be quite limiting, especially if someone's religious affiliation is not listed. For example, an individual, even a very religious one, might be inclined to choose "None" if that specific religion is not on the list. This is why surveys should be developed *after* the researcher has conducted some exploratory qualitative research in the area and has pilot-tested survey questions to ensure that the surveys are culturally relevant and socially acceptable. With such preparation, targeted questions that attend to specific localized phenomena can be extremely useful. This is the approach taken by many contributors to this book.

## PSYCHIATRIC INVENTORIES

Targeted questions around localized idioms of psychological distress have also been developed by anthropologists to capture unique ways in which people experience and express mental illness. For example, the term "tension" is increasingly used in South Asia to refer to aspects of depression and anxiety but does not carry the stigma of these more specific terms (Andrew et al. 2012; Chase et al. 2013; Weaver and Hadley 2011). To differentiate between localized symptoms and "universal" symptoms of distress, medical anthropologists Lesley Jo Weaver and Craig Hadley (2011) used a combination of ethnographic methods and more structured interviewing to develop a means of measuring the symptoms that women described as "tension" and then used this measurement in a broader sample to show that tension overlapped with depression but remained a distinct cultural expression of distress. Similarly, working in Haiti, Bonnie Kaiser and colleagues (2013) combined open-ended and structured interviewing to develop an instrument to assess mental health in culturally relevant ways. Such an approach has been tested in culturally adapted interventions and training, revealing that "tension" can elicit appropriate treatment modalities in South Asia (Chatterjee et al. 2008; Patel et al. 2011).

Developing such a tool requires extensive ethnographic research as well as devoted clinical opportunities to assess the validity of a tool that measures clinical symptoms of psychological distress. Therefore, many mental health researchers use standardized psychiatric inventories to evaluate the types and/or severity of mental illnesses afflicting the people with whom they work. One of the most widely utilized inventories is called the General Health Questionnaire (GHQ). This tool comes in many forms—with names such as the GHQ-12, GHQ-28, and GHQ-60—and helps to identify individuals who experience different types of psychological symptoms and therefore may correspond with diagnostic categories of mental disorders. The GHQ-12 is the most widely used because of its brevity (12 questions) and its ability to identify people experiencing psychological problems in a community setting. The GHQ-28 also is commonly used and incorporates four seven-item scales to identify different types of psychological problems: somatic symptoms, anxiety and insomnia, social dysfunction, and severe depression (Goldberg et al. 1997). Although not a diagnostic, this screening tool allows for mental health assessment of these four dimensions to better discern the prominence of various symptoms in a population. What is also useful about the General Health Questionnaire, as well as the Patient Health Questionnaire, used mostly in clinical settings, is that they have been translated and validated in multiple languages and therefore are extremely valuable in global mental health, and particularly cross-cultural, research.

However, these brief questionnaires do not replace clinical diagnoses. In the United States and elsewhere in the world, the American Psychiatric Association's *Diagnostic and Statistical Manual of Mental Disorders* (*DSM*) serves as a "universal authority" for the diagnosis of psychiatric disorders. Clinicians and researchers have relied upon the *DSM-IV* since 1994, but the *DSM-5* was released in May 2013. Each subsequent publication of the *DSM* presents new "categories" of mental disorders and interpretations of what those disorders means, underscoring the flexibility and cultural relativity of these disorders in psychiatric practice.

As medical and psychological anthropologists, some of whom are also psychiatrists, many of the contributors to this book concurrently accept the *DSM* as an important book that provides important insight into mental illness and recognize that how people experience and express psychological distress around the world can differ as a result of cultural and social factors. This brings to the forefront a major anthropological critique of global mental health, which is that biomedical definitions of mental illness as "universals," as posed in the *DSM*, can overshadow how people experience and express psychological distress cross-culturally. In this book, we recognize this critique but also believe that the symptoms revealed through these diagnoses provide insight into mental illnesses experienced worldwide. Notably, the *DSM* does incorporate some culturally defined expressions of psychological distress (e.g., *susto*, meaning fright or "magical fright" among Latin American populations), and the number of these variants included in the *DSM* tends to increase with each subsequent publication.

Many researchers studying specific diseases use targeted psychiatric inventories that, although not diagnostics, can provide very reliable measures of psychological burden. For example, researchers may administer the Beck Depression Inventory (BDI-I or BDI-II) or the Beck Anxiety Inventory (BAI) to evaluate their study participants' likelihood of having depression and anxiety, respectively. These inventories are reliable measures of *DSM*-defined symptoms, therefore providing a "universal" measure of psychological distress—although some symptoms associated with common mental disorders, including depression, anxiety, and post-traumatic stress disorder (PTSD), might vary cross-culturally, which is why an anthropological approach is useful. Coupled with localized tools to measure distress, anthropological studies of mental illness can provide unique insight into the global mental health burden and how people's experiences in one context may differ from another.

One of the best examples of this is Erin Finley's chapter, "The Few, The Proud" (Chapter 13), which discusses the social experiences of women veterans who present symptoms of PTSD. Detailed further in her book, *Fields of Combat: Understanding PTSD among Veterans of Iraq and Afghanistan* (2010), Finley employs the commonly used PTSD Checklist (PCL) to evaluate 17 *DSM-IV* symptoms of PTSD. The PCL has a variety of purposes, from screening individuals for PTSD, "diagnosing" PTSD, and monitoring symptom change during and after treatment. In many cases, the PCL-M ("M" for military personnel) provides a way to monitor the effect of a specific traumatic event on an individual's mental health over time, which can be extremely important in the case of military veterans. Finley employed this military version in part because of its extensive use, as well as the fact that her research was conducted through the Veteran Affairs (VA) medical system. However, there is also a version for civilians (PCL-C—the "C" denoting civilian) and another to be administered immediately following a traumatic event. Finley's research demonstrates how useful such a tool can be, while detailing the unique individual- and community-level factors that shape people's traumatic experiences, related symptoms, and coping strategies immediately as well as long after the event.

## BIOCULTURAL METHODS

Biocultural anthropology is a discipline that takes into account biological and structural factors as well as variable models of beliefs systems, both implicit and explicit (Armelagos et al. 1992; Hinton 1999; Lende 2005). This field relies on mixed-methods research with an emphasis on the interaction of biology and culture (Hruschka, Daniel, and Worthman 2005) to examine how culture and social experiences "get under the skin" through connections among culture, biology, and behavior (Lende 2005; Worthman and Brown 2005; Worthman and Kohrt 2005). One objective of biocultural anthropology is to account for both explicit and implicit associations by trying to study actual mechanisms—often with biomarker measurement—and by taking into account context that affects how stimuli are perceived and responded to (Worthman 2009; Worthman and Costello 2009). For example, political and economic constraints, the physical and symbolic environment, and especially the social environment frame what and how stimuli are perceived and the possible world of behavioral responses.

Mental disorders are often conceived to be problems associated with the brain, although mental disorders can stem from a diverse range of factors, from biology to the environment. It is important to remember that mental distress can have an impact on the body itself and therefore must be recognized as a problem that can be measured within the body. Thus, biocultural approaches that entail both traditional cultural anthropology methods and an expanding array of field-based biological measures are ideal for studying global mental health. The relative impact of social and psychological distress on the body can be measured through different types of "stress biomarkers" found in the hair, saliva, and blood (Worthman and Costello 2009). For example, a common way to measure stress is by collecting vials of saliva throughout the day to measure the stress hormone cortisol.[1] Cortisol is part of the stress response system, and elevated levels at baseline can indicate that life stressors have modified the body's stress threshold. Likewise, some researchers measure inflammation via C-reactive protein (CRP) or Epstein Barr virus (EBV) antibody titers. These biomarkers are measured through blood samples, which are often obtained, particularly in resource-poor settings, via finger-stick blood collection (see McDade, Williams, and Snodgrass 2007). Then the researchers can take the blood samples back to the lab to examine elevated biomarkers across and within a population (see Lindau and McDade 2008). Triangulated with survey or qualitative interviews and psychiatric inventories, evaluating biomarkers can provide insight into how social and psychological distress can affect the body.

On the Caribbean island of Dominica, child development research with longitudinal cortisol collection was conducted over two decades by Mark Flinn and colleagues, one of the few studies undertaken outside of high-income settings (Flinn 2009; Flinn and England 1997; Flinn, Muehlenbein, and Ponzi 2009). This study also stands out because it pays attention to the "causal arrow from culture to biology" (Konner 2010: 542). By collecting daily saliva samples during various household activities, Flinn demonstrated that family disruptions such as marital conflict and separation were associated with aberrant cortisol levels. Furthermore, through long-term monitoring, he found that children with single mothers or stepparents experienced a greater burden of physiological stress, often displaying elevated cortisol levels. A growing number of anthropologists are combining biological methods with ethnographic techniques such as this in order to understand mental health across populations throughout the world (see Kohrt et al. 2014).

## WHAT'S MISSING?

Rarely have anthropologists conducted an ethnographic study of mental health institutions or of the people who care for people living with and suffering from mental illness. As we illustrated above, most of the anthropological research on global mental health has focused on sufferers. Yet, the ways in which providers and policy makers conceive of mental illness and provide care for people suffering from those conditions play a pivotal role in how people understand, interact, and care for people with mental illness. Some of these issues are fundamentally rooted in problems of stigma and health expenditures, as many low- and middle-income countries have poor (if not nonexistent) mental health systems. The lack of mental health care in such settings has motivated the transnational movement for global mental health and the increasing attention directed toward it in research and policy (cf. Lancet Global Mental Group 2007; Prince et al. 2007). Indeed, a growing group of global mental health researchers in public health have begun to focus on the dearth of research and policy in this arena and are beginning to make a big impact.

Despite the growing body of anthropological research on people living with mental illness or experiencing mental distress as a result of social suffering, few anthropologists have critiqued mental health providers or systems. Perhaps the most well-known ethnography of psychiatrists comes from research in the United States. In a seminal book, *Of Two Minds: An Anthropologist Looks at American Psychiatry*, Tanya Luhrmann explains that even medical training for psychiatrists in the United States requires psychiatric residents to learn a new cultural system of interpreting mental illness and how to treat it. She explains:

> I was, after all, watching people learn. They came into psychiatric residency as nonpsychiatrists and left as qualified psychiatric professionals. I could see what they were taught explicitly, by those appointed to teach them; I could also see what everyday experience with psychiatric patients confronted them with and how they learned from one another to defend themselves against its assaults. I saw how they learned to find significance and meaning in behavior other people might not even notice and how they learned to communicate their sense of that behavior in an ordinary language other people might not grasp, even when understanding each individual word. (Luhrmann 2000: 20)

Understanding how biomedical training shapes the way psychiatrists interpret mental disorders and care for people suffering from these health problems is fundamental for anthropological research on the illnesses themselves. In this volume, Sarah Willen and Anne Kohler's "Cultural Competence and Its Discontents" (Chapter 14) illustrates how such training conditions psychiatrists to distance themselves from patients, even when those patients might share some cultural histories.

Despite the dearth of research in the anthropology of health systems, calling for more research around mental health care providers and systems is not a new concept. The seminal work of anthropologist Laura Nader in the late 1960s called for anthropologists to "study *up*," meaning to focus on those who hold the power within systems. Within the fields of anthropology and global health, there have been limited studies of policy makers and corporate and government leaders who shape diagnostic categories, make treatment guidelines, and determine funding in low- and middle-income countries (Petryna, Lakoff, and Kleinman 2006). One of the rare exceptions is the work of Stefan Ecks (2013) on psychopharmaceuticals in South Asia. And the work of Kalman Applbaum (2010, 2012) addresses this issue in Japan, a high-income country. In "studying up," methodological approaches are not necessarily different, but the type of participant shifts from end users and general community members to persons in positions of power within corporations, governments, and other organizations. Additionally, studying up entails poring through annual reports, budgets, and profit reporting to national governments, and other publicly available documents. Still more anthropological research is needed around those who hold the power to implement mental health programs and policies in resource-poor settings.

Problematizing pharmaceutical companies and the role they play within global mental health research, programs, and policies has been a focus of anthropologists. However, in global mental health, studies of nongovernmental organizations are crucial to understanding how policies become praxis and affect the experience of service providers, including their supervisors. A recent global mental health study by anthropologist Sharon Abramowitz (2008, 2010) explored this issue by investigating the psychosocial and mental health services in post-conflict Liberia. Abramowitz conducted participant observation with an NGO in Liberia that offered mental health services. In high-income countries, one can find a range of anthropologists conducting participant observation at the level of service providers and not limiting their studies only to beneficiaries. Such approaches yield vital on-the-ground understanding of the opportunities and challenges for implementing mental health interventions in varied cultural contexts.

Thus, the project of the anthropologists in this volume is to move beyond simply recognizing mental illness or how it is situated in the social world. We achieve this through applying multiple methods—from ethnography to biology—and working at the intersection of multiple disciplines—from anthropology to epidemiology, psychiatry, and policy. In doing so, we problematize the complexities around those who suffer from, thrive in spite of, and care for those with or associated with mental illness. We also shed some light on some of the political and programmatic issues associated with providing mental health care to those who need it most.

## Note

[1] Refer to Sapolsky's *Why Zebras Don't Get Ulcers* (1998).

## Further Reading Related to Chapters in this Volume

For further reading on the topics presented in this book, and more insight into specific methods utilized, please refer to the following references supplied by the contributors:

Anderson-Fye, Eileen P. (2010). The role of subjective motivation in girls' secondary schooling: the case of avoidance of abuse in Belize. *Harvard Educational Review*, 80 (2): 174–202.

El-Shaarawi, Nadia. (2012). Living an uncertain future: an ethnography of displacement, health, psychosocial well-being and the search for durable solutions among Iraqi refugees in Egypt. Electronic thesis or dissertation. Case Western Reserve University. https://etd.ohiolink.edu/.

Finley, Erin. (2010). *Fields of Combat: Understanding PTSD among Veterans of Iraq and Afghanistan*. Ithaca, New York: Cornell University Press.

Friedman, Jack R. (2009). The "Social Case": illness, psychiatry, and deinstitutionalization in postsocialist Romania. *Medical Anthropology Quarterly*, 23 (4): 375–396.

Kaiser, B., McLean, K., Kohrt, B., Hagaman, A., Wagenaar, B., Khoury, N., and Keys, H. (2014). *Reflechi twòp*—Thinking too much: description of a cultural syndrome in Haiti's Central Plateau. *Culture, Medicine, and Psychiatry*, 38 (3): 448–472.

Kalofonos, I. (2014). "All they do is pray": community labour and the narrowing of "care" during Mozambique's HIV scale-up. *Global Public Health: An International Journal for Research, Policy and Practice*, 9 (1–2): 7–24.

Keys, H., Kaiser, B. N., Foster, J. W., Burgos, R. M., and Kohrt, B. A. (2014). Perceived discrimination, humiliation, and mental health: a mixed-methods study among Haitian migrants in the Dominican Republic. *Ethnicity and Health*, 14:1–22.

Kohrt, B. A., and Hruschka, D. J. (2010). Nepali concepts of psychological trauma: the role of idioms of distress, ethnopsychology and ethnophysiology in alleviating suffering and preventing stigma. *Culture, Medicine, and Psychiatry*, 34 (2): 322–352.

Kohrt, B. A., Jordans, M. J. D., Tol, W. A., Luitel, N. P., Maharjan, S. M., and Upadhaya, N. (2011). Validation of cross-cultural child mental health and psychosocial research instruments: adapting the depression self-rating scale and child PTSD symptom scale in Nepal. *BMC Psychiatry*, 11 (1): e127.

Kohrt, B. A., Speckman, R. A., Kunz, R. D., Baldwin, J. L., Upadhaya, N., Acharya, N. R., Sharma, V. D., Nepal, M. K., and Worthman, C. M. (2009). Culture in psychiatric epidemiology: using ethnography and multiple mediator models to assess the relationship of caste with depression and anxiety in Nepal. *Annals of Human Biology*, 36 (3): 261–280.

Lende, D. H. (2005). Wanting and drug use: a biocultural analysis of addiction. *Ethos*, 33, (1): 100–124.

Maes, K., and Shifferaw, S. (2011). Cycles of poverty, food insecurity, and psychosocial stress among AIDS care volunteers in urban Ethiopia. *Annals of Anthropological Practice*, 35: 98–115.

Mains, D. (2012). *Hope is Cut: Youth, Unemployment and the Future in Urban Ethiopia*. Philadelphia: Temple University Press.

Mains, D., Hadley, C., and Tessema, F. (2013). Chewing over the future: khat consumption, anxiety, depression, and time among young men in Jimma, Ethiopia. *Culture, Medicine, and Psychiatry*, 37 (1): 111–130.

Mendenhall, E. (2012). *Syndemic Suffering: Social Distress, Depression, and Diabetes among Mexican Immigrant Women*. Walnut Creek, alifornia.: Left Coast Press, Inc.

Mendenhall, E., and Jacobs, E. A. (2012). Interpersonal abuse and depression among Mexican immigrant women with Type 2 diabetes. *Culture, Medicine, and Psychiatry*, 36 (1): 136–153.

Willen, S. S. (2013). Confronting a "big huge gaping wound": emotion and anxiety in a cultural sensitivity course for psychiatry residents. *Culture, Medicine, and Psychiatry*, 37 (2): 253–279.

Wutich, A., and Ragsdale, K. (2008). Water insecurity and emotional distress: coping with supply, access, and seasonal variability of water in a Bolivian squatter settlement. *Social Science and Medicine*, 67: 2116–2125.

Yarris, K. E. (2014). "Quiero ir y no quiero ir" (I want to go and I don't want to go): Nicaraguan children's ambivalent experiences of transnational family life. *The Journal of Latin American and Caribbean Anthropology*, 19 (2): 284–309.

Zahran, S., Snodgrass, J. G., Maranon, D., Upadhyay, C., Granger, D., and Bailey, S. (in preparation). Stress and telomere shortening among central Indian "wildlife refugees." *Proceedings of the National Academy of Sciences.*

## References

Andrew, G., Cohen, A., Salgaonkar, S., and Patel, V. (2012). The explanatory models of depression and anxiety in primary care: a qualitative study from India. *BMC Research Notes* 5 (1): 499.

Armelagos, G. J., Leatherman, T., Ryan, M., and Sibley, L. (1992). Biocultural synthesis in medical anthropology. *Medical Anthropology*, 14 (1): 35–52.

Abramowitz, S. (2010). Trauma and humanitarian translation in Liberia: the tale of open mole. *Culture, Medicine, and Psychiatry*, 34 (2): 353–79.

Abramowitz, S., and Kleinman, A. (2008). Humanitarian intervention and cultural translation: a review of the IASC guidelines on mental health and psychosocial support in emergency settings. *Intervention: International Journal of Mental Health, Psychosocial Work and Counselling in Areas of Armed Conflict*, 6 (3–4): 219–227.

Applbaum, K. (2010). Shadow science: Zyprexa, Eli Lilly and the globalization of pharmaceutical damage control. *BioSocieties*, 5 (2): 236–255.

——. (2012). Depression in Japan: psychiatric cures for a society in distress. *Anthropological Quarterly*, 85 (2): 593–604.

Bernard, H. R. (1998). *Research Methods in Anthropology: Qualitative and Quantitative Approaches*. New York: AltaMira Press.

Bourgois, P. (2002). *In Search of Respect: Selling Crack in El Barrio*. Cambridge: Cambridge University Press.

Chase, L. E, Welton-Mitchell, C., and Bhattarai, S. (2013). "Solving tension": coping among Bhutanese refugees in Nepal. *International Journal of Migration, Health and Social Care*, 9 (2): 71–83.

Chatterjee, S., Chowdhary, N., Pednekar, S., Cohen, A., Andrew, G., Araya, R., Simon, G., King, M., Telles, S., Verdeli, H., Clougherty, K., Kirkwood, B., and Patel, V. (2008). Integrating evidence-based treatments for common mental disorders in routine primary care: feasibility and acceptability of the MANAS intervention in Goa, India. *World Psychiatry*, 7 (1): 39–46.

Desjarlais, R. (1997). *Shelter Blues: Sanity and Selfhood among the Homeless*. Philadelphia: University of Pennsylvania.

Ecks, S. M. (2013). *Eating Drugs: Psychopharmaceutical Pluralism in India*. New York: NYU Press.

Flinn, M. V. (2009). Are cortisol profiles a stable trait during child development? *American Journal of Human Biology*, 21 (6): 769–771.

Flinn, M. V., and England, B. G. (1997). Social economics of childhood glucocorticoid stress response and health. *American Journal of Physical Anthropology*, 102 (1): 33–53.

Flinn, M. V., Muehlenbein, M. P., and Ponzi, D. (2009). Evolution of neuroendocrine mechanisms linking attachment and life history: the social neuroendocrinology of middle childhood. *Behavioral and Brain Sciences*, 32 (1): 27–28.

Goldberg, D., Gater, R., Sartorius, N., Ustun, T., Piccinelli, M., Gureje, O., et al. (1997). The validity of two versions of the GHQ in the WHO study of mental illness in general health care. *Psychological Medicine*, 27: 191–197.

Hinton, A. L. (1999). *Biocultural Approaches to the Emotions*. Cambridge/New York: Cambridge University Press.

Hruschka, D. J., Daniel, H., and Worthman, C. M. (2005). Biocultural dialogues: biology and culture in psychological anthropology. *Ethos* 33 (1): 1–19.

Kaiser, B. N., Kohrt, B. A., Keys, H., Khoury, N. M., and Brewster, A. (2013). Strategies for assessing mental health in Haiti: local instrument development and transcultural translation. *Transcultural Psychiatry*, 50: 532.

Kohrt, B. A., Hruschka, D. J., Kohrt, H. E., Carrion, V. G., Waldman, I. D., and Worthman, C. M. (2014). Child abuse, disruptive behavior disorders, depression, and salivary cortisol levels among institutionalized and community-residing boys in Mongolia. *Asia-Pacific Psychiatry*. doi: 10.1111/appy.12141. (Epub ahead of print)

Konner, M. (2010). *The Evolution of Childhood: Relationships, Emotion, Mind*. Cambridge, Massachusetts: Belknap Press of Harvard University Press.

Lancet Global Mental Health Group. (2007). Scale up services for mental disorders: a call for action. *The Lancet*, 370: 1241–1252.

Lindau, S. T. and McDade, T. W. (2008). Minimally-invasive and innovative methods for biomeasure collection in population-based research. In M. Weinstein, J. W. Vaupel, and K. W. Wachter (eds.), *Biosocial Surveys*, pp. 251–277. Washington, DC: Committee on Advances in Collecting and Utilizing Biological Indicators and Genetic Information in Social Science Surveys, National Academies Press.

Luhrmann, T. M. (2000). *Of Two Minds: The Growing Disorder in American Psychiatry*. New York: Knopf.

Lende, D. H. (2005). Wanting and drug use: a biocultural approach to the analysis of addiction. *Ethos,* 33 (1): 100–124.

McDade, T. W., Williams, S., and Snodgrass, J. J. (2007). What a drop can do: dried blood spots as a minimally-invasive method for integrating biomarkers into population-based research. *Demography*, 44: 899–925.

Nakamura, K. (2013). *A Disability of the Soul: An Ethnography of Schizophrenia and Mental Illness in Contemporary Japan*. Ithaca, New York: Cornell University Press.

Ochs, E., and Capps, L. (1996). Narrating the self. *Annual Review of Anthropology*, 25: 19–43.

Patel, V., Chowdhary, N., Rahman, A., and Verdeli, H. (2011). Improving access to psychological treatments: lessons from developing countries. *Behaviour Research and Therapy*, 49 (9): 523–528.

Petryna, A., Lakoff, A., and Kleinman, A. (2006). *Global Pharmaceuticals: Ethics, Markets, Practices*. Durham, North Carolina: Duke University Press.

Prince, M., Patel, V., Saxena, S., Maj, M., Maselko, J., Phillips, M. R., and Rahman, A. (2007). No health without mental health. *The Lancet*, 370 (9590): 859–877.

Sapolsky, R. M. (1998). *Why Zebras Don't Get Ulcers—A Guide to Stress, Stress-Related Disorders and Coping*. New York: WH Freeman Publishers.

Weaver, L. J., and Hadley, C. (2011). Social pathways in the comorbidity between Type 2 diabetes and mental health concerns in a pilot study of urban middle- and upper-class Indian women. *Ethos*, 39 (2): 211–225.

Worthman, C. M. (2009). Habits of the heart: life history and the developmental neuro-endocrinology of emotion. *American Journal of Human Biology*, 21 (6): 772–781.

Worthman, C. M., and Brown, R. A. (2005). A biocultural life history approach to the developmental psychobiology of male aggression. In D. M. Stoff and E. J. Susman (eds.), *Developmental Psychobiology of Aggression*, pp. 187–221. New York: Cambridge University Press.

Worthman, C. M., and Costello, E. J. (2009). Tracking biocultural pathways in population health: the value of biomarkers. *Annals of Human Biology*, 36 (3): 281–297.

Worthman, C. M., and Kohrt, B. (2005). Receding horizons of health: biocultural approaches to public health paradoxes. *Social Science and Medicine*, 61 (4): 861–878.

# Part I

## SOCIAL AND STRUCTURAL ORIGINS OF MENTAL ILLNESS IN GLOBAL CONTEXT

## Brandon A. Kohrt and Emily Mendenhall

Placing focus on the social and structural origins of mental illness highlights that low- and middle-income countries bear the burden of social risk factors such as poverty, war, infectious disease, child mortality, and food and water insecurity. On a population level, one social epidemiological fact is clear: poor mental health is correlated with poverty (Lund et al. 2010; Lund et al. 2011). Stressful living conditions associated with poverty, such as interpersonal violence, political violence, food insecurity, limited access to health care, untreated physical illness, and a variety of other variables, have been examined in detail in research about the *social determinants of health* (Wilkinson and Marmot 2003). Different from behavioral facts, the social determinants of health are almost never modifiable by individuals. Rather, they are taken-for-granted aspects of unequal socioeconomic systems characterized by political ideologies that systematically oppress the poor.

Understanding how social and structural factors underlie and shape mental illness is a central theme of medical anthropology. Calling it the *new cross-cultural psychiatry*, Harvard anthropologists Arthur Kleinman, Byron Good, Mary-Jo Delvecchio Good, and colleagues placed focus on how social suffering fuels mental illness (Kleinman 1997; Kleinman and Good 1985). For example, Kleinman's research and collaborations focused on the social origins of suffering, stigma, and morality, including the role of medical systems, in shaping trajectories of suffering differently in China and the West (Kleinman 1982, 1997, 2006). The research on social suffering also built upon the writings of Norwegian scholar Johan Galtung (1969) on *structural violence*. Galtung's original definition of structural violence refers to processes that erode human needs, and has since been amended to incorporate social and material needs. Through the work of Kleinman's students Paul Farmer and Jim Kim, the importance of structural violence became a central focus

*Global Mental Health: Anthropological Perspectives*, edited by Brandon A. Kohrt and Emily Mendenhall, 51–55. © 2015 Left Coast Press, Inc. All rights reserved.

in global health research (Farmer 2003, 2004). Farmer describes structural violence as constrained agency: "the degree to which agency is constrained is correlated inversely, if not always neatly, with the ability to resist marginalization and other forms of oppression" (2004: 307).

Global health advocates focusing on infectious diseases have called this situation of constrained agency "structural violence" because it results in stressful and hopeless living conditions that are dangerous to both physical health (Farmer 2001, 2004; Farmer et al. 2006) and mental health (Kelly 2005; Kohrt and Worthman 2009). Others have emphasized how structural violence is a fundamental factor in the clustering of diseases, including social, psychological, and physical problems that cultivate individual- and community-level disease and suffering (Mendenhall 2012; Singer and Clair 2003). Structural violence is obviously an underlying contributor to mental health problems.

Humanitarian disasters and other complex emergencies, which represent an extreme example of social determinants of mental health problems, have received increasing attention in medical anthropology. This can be attributed to, in part, the introduction of post-traumatic stress disorder (PTSD) into psychiatry in the 1980s, with the intention to understand and care for those affected by war, environmental disasters, and other complex catastrophes. While mental health and psychosocial support (MHPS) programs pale in comparison to other health programs in humanitarian settings, it is now commonplace to consider what types of MHPS services also should be provided when considering services for Syrian refugees in Jordan or typhoon survivors in the Philippines. Cultural psychiatrists and medical anthropologists have put forward a range of critiques of these programs, with some concerns that mental health services in these settings medicalize suffering and detract from other needed services as well as from indigenous ways of understanding and responding to such crises (Abramowitz 2010; Abramowitz and Kleinman 2008; Breslau 2004; James 2010; Summerfield 1999). Similar critiques of medicalizing suffering have been expressed about global mental health (Summerfield 2008, 2012).

In this first section, we explore the sociocultural determinants and origins of mental health problems. Anthropologists Charles Seligman and psychiatrist Emil Kraepelin, in their work a century ago, posited that the sociocultural environment shaped, and even caused, mental illness. The six chapters in Part I draw on this legacy of anthropological critique by examining how structural inequalities, such as poverty and water insecurity, and social inequalities, such as racism and marginalization, influence people's experiences of "being in the world" and coping with what's placed before them. These are stories not only of extreme suffering but also, in most cases, stories of resilience that illuminate the strength people demonstrate amid adversity. Narrative by narrative, the following chapters illustrate how various structural and social inequalities cultivate an experience of heightened stress and psychological distress that impedes mental health and social well-being.

In "Water, Worry, and Doña Paloma," Amber Wutich and colleagues (Chapter 3) write, "Fear, anxiety, and hopelessness are normal emotional responses to living in a system where one's survival and dignity are constantly under siege." Their research presents a larger narrative of how living in a water-insecure world can give rise to chronic, everyday stress and psychological distress that manifests in mental disorders, including depression, anxiety, PTSD, and substance abuse. In many cases, it is the geopolitical orientation of inequality that shapes individual psychological distress—people trying to maneuver in an unequal system that presents challenges in everyday life—that cannot be underestimated. For example, Nadia El-Shaarawi's "Life in Transit" (Chapter 4) outlines the case of Iraqi refugees surviving in Cairo with limited access to education, work, or family networks in Iraq because of Egyptian policies around refugee rights, their tenuous status in Cairo, and the ongoing violence in Iraq. Daniel Mains, then, in "Reconnecting Hope" (Chapter 5), illustrates how chronic unemployment contributes to substance abuse and mental distress among young Ethiopian men. Kristin Yarris's chapter (Chapter 7) on intergenerational distress from labor migration portrays the grief of migrants and their families when parents migrate from Nicaragua to Costa Rica for work, leaving grandparents to rear grandchildren. While these macro-social forces can play a fundamental role in people's mental health, micro-social factors, such as interpersonal relationships, can have a profound effect on people, too, and these factors are often overlapping. Daniel Lende and Sarah Fishleder's "Addiction in Colombia" (Chapter 8) demonstrates this by exemplifying how peer relationships influence substance abuse, and this dynamic is negotiated differently in contexts of poverty and affluence. In "The Greater Good," Eileen Anderson-Fye (Chapter 6) shows how young women negotiate unwanted sexual advances from benefactors in order to attain their goals, and move beyond interpersonal abuse. Together these chapters illustrate the structural and social origins of mental illness in global context.

## References

Abramowitz, S. A. (2010). Trauma and humanitarian translation in Liberia: the tale of open mole. *Culture, Medicine, and Psychiatry*, 34 (2): 353–379.

Abramowitz, S. A., and Kleinman, A. (2008). Humanitarian intervention and cultural translation: a review of the IASC Guidelines on Mental Health and Psychosocial Support in Emergency Settings. *Intervention: International Journal of Mental Health, Psychosocial Work and Counselling in Areas of Armed Conflict*, 6 (3–4): 219–227.

Breslau, J. (2004). Cultures of trauma: anthropological views of posttraumatic stress disorder in international health. *Culture, Medicine, and Psychiatry*, 28 (2): 113–126; 211–120.

Farmer, P. (2001). *Infections and Inequalities: The Modern Plagues*. Berkeley: University of California Press.

———. (2003). *Pathologies of Power: Health, Human Rights, and the New War on the Poor*, Vol. 4. Berkeley: University of California Press.

———. (2004). Sidney W. Mintz Lecture for 2001—an anthropology of structural violence. *Current Anthropology*, 45 (3): 305–325.

Farmer, P. E., Nizeye, B., Stulac, S., and Keshavjee, S. (2006). Structural violence and clinical medicine. *PLoS Medicine*, 3 (10): 1686–1691.

Galtung, J. (1969). Violence, peace, and peace research. *Journal of Peace Research*, 6 (3): 167–191.

James, E. C. (2010). Ruptures, rights, and repair: the political economy of trauma in Haiti. *Social Science and Medicine*, 70 (1): 106–113.

Kelly, B. D. (2005). Structural violence and schizophrenia. *Social Science and Medicine*, 61 (3): 721–730.

Kleinman, A. M. (1982). Neurasthenia and depression: a study of somatization and culture in China. *Culture, Medicine, and Psychiatry*, 6: 117–190.

———. (1997). *Writing at the Margin: Discourse between Anthropology and Medicine*. Berkeley: University of California Press.

———. (2006). *What Really Matters: Living a Moral Life amid Uncertainty and Danger*. New York: Oxford University Press.

Kleinman, A., and Good, B. (1985). *Culture and Depression: Studies in the Anthropology and Cross-Cultural Psychiatry of Affect and Disorder*. Berkeley: University of California Press.

Kohrt, B. A., and Worthman, C. M. (2009). Gender and anxiety in Nepal: the role of social support, stressful life events, and structural violence. *CNS Neuroscience and Therapeutics*, 15: 237–248.

Lund, C., Breen, A., Flisher, A. J., Kakuma, R., Corrigall, J., Joska, J. A., and Patel, V. (2010). Poverty and common mental disorders in low and middle income countries: a systematic review. *Social Science and Medicine*, 71: 517–528.

Lund, C., De Silva, M., Plagerson, S., Cooper, S., Chisholm, D., Das, J., and Patel, V. (2011). Poverty and mental disorders: breaking the cycle in low-income and middle-income countries. *The Lancet*, 378 (9801): 1502–1514.

Mendenhall, E. (2012). *Syndemic Suffering: Social Distress, Depression, and Diabetes among Mexican Immigrant Women*. Walnut Creek, California: Left Coast Press, Inc.

Singer, M., and Clair, S. (2003). Syndemics and public health: reconceptualizing disease in bio-social context. *Medical Anthropology Quarterly,* 17 (4): 423–441.

Summerfield, D. A. (1999). A critique of seven assumptions behind psychological trauma programmes in war-affected areas. *Social Science and Medicine,* 48 (10): 1449–1462.

——. (2008). How scientifically valid is the knowledge base of global mental health? *British Medical Journal,* 336 (7651): 992–994.

——. (2012). Afterword: against global mental health. *Transcultural Psychiatry* 49 (3): 519.

Wilkinson, R., and Marmot, M. (2003). *The Social Determinants of Health: The Solid Facts.* 2nd ed. Geneva: World Health Organization.

Chapter 3

# Water, Worry, and Doña Paloma: Why Water Security is Fundamental to Global Mental Health

Amber Wutich, Alexandra Brewis, Jose B. Rosales Chavez, and Charu L. Jaiswal

FOR MILLIONS OF PEOPLE AROUND THE WORLD, dealing with water shortages is a daily struggle with a high human toll. In rural settings, where people are vulnerable to drought and often lack adequate water infrastructure, water scarcity poses an enormous threat to agricultural livelihoods. Even in urban settings, where it is often assumed that people have good access to water infrastructure, the scarcity and commodification of water means many people don't have enough to cook or wash with, or even to drink. Water shortages undermine not only the physical health of community members—putting them at risk of dehydration, hunger, and waterborne disease—but also damages mental health.

Injustice in how water is distributed also can lead to water becoming highly politicized. In 2000, the people of Cochabamba, Bolivia, launched a series of protests against their government's privatization of water. While many around the world hailed the Cochabambans as "winners" of the Water War after the privatization deal ended, years later nearly half the population of the city of Cochabamba still lacks stable access to the municipal water supply. In Cochabamba's squatter settlements, as in many other parts of the world, it is usually women who are responsible for solving the daily problem of where their families' water will come from. Doña Paloma is one of them.

## DOÑA PALOMA AND VILLA ISRAEL

> We have run out of water. I don't even have water to make breakfast. Without water, we have absolutely nothing. I worry about water all the time.
>
> —Doña Paloma

*Global Mental Health: Anthropological Perspectives*, edited by Brandon A. Kohrt and Emily Mendenhall, 57–71. © 2015 Left Coast Press, Inc. All rights reserved.

Amber Wutich[1] first met Doña Paloma in 2004, when she was managing a team of researchers studying water insecurity in Villa Israel,[2] a squatter settlement at the extreme southern end of the city of Cochabamba, Bolivia. Doña Paloma was a 29-year-old working mother. She lived with her husband, four children, mother-in-law, and brother-in-law in a small but sturdily built concrete home with a large, open courtyard. Like many of the women in Villa Israel, she was hard-working, enterprising, and earned a steady income while cooking and caring for her family. She also had a sly sense of humor and a knack for frankly appraising a situation.

Doña Paloma was among Villa Israel's longest-standing residents; she had come to the young community more than nine years before our team first met her. As a result, Doña Paloma knew most of the local families and had participated in the squatter settlement's struggle to establish itself as a legal community with basic public services. Doña Paloma worked together with her neighbors to build local schools, daycare centers, churches, streets, and stormwater channels, two public transport lines, and a medical clinic. In the stormwater project, for instance, the women of Villa Israel spent months digging out storm channels, hauling boulders, and stacking them laboriously along the channels to ensure that the community would not suffer dangerous flash flooding. But, despite these collective efforts, safe and sufficient water access, their top priority, remained elusive.

Most of the water and nearly all municipal water infrastructure in the Cochabamba Valley are located in the north. In the south, squatter settlements have little or no surface water, and groundwater is scarce and often inaccessible. Throughout Cochabamba's south side, squatter settlements are dry, dusty, and desiccated. Families lovingly tend tiny garden plots, only to see their corn stalks and other vegetables wither and die before ripening. Rainfall comes in quick bursts and mostly in summer. Early on, Doña Paloma and her neighbors built rainwater-harvesting systems, lining their roofs with gutters to catch water and channel it to homemade storage tanks. But for most of the year, these sustainable rainwater-harvesting systems remain empty.

After putting in years of hard physical labor to dig their own groundwater system, investing their own meager funds, and courting nongovernmental organizations (NGOs) for financial assistance, members of Dona Paloma's community finally managed to build a small tapstand system. Tapstand systems are owned, maintained, and administered by the community itself; they are often called "urban commons" water systems (see Wutich 2009). Only established community members who own homes, participate in community labor projects, and pay a monthly maintenance fee are eligible to receive water from the tapstand system. But the community's water was so scarce that their tapstands could provide at best four buckets of water (40 liters) per family—once a day, six days a week—and only for a minority of people who lived in Villa Israel. Renters, new homeowners, and households too poor to pay the monthly fee were excluded from the taps.

Doña Paloma's family is one of the lucky few (only 28% of the community) that had steady access to the tapstand system. They also were fortunate to have enough income to pay the monthly maintenance fees and enough household members to send someone to get the water during once-a-day collection times. But with such a large household, the tapstand allotment provided only 5 liters per person per day—just a bit more than each household member needed to drink. It was not enough water for cooking, bathing, and other household chores. "Sometimes," said Doña Paloma, "we run out of water and we are forced to go into town to eat." Water from the tapstands could not be bought, and no family was allowed to exceed its daily allotment. These rules have a deep history in the Andes and ensure that communities distribute their scarce water stores fairly and equitably. But it also means that even when families like Doña Paloma's had money, it did not help them get more water from the tapstands.

The only alternative was to buy water from vending trucks. But the vendors did not like driving to Villa Israel, and they worried about the high cost of gas and the risk of damaging their trucks on rough, unpaved roads. On most days, just one or two trucks came to Villa Israel. And, "some days," Doña Paloma explained, "the vendors just don't come at all." When they did, people were sometimes forced to run up and down the streets, chasing the water vendors and pleading with them for water. They were often refused. Then came the added humiliation of begging their neighbors to lend them a bit of water—a bucket, a jerrycan—just enough to prepare a simple meal and quench the thirst of their family.

Over two years, Doña Paloma sat down with us many times to tell us about her life, her struggle to make ends meet, and, above all, the anguish she felt over the water situation. That year, the family's rainwater-harvesting system had already run dry by the time the dry season began. Although they could still get water from the tapstand or vendors, their tiny household storage capacity (240 liters, or a little less than one bathtub full of water) meant that each member of Doña Paloma's family had only 14 liters (less than 1½ buckets) of clean water to make it through each day. "Look at how we wash here," said Doña Paloma, motioning to graywater she had reused repeatedly. "I can reuse this water for the toilet, but not for washing because it's so dirty." Having a 14-liter allotment meant it was difficult, and sometimes impossible, for Doña Paloma's family to cook, wash their bodies and clothes, clean their home, or even flush their toilet.

Doña Paloma reminisced about water in the early days of the squatter settlement, when "there were fewer people and there was enough to plant corn and potatoes." As the community grew, the meager local groundwater was no longer enough to support the population's needs. The community water council initiated an ambitious plan to bring taps into homes and build a community pump on shared land. But the plan failed and "now the land just sits there and our investments are lost." In our discussions about water problems, past and present, Doña Paloma showed the struggle's emotional toll; she often complained of fatigue, worried constantly, and said she preferred to withdraw from others. When we asked about her friendships with other families in Villa Israel, she said, "I don't really have any friends. I say hello to my neighbors, but I don't like to talk to people." Instead of socializing with others, she said she prefers to "sleep when I have free time."

As the dry season hit Villa Israel families in full force, Doña Paloma's family was still managing to get water from the tapstand, but the effort was proving increasingly stressful. The family had gone to their home village to help with the harvest, as is customary for many urban migrants, and had lost their regular income as a result. "We are living on our savings," Doña Paloma explained, "and it is about to run out. I am so worried about money." Since water costs money, whether in tapstand fees or purchases from the vending truck, the cost of water was becoming the main family concern. She worried about the water vendor not coming, or refusing to sell her water. As the situation got worse, Doña Paloma had gone to her neighbors and borrowed 10 liters of water from one and bought 100 liters from another. Dealing with her equally water-short neighbors was adding to her stress. "At the tapstand," Doña Paloma explained, "there is a neighbor that I can't stand. We are constantly arguing because this woman does not think that my family should receive water from the same tapstand as hers." There had also been anger and fighting among her family members over water. At the end of that visit, it seemed Doña Paloma and her family were nearing a breaking point.

"One day the water ran out and I could not cook anything," Doña Paloma stated when we visited her again two months later, in the height of the dry season. The family was in crisis. Doña Paloma's husband was out of town, trying to land a better-paying job in their home village. Doña Paloma's mother-in-law had gone to stay with relatives. Doña Paloma herself was working from three in the morning to six in the evening each day, leaving little time for her to wait at the tapstand or chase down the water vendor even when they could afford it. On top of this, she exclaimed, "My little son has diarrhea because of the water." The arguments and anger among family members had continued as the situation deteriorated. Doña Paloma summed up her frustration by saying, "There is nothing I like about living here anymore. I am sick of not having any water. I want to sell my house and move away."

We visited Doña Paloma again as the dry season neared its end, but we had trouble finding her. By that time, her family was only occasionally visiting Villa Israel; they were building a new home in another, less-established squatter settlement. Selling the old home enabled them to liquidate their assets and start over again. When they moved away, Doña Paloma and her family lost access to Villa Israel's tapstands and became completely dependent on the water vendors. She said,

"I am still worried about money, as finishing construction of the house will be expensive." Her husband added that they had stopped construction of the house the previous week because there was not enough water to mix the concrete. With no hope of gaining access to piped water in her new community, Doña Paloma told us she still felt as angry, worried, and scared as before; the move had not helped solve the water problem at all, and now they were back struggling as ever.

## WATER SCARCITY: IMPACTS ON EMOTIONAL AND MENTAL HEALTH

Doña Paloma's story exemplifies the struggles that many families in Villa Israel face. And others are doing even worse: while Doña Paloma's household contained as many as four working adults and had stable access to the community tapstand system in Villa Israel, other families were not so lucky. Many households had only one income-earner; some had dependent minors and no steady income; and a few households were made up entirely of children who had been abandoned by their parents and lived on what little charity their neighbors could afford. Yet, Doña Paloma's relative good fortune did not protect her from suffering the physical, emotional, and mental health costs of water scarcity. Doña Paloma's experiences illustrate why water insecurity is so very damaging to those who live with it.

The issue of water and mental health is just beginning to receive international attention. In contrast, the relationship between poverty and mental health is a central topic in global mental health research. However, the causal pathways and best approaches to intervention are highly contested. Some have argued, using cross-national data, that poverty does not predict mental health problems (cf. Das et al. 2007). Other studies have argued that poverty leads to mental illness, as well as the converse (cf. Lund et al. 2011). In this volume, Mains demonstrates how employment alone is not a guarantee of psychological well-being. Our ethnographic exploration below argues that an understanding of the role water insecurity plays in the lives of the poor may help clarify this relationship. Water can mediate the relationship between poverty and mental health through multiple mechanisms. In the next section, we focus on three key factors that our own and others' research studies suggest are especially important to shaping the emotional costs of water insecurity: uncertainty, injustice, and stigma.

### Uncertainty

In Villa Israel and other squatter settlements in south-side Cochabamba, people could look forward each year to the arrival of the rainy season and a little relief from the difficulties of finding scarce and costly water. When this predictability is undermined by drought, people often experience terrible distress. Droughts pose a huge threat to all human settlements: they wither fields of crops, empty wells and water reservoirs, and can force massive waves of unplanned migration. Drought can also trigger the proliferation of anxiety, depression, and other mental health issues because they threaten people's ability not only to thrive but in many cases to survive (cf. Berry, Bowen, and Kjellstrom 2010). Australia, where people enjoy much better water infrastructure than the squatter settlements of Bolivia, experienced a drought from 2000 to 2012. As farmers saw their crops devastated, their incomes and savings lost, and their long-term ability to farm threatened, they were plagued by financial strain, feelings of loss, and fears for the future. Ultimately, Australian farmers suffered a significant increase in stress, anxiety, and depression (e.g., Stain et al. 2008), and suicides (cf. Hanigan et al. 2012), a fundamental visible marker of mental distress.

Other studies indicate that similar trends may exist in urban areas. In a drought-hit city of northeastern Brazil, for example, residents were significantly more anxious and emotionally distressed than residents of a similar city that was unaffected by drought (Coêlho, Adair, and Mocellin 2004). In other urban settings, like Indian slums (Siddiqui and Pandey 2003) and Mexican squatter settlements (Rios et al. 2003), people who experience water insecurity suffer more emotional distress or mental illness than people who are not water insecure. This may be due to the uncertainties involved in obtaining water for drinking, cooking, and maintaining income-generating activities. Yet, unlike the case of drought-struck rural farmers, the social and emotional mechanisms that cause anxiety and emotional distress in poor urban areas are not well documented. It is widely believed that municipal water planning and infrastructure buffer urbanites from water insecurity. So why are some urbanites at increased risk of mental illness? The Cochabamba case offers some clues.

Doña Paloma's story clearly shows that water vendors can cause uncertainty and emotional distress for urban clients. Unlike other urban services, such as public transport and trash removal, water vending was not part of an organized municipal delivery system in Cochabamba. Rather, water vendors were independent or unionized entrepreneurs who were free to pursue profits without any obligation to serve less-desirable neighborhoods and clients. In other words, instead of water supply being a social service provided by the government, it was something that was marketed and sold for a profit. While many of Cochabamba's water vendors professed a social conscience, their unregulated service structure also clearly produced systemic inequity and unpredictability. Although Doña Paloma lived near the cobblestoned and easily accessible center of Villa Israel, her family—like a third of Villa Israel households—owned only one 200-liter water storage tank. While tanker truck vendors could be convinced to sell as little as 200 liters, they strongly preferred clients who bought in bulk. In Villa Israel, nearly a third of families (28%) had bought or built huge underground storage tanks holding

3,000–10,000 liters. When in competition against bulk buyers like those, it was almost impossible for Doña Paloma and other small-scale buyers to convince the water vendors to deliver to their homes.

Reliance on unpredictable water vendors was closely associated with emotional distress in the less established, more marginal, and more impoverished Cochabamba squatter settlements. We believe there may be a spatial relationship among where people lived, how they accessed water, and the emotional distress they experienced. We found in interviews that in more central, better established, and more economically stable squatter settlements, water-vending services were more predictable and less stressful. While the difficulty of finding money to pay for a high-priced water service (compared with the cost of municipal water) was a potential concern for all families, unpredictability around when water would be available and when severe shortages might strike a family next were really the major source of worry.

*Injustice*

Just before she decided to leave the community, Doña Paloma told us, "We don't participate in community governance anymore. It's just for suckers." Doña Paloma's stories of life in Villa Israel conveyed her sense that community leaders had mismanaged and unfairly administered residents' investments toward solving the water problem. She described all of Villa Israel's efforts to truly solve its water problems, including getting a groundwater well with enough output to support the community and installing taps in each home, as failed projects. Furthermore, Doña Paloma felt that corruption and incompetence in Villa Israel's community governance was at the root of these failures. Her sense of injustice led her to disengage from community governance and, ultimately, to leave the community itself. Doña Paloma's perspective on the community water system was relatively unusual for Villa Israel. While many people expressed frustration with aspects of the tapstand system—the shortages, exclusion of renters, timing of water distribution, or squabbling of neighbors—most agreed that the rules themselves were fair and equitable.

In other Cochabamba squatter settlements, however, this was not always the case. Interviews with people from 23 Cochabamba squatter settlements showed a deep-seated sense of injustice and even outrage about malfeasance in community-owned and administered water systems. In one squatter settlement, for example, a respondent said, "The leaders are . . . just swindling us." In another, a respondent grumbled, "A new leader has come to power, but he does nothing." In many communities, we were told there is no water because "the leaders are not *caminando* [pounding the pavement]" to find financing for building infrastructure. There were many other aspects of the water situation in south-side Cochabamba that people also found unjust, including their exclusion from the municipal system and the commoditization of water. But the local community water system was one of the few city functions that, for those who did not have access, was consistently associated with symptoms of anxiety and depression.[3]

Around the world, new research (including our own) is beginning to indicate that when people perceive injustice—that is, a sense of unfairness or inequity—in water distribution, they may be more likely to feel psychosocial distress. In South Africa, for instance, apartheid produced long-standing inequities and exclusions in water distribution. For Blacks, this exclusion has been a source of profound shame, which has further hampered their participation in reforming the water sector and thus put them at greater risk for water insecurity (Goldin 2010). In an ethnographic study of a Mexican town, many people reported *sufriendo del agua* (suffering from water), which involved feelings of frustration, anguish, bother, worry, and anger over water scarcity (Ennis-McMillan 2006). Those most at risk were residents who depended on the community water system, experienced water shortages, and felt that new and wealthy residents had taken advantage of the system. In both the Mexican and South African cases, psychosocial distress is borne of the twin stresses of water shortages and injustices in water distribution. Farhana Sultana (2011), in a study of water scarcity and contamination in Bangladesh, argues more broadly that inequitable power and control over water—based on class, gender, and other social divisions—produces negative emotions such as suffering, belittlement, shame, pain, fear, worry, sadness, emotional distress, anxiety, and depression.

While the local, on-the-ground realities in each case vary widely—ranging from racial divisions in South Africa, income inequity in Mexico, gender and class divisions in Bangladesh, or perceived corruption in Bolivia—these cases together seem to indicate that feelings of unfairness or injustice may be linked with emotional distress.

## Stigma

Doña Paloma once exclaimed in frustration, "I feel dirty because there is not enough water . . . with more water I could clean the rooms, the bathroom, grow plants, *everything!*" As she explained it, water scarcity prevented Doña Paloma from living what she considers to be a good life—being able to be proud of well-groomed children, a tidy home, and a green garden. The inability to be respectable in these ways was a source of shame and sadness for her. This is echoed in research from around the world, where uncleanliness is widely associated with disgust and shame (Curtis, Danquah, and Aunger 2009). In Madagascar, for instance, "It is shameful to be dirty in front of your friends" (Curtis, Danquah, and Aunger 2009: 662). When people are perceived to be "dirty," this can lower their social status and even cause them to be shunned by neighbors. In Tanzania, it was reported that "[a] person who is not clean is like a mad person . . . people avoid him but feel sorry for him" (Curtis, Danquah, and Aunger 2009: 662). When water scarcity produces disease, that sickness too can be profoundly stigmatizing if it is perceived as a marker of poverty, filth, and contamination. In Brazil's cholera-stricken *favelas* (slums), for instance, the urban poor came to feel that "We ARE the cholera!"—a powerful statement conveying their feelings of culpability, stigma, and social exclusion (Nations and Monte 1996: 1017).

The social pressure to maintain clean homes and hygienic bodies can have a particularly devastating emotional effect on women like Doña Paloma (cf. UNDP 2006) because they are the ones responsible for water acquisition, housekeeping, and health care. Women in the slums of Andhra Pradesh, India, for example, suffer scolding by their husbands and humiliation before neighbors when they are unable to keep their families and homes clean (Reddy and Snehalatha 2011). It is possible that the shame associated with poor hygiene may even partially explain why the association between poverty and mental illness is so much stronger for women than men around the world (cf. Patel and Kleinman 2003).

While poor hygiene and unclean living conditions appear to be universally stigmatized, there are also locally unacceptable dimensions of water insecurity that are sources of enormous stigma and shame. In Cochabamba's squatter settlements, for example, many families rely on kin, neighbors, and friends for gifts and loans of water. In some cases, they form long-standing bonds of mutual assistance. When families lack stable or reliable sources of assistance and are forced to beg their neighbors for water, the experience is felt as deeply degrading and, when refused, is compounded by humiliation. In Doña Paloma's case, her long-standing local residence and insight into community norms helped her avoid the stigma of borrowing water. As she explained to us, "I always buy from my neighbors when I need a lot. When I only need a little, I borrow." This was, however, unusual. Few people we interviewed across Cochabamba's 23 squatter settlements had the deep community connections, social acumen, or financial resources to navigate the social complexities of water loans and purchases as successfully as Doña Paloma. Often, people saw water loans as a stigmatized source of last resort, and feared that a request for help from neighbors was as likely to bring them rejection and shame as a bucketful of water (see Wutich 2011 for details). As one woman who steered clear of such social difficulties said, "I always try to avoid borrowing water; I just make do with the tapstand water."

Across a wide variety of studies, there is strong and mounting evidence of a connection among resource insecurity, stigma, and mental illness. In the realm of food insecurity, for instance, people who resort to socially stigmatized forms of eating and food acquisition are more likely to feel shame, anxiety, and depression (cf. Weaver and Hadley 2009). In Cochabamba, people who adopt stigmatized water-acquisition strategies—such as begging for water—or who borrow water from neighbors are also more likely to experience anxiety and depression.[3] More universally, there is strong evidence of a link among water insecurity, uncleanliness, stigma, and negative emotions such as shame. The potential mental health implications deserve greater attention in the global health community, especially in light of "shaming interventions" that have been designed to stigmatize "dirty" people in order to increase hand-washing and sanitation in poor communities (cf. Pattanayak et al. 2009).

## CHANGE THE SYSTEM, CHANGE THE OUTCOME

Any study that connects resource insecurity to mental illness runs a very real risk of contributing to the "medicalization of poverty" (Moreira 2003). This is the mistake we make when we recast normal emotional and physiological responses to poverty as pathologies, and focus on treating the symptoms of poverty rather than the root of the problem. In Brazil, for instance, doctors counseled the urban poor to take psychiatric medication to treat such symptoms as weakness, shaking, and irritability (Scheper-Hughes 1992). The real source of these symptoms was hunger, and people ended up spending precious income on antidepressants instead of food. As Moreira explains, "The poor are thus transformed into patients. Poverty becomes a mental illness. A problem that is principally social and political is treated like a psychiatric symptom" (2003: 70).

When poverty is medicalized, the purses of the poor are emptied to pay for costly medicines and treatments without attending to the root causes of their distress. To avoid this kind of injustice, it is important to understand that the best cure for emotional distress caused by poverty is to change the system that produces it. This is a difficult undertaking, and very little research has investigated the effects of poverty interventions on mental health in low- and middle-income countries. But there is encouraging evidence that some interventions, such as conditional cash transfer and asset promotion programs, can make a difference (Lund et al. 2011). Another promising but unexplored approach may be to intervene directly in processes—such as water insecurity—that mediate the cycle of poverty and mental ill health.

### Municipal Water System

In Cochabamba, the most direct way to address mental distress and illness related to water insecurity is to extend the municipal water system to the city's squatter settlements. People living in the squatter settlements and their advocates have made many efforts to achieve this. After the end of Cochabamba's Water War, the municipal water authority, SEMAPA (Municipal Water and Sewage Service), regained control of water distribution. The protesters demanded that they be given a larger voice in water decision-making and won a place at the table for community organizations that represented south-side communities. In 2004, SEMAPA expanded its service area to include the south-side squatter settlements. With funding from the Inter-American Development Bank and others, SEMAPA committed to expand the municipal water grid to the south side.

Unfortunately, it is much easier to promise such changes on paper than to make them a reality in the poorest neighborhoods. Historical inequities, power imbalances, and corruption—all problems that existed long before the Water War and continue to persist—have derailed these plans to extend SEMAPA infrastructure. In 2007 alone, for example, external reviews of SEMAPA found 51 "irregularities" (i.e., potential incidents of corruption) representing misuses or losses of between $600,000 and $1,000,000 of funds meant for managing and improving the water system (Driessen 2008: 93). And so, even in Cochabamba—where SEMAPA stands as a global symbol of the triumph of common people against private water interests—the poor remain excluded from municipal water service, left with only the hope that the municipal system will one day be reformed.

## Community-Owned Delivery Tanks

Although efforts to reform SEMAPA were disappointing, the activists empowered by the Water War have found other ways to make an impact. One particularly innovative and effective organization is Cochabamba's Association of South-Side Community Water Systems (ASICA SUR). In addition to protesting against SEMAPA and pushing for political reform, ASICA SUR has taken the lead in finding small-scale solutions for water-scarce squatter settlements. After the local mayor's office reneged on its promise to build a major subterranean tank for the south-side community of Vera Cruz, ASICA SUR stepped in with a solution. They negotiated directly with the European Union for a $150,000 grant to buy five water tanker trucks for Vera Cruz (Los Tiempos 2007). Instead of forcing community members to rely on water vendors, who can be unreliable, sell water of unknown quality, and charge more than municipal suppliers, the community will be able to provide water to 20,000 of its residents. The water will be distributed to residents of Vera Cruz using the five community-owned water tanker trucks. This project is a clever one—with a very high likelihood of success—because it builds on existing local social organization, familiar technologies, and well-established behavioral habits to create a community-owned, community-administered solution.

## Enhancing Water Storage Capacity

In addition to community organizations like ASICA SUR, many south-side communities have found affordable, small-scale solutions to their water problems. In Villa Israel, for instance, the community had already built its own local water distribution system. When they discovered that the system did not yield enough water to support its growing population, community leaders bought land in an adjacent community, with the hope that they could install a groundwater well and pump the water to Villa Israel. Once the other community got wind of the plan, however, they legally blocked the export of their water.

Most recently, Villa Israel succeeded in executing the plan that the nearby settlement of Vera Cruz, described above, had presented to its local mayor: the construction of a major subterranean water tank. Such tanks typically have a capacity of 50 cubic meters of water. This is about the same amount of water that two tanker trucks could deliver in one day if they served only Villa Israel. While this storage capacity alone is not enough to support the community permanently, it provides an important buffer against water scarcity and lowers community dependence on the water truck vendors. Like the community-owned truck solution in Vera Cruz, it represents a partial but important step toward secure and affordable water provision for a south-side community.

As these examples demonstrate, there are rarely easy solutions for the poor. The case of Cochabamba shows that although activists have been able to shift the system in their favor—securing the right to water and promises of infrastructure extension—they have not been able to fully reform the local power structures that produced those inequities in the first place (Driessen 2008). Even so, the examples of the community-owned water trucks and storage tanks show that targeted interventions can make a big difference.

## CONCLUSION

Water scarcity is a source of profound struggle for many across the globe, most especially women who bear the burden of seeking and carrying water and using it to care for their families. It undermines both physical and mental health, as people struggle to operate in unfair water distribution systems, like many in Cochabamba who have too little money, time, and options to draw on. It pits neighbors and family members against one another and is a terrible source of humiliation, shame, and other forms of social stress. As the demand for water grows and water becomes more commodified, the everyday struggles it creates for the poor will only proliferate. Unless real structural solutions are implemented that meet the human need for stable and safe water supplies, there is every reason to anticipate even more damaging mental health effects in the years ahead. Since water appears to be a mediator of the relationship between poverty and mental health, direct interventions to improve water provision and accessibility may offer an efficient approach to breaking the cycle of poverty and mental illness. This contrasts with general poverty reduction models that do not necessarily have the same direct benefit on health and well-being. From the perspective of mental health provision to the world's poor, this reminds us that all mental health policies ultimately start with delivering the very basics of life's necessities to all, beginning with the most fundamental of all: water.

## ACKNOWLEDGMENTS

Many thanks to our Bolivian colleagues Wilda Valencia, Richard Aguilar, Wilfredo Valencia, and Dominga Choque for lending their talent and insight to this research. We received financial support from Fulbright-IIE, the Tinker Foundation, Paul and Polly Doughty, NSF Grant BCS-0314395 (Cultural Anthropology) and SES-0951366 (Decision Center for a Desert City II: Urban Climate Adaptation). Opinions, findings, and recommendations expressed in this material are those of the authors and do not necessarily reflect the views of the funding agencies.

## Notes

[1] Dr. Amber Wutich directed this research. In the field, Wutich worked with a team of three Bolivian researchers: Wilda Valencia, Richard Aguilar, and Wilfredo Valencia. Wilda Valencia and Richard Aguilar were both advanced *licenciatura* students in Education Sciences at Cochabamba's Universidad Mayor de San Simon. Wilfredo Valencia is a Quechua translator for a local Baptist church. At Arizona State University, Wutich collaborates with Dr. Alexandra Brewis, a biocultural anthropologist, on the analysis of data on physical and mental health. Jose Rosales Chavez and Charu Jaiswal are students who worked in the Culture, Health, and Environment Lab, the research unit that Wutich and Brewis co-direct.

[2] This research is based on long-term ethnographic fieldwork in the squatter settlements of Cochabamba. For more information, consult Wutich 2009, 2011; Wutich and Ragsdale 2008; and Wutich et al. 2013. Names and some minor details have been changed to protect informants. No analytically relevant details have been altered. The real name of the community is used here: community members want their story told and their identity known to the world.

[3] Assessments of anxiety and depression were based on scores past the cut-points on the Standard Reporting Questionnaire (SRQ; Mari and Williams 1986) and the Hopkins Symptom Checklist (HSCL; Sogaard et al. 2003). These results are based on interviews with 42 women sampled from 23 Cochabamba squatter settlements.

# References

Berry, H. L., Bowen, K., and Kjellstrom, T. (2010). Climate change and mental health. *International Journal of Public Health*, 55: 123–132.

Coêlho, A., Adair, J., and Mocellin, J. (2004). Psychological responses to drought in northeastern Brazil. *Revista interamericana de psicologia*, 38 (1): 95–103.

Curtis, V., Danquah, L., and Aunger, R. (2009). Planned, motivated and habitual hygiene behaviour: an eleven country review. *Health Education Research*, 24 (4): 655–673.

Das, J., Do, Q. T., Friedman, J., McKenzie, D., and Scott, K. (2007). Mental health and poverty in developing countries: revisiting the relationship. *Social Science and Medicine*, 65 (3): 467–480.

Driessen, T. (2008). Collective management strategies and elite resistance in Cochabamba, Bolivia. *Development*, 51: 89–95.

Ennis-McMillan, M. (2006). *A Precious Liquid: Drinking Water and Culture in the Valley of Mexico*. Belmont, California: Thomson Wadsworth.

Goldin, J. (2010). Water policy in South Africa. *Review of Radical Political Economics*, 42 (2): 95–212.

Hanigan, I. C., Butler, C. D., Kokic, P. N., and Hutchinson, M. F. (2012). Suicide and drought in New South Wales, 1970–2007. *Proceedings of the National Academy of Sciences of the USA*, 109 (35): 13950–13955.

Los Tiempos. (2007). Asicasur entrega 2 de 5 cisternas. Aug. 20, 2007. Online: http://www.lostiempos.com/diario/actualidad/local/20070820/asicasur-entrega-2-de-5-cisternas_28308_35755.html (accessed May 17, 2013).

Lund, C., De Silva, M., Plagerson, S., Cooper, S., Chisholm, D., Das, J., Knapp, M., and Patel, V. (2011). Poverty and mental disorders: breaking the cycle in low-income and middle-income countries. *The Lancet*, 378 (9801): 1502–1514.

Mari, J. J., and Williams, P. (1986). A validity study of a psychiatric screening questionnaire (SRQ-20) in primary care in the city of São Paulo. *British Journal of Psychiatry*, 148 (1): 23–26.

Moreira, V. (2003). Poverty and psychopathology. In S. Carr and T. Sloan (eds.), *Poverty and Psychology: From Global Perspective to Local Practice*, pp. 69–86. New York: Kluwer Academic.

Nations, M. K., and Monte, C. M. G. (1996). "I'm not a dog, no!": cries of resistance against cholera control campaigns. *Social Science and Medicine*, 43 (6): 1007–1024.

Patel, V., and Kleinman, A. (2003). Poverty and common mental disorders in developing countries. *Bulletin of the World Health Organization*, 81 (8): 609–614.

Pattanayak, S., Yang, J.-C., Dickinson, K., Poulos, C., Patil, S., Mallick, R., Blitstein, J., and Praharaj, P. (2009). Shame or subsidy revisited. *Bulletin of the World Health Organization*, 87: 580–587.

Reddy, B., and Snehalatha, M. (2011). Sanitation and personal hygiene: what does it mean to poor and vulnerable women? *Indian Journal of Gender Studies*, 18 (3): 381–404.

Rios, J., Palacios, F., Gonzalez, M., and Sandoval, M. (2003). Construcción de significados acerca de la salud mental en población adulta de una comunidad urbana marginal. *Salud mental*, 26 (5): 51–60.

Scheper-Hughes, N. (1992). *Death without Weeping: The Violence of Everyday Life in Brazil*. Berkeley: University of California Press.

Siddiqui, R., and Pandey, J. (2003). Coping with environmental stressors by urban slum dwellers. *Environment and Behavior*, 35 (5): 589–604.

Sogaard, A. J., Bjelland, I., Tell, G. S., and Roysamb, E. (2003). A comparison of the CONOR mental health index to the HSCL-10 and HADS measuring mental health status in the Oslo health study and the Nord-Trøndelag health study. *Norsk Epidemiologi*, 13 (2): 279–284.

Stain, H. J., Kelly, B., Lewin, T. J., Higginbotham, N., Beard, J. R., and Hourihan, F. (2008). Social networks and mental health among a farming population. *Social Psychiatry and Psychiatric Epidemiology*, 43 (10): 843–849.

Sultana, F. (2011). Suffering for water, suffering from water: emotional geographies of resource access, control and conflict. *Geoforum*, 42: 163–172.

United Nations Development Programme (UNDP). (2006). *Beyond Scarcity: Power, Poverty and the Global Water Crisis*. New York: UNDP.

Weaver, L., and Hadley, C. (2009). Moving beyond hunger and nutrition: a systematic review of the evidence linking food insecurity and mental health in developing countries. *Ecology of Food and Nutrition*, 48 (4): 263–284.

Wutich, A. (2009). Water scarcity and the sustainability of a common pool resource institution in the urban Andes. *Human Ecology*, 37 (2): 179–192.

——. (2011). The moral economy of water reexamined. *Journal of Anthropological Research*, 67 (1): 5–26.

Wutich, A., and Ragsdale, K. (2008). Water insecurity and emotional distress: coping with supply, access, and seasonal variability of water in a Bolivian squatter settlement. *Social Science and Medicine*, 67: 2116–2125.

Wutich, A., Brewis, A., York, A., and Stotts, R. (2013). Rules, norms, and injustice: a cross-cultural study of perceptions of justice in water institutions. *Society and Natural Resources*, 26 (7): 795–809.

Chapter 4

# Life in Transit: Mental Health, Temporality, and Urban Displacement for Iraqi Refugees

Nadia El-Shaarawi

## Ali's Story

I FIRST MET ALI, A 20-YEAR-OLD IRAQI REFUGEE, in an NGO that provides legal and psychosocial assistance to urban refugees in Cairo, Egypt. Like millions of other Iraqis, Ali had been forced to flee his home as a result of violence and unrest following the 2004 invasion of Iraq. At the height of the sectarian conflict and resultant forced migration, over two million Iraqis were internally displaced within Iraq's borders, and nearly as many people crossed an international border to become refugees in surrounding countries. In 2010, when Ali and I met, many Iraqi refugees had been displaced for three or more years and were already feeling the strain of what they had imagined would be a temporary displacement becoming increasingly prolonged.

Straining to hear each other over the din of Cairo traffic outside, Ali and I sat over steaming cups of Nescafé and discussed his life in Egypt. Ali told me how he suffered from a congenital lung condition, which made it difficult for him to breathe and essentially confined him to his apartment, a haven from the persistent smog of urban Cairo. He had been forced to flee Iraq as a teenager in 2006 after terrorists burned down his family's business, robbed his family home, and threatened his life. His high school education, which he described as "the first priority of my life," had been disrupted by exile. In Egypt, he had been unable to resume his studies because he could not procure the reports that would allow him to register in school, and did not have sufficient money to pay the school fees. Ali was also unable to find work because most Iraqis are not legally permitted to work in Egypt, and he had not managed to find work in the informal economy. His medical condition also

*Global Mental Health*: *Anthropological Perspectives*, edited by Brandon A. Kohrt and Emily Mendenhall, 73–86. © 2015 Left Coast Press, Inc. All rights reserved.

made work challenging, particularly in the kinds of occupations available to him as a refugee.

Although he had initially fled to Egypt in the company of his father and brother, Ali's father had developed cancer and traveled to Syria where medical treatment for his condition was more affordable. Ali lived in a small apartment with his brother and two other young Iraqi men who were also living apart from their families. None of the young men were able to find work, so they survived on remittances from their families. As we sat talking, Ali listed his problems in Egypt. Finally, he told me that, despite all of it, his biggest problem in Egypt was his *hala nufsia*:

> My *hala nufsia*, more than my medical condition, is the biggest problem I face in Egypt. There is nothing here that could make me feel like I am living like a normal human being. It's the same place, the same bed, the same apartment every day. Sometimes I feel seriously like I'm in prison. I sleep very little. And most of the time I spend thinking. And all my thinking is worry. Are we going to stay in the same situation? What are we going to do? Since I can't go back to my home country . . . it's impossible (to go back). Because our life is at risk there, they will kill us, and I cannot go back—so what can I do?

*Hala nufsia* is a holistic term, referring to a whole spectrum of ways of being and feeling. But it was primarily spoken here in the context of displacement to denote various types of distress, ranging from discomfort caused by social problems to diagnosable mental disorders. Some Iraqis told me that their *hala nufsia* was fine, but others, like Ali, explained that their *hala nufsia* was not good in Egypt. The use of this term by Iraqi refugees in Cairo, instead of other terms that might also capture suffering or poor mental health, can tell us something about how Iraqis themselves experience, understand, and negotiate mental health and displacement. In conversations and observed interactions, Iraqi refugees never used the term *mareed nufsi*, the polite term for mental illness, even when discussing cases of severe mental illness; nor did they use more pejorative terms such as *mukhabil/a* or *majnoon/a*, both of which translate to "crazy" or "mad." Instead, they always spoke of *hala nufsia*, whether referring to themselves or others. *Nufs* is a word with multiple meanings in Arabic, but it generally refers to the self, person, or soul. When I asked one informant what *hala nufsia* meant, he explained to me that *al nufs* was "the part of the soul that allows one to exist in the world." Translated literally, *hala nufsia* then refers to the situation or condition of one's *nufs*.

In speaking about his *hala nufsia*, Ali recounted how he was afraid to return to Iraq because the situation continued to be violent. His family had lost their home, business, cars, and other property, so going back would have not meant returning to his previous life. "It's very difficult to live here. But it's not a choice for us. We can't go anywhere and we can't go back to Iraq, so we don't have any other option." When Ali spoke of his *hala nufsia*, he spoke not so much about the experiences he and his family suffered in the war in Iraq, but about the disruption of his life trajectory that exile had provoked, and the anxiety about the future and depression he felt as a result. Life in Egypt, for many Iraqis, is a liminal space between an old life in Iraq and an unknown, anxiety-provoking future.

For Ali, displacement was a source of suffering and a threat to his mental health. He likened his political asylum to "prison," lamenting that he was trapped, since he could not safely return to Iraq, was prohibited from traveling elsewhere, and could not live "like a normal human being" in Egypt. As a result, Ali reported being unable to sleep, thinking too much, and worrying about the future. Ali's medical condition, which limited his ability to leave his apartment, certainly contributed to his feeling of being imprisoned. However, many other Iraqis with whom I spoke in Egypt echoed his sentiments.

Ali identified uncertainty and worry for the future as important causes of his difficult *hala nufsia* in Egypt. While much of the literature about refugee mental health considers displacement in terms of past trauma or, more recently, stresses in contexts of asylum, Ali's case demonstrates how concern for the future can also be important for understanding displacement and mental health. These themes highlight the need to emphasize refugees' experiences of exile when we attempt to understand mental health in contexts of displacement. In this chapter, I draw on Ali's case to consider how a focus on experience bridges different dimensions of displacement and mental health. Iraqi refugees' accounts of displacement in Egypt indicate that displacement for them is not only about dis-place-ment, but also about an alteration in experiences of time (cf. Mains, Chapter 5, this volume). These changes have important implications for refugees' mental health and well-being. By taking Iraqis' narratives about *hala nufsia* seriously, we learn about how displacement refigured refugees' experiences of time and their life trajectories, and how this refiguring itself was a source of suffering.

In this chapter, I argue for a way of thinking about refugee mental health that seriously engages with subjective experience. While not by any means a resolution to ongoing debates about displacement and mental health, attention to refugees' experiences and expressions of distress and well-being allows us to uncover some of the meaning and stakes involved in questions of mental health. Instead of focusing exclusively on signs and symptoms, or on social conditions in exile, refugees' accounts of their experiences of displacement illuminate some of the hybrid ways that the social, political, and medical collide (Hamdy 2012). I argue that this approach, which draws on anthropological theory that challenges us to take subjective experience seriously, especially in moments of crisis and upheaval (Biehl,

Good, and Kleinman 2007), can contribute to ongoing debates about how best to understand post-displacement and post-conflict mental health. In particular, I am interested in thinking about mental health in contexts of displacement as an unfolding, indeterminate, experienced process, a process of "becoming" (Biehl and Locke 2010). Understanding that displacement is often characterized as an in-between, or liminal, experience, I draw inspiration from Jason Throop's assertion that anthropological accounts of subjective experience have tended to focus more on "fully articulated forms" of experience (Throop 2010), and I therefore look to the importance of considering the uncertain and emergent in understanding refugee mental health.

In recent years, a large body of anthropological work has engaged with the particularities and varieties of experience in a range of domains (see Willen and Seeman 2012 for a good review). Likewise, investigations of lived experience give us opportunities to consider aspects of refugee mental health to which we seldom attend. In displacement, where asylum is often characterized by radical forms of uncertainty, temporal experience is particularly salient. For Iraqi refugees in Egypt, problems with *hala nufsia* were often a result of experiencing time in a particular and challenging way.

IRAQI REFUGEES IN EGYPT

Iraqi refugees fled to Egypt as part of a regional process of forced migration that followed the 2003 invasion of Iraq and the sectarian violence and unrest that followed. More than 2.5 million Iraqis were internally displaced, and millions more became refugees in the region, especially in Syria, Jordan, Egypt, Lebanon, and Turkey. In the period of lawlessness and sectarian violence that reached its height in 2007 and which to some extent continues today, Iraqis suffered from kidnappings, death threats, bombings, and the redrawing of communities along sectarian lines. Religious and ethnic minorities, physicians, journalists, academics, and Iraqis associated with or perceived to be associated with the former regime or the invasion were particularly at risk.

Iraqi refugees are primarily urban refugees, meaning they mostly must fend for themselves in cities such as Cairo, Amman, Damascus, and Beirut. While the United Nations High Commissioner for Refugees (UNHCR) notes that the majority of the world's refugees now live in urban environments, the enduring image of refugees housed in sprawling refugee camps continues to dominate both the public imagination and, to a lesser extent, policy, practice, and research. Ali's situation is also not unusual in that he was displaced to a country geographically near the one he fled. Most refugees seek asylum in countries bordering or near their own, primarily in the Global South.[1]

Egypt is host to one of the largest urban refugee populations in the world. With the large Iraqi refugee populations in Syria and Jordan, humanitarian actors and media sources have paid less attention to Iraqi populations in Egypt and other countries in the region. However, at the height of the refugee crisis, Egypt hosted an estimated 100,000–150,000 Iraqi refugees (Yoshikawa 2007), although numbers are hard to estimate in urban refugee populations, and later estimates placed the numbers lower (Fargues et al. 2008). At the time, Iraqis were the second largest refugee population in Egypt, after Sudanese refugees. In 2013, more than 157,000 refugees were registered with UNHCR Egypt, a number that is likely significantly below the total number of refugees in the country.[2] Not all Iraqi refugees have registered with UNHCR; some were able to gain residency by other means.

Life in Egypt is difficult for refugees. Sadek (2010) has characterized Egypt's response to refugees, and to Iraqi refugees more specifically, as one of "indifference." Egypt is a signatory to the 1951 Refugee Convention but has entered reservations to several articles. Most refugees in Egypt are unable to work legally, cannot send their children to public schools, and are unable to access public assistance. The government leaves most of the administration and assistance of refugees to UNHCR, which manages refugee aid, including health care. In addition to these challenges, refugees face the uncertainty of the future, not knowing if or when conditions will improve, if or when they will be able to return home, or if they will be able to remain in Egypt or travel elsewhere.

Like Ali, most refugees whom I met during my fieldwork had been living in Egypt for a period of about four or more years. Yet Iraqis overwhelmingly referred to life in Egypt as "temporary." It is easy to see why Iraqis could not conceive of Egypt as a possible home; for most refugees in Egypt, many human rights are denied or at risk, including stable residency, the right to work, and the right to attend school. Despite long-standing historical, political, and religious ties between the two countries, many Iraqis spoke of feeling a sense of alienation (*al ghorba*) in Egypt. For many, the insecurity and uncertainty of life in Egypt was seen as the cause of suffering and health problems, including mental health problems.

Research on the mental health of Iraqi refugees in exile has generally shown higher rates of mental health problems than among non-conflict-affected populations (Jamil et al. 2002; Gorst-Unsworth and Goldenberg 1998). However, most studies have been conducted in resettlement contexts. In countries of first asylum, higher rates also have been found. For example, in Jordan and Lebanon, the International Organization for Migration (IOM) found high levels of psychosocial distress among more than half the respondents (IOM 2008). A UNHCR-commissioned survey in Syria found similarly high levels of distress and PTSD (Ipsos and UNHCR 2007). Studies also have indicated that stigma toward mental health issues may inhibit Iraqi refugees from seeking mental health care.

## BACKGROUND: DISPLACEMENT AND MENTAL HEALTH

Displacement is arguably a greater global concern now than ever. Since the Second World War, changes in the types and nature of armed conflict have resulted in massive displacement, with important implications for health and well-being (Pedersen 2002). Globally, 45.2 million people are forcibly displaced from their homes as a result of conflict, persecution, and human rights violations (UNHCR 2013). Yet in this context of mass displacement, fewer spaces of refuge exist globally, as countries respond to concerns about uncontrolled migration by adopting increasingly stringent policies and practices as part of deterrence and security initiatives (Silove, Steel, and Watters 2000; Gibney 2004). Despite rhetoric about floods of asylum-seekers landing on the shores of Western countries, the majority of displaced persons seek refuge, at least initially, in the Global South, either within the borders of their own country or in a neighboring country. While only some of these people meet the legal criteria of a refugee, most share the experiences of loss, dislocation, and exile associated with forced migration. For those who cross an international border, conditions of displacement in countries of asylum may be difficult and unstable, both in camps and urban contexts. In addition, displacement is often protracted,[3] with refugees living in exile for an average of about 20 years before being able to return home, successfully integrate in a country of asylum, or be resettled in a third country (Milner and Loescher 2011). Some refugees live in exile for generations, waiting for the opportunity to return home or begin their lives anew in another place.

Given their flight from violence and persecution as well as the frequently adverse and unstable conditions of exile, it is not surprising that refugees experience challenges to their mental health and well-being. Forced migration does not in itself lead to mental illness, but rates of mental illness among migrants also do not simply reflect the rates in their country of origin (Kirmayer et al. 2011). Instead, adversity is important to our understanding of mental health and migration, especially among displaced persons. Exposure to conflict is associated with increased psychopathology, but data suggest that displaced persons suffer more psychological sequelae than conflict-affected populations not forced to move (Porter and Haslam 2001), and conditions after migration often overshadow conflict-related exposures as the primary determinants of mental health (Porter and Haslam 2005; Porter 2007). In addition to conflict, then, displacement has implications for mental health that are worth considering.

While there are many shared experiences between displaced people and other types of migrants, refugees and other forced migrants are often more likely to have experienced violence and torture or to have been exposed to treacherous conditions during flight or asylum, such as in refugee camps. As a result, studies have consistently found refugees to be at a significantly higher risk of such mental illnesses as post-traumatic stress disorder, depression, and somatic complaints as compared with the general population or other types of migrant (Fazel, Wheeler, and Danesh 2005; Kirmayer et al. 2011; Lindert et al. 2009). Refugees may be exposed to multiple traumas or stressful events, further complicating ideas of refugee trauma (Hollifield et al. 2002). In addition to violence experienced before displacement, refugees and asylum seekers may experience powerlessness and precariousness if they are in contexts where their rights are circumscribed, such as refugee camps or detention (Steel et al. 2006). These conditions may provoke or exacerbate mental health problems. Legal status, or the lack of it, may also adversely affect mental health status. For example, asylum seekers exposed to policies of deterrence may be at higher risk for psychiatric disturbance (Silove, Steel, and Watters 2000), as are refugees who receive only temporary, short-term legal protection (Momartin et al. 2006).

## DEBATING REFUGEE MENTAL HEALTH IN GLOBAL MENTAL HEALTH

In the rapidly growing field of global mental health, mental illness and care in complex emergencies is of increasing concern. Mental health for refugees and other displaced persons is one important area of research and intervention. However, decades of research on post-conflict and post-migration mental health and illness have led to yet unresolved debates about the best ways to conceptualize and address the mental health needs of displaced populations. One key area of contention is the effectiveness of trauma-focused versus psychosocial approaches, as identified by Miller and Rasmussen (2010). Trauma-focused approaches, which have become the dominant approach to understanding refugee mental health, build on the explosive growth in the identification and elaboration of post-traumatic stress disorder among conflict-affected populations. Psychosocial approaches (see, for example, the IASC [2007] guidelines for mental health in complex emergencies) were developed, to some extent, as a response to this bias and point out that only some of the people who experience conflict, violence, and displacement will develop PTSD. Psychosocial approaches instead consider the social conditions and dynamics that can lead to or exacerbate distress and seek to address those without resorting to specialized psychiatric care except in cases where clearly indicated.

Trauma-focused approaches have most often been associated with large, epidemiological studies that use Western psychological measures of PTSD to evaluate the mental health of refugee and other displaced populations (Silove 2005). These approaches have been heavily criticized from a number of different perspectives. Some have argued that PTSD has been vastly overestimated in refugee populations (Summerfield 1999). Others have argued that an emphasis on PTSD draws attention away from other diagnoses, while still others believe that an overwhelming emphasis on psychological trauma misses broader structural causes and effects of conflict and displacement.

Increasingly, the field of refugee mental health is characterized by integrated approaches that seek to take into account both trauma and structural and social aspects of mental health. Despite this, questions remain about how best to conceptualize the mental health effects of displacement. Approaches from medical anthropology and related fields contribute to these questions in a number of ways. While ethnographic evidence contributes to our understanding of both trauma and the social determinants of suffering and ill health, anthropology can also widen the parameters of debate in additional ways. Studies of idioms of distress, for example, have demonstrated how purely clinical accounts of disease may fail to capture people's experiences of illness and how attention to the ways in which people speak about suffering can be important for providing care (Hinton and Lewis-Fernández 2010). Locally salient psychological frameworks, or ethnopsychologies, are crucial for understanding how people experience suffering, and for developing and implementing effective interventions as well as minimizing the risk of harm (Kleinman and Desjarlais 1995; Kohrt and Hruschka 2010). Scholars increasingly focus on emic ways of experiencing and expressing the suffering associated with displacement, an approach that draws heavily on medical anthropology. Ethnopsychology more broadly helps us to understand how a distinction between mental and physical health may not be clinically or analytically helpful in contexts where mind and body are not understood as different entities.

### Living in Transit: Displacement, Mental Health, and Temporality

While displacement is inherently about the loss of place—home, community, and country—it is also inextricably about temporality. This is particularly true in conceptualizations of the mental health effects of migration, and forced migration more specifically, which are often understood in terms of temporal, processual components, such as pre-migration, migration, and post-migration. Debates about trauma-focused versus psychosocial approaches are in some ways debates about what time period is most salient for understanding and treating refugee mental health. Should we focus on past traumas or on daily stressors? How are these interrelated? By definition, trauma-focused approaches tend to emphasize the past. In a framework that privileges PTSD, the past is a specter that haunts and predicts current and future mental health outcomes. Famously, past traumatic experience is the defining feature of PTSD, without which the diagnosis loses its rhythm and sense. Psychosocial approaches are more focused on the now: rather than emphasizing past trauma, advocates of a psychosocial framework consider conditions in displacement as being important stressors.

Ali's case, and that of many Iraqis I met, illustrates the importance of temporality for understanding mental health in contexts of displacement. For Ali, mental health was not about pre-migration, migration, or post-migration stressors; instead, it was primarily about the disruption of his life trajectory and the uncertainty of his future. His experience of the time of his life, and the ways in which time had been brought into his awareness, were the primary cause of his suffering. Iraqis often described life in Egypt as "temporary," "a station," or "transit"—a sentiment that echoes research with other refugee populations, which suggests that refugees tended to see Egypt as a place of transit, even though opportunities for resettlement or relocation were limited and difficult (Coker 2004). Yet the reality of life in exile was that Iraqis found themselves in Egypt for years, in conditions of prolonged and uncertain waiting for the future. Displacement has often been likened to liminality or limbo, with the idea that refugees are caught between places, categories, and identities (Malkki 1992; Harrell-Bond and Voutira 1992; Coker 2004).

Debates about refugee mental health are particularly challenging because of the radical disagreement between trauma-focused and psychosocial approaches. Recently, scholars have paid increased attention to other diagnoses, focused on protective factors (Fazel et al. 2012), and have made attempts to synthesize approaches using models such as the biopsychosocial model (Porter 2007). My fieldwork has emphasized how complex the experiences of poor *hala nufsia* could be. For example, perceptions of worsening security concerns in Iraq increased worry for the future by limiting the possibility of return, while also affecting conditions in Egypt through a number of means, such as creating anxiety about family members still in Iraq, raising concerns about property or other sources of income still in Iraq, and contributing to feelings of *al ghorba*, or alienation, in Egypt.

When Ali described his *hala nufsia,* it was often in terms of anxiety about the future and frustrations about conditions in Egypt, which impeded his ability to pay for the operation that would allow him to be more mobile. To make matters worse, worry about where he would be in the future, and dwindling family resources, further affected Ali's *hala nufsia.* For example, he told me that although his biggest desire was to resume his studies, he worried that he did not have the money to complete his high school education in the private system, and he knew in any case that as a refugee he would not be permitted to attend public university in Egypt, and the cost of private university rendered it out of the question. With limited money and constraints on his choices, Ali focused on how his *possibility* as a person had been constrained by displacement:

It has a very severe effect on my *hala nufsia*. I live a severe life. You can imagine my life. I am sitting in the house all the time while I have the possibility to live a normal life. But I can't have that life and I keep watching myself getting worse.

This focus on the loss of possible futures and the disruption of an imagined life trajectory was echoed in other conversations with Iraqi refugees in Cairo and illustrates the ways in which the personal and the political intersect. Iraqis reported experiencing poor *hala nufsia* on an intimately personal level when they described how they could not work, how they missed their families, how they were afraid of what the future might, or might not, hold. Yet this personal and familial suffering was inseparable from the social, political, and institutional conditions and processes of their displacement. Restrictions on refugees' ability to work and study in Egypt led to lowered socioeconomic status and limited their ability to feel that their time in Egypt was meaningful. The impermeability of borders and their inability to safely return to Iraq made refugees feel trapped in limbo. Impenetrable and lengthy bureaucratic processes for refugee status or resettlement caused Iraqis to worry about whether or not they would be able to stay in Egypt and when, if ever, they might have the opportunity to move elsewhere. Refugee status is, in legal terms, temporary by definition. However, for Iraqi refugees in Egypt, the years they had spent in Egypt and the challenge of imagining a future alternative rendered this temporariness distressing.

Most of the Iraqi refugees I met in Egypt identified problems with their *hala nufsia* or the *hala nufsia* of at least one close member of their household. This term referenced their experiences of displacement in Egypt, and was often used to describe distressing feelings or psychopathological conditions. In many ways, *hala nufsia*, with its emphasis on one's situation, was a way in which Iraqi refugees like Ali tied their experiences of distress to their ongoing conditions of displacement and their worries about the future. When people told me "the unknown future . . . that's what makes people sick," they were making a statement about the condition of being a refugee; but in a sense, these utterances index something important about the role of experience in our understanding of mental health. While refugee mental health may be about past trauma, or conditions in exile, or a number of other interrelated conditions and factors, a focus on refugees' experiences and expressions helps to highlight what matters most. In the case of Ali and other Iraqi refugees in Egypt, what mattered most was the ways in which being stuck in exile rendered the future unattainable and unimaginable.

## RECOMMENDATIONS

To date, the vast majority of research on refugee mental health has considered the mental health outcomes of refugees resettled in countries in the Global North.

Given that most refugees live in the Global South, and only about 1% of refugees are ever resettled, more attention should be paid to the mental health of refugees in countries of first asylum, particularly in conditions of urban displacement. Experiences of displacement in urban or camp settings in countries of first asylum in the Global South are different from contexts of resettlement, and even the small proportion of refugees who are resettled often spend years in contexts of first asylum prior to resettlement. While post-resettlement mental health is certainly an important topic of study, more research is necessary to understand the mental health of the vast majority of refugees who may never have access to resettlement.

I have argued here for a focus on subjective experience as a way of understanding how diagnoses and the social, cultural, and political intersect in contexts of asylum and resettlement. Aspects of the experience of displacement may be more or less meaningful for refugees, and may contribute to suffering, illness, and recovery in different ways. In the therapeutic context, this could mean turning to therapeutic modalities that incorporate refugees' narratives. In the realm of broader policy and practice, improvements in health and well-being may result from efforts to minimize the disruption of life experienced by refugees like Ali, and to support refugees' rebuilding of their lives in displacement.

## Notes

[1] The term "Global South" does not refer to a directional distinction but is a designation often used to divide the world into hemispheres based on economic and political power. Like all such terms that seek to make sweeping generalizations about the world, the designation and its utility are contested. Importantly, such terms obscure the vast diversity of cultures and societies encompassed in the north–south distinction. I use this term here not for its utility in describing any one context of displacement but to highlight some broad global trends in displacement and asylum.

[2] For example, this number does not include Palestinian refugees, who do not receive assistance from UNHCR.

[3] Collecting statistics about refugees is an enormously difficult task, given the geographic, bureaucratic, and logistical complexity of displacement on a global scale. This estimate fails to include some important protracted refugee situations, most notably Palestinian refugees. However, as Milner and Loescher note (2011: 3), there has been an increase in recent decades of both the number of refugees stuck in protracted situations and the length of time during which they are displaced.

## References

Biehl, J., Good, B., and Kleinman, A. (2007). *Subjectivity: Ethnographic Investigations.* Berkeley: University of California Press.

Biehl, J., and Locke, P. (2010). Deleuze and the anthropology of becoming. *Current Anthropology*, 51 (3): 317–351.

Coker, E. M. (2004). "Traveling pains": embodied metaphors of suffering among Southern Sudanese refugees in Cairo. *Culture, Medicine, and Psychiatry*, 28 (1): 15–39.

Fargues, P., El-Masry, S., Sadek, S., and Shaban, A. (2008). *Iraqis in Egypt: A Statistical Survey in 2008*. Cairo: Center for Migration and Refugee Studies, The American University in Cairo. http://www.aucegypt.edu/GAPP/cmrs/Documents/Iraqis%20in%20Egypt%20Provisional%20Copy.pdf.

Fazel, M., Reed, R. V., Panter-Brick, C., and Stein, A. (2012). Mental health of displaced and refugee children resettled in high-income countries: risk and protective factors. *The Lancet*, 379 (9812): 266–282.

Fazel, M., Wheeler, J., and Danesh, J. (2005). Prevalence of serious mental disorder in 7000 refugees resettled in Western countries: a systematic review. *The Lancet*, 365 (9467): 1309–1314.

Gibney, M. J. (2004). *The Ethics and Politics of Asylum: Liberal Democracy and the Response to Refugees*. Cambridge: Cambridge University Press.

Gorst-Unsworth, C., and Goldenberg, E. (1998). Psychological sequelae of torture and organised violence suffered by refugees from Iraq. Trauma-related factors compared with social factors in exile. *British Journal of Psychiatry*, 172 (1): 90–94.

Hamdy, S. (2012). *Our Bodies Belong to God: Organ Transplants, Islam, and the Struggle for Human Dignity in Egypt*. Berkeley: University of California Press.

Harrell-Bond, B. E., and Voutira, E. (1992). Anthropology and the study of refugees. *Anthropology Today*, 8 (4): 6–10.

Hinton, D. E., and Lewis-Fernández, R. (2010). Idioms of distress among trauma survivors: subtypes and clinical utility. *Culture, Medicine, and Psychiatry*, 34 (2): 209–218.

Hollifield, M., Warner, T. D., Lian, N., Krakow, B., Jenkins, J. H., Kesler, J., Stevenson, J., and Westermeyer, J. (2002). Measuring trauma and health status in refugees. *JAMA*, 288 (5): 611–621.

IASC. (2007). *Guidelines on Mental Health and Psychosocial Support in Emergency Settings*. Geneva: Inter-Agency Standing Committee.

International Organization for Migration (IOM). (2008). Assessment on psychosocial needs of Iraqis displaced in Jordan and Lebanon. Amman and Beirut: IOM. http://www.iom.int/jahia/webdav/shared/shared/mainsite/published_docs/brochures_and_info_sheets/report_psy_assessment.pdf.

IPSOS Marketing, and United Nations High Commissioner for Refugees (UNHCR). (2007). Second IPSOS survey on Iraqi refugees. http://www.unhcr.org/4795f96f2.pdf.

Jamil, H., Hakim-Larson, J., Farrag, M., Kafaji, T., Duqum, I., and Jamil, L. H. (2002). A retrospective study of Arab American mental health clients: trauma and the Iraqi refugees. *American Journal of Orthopsychiatry*, 72 (3): 355–361.

Kirmayer, L. J., Narasiah, L., Munoz, M., Rashid, M., Ryder, A. G., Guzder, J., Hassan, G., Rousseau, C., and Pottie, K. (2011). Common mental health problems in immigrants and refugees: general approach in primary care. *Canadian Medical Association Journal*, 183 (12): E959–E967.

Kleinman, A., and Desjarlais, R. (1995). Violence, culture, and the politics of trauma. In A. Kleinman, *Writing at the Margin: Discourse between Anthropology and Medicine*, pp. 173–189. Berkeley: University of California Press.

Kohrt, B. A., and Hruschka, D. J. (2010). Nepali concepts of psychological trauma: the role of idioms of distress, ethnopsychology and ethnophysiology in alleviating suffering and preventing stigma. *Culture, Medicine, and Psychiatry*, 34 (2): 322–352.

Lindert, J., von Ehrenstein, O. S., Priebe, S., Mielck, A., and Brähler, E. (2009). Depression and anxiety in labor migrants and refugees—a systematic review and meta-analysis. *Social Science and Medicine*, 69 (2): 246–257.

Malkki, L. (1992). National geographic: the rooting of peoples and the territorialization of national identity among scholars and refugees. *Cultural Anthropology*, 7 (1): 24–44.

Miller, K. E., and Rasmussen, A. (2010). War exposure, daily stressors, and mental health in conflict and post-conflict settings: bridging the divide between trauma-focused and psychosocial frameworks. *Social Science and Medicine*, 70 (1): 7–16.

Milner, J., and Loescher, G. (2011). *Responding to Protracted Refugee Situations: Lessons from a Decade of Discussion*. Forced Migration Policy Briefing 6. Oxford: Refugee Studies Center. http://www.refworld.org/docid/4da83a682.html.

Momartin, S., Steel, Z., Coello, M., Aroche, J., et al. (2006). A comparison of the mental health of refugees with temporary versus permanent protection visas. *Medical Journal of Australia*, 185 (7): 357–361.

Pedersen, D. (2002). Political violence, ethnic conflict, and contemporary wars: broad implications for health and social well-being. *Social Science and Medicine*, 55 (2): 175–190.

Porter, M. (2007). Global evidence for a biopsychosocial understanding of refugee adaptation. *Transcultural Psychiatry*, 44 (3): 418–439.

Porter, M., and Haslam, N. (2001). Forced displacement in Yugoslavia: a meta-analysis of psychological consequences and their moderators. *Journal of Traumatic Stress*, 14 (4): 817–834.

——. (2005). Predisplacement and postdisplacement factors associated with mental health of refugees and internally displaced persons. *JAMA*, 294 (5): 602–612.

Sadek, S. (2010). Iraqi "temporary guests" in neighbouring countries. In E. Laipsan and A. Pandya (eds.), *On the Move: Migration Challenges in the Indian Ocean Littoral*. Washington, DC: The Henry L. Stimson Center.

Silove, D. (2005). From trauma to survival and adaptation. In D. Ingleby (ed.), *Forced Migration and Mental Health: Rethinking the Care of Refugees and Displaced Persons*, pp. 29–51. New York: Springer.

Silove, D., Steel, Z., and Watters, C. (2000). Policies of deterrence and the mental health of asylum seekers. *JAMA*, 284 (5): 604–611.

Steel, Z., Silove, D., Brooks, R., Momartin, S., Alzuhairi, B., and Susljik, I. (2006). Impact of immigration detention and temporary protection on the mental health of refugees. *British Journal of Psychiatry*, 188 (1): 58–64.

Summerfield, D. (1999). A critique of seven assumptions behind psychological trauma programmes in war-affected areas. *Social Science and Medicine*, 48 (10): 1449–1462.

Throop, C. J. (2010). *Suffering and Sentiment: Exploring the Vicissitudes of Experience and Pain in Yap*. Berkeley: University of California Press.

UNHCR. (2013). *UNHCR Global Trends 2012*. Geneva: UNHCR. http://www. unhcr.org/51bacb0f9.html.

Willen, S. S., and Seeman, D. (2012). Introduction: experience and inquietude. *Ethos*, 40 (1): 1–23.

Yoshikawa, L. (2007). Iraqi refugees in Egypt. *Forced Migration Review*, 29: 54.

Chapter 5

# Reconnecting Hope: Khat Consumption, Time, and Mental Well-Being among Unemployed Young Men in Jimma, Ethiopia

Daniel Mains

"I AM AFRAID OF THE FUTURE. Every day is the same. Next year I need to have change, either good work or education. If I can't do this then I would rather die than continue this way." At age 24, Habtamu had been unemployed for around three years. He explained to me that unemployment was the worst part of his life. "There is constant stress thinking, 'how long will this last?' You get older, you are dependent on your family, and there is conflict everywhere. Somehow I must find change. I always argue with my father. He comes home in the evening and sees me watching television. He bothers me about getting a job, but I just turn up the volume on the TV and ignore him until he leaves."

During the early 2000s, when I first interviewed Habtamu, unemployment among young people in urban Ethiopia was close to 50%, and lengths of unemployment averaged three to four years (Serneels 2007). Like many unemployed young men in Jimma, Ethiopia, Habtamu associated unemployment with having too many thoughts and too much time. "Too many thoughts" and "thinking too much" are local idioms identified in other studies in Africa to describe worries about one's future (Johnson et al. 2009; Okello and Ekblad 2006; Patel et al. 1995; Weiss 2005), and in some of these cases, it is associated with poor mental health (Johnson et al. 2009; Okello and Ekblad 2006; Patel et al. 1995).

Habtamu tried to solve his struggles with time and thoughts by chewing khat, a green leaf that functions as a stimulant when consumed. He explained:

> Every day is the same for me. It has been this way for years. This is why I chew khat. When I chew I forget everything else. I lose myself in conversation.[1] My mind is free from thoughts. On days when I don't get khat, I don't want to do anything. Last Friday I didn't want to chew, so I just stayed at home and slept in

*Global Mental Health: Anthropological Perspectives*, edited by Brandon A. Kohrt and Emily Mendenhall, 87–102. © 2015 Left Coast Press, Inc. All rights reserved.

the afternoon. My older sister found me there and started bothering me. Finally she gave me money and told me to go buy khat. When I chew, I forget that I've been doing the same thing every day for years. If I don't get khat for a couple of days, I feel terrible sadness and nothing makes me happy.

In conducting intermittent research among youth in Jimma between 2003 and 2012, I encountered many narratives like Habtamu's. My interest in Ethiopia and youth initially came out of my experience as a Peace Corps volunteer. I was randomly assigned to Ethiopia, and from 1998 to 1999 I taught English as a second language to secondary students in Goha Tsion, a small town near the Blue Nile gorge. I noticed that many of my students were heavily invested in their education and had desires for future employment that would be nearly impossible to realize. After my experience in the Peace Corps, I began pursuing my PhD in anthropology, and for my dissertation I conducted 18 months of research, from 2003 to 2005, in Jimma. I investigated how young people negotiate the gap between economic realities and their desires for the future. I returned to Jimma for brief visits in 2008 and 2009 to work on a collaborative project that investigated the relationship between young people's aspirations for the future and mental health. For this project, I explicitly asked young people about particular symptoms of anxiety and depression.

Young men consistently described relationships among long-term unemployment, khat consumption, and symptoms of depression and anxiety, such as difficulties sleeping and a lack of satisfaction with day-to-day life. These relationships were particularly apparent in focus group discussions I conducted in 2009. In describing specific symptoms of anxiety and depression, young men consistently spoke about the importance of khat (Mains, Hadley, and Tessema 2013). However, survey data from Jimma and the surrounding countryside indicate that there is no correlation between khat consumption and symptoms of anxiety and depression (Mains, Hadley, and Tessema 2013). In other words, those with high symptom loads were no more likely to consume khat than other youth. How, then, can the relationship between khat and symptoms of anxiety and depression in youth narratives be understood? Rather than seeking to identify a causal link between khat and symptoms of anxiety and depression, I argue that both emerge out of a context characterized by high levels of youth unemployment and struggles with time.

In the first half of this chapter, I argue that unemployed young men have difficulty constructing narratives in which they are progressing toward a desirable future. They experience mental distress as they negotiate overabundant amounts of unstructured time in the present. Young men want their lives to improve with the passage of time, but they have little faith that this will occur. I examine young men's self-reported experience of having "too many thoughts" to better understand the relationship between symptoms of anxiety and depression and time. Although this relationship is specific to the case at hand, it may also be applicable to the growing number of youth throughout the world who struggle to take on the responsibilities of adults. In the second half of the chapter, I argue that the power of khat to both alleviate and exacerbate symptoms of anxiety and depression is based in the particular way that khat consumption repositions young men in relation to time and influences their construction of narratives concerning the future.

The relationship between mental health and poverty is a central issue in the field of global mental health (Das et al. 2007; Lund et al. 2011). Multi-country analyses have suggested that poverty is not consistently associated with poor mental health when controlling for gender, age, marital status, and physical health. When examining the relationship from an intervention perspective, there is more support for mental health interventions that aim to reduce poverty than there is support for interventions aimed at improving mental health (Lund et al. 2011). Recently, studies in the United States have demonstrated that the implications of poverty for poor mental health vary with ethnicity (Costello et al. 1997). Studies of Cherokee and white youth in the Great Smoky Mountains region indicate that it is not individual poverty but rather other neighborhood attributes that determine mental health (Brown et al. 2008). One of the reasons for inconsistent correlations between poverty and mental health may be assumptions about what employment and economic status mean and their consequences for mental health. For example, among the Cherokee, local expectations for one's life course can explain mental health outcomes beyond traditional economic markers (Brown et al. 2008; Brown, Hruschka, and Worthman 2009).

Drawing upon ethnographic research in Ethiopia, I develop two primary arguments to convey why economic and employment status alone is insufficient to understand well-being, mental health, and substance use disorders. First, youth mental health is closely related to the construction of desirable temporal narratives. That is, the ability of young people to see themselves moving toward a desirable future supports their mental well-being. Second, the importance of temporal narratives has policy implications for addressing youth unemployment and mental well-being. For urban young men, the experience of time is at the center of the relationship among khat, mental health, and unemployment. The significance of young people's temporal experiences suggests that policy makers must think of unemployment not only as an economic problem but also as a problem of time. Solving unemployment is not just a matter of creating work but of supporting processes in which young people can generate hopeful narratives and believe that they are progressing toward desirable futures. In other words, for youth, employment opportunities must support the perception that one's life can improve with the passage of time. Thus, rather than offer suggestions for specific policy changes, I seek to build on my analysis of khat and mental health to demonstrate the relevance of the experience of time for employment and economic policy more generally.

## ETHNOGRAPHIC AND HISTORICAL BACKGROUND

This paper is based on intermittent ethnographic research in Jimma, Ethiopia, from 2003 to 2012. Jimma is located in a lush, green, coffee-growing area around 350 kilometers to the southwest of Addis Ababa. With a population of 150,000, Jimma is the major urban center in southwestern Ethiopia. Jimma has a large university, a hospital, cinema, athletic stadium, and many multistory hotels. The city of Jimma is very diverse. Significant populations of Oromo, Dawro, Amhara, Gurage, Kaffa, Yem, and Tigrean people make their homes in Jimma. Nearly all urban residents are fluent in Amharic, which is the language used for most day-to-day social interactions. The city is split almost evenly between Muslims and Orthodox Christians, and there is a small population of Protestant Christians and Catholics.

The lives of young people in Jimma and many other urban areas of Ethiopia, including small towns, are shaped by the experience of chronic unemployment. Although urban youth unemployment has recently decreased (Broussard and Teklesellasie 2012), in the late 1990s and early 2000s, rates of unemployment among urban youth (ages 18–30) were around 50%, and lengths of unemployment averaged three to four years (Serneels 2007). High urban unemployment rates in Ethiopia are partially a result of the dramatic gap between young people's expectations for the future and economic opportunity (Mains 2007, 2012). During the 20th century, an ideal urban male life course involved education, which led to government employment, the establishment of a family, and eventually a prestigious position within one's community; but economic changes have made the actualization of this life course extremely difficult (Mains 2012).

Like many African nations, in order to access support from the International Monetary Fund (IMF) and the World Bank, during the 1990s the Ethiopian state implemented various *structural adjustment* policies aimed at liberalizing the economy. The most important of these policies for urban youth unemployment was a massive downsizing of the public sector. Previously, completing secondary school was a virtual guarantee of government employment (Markakis 1974: 183). Today, despite the growing population of educated young people who expect to access government employment, there quite simply has been no work available in the public sector. Young urban Ethiopians often choose not to take up the income-generating opportunities that exist in the informal economy because they do not believe this type of work will help them attain their aspirations (Mains 2012). In the late 1990s, rates of unemployment were highest among young people with a secondary education (Krishnan 1998; Serneels 2007), suggesting that it is partially the contrast between expectations and economic realities that led to such high rates of youth unemployment in Ethiopian cities.

Although rates of unemployment were virtually the same between urban young men and women, I focus on young men because of their particular relationship to mental well-being, time, and khat. Unlike unemployed young women, who are nearly always busy with household chores, urban young men have large amounts of unstructured free time. Throughout Ethiopia, khat consumption is also much more common among young men than young women.

## PROGRESS, THOUGHTS, AND TIME

Young men's symptoms of depression and anxiety are rooted in their inability to attain their aspirations and their accompanying struggles with time. Young men often claimed, "We live like chickens, we are just eating and sleeping." Living like chickens implies that life lacks meaning, simply moving here and there without any purpose besides filling one's stomach. They contrasted a life of "eating and sleeping" or "simply sitting" with one that involved change or "progress."[2] Progress involves incremental movements through time in a particular direction. Young men's progressive desires have been generated partially through their engagement with formal education, and young men assess progress based on local values concerning social relationships (Mains 2007, 2012). Their ideal life course is based on achieving progressive changes within social relationships. The shift from living with one's parents to marriage, having children, supporting extended family, and eventually helping one's community entails movement from a position of economic dependence, to independence, and then gradually providing support to an increasing number of dependents. This represents a particularly masculine notion of adulthood, one that has been noted in other ethnographies of Africa (Ferguson 1985; Guyer 1993; Johnson-Hanks 2006). Like many young men, Habtamu was able to attain the first step in this narrative of becoming, by finishing secondary school, but he was unable to find a job.

Although he was in his mid-twenties, Habtamu did not see marriage and a family in his near future. He told me that dating, marriage, and having children were nearly impossible, and that he would not marry before the age of 30 or 35, and then only if he had become wealthy. For young men like Habtamu, raising children was even more daunting than marriage. To simply raise children does not involve any great costs, but he wanted a better future for his children. In response to questions about the qualities of a good father, young men consistently explained that a good father must provide an expensive private education for his children. There was a notion that progressive change must occur not only in one's own life but also between generations. One young man explained, "In order for my children to reach a good place they must have everything. Good school, good clothes, and good food. If my father had been a driver, I could have been a doctor" (Mains 2012:81).

Primarily as a result of their inability to move toward adulthood by achieving progressive changes in their position within social relationships, young men experience unstructured time as overabundant and potentially dangerous. For young men, the most salient quality of time is its lack of structure, and time is often described as something to be "passed" (*yasallefal*) or "killed" (*yasgedal*). One unemployed young man explained, "In Ethiopia there is only spare time. Tomorrow is very far from today. The evening is far from the afternoon. There is no difference between today, yesterday, and tomorrow." This experience of time is increasingly common in Africa and much of the Global South. As young people fail to attain their aspirations, they become frustrated and cannot manage to place their own lives within a hopeful narrative (Hansen 2005; Jeffrey 2010; Jeffrey, Jeffrey, and Jeffrey 2008; Musharbash 2007; Ralph 2008; Schielke 2008; Weiss 2004).

The emotional state associated with "too much time" is generally described with the Amharic word *debirt*. Native Amharic speakers who are also fluent in English define *debirt* as both depression and boredom. They are not referencing a clinical psychiatric disorder. *Debirt* encompasses a range of emotions and experiences that are associated with feelings of sadness and boredom. In practice, both the sight of a person suffering from a physical injury and a day spent alone with nothing to do are described with the adjectival form of *debirt*, although in casual conversation with young men the word was used more commonly in the case of the latter. The burden of too much time that is associated with a failure to attain social milestones, then, appears to produce emotional responses similar to those created by exposure to another person's suffering.

In her investigation of discourses of boredom in 19th-century Europe, the philosopher Elizabeth Goodstein (2005) argues that boredom results from failed expectations of progress. In the Ethiopian case, unmet expectations for progress are also essential to young men's experience of too much time. Notions of progress, however, are inextricable from changes in one's position within social relationships. Feelings of *debirt* arise from the social processes associated with young men's failure to achieve normative adult responsibilities.

The relationship between boredom and symptoms of clinical depression and anxiety appears to be based in the experience of time and "thinking too much."[3] The problem of too much unstructured time is that it leads to thinking too much about one's problems. For Habtamu and many other young people, thinking too much involved rumination about the future. He continually asked himself, "how long will this last" and "what will I do in the future?" Rather than developing satisfactory answers to these questions, he found himself asking them again and again. For some youth, thoughts were not necessarily concerned with the future, but young people consistently described thinking too much in relation to repetitive thoughts about one's problems that do not lead to solutions. In focus groups, young people associated too many thoughts with symptoms of depression and anxiety, like problems with sleeping and thinking. Young men evaluate day-to-day activities specifically in terms of their ability to focus their mind away from their present condition. "Thought" (*assab*) is a key term in these narratives, representing a broad range of feelings, including stress and sadness. Some young men even went as far as defining a "good life" in terms of being "free from thoughts."

In focus groups, young men explained struggles with too many thoughts in relation to the passage of time and unemployment. One young man noted, "Yes, there is a problem of thinking too much, it is because youth lack jobs. They think, 'when will we be like our friends?' They worry about this. They also worry about how to change their families and help their families. If they get jobs they will not have too many thoughts." In this case, thoughts are associated with frustration at stagnation and a lack of participation in a process of becoming—thinking about how to become more like one's successful peers or how to help one's family improve its economic status. In terms of the actual direction of one's thoughts, these are consistently focused on the future. As one unemployed young man explained, "When I am alone with too much time I think too much. This is the worst part of the day. I think about my future. For how long will I live with my parents? Will my life ever change?"

Susan Nolen-Hoeksema (2000) argues that rumination may be a key reason behind the common comorbidity of anxiety and depression. She describes a cycle between depression and anxiety that occurs among ruminators. Ruminations are associated with anxiety in the sense that they reflect an uncertainty regarding one's ability to manage or control the future. As ruminators negatively evaluate future possibilities, hopelessness and negative evaluations of the past and present that are associated with depression are increasingly likely; depressive symptoms may "revert to anxiety symptoms when ruminators have some glimmer of hope that they may be able to wrest some control over their circumstances" (Nolen-Hoeksema 2000: 509).

Nolen-Hoeksema's analysis may be usefully complemented with more explicit attention to the qualitative experience of the passage of time and perceptions of the future. Anxiety involves a sense of fear or trepidations about what the future will bring. It is related to the belief that the future may not be desirable and in fact may be quite unpleasant (Hay 2009). In urban Ethiopia, youth as a social category is future oriented. Young people expect to be in the process of becoming something else, for which chronic unemployment is a barrier. The future for young men is not necessarily uncertain, but it is definitely not desirable, and this brings on feelings of anxiety. A growing number of studies of youth in the Global South indicate the importance of the experience of time and the disrupted processes of becoming an adult (Amit and Dyke 2012; Cole 2005; Hansen 2005; Jeffrey 2010; Jeffrey, Jeffrey, and Jeffrey 2008; Musharbash 2007; Ralph 2008; Schielke 2008; Weiss 2004). The Ethiopian case demonstrates that for these young people, mental health and the experience of time may be inseparable.

M. Cameron Hay argues that anxiety focuses the mind and generates creative solutions to problems that may disturb one's future (2001: 308). For urban young men, anxieties about the future are combined with a sense that it is nearly impossible to act in a way that will bring about a more desirable future. Young men argue that there is little they can do to solve their problem of unemployment. Certainly, some utilize strategies like reentering the education system or migrating for work, but many young men lack the means or the desire to pursue these possibilities. Most young men are concerned about their future but feel that they are powerless to find work, which causes them to experience the pain of "too much time" as particularly acute.

For many young men, khat provides a potential solution to their problems of anxiety, depression, and time. As a focus group of young men noted, "Most of the time chewing khat makes people happy." Khat provides a sort of freedom from thoughts, but not by simply preventing young men from thinking too much. Khat promotes thoughts about the future, but it also facilitates a change in the nature of these thoughts and helps young men envision a future in which achieving progress within their social relationships is possible.

## CHEWING, DREAMING, AND KILLING TIME

For young men in Jimma, khat offers a socially appropriate solution to their problems. Khat has long been chewed by Muslim men in Ethiopia at important social events (Gebissa 2004). More recently, Orthodox Christians have begun using khat recreationally, particularly young men living in urban areas. Based on participant observation in Jimma, khat consumption appears to increase among young men after they finish secondary school. Although not all parents approve of their sons' khat consumption, for the most part khat is less stigmatized than alcohol or tobacco, and pressure from parents or peers is not a common reason for avoiding khat. Khat is an affordable recreational option for urban young men. Although food prices were rising rapidly in the late 2000s, the price of khat remained relatively stable, partially because it is grown near Jimma and consumed fresh. In 2009, a bundle of khat (enough for one or two people) cost about 5 birr (about $0.40).

To understand the relationship among khat, time, and symptoms of anxiety and depression, it is necessary to examine *mirqana* (a high specifically associated with khat). For most youth, the purpose of chewing khat is to reach *mirqana*, a high achieved approximately an hour after beginning to chew. During *mirqana*, the heartbeat is notably faster, one begins to sweat, and there is a general sense of happiness and satisfaction with life. It is during *mirqana* that thoughts and conversations turn to the future, and youth begin to "dream."

Youth generally chew for at least three or four hours, finishing at some point in the evening. It is this aspect of khat consumption that solves one of young men's problems of time. When asked why they chew khat, young men often responded with the simple answer that it "kills time," and in a very literal sense, khat chewing occupies a great deal of time. It provides an activity to fill one's day. The act of first acquiring khat and then chewing and talking with friends takes hours and provides structure, focus, and rhythm to one's life. Khat chewing eliminates free time, but perhaps more importantly, it transforms the nature of thoughts that often plague unemployed young men.

It is during the state of *mirqana* that the particular social interactions associated with khat begin to emerge. Among unemployed young men, the state of *mirqana* is associated with intense discussions and "dreams" about one's desires for the future. Chewers describe the opening of the mind (*aimro yikeftal*) and thinking about wishes (*miññot*). Youth use a variety of terms, including dream (*hilm*), goal (*alama*), wish (*miññot*), and hope (*tesfa*), to describe where the mind is directed during *mirqana*.

In Jimma, while young men chewed and talked, one young man explained, "This is my favorite thing to do—chewing khat, talking, and joking. In the afternoon you will always find me here. It's better than any other way of passing time—reading the paper or watching movies. When I chew I think about the future. I plan everything for tomorrow, I make a schedule for everything. I feel very good about myself. Any problems that I have are forgotten. If a person is strong they can follow through on their plans and they might succeed, but usually, the next morning all of this is forgotten."

The dreaming that is associated with khat consumption is not a passive activity, and the social dynamics of khat consumption are very important. Chewers exchange ideas, and plans for the future are formed through intensive dialogue. It is the process of "dreaming" that appears to bond khat chewers together as a social group. One young khat chewer classified others in terms of chewers and non-chewers. Especially during *mirqana*, he prefers to be around chewers, who are dreamers who go places in their mind, while non-chewers are continually caught up in day-to-day affairs. During *mirqana*, everyday reality seems very dull. Chewers do not want to talk about anything "normal" (the English word is often contrasted with "dreaming"). They prefer an atmosphere that allows them to escape into explorations of hopes and desires for the future.

The conversations I observed while young men were chewing were often repetitive. Many young men chewed daily, and what began as fantasy could eventually be perceived as a realistic possibility, in a way that changed young men's relationships to their future. The following comes from a conversation between Habtamu and two unemployed friends. They are describing the types of conversations that they have during *mirqana*. They are also experiencing *mirqana* as they are describing it, and this most likely influences the flow of the discussion.

Tawfiq: If you are thinking about the *future*[4] or another thing . . .

Habtamu: *Future*?! In the name of God! Stop! [Implying that this is something that he could talk about all day.]

Tawfiq: If you buy khat today you will become bright. You will plan ten years ahead. [He names one thing after another—work, marriage, children—snapping his fingers between each one.] Now if I am experiencing mirqana and you ask me, I will tell you about America. After arriving in America I will go to Atlanta.

Habtamu: Is it Atlanta today?

Daniel Mains: My town.[5]

Tawfiq: Yes, yours. There, good work. A private car. A good house.

Yonas: *Palace*.

Tawfiq: After I win the DV [Diversity Visa Lottery], I will do all of this. But sometimes it gives me a headache. Thinking, "why can't I do this?"

Tawfiq: Why is it this way? *America life* and *Ethiopia life*—there is one hundred years *difference*. An American will never think about finding something to drink or something to eat. For us we eat breakfast at home, after that we don't know where we will find lunch. This is a problem. (Mains 2012:59)

Khat appears to alleviate both young men's anxieties about the future and the sense of depression that is associated with feeling trapped in the present. The comments in the discussion quoted here are an exaggerated form of what young men often express concerning their desires for the future. In other discussions, the desire to travel abroad and own a house and car that is expressed here is less common than simply finding work, supporting one's parents, and starting a family of one's own.

As young men chew and talk with their friends, the future appears to be desirable and attainable. Khat is effective not because it eliminates or reduces thoughts, but because it qualitatively changes them. During *mirqana*, time is no longer a source of anxiety because introspective thought about one's future brings pleasure rather than stress. Khat also frees young men from the present. The association between dreaming and chewing among unemployed young men clearly indicates that their minds are not focused on their problems while they chew. In contrast to the patterns of negative rumination discussed above, increased thinking during khat chewing sessions does not dwell on past failures or the absence of future opportunities. Khat appears to break the relationship between anxiety and depression that Nolen-Hoeksema (2000) describes as being cemented by rumination. The perceived possibility of moving toward the future removes young men from the present. Not only are day-to-day struggles forgotten, but also during *mirqana* it is possible to believe that tomorrow will be better than today.

The shift is not complete. As the comment about the headache indicates, the ability to achieve this fantasy is continually questioned. If khat facilitates dreams that help young men escape from depressive symptoms, it also may reproduce these same symptoms. In the group discussion quoted above, Habtamu described how one feels the morning after chewing khat.

> In the morning you don't want to talk with anyone. You won't even greet your friends. You try to remember what you were thinking about the day before, but it just won't come. Nothing helps, you can drink coffee or try anything, but you just feel bad. In the afternoon, after khat, you can deal with people again and all of the plans from yesterday come flooding back. The only thing that will bring back the feeling of brightness and hope for the future is to chew more khat. (Mains 2012: 57)

In focus groups, young men often contradicted the claims of others that khat alleviates symptoms of anxiety and depression. They claimed that khat consumption causes a lack of satisfaction with one's life. Young men in focus groups also frequently noted that the effects of khat as a stimulant disrupt one's sleep and appetite.

Unemployed chewers spoke of an intense sadness that occurs on the days when one does not obtain khat. One young man simply stated, "If I don't get khat, I hate everything." Young chewers explained that the best part of their day was when *mirqana* was beginning to set in, and they dreaded those days when they could not scrape together the money for a small bundle of khat. A different young man who occasionally worked as a barber explained, "Without khat, life is very boring and depressing (*betam yideberal*). With khat I will always find something fun to do, even if it is just visiting a sick friend, going to a mourning tent, watching television, or reading a book. Without khat I usually just stay home and sleep. Everything is more fun with khat. Even if it is just talking and watching soccer, khat makes it great."

## CONCLUSIONS

A close analysis of the day-to-day realities concerning mental distress and khat draws attention to the importance of time in a young man's life. My ethnographic research in Jimma suggests that young men's inability to create a desirable narrative in which they project themselves into the future is a key source of their mental distress. The importance of time and progress has significant implications for addressing issues of mental health and employment among young people. Khat is functional in negotiating mental distress because of its utility in repositioning oneself in relation to the future. This indicates that for young men, symptoms of depression and anxiety cannot be understood simply in economic terms. Alleviating these symptoms requires addressing how young people perceive their lives in relation to time.

Khat acts as an intervening force to overcome the present struggle to envision a desirable future. While khat simultaneously exacerbates many anxiety symptoms that are associated with battles with time, such as a loss of happiness when one is not chewing, sleeplessness, and a lack of desire for food, it also enables people to see a possible resolution to achieving what they understand to be progress. In focus group discussions, young men and women claimed that employment and other forms of financial support are the primary solutions to problems like sleeplessness or lack of satisfaction with day-to-day life. They envisioned economic changes that would alleviate their mental distress. I argue, however, that the solution to their problems is not as straightforward as many young people imagine, as work alone would not transform their experience of time. Employment would certainly alleviate young men's problem of having too much time, but it would not necessarily allow them to actualize a temporal narrative in which they gradually become the person they wish to be in the future.

When I visited Jimma in 2008, Habtamu invited me to the house he shared with his older sister. We sat on overstuffed sofas, sipping strong cups of coffee, gossiping about other young men from the neighborhood, and discussing his plans for the future. His siblings, who live in the United States, had begun paying for him to study toward his bachelor's degree in Jimma University's engineering program.[6] He was currently in his third year of the six-year evening study program, and he was confident of finding employment at the government telecommunications center after graduation. I did not get the impression that he was in a hurry to complete the program. Returning to school seemed to provide Habtamu with a sense of satisfaction and direction that he previously lacked. He still chewed khat, but now studying in the afternoon and attending classes in the evening gave him a focus for his mental energy. His studies would qualify him to teach at the university level and enable him to continue his involvement in education for the foreseeable future.

Like Habtamu, Mulugeta was an unemployed young man who participated in my 2003–2005 research. I spent a good deal of time with Mulugeta in 2012. He was working on a joint government- and international-NGO-supported project, constructing cobblestone roads in Jimma. Although the work required heavy manual labor and was not highly paid, Mulugeta took great pride in it. He described his work with phrases like "working for injera,"[7] "working to live," and "living hand to mouth." These were nearly the exact phrases that had been used to denigrate available work during in the early 2000s, but now Mulugeta claimed that even if work did not bring great profit, it still had value. Certainly there were many young men in Jimma who still argued against the value of "working to live," but Mulugeta demonstrated an attitude that I found among other formerly unemployed young men, in which there was an increased emphasis on the present and less concern with achieving linear progress toward a desirable future. He explained that the biggest change from his work was related to his mental health: "This is the most important thing. Before life was very stressful, with constant thoughts about the future. Now I am so busy with work that I have no time for thoughts. I work, take a shower, eat, and then sleep. My mind is free and it feels good." The creation of opportunities for education and work were certainly important for Mulugeta and Habtamu, but for both, shifts in their relationship to the future and the passage of time were equally significant in easing their mental distress.

This may explain why some unemployed youth in Ethiopia choose volunteering despite its financial detriment to their family (see Maes, Chapter 17), and therefore may provide further insight into some work-related decisions Ethiopian men make. The young men I met in Ethiopia would benefit from jobs that lead to progressive movement within their social relationships. This requires jobs that not only allow young men to be independent from their parents, but also to begin to provide support for a growing network of dependents. Reentering the education system provided Habtamu with a sense of satisfaction because it enabled him to believe that he would eventually achieve progress within his relationships. While this supports the need for more job creation at a level commensurate with the desires of educated Ethiopian young men, it also opens opportunities for other forms of mental health and psychosocial interventions. For example, assisting young men in finding value in other activities or redefining the meaning associated with different forms of employment may help them to envision narratives in which they are moving toward a desirable future. To solve young men's problems of time and improve their mental well-being, alternatives to khat chewing must not only qualitatively change one's experience of the present but support a desirable relationship to the future.

## Notes

1  *Chewata* is literally "play" in English, but in this context it is best translated as "conversation" or "joking."

2  I use "progress" for the Amharic *lewt*, which is sometimes used to refer to any type of change, but in youth narratives it took on a meaning of gradual improvement over time. *Idget*, meaning "growth," was sometimes used as well.

3  See also Kaiser and McLean, Chapter 16, this volume.

4  Italics indicates words that were spoken in English.

5  It was not simply the fact that Mains lived in Atlanta prior to conducting research that caused these young men to reference the city. Both Habtamu and his friends had family living in the Atlanta area.

6  Habtamu's relatives in the United States paid for evening courses. Most youth did not have these resources, but the expansion of the post-secondary education system created numerous opportunities for students to attend government universities at very little cost.

7  *Injera* is a flat, spongy bread that is the staple food in Ethiopia.

## References

Amit, V., and Dyke, N. (eds.) (2012). *Young Men in Uncertain Times*. New York: Berghahn Books.

Broussard, N., and Tekleselassie T. G. (2012). Youth Unemployment: Ethiopia Country Study. Working Paper 12/0592. London: International Growth Centre.

Brown, R., Hruschka, D., and Worthman, C. (2009). Cultural models and fertility timing among Cherokee and white youth in Appalachia: beyond the mode. *American Anthropologist*, 111 (4): 420–431.

Brown, R., Adler, N., Worthman, C., Copeland, W., Costello E. J., and Angold, A. (2008). Cultural and community determinants of subjective social status among Cherokee and white youth. *Ethnicity and Health*, 13 (4): 289–303.

Cole, J. (2005). The Jaombilo of Tamatve (Madagascar), 1992–2004: reflections on youth and globalization. *Journal of Social History*, 38 (4): 891–914.

Costello, E. J., Farmer, E. M., Angold, A., Burns, B. J., and Erkanli, A. (1997). Psychiatric disorders among American Indian and white youth in Appalachia: the Great Smoky Mountains study. *American Journal of Public Health*, 87 (5): 827–832.

Das, J., Do, Q.-T., Friedman, J., McKenzie, D., and Scott, K. (2007). Mental health and poverty in developing countries: revisiting the relationship. *Social Science and Medicine*, 65 (3): 467–480.

Ferguson, J. (1985). The bovine mystique: power, property and livestock in rural Lesotho. *Man*, 20 (4): 647–674.

Gebissa, E. (2004). *Leaf of Allah: Khat and the Transformation of Agriculture in Harerge, Ethiopia, 1875–1991*. Oxford: James Curry.

Goodstein, E. (2005). *Experience without Qualities: Boredom and Modernity*. Stanford, California: Stanford University Press.

Guyer, J. (1993). Wealth in people and self realization in equatorial Africa. *Man*, 28: 243–265.

Hansen, K. T. (2005). Getting stuck in the compound: some odds against social adulthood in Lusaka. *Africa Today*, 51 (4): 2–17.

Hay, M. C. (2001). Anxiety, remembering, and agency: biocultural insights for understanding Sasaks' responses to illness. *Ethos*, 37 (1): 1–31.

——. (2009). *Remembering to Live: Illness at the Intersection of Anxiety and Knowledge in Rural Indonesia*. Ann Arbor: University of Michigan Press.

Jeffrey, C. (2010). *Timepass: Youth, Class, and the Politics of Waiting in India*. Stanford, California: Stanford University Press.

Jeffrey, C., Jeffery, P., and Jeffery, R. (2008). *Degrees without Freedom? Education, Masculinities and Unemployment in North India*. Stanford, California: Stanford University Press.

Johnson, L., Mayanja, M. K., Bangirana, P., and Kisito, S. (2009). Contrasting concepts of depression in Uganda: implications for service delivery in a multicultural context. *American Journal of Orthopsychiatry*, 70 (2): 275–289.

Johnson-Hanks, J. (2006). *Uncertain Honor: Modern Motherhood in an African Crisis*. Chicago: University of Chicago Press.

Krishnan, P. (1998). *The Urban Labour Market during Structural Adjustment: Ethiopia 1990–1997*. Oxford: Center for the Study of African Economies.

Lund, C., de Silva, M., Plagerson, S., Cooper, S., Chisholm, D., Das, J., Knapp, M., and Patel, P. (2011). Poverty and mental disorders: breaking the cycle in low-income and middle-income countries. *The Lancet*, 378 (9801): 1502–1514.

Mains, D. (2007). Neoliberal times: progress, boredom, and shame among young men in urban Ethiopia. *American Ethnologist*, 34 (4): 659–673.

——. (2012). *Hope_is Cut: Youth, Unemployment and the Future in Urban Ethiopia*. Philadelphia: Temple University Press.

Mains, D., Hadley C., and Tessema, F. (2013). Chewing over the future: khat consumption, anxiety, depression, and time among young men in Jimma, Ethiopia. *Culture, Medicine, and Psychiatry*, 37 (1): 111–130.

Markakis, J. (1974). *Ethiopia: Anatomy of a Traditional Polity*. Oxford: Clarendon Press.

Musharbash, Y. (2007). Boredom, time, and modernity: an example from aboriginal Australia. *American Anthropologist*, 109 (2): 307–317.

Nolen-Hoeksema, S. (2000). The role of rumination in depressive disorders and mixed anxiety/depressive symptoms. *Journal of Abnormal Psychology*, 109 (3): 504–511.

Okello, E., and Ekblad, S. (2006). Lay concepts of depression among the Baganda of Uganda: a pilot study. *Transcultural Psychiatry*, 43 (2): 287–313.

Patel, V., and Gwanzura, F., Simunyu, E., Lloyd, K., and Mann, A. (1995). The phenomenology and explanatory models of common mental disorder: a study in primary care in Harare, Zimbabwe. *Psychological Medicine*, 25 (6): 1191–1200.

Ralph, M. (2008). Killing time. *Social Text*, 26 (4): 1–29.

Schielke, S. (2008). Boredom and despair in rural Egypt. *Contemporary Islam*, 2: 251–270.

Serneels, P. (2007). The nature of unemployment among young men in urban Ethiopia. *Review of Development Economics*, 11 (1): 170–186.

Weiss, B. (2004). The barber in pain: consciousness, affliction, and alterity in urban East Africa. In A. Howanda and F. De Boeck (eds.), *Makers and Breakers: Children and Youth in Postcolonial Africa*. Oxford: James Curry.

——. (2005). Introduction: contentious futures: past and present. In B. Weiss (ed.), *Producing African Futures: Ritual and Reproduction in a Neoliberal Age*, pp. 1–20. Leiden: Brill.

Chapter 6

# The Greater Good: Surviving Sexual Violence for Schooling

Eileen Anderson-Fye

## INTRODUCTION

JUANA WAS NOT UNLIKE OTHER YOUNG WOMEN in impoverished, post-colonial communities—especially those undergoing rapid change. She felt great ambition for a better life than she observed among her mother and aunts. Juana's broad smile, friendly demeanor, and easy laugh stood out for their particular charm, though most young women in her rural secondary school in San Andrés,[1] Belize, also prided themselves on their friendliness at the time.

Belize, post-colonial for only the past 15 years, was in a period of nation-building, and it professed a friendly and welcoming multiculturalism as core to its identity. In fact, "friendliness" topped the list of desired and proclaimed personality traits cited in a survey of every high school girl ($n = 80$) in San Andrés, the country's most tourism-driven town, neatly matching the national rhetoric begun when these young women were born (Anderson-Fye 2002, 2003).

Juana, aged 13 at the time, was the first young woman to approach me on my first day of fieldwork in San Andrés. The research that began that winter morning has since evolved into an 18-year longitudinal study of the first mass high-school-educated cohort of young women in the region. That morning, the principal announced my arrival and interest in speaking with students during their study halls. I was a doctoral student in human development and anthropology, but he introduced me as "training to be a doctor." Juana, a petite young woman of multicultural Mayan, mestizo,[2] and Garifuna heritage, ran to the front of the line when the bell rang to signal the start of her study hall.

"Miss! Miss!" she called. "I want to talk with you, and I want you to check me" (field notes 12/96). When I asked her what she wanted me to check, she answered, "I want you to check me that I'm a virgin."

*Global Mental Health: Anthropological Perspectives*, edited by Brandon A. Kohrt and Emily Mendenhall, 103–116. © 2015 Left Coast Press, Inc. All rights reserved.

After I explained that I was not training to be a medical doctor, she explained:

Miss, my stepfather told my mother I'm not a virgin. And I AM! I AM! I want you to check me and tell her, prove to her. My stepfather told her my uncle molested me and so I'm not a virgin. But HE [stepfather] was the one who do that to me. HE was the one who try to sleep with me. That don't count! I did not want that and I am still a virgin! (Juana; LI1; 12/96)[3]

Juana's impassioned words about molestation by her stepfather took me aback at first. But as I met with other students, I learned she was one of a remarkable group of young women, young women whose courageous pursuit of well-being and freedom from sexual violence have changed their society.

## THE CONTEXT: WHAT'S AT STAKE IN A SECONDARY SCHOOL DIPLOMA?

Juana entered secondary school in the 1990s. At this time, young women from all social strata were just beginning to have the chance to continue their education beyond the primary level. Like many of her peers, Juana fought hard to have family resources directed toward *her*, to cover *her* school fees. Until that historical moment, families that had enough money to send a child or children to school usually sent the boys; they had better employment and economic prospects, and their future social roles hinged on being breadwinners. But as eco-tourism ballooned in San Andrés, a new, feminized service sector offered many "good" jobs for young women with high school diplomas. Girls seized these opportunities, seeing education not only as a way *toward* financial independence but also as a future way *out* of difficult situations, including sexual and physical violence in the home (Anderson-Fye 2010b). Moreover, tourism and its attendant economic development brought a substantial influx of money to San Andrés, bolstering most families' incomes to the level that even unskilled laborers could send a child to secondary school for the first time in the community's history.

This widespread hope for a better life through secondary education, coupled with actual pathways to employment for young women, created an intense hunger for a secondary diploma among Juana and her peers. The secondary diploma became their linchpin for future well-being. Juana's peers all had either experienced or witnessed significant domestic violence in some way, a phenomenon disturbingly common in recently post-colonial contexts. The idea of secondary school leading to a diploma, and in turn to a service sector job, represented a path out of future violence. If they could secure a job that paid above subsistence level, young women would be able to remove themselves from abusive situations, a future peril that every young woman saw as possible, even likely (Anderson-Fye

2010b). As a result, a diploma carried immense value on multiple levels. The stakes to achieve that diploma could not be higher for most young women. Yet, as is the case in many places where secondary schooling is not yet universal (as well as many where it is), the four years of secondary school can be full of unexpected pitfalls and potential derailments.

In our subsequent conversations, Juana recounted a heartbreaking set of choices that proved tragically common. To stay in school, she needed her stepfather to pay for her school fees. For her stepfather to continue to pay those expenses, she had to accept his ongoing sexual molestation. If she moved out, she would have to leave school. Without that diploma, she would be limited to subsistence-level jobs, which in turn meant she would risk being unable to afford to escape further abuse for the rest of her life. Would she endure shorter-term abuse to increase the odds of longer-term gain?

This hideous dilemma is only one version of the decisions that young women face as they seek to attend and stay in secondary school around the world. Some of Juana's peers who could not muster family resources pursued sex work to pay for school. Others would move in with "benefactors" who traded sex for school fees. Not surprisingly, girls who feel these pathways are their only options have low rates of school completion globally (Annitto 2011; Birdsall, LeVine, and Ibrahim 2005; Gerver 2013; Williams, Binagwaho, and Betancourt 2012). Yet Juana and her cohort defied those trends, with most earning their diplomas and securing promising positions. Even when a young woman gains her diploma and escapes abuse, however, these brutal situations leave harmful residue that can impair mental health for the rest of a young woman's life. The persistence of Juana and her cohort underscores the increasing importance of educational experience and success as key components of well-being for young people around the world. They also offer lessons about well-being in contexts of enormous constraint as well as clues about how to reduce these unconscionable dilemmas.

### An Uneasy Arithmetic: Short Violation of Self for Long-Term Preservation of Self

Throughout high school, Juana continued to endure sexual advances and abuse from her stepfather. Like many other young women, she spoke about it in a matter-of-fact way. "I hate it when he [stepfather] does that to me. I hate it. And I hate him. I hate that he makes me leave myself" (Juana; LI2; 12/97). In the third follow-up year, I began to unpack the ethnopsychological concept of "leaving the self." I asked her about it.

I: What does it mean that he makes you leave yourself?

J: He makes me leave myself.

I: I'm not sure I know what that means.

J: You don't know what that means?

I: Could you explain it to me to make sure I understand what *you* mean?

J: You should never leave yourself . . . never let a man take advantage of you . . . never let them sleep with you, hurt you, or touch you . . . you know, do those things men do. . . . With my stepfather he *made* me leave myself. I didn't *want* to. I never do. I never do those things like sleep with boys, drink beer, you know, those bad things. I always carry myself, maintain myself. . . . He [stepfather] made me leave myself but *I* would never leave myself. (Juana; LI3; 1/99)

Initially surprised that I did not know implicitly about "leaving the self," Juana explained that maintaining the self includes staying away from "bad things" like boys' sexual advances, alcohol, and drugs. Nevertheless, she noted, sometimes someone can *make* you leave yourself, which is an additional violation to the physical and emotional aspects of violation. Her stepfather's abuse was a violation of the *self* and the ethnopsychological structures set up to take care of the self.

## ETHNOPSYCHOLOGY, COPING, AND CULTURES OF GENDER-BASED VIOLENCE

Juana and her cohort managed awful experiences of gender-based maltreatment through an ethnopsychology organized around self-care and self-protection. Ethnopsychology, like other "ethno" theories, refers to local orientations and theories about "how people work." The young women of this community across ethnic and class lines articulated their heavily gendered Belizean ethnopsychology as "Never leave yourself" (English); "Neva' lef yo'sef" (Creole); and "No te dejes" (Spanish); (see Anderson-Fye 2003 for extensive discussion of this ethnopsychology).

By applying the principles of "Never leave yourself" to the changing world around them, these young women persevered through deeply painful experiences to achieve extraordinary goals on personal, social, and institutional levels. Their ethnopsychology provided a way to survive in the moment of harm, and also enabled them to *filter* symbolic and material opportunities of globalization through a lens that emphasized self-protection and self-care.

This approach framed their engagement with transnational media, for example, in that they quickly incorporated notions consistent with this principle found on television programs (Oprah Winfrey's shows were a perennial favorite) and the Internet. In particular, ideas and language regarding individual rights, gender equality, and strategies that women elsewhere in the world employed for success resonated the most for them. On the other hand, these young women filtered out messages that contradicted this ethnopsychology, such as pressures for a thin body that had been influential in many other parts of the globe (Anderson-Fye 2003, 2004). These young women engaged this ethnopsychology in a profoundly intentional, multilevel, and individual way. And, while they did not intend to act as a cohort, their behaviors simultaneously accumulated and ultimately changed their community—and their children's lives (Anderson-Fye 2010b).

Indeed, prioritizing long-term gain over short-term harm requires an environment where such aspirations carry at least some credibility. Rapid economic and sociocultural change generally tends to shift gender roles. In Belize's context of global eco-tourism, it opened up an entire feminized service sector where women with a high school diploma could earn wages above subsistence level for the first time in the country's history. In San Andrés, those who earned a high school diploma could expect economic independence, particularly when they also possessed a friendly demeanor and physical attractiveness (cf. Anderson-Fye 2004). Over the next decade, Juana and many of her peers realized that once-unattainable goal—and went on to experience its promise.

The culture of gender in Juana's community in the mid- to late 1990s was fundamental to the way Juana and her peers experienced and responded to sexual violence. The eco-tourism boom meant that gender roles for girls and women began to expand dramatically. Feminine roles were already complex in San Andrés because of the coexistence of Latin American patriarchal family structures and Caribbean matriarchal roles among some sub-groups. Multiple systems of gender existed in the community even before the explosion of television, tourism, Internet access, and other routes of cultural globalization (Sutherland 1998).

The 1990s brought new forms of gender role change. Eco-tourism's growth brought an enormous influx of cash into the community. The increased circulation of money had multiple effects, including ones directly relevant to Juana and other young women. First, more families could afford to pay secondary school fees for at least some of their children. Second, the ability to acquire alcohol increased exponentially, which in turn led to more frequent and severe bouts of inebriation among residents—particularly men. The narratives that young women shared of gender-based violence often included drunkenness on the part of aggressors. To be clear, such gender-based violence had long existed in this community, but the upheaval generated by eco-tourism created new contexts. Increased availability of alcohol made the incidents more common, while new economic opportunities signaled pathways women could follow to escape cycles of abuse (Anderson-Fye 2010b).

Attending secondary school represented the first and most significant step along that journey. The young women in this study, including Juana, immediately recognized the potential rewards of a degree and seized the opportunity to enroll. In fact, young women far outstripped men in attendance and graduation rates as well as in regional benchmarks (Anderson-Fye 2010b). Their impressive educational attainment made them the first female mass-educated secondary cohort in the community, and began a significant shift in gendered power. These young women quickly began to ascend career ladders in nearly every profession, with the minor exceptions of those deemed most masculine (e.g., construction and dive guiding).

Even as feminine influence grew, masculinity faced growing challenges. For decades, a deeply rooted "machismo"-based masculinity (Gutmann 2006; Sutherland 1998) had allowed men a sort of ownership over the bodies of women and children. As recently as 1997, a man had bragged publicly how he had "had" his teenage daughter sexually to ensure she was initiated well. Mothers regretfully discussed their inability to keep their partners from instigating sexual contact with their daughters. Sexual abuse of children did not become illegal until 1995, and even then officials prosecuted few cases. It was not until 2011 that the first case of child sexual abuse in San Andrés appeared in the local news.

This long-standing history of child sexual abuse as common, even accepted behavior (Cameron 1997), inevitably influenced the way young women like Juana viewed the behavior, even when they experienced it themselves. In their early conversations with me, the schoolgirls reported, "that's just how men are" and "that's just what men do" (field notes, 5/97). In 1997, 58 of the 60 schoolgirls interviewed (of 80 enrolled) endorsed such beliefs about male nature. Men's sexual aggression was seen as typical and unavoidable. Since "men don't know otherwise" (field notes, 5/97), girls sometimes hardly blamed their sexual aggressors. While universally "hating" the treatment, many young women showed more fury toward their mothers, "who should know better," than their abusers (Anderson-Fye 2010a, 2010b). In this culture of gender, girls also tended not to blame themselves or perseverate that they somehow caused the abuse, patterns common in the United States (Herman 1997). The absence of self-reproach during this period played a pivotal role in the ways girls like Juana coped with what they later came to consider abuse.

Juana had friends with their own apartments and several aunts with whom she might live. When I asked why she did not move out of her house, she explained:

> I have to endure it. I have to live it for now. It's not my mother's fault. Men do these things. My stepfather makes good money in his [construction] job. . . . He pays my school fees. If I move, no one pays my fees and I drop out. I need my [secondary school] diploma . . . you see what happens here with no diploma . . . girls, like my mother, they have to stay like this. They get treated bad all their life. I don't want that. I get my diploma, and I'll get a good job, and I'll get my apartment. I won't take it, and if he does it to my sister when I leave, I can take her. And if he does it to my mother, I can take her. And if my husband does it to my daughter, I can take her away. So I think I only have one more year and then I

don't take it ever again . . . and I don't leave myself ever again . . . that's worth it to me. (LI3; 1/99)

Juana articulated a temporally based logic I came to hear repeatedly. If she could endure violation of her body, her emotions, her daily life, and her articulated *self* for a limited time (i.e., until graduation), she could obtain a future free from this treatment for herself, any future children, and possibly even her sister and mother. That highly desirable goal—the most important aspiration that Juana and other girls reported individually (Anderson-Fye 2010a) and as a group (Anderson-Fye 2010b)—gave them reason to bear almost anything until they could graduate and ultimately get "a good job" that allowed them to support themselves—and, if necessary, their families. Fifteen years after Juana first asked me to confirm her virginity, she achieved economic independence and went on to support her child herself. Juana removed two abusive partners from their lives, including the biological father.

## *"She Should Know Better": Who is to Blame?*

While Juana did not express anger at her mother, many of the other young women articulated outright rage that their mothers did not prevent the abuse. As one young woman put it, "she [my mom] should know better . . . after all, she's been through it!" Because they believed their mothers should "know better" since they had suffered "the same things," these daughters expressed complex sets of feelings—immense love for their mothers, combined with enormous hurt and anger that they did not stop the behaviors. Several young women who showed depressive symptoms attributed the onset or worsening of these symptoms to what they considered their mothers' betrayal—condoning gender-based maltreatment in the home. Many years later, they tended to express a new understanding that their mothers did not have the same educational or employment opportunities that they did, and asserted that their mothers had done the best they could. In fact, several went on to take in their mothers to remove them from domestic violence. In longitudinal narratives 10 years post-graduation, almost the entire sample described reconciliation with mothers. Now that they were adult women managing a household, they felt a new kind of compassion for the constraints their mothers experienced.

Also notable was the virtual absence of the concept of "victim" in the initial five-year study, a finding especially surprising in light of the sexual trauma literature (e.g.,Herman 1997; van der Kolk, McFarlane, and Weisaeth 2006). The young women did not report feeling idiosyncratically targeted. They also expressed understanding that sexual abuse was widely prevalent despite the lack of public discourse (Anderson-Fye 2010b). Finally, they recognized that they no had immediate recourse to stop the abuse. As a result, the perpetrator-victim construct did not appear to serve a psychological or legal purpose.

In subsequent years, however, I began to see evidence of the emergence of "victim" as a construct. Young women started to exhibit post-traumatic stress symptoms in the wake of cultural globalization and went on to seek psychiatric help, some of it in transnational contexts (Anderson-Fye 2010a). In 2011, after a string of high-profile rape-murders of young women in urban areas of Belize, the concept of "victim" became ensconced in public discourse. It was cited in litigation and cropped up in women's private conversations and public social networking communications.

This shift to a model of perpetrator-victim is significant in that it places willful blame on the aggressor. Once sexual violence is a matter of "will" and not "nature," room for nonviolent masculinities can appear in the communal imagination. The young women in this study actively sought nonviolent male romantic and sexual partners in their adolescence and early adulthood. For most of them, they either found a partner who met their criteria or rejected those who later acted violently. Because of the women's earlier successful pursuit of educational advancement, they were able to take action to support themselves if necessary, an option earlier generations largely lacked (Anderson-Fye 2010b).

When gender norms and expectations change rapidly and continue to evolve, the question of young men's developing masculinity also demands consideration. Although a full discussion is beyond the scope of this chapter, ethnographic data and interviews provide powerful evidence of struggle and uncertainty among the male peers of the focal research participants. These young men have felt significant distress regarding the transition to adulthood in an environment where gender roles, and masculinity itself, were in such rapid flux. This question of how boys plot a new course of successful masculinity without clear role models and rules remains a pressing one.

## NAMING AND ENDURING "AWFUL" EXPERIENCES FOR A GREATER GOOD

It is in this context of gender and cultural change in San Andrés that girls navigated their experiences of sexual abuse inside the home and their responses to them. While about one-third of the young women enrolled in the high school in 1997 reported having experienced "abuse," all were highly aware of it (Anderson-Fye 2010b). In cross-sectional interviews with nearly half of the high school girls, the majority spoke spontaneously of gender-based violence. In close longitudinal interviews over the course of five years, all 16 girls in this subsample discussed abuse as a central life issue—whether or not they personally experienced it. Ninety-four percent of the total schoolgirl population listed maltreatment at the hands of men as one of their top three life concerns (education and social relationships were the others).

Juana was the first in her family to graduate from high school, and she collected multiple achievements and accolades in the process. She worked part-time during high school in various tourism-related jobs and easily secured a "good job" with her diploma. Immediately upon graduation, she moved into her own apartment. By delaying her departure until she earned her diploma, Juana not only secured ongoing school fee payments, but also, she said, kept critically important peace with her mother. If she had moved out earlier, all eyes in the community would have been on her mother. Peers likely would have blamed her mother for some sort of idiosyncratic failure, or possibly even blamed Juana for being a "bad daughter." This potential individual failure stands in contrast to what many young women later came to see as a larger structural failure—namely, that so many girls like Juana felt their best option was to endure temporary maltreatment to escape it permanently. Moving out after graduation but before marriage was a nascent cultural pattern; that is, enough girls had done so that Juana's choice was a culturally intelligible action. Therefore, waiting allowed her family to save face and let Juana achieve the educational milestone she needed. She swiftly attained her economic goals after graduation.

Since graduation, Juana has won a series of promotions and now manages a large tourist resort. She has taken in a sister and her mother, and her mother continues to live in her home. Juana also committed to a common-law marriage with a man who was the biological father of her child. When he began to drink and act irresponsibly, she kicked him out of the house. She later entered into a common-law marriage with a man she has known her entire life and who, she says, treats her well. She makes a higher salary than he does, which she feels helps to justify her support of her mother. Juana also paid her sister's school fees before her new husband moved in, and this sister since has found her own apartment. Juana also has a young son she intends to raise to be "different" from "those bad men"—one who is more like her current husband. Again, this child-rearing goal echoes those of her contemporaries and suggests an expansion of masculine gender roles. Unlike the near-ubiquitous sense among young women in the mid-1990s that "that's how men are" in relation to abusive behavior, this cohort of young women has sought nonviolent masculinities in their relationships with partners. In addition, they actively attempt to socialize this masculinity in their children.

Today, Juana describes her greatest burden as "the stress of being a working mother." She says that enduring the "bad behavior" was worthwhile because it ultimately allowed her to achieve her educational, career, and life goals. Like many of her peers, Juana felt her only choice was to endure sexual molestation (her term) to get the education she needed while also remaining loyal to her mother. "Would I rather have not had that bad stuff happen and instead just go to school? Of course!" she recounted. "But if I had to choose again, I'd make the same choice."

Ten years after graduation, every young woman in this study found an actual or possible way to economic self-sufficiency.[4] They work in tourism, banking, utilities, education, and politics. Some have taken breaks from employment for family reasons, but all remain employable. Most gained additional education in junior college and further expanded their professional options. In a dramatic contrast to their mothers, none has remained in relationships with men who hurt them or their children. Generally, their mental health reports are positive, although they encounter everyday stress and now worry about their own children. Juana's experience and the life pathway she has navigated share many commonalities with her peers' stories.

## A DOUBLE-EDGED SWORD: MENTAL HEALTH PRESENT AND FUTURE

Juana's achievements are remarkable but have not come without costs. As an adolescent, Juana battled what she called "problems in my head and heart." Over the five years of the initial study, she suffered periods of despondency when she would burst into tears, stop eating, and complain of overwhelming lethargy.

Once, after a difficult incident, she approached me sobbing, finally choking out that she wondered if she should go on living, or if things might be easier for herself and her mother if she ended her own life. Today, she reports no symptoms of depression but also acknowledges doubts of "the kind everyone has like on a bad day where I feel I didn't do a good enough job at work or being a mom." She does, however, continue to have flashbacks, particularly in the middle of the night. She reports hating them but also notes that "they remind me of how good I did. I got me and my mom out" [LI15, 5/2012].

Among the entire cohort of young women, a range of mental health problems were identified in relation to sexual violence. Most common were depressive symptoms. Young women reported sadness, changes in sleep and eating, stomachaches, and social withdrawal, and a few turned to drugs or alcohol to "block out the feelings." They also cited anxiety symptoms of "too much worry," hypervigilance (which seemed highly rational to me, albeit stressful), and obsessive thoughts. Under the condition of "that's just how men are" described above, post-traumatic stress per se proved rare, though reports of it since have increased. Elsewhere, I described the first young woman to receive a PTSD diagnosis after sexual abuse (Anderson-Fye 2010a).

Every girl reported these experiences as "awful" and "stressful," whether they classified them as "abuse" or "just how life is" (Anderson-Fye 2010b). It is unequivocal that enduring gender-based maltreatment generally and sexual violence in particular caused a cascade of struggles and symptoms for these young women, impairing the quality of their lives. Across the globe, the World Health Organization (2013b) documents that the rates of depression and substance abuse are approximately twice as high for those who have experienced sexual violence compared with those who have not. Also important, though, are the effects that a culture of sexual violence had on the 70% of young women *not* reporting personal experiences in this domain. In the initial five-year study, every young woman reported some degree of stress and anxiety regarding the possibility of sexual violence. Many reported profound sadness at times, especially because all personally knew someone who had been a target of sexual violence. Negative mental health effects were found not only for young women like Juana who experienced sexual violence, but also among the entire population of schoolgirls citing the *possibility* of sexual violence (see Anderson-Fye 2010a).

Notably, a key dimension mostly absent from the majority of narratives in this longitudinal study was hopelessness. Young women seized upon the prospect of future employment and financial independence to sustain themselves emotionally through difficult and uncontrollable experiences. Through the lens of trying to "never leave yourself," Juana and her peers fought moment to moment to preserve their psychological well-being and work toward a better future in a particular historical moment where actual opportunity existed. In doing so, as a cohort, they have changed the local landscapes for themselves and their children. While other challenges to adolescent mental health have emerged, protections around this common set of issues of sexual violence have expanded dramatically at family, institutional, legal, and community "ethos" levels.

## THE GLOBAL PICTURE

The tradeoffs Juana explicitly made between shorter-term endurance and longer-term educational and employment security are not unique. Young women around the globe are affected by sexual violence and also face inconceivable choices between enduring an awful present for a better imagined future. A discussion of further constrained circumstances—where girls have no choice—is beyond the scope of this chapter (Annitto 2011; Rafferty 2013; WHO 2013a, 2013b).

The kind of endurance of intra-family sexual violence that Juana suffered to stay in school is found around the world, particularly in places without services and other structural options (Ganju et al. 2004; WHO 2013a, 2013b). A related dynamic documented in multiple world regions involves more explicit transactional sex for school fees among secondary schoolgirls (e.g., IRIN 2011; Roberts, Jones, and Sanders 2013; Rupapa 2013). In this circumstance, girls engage in local sex work markets, or non-familial guardians offer school fees in exchange for sex. Engaging in sex work for tertiary educational tuition also has been documented in both the Global North and Global South (e.g., Gerver 2013; Roberts, Jones, and Sanders 2013). All of these forms of exchange of sex for school fees have profound negative mental health consequences for young women. In addition, the ultimate success of Juana and her peers may represent an outlier or anomalous situation. Data on how many of these young women actually finish their schooling are difficult to obtain, but evidence suggests that many never meet their educational goals due to exploitation.

Education has been shown to be a critical piece of adolescent well-being generally (Ben-Arieh et al. 2014) and in terms of health for individuals, families, and societies (LeVine 2010; LeVine, LeVine, and Schnell 2001). When girls encounter sexual violence and exploitation in their pursuit of paying for school, they not only endure psychological, emotional, and physical harm through sexual violence, but they also risk losing one of the largest buffers of mental health and overall well-being at present and in their futures—their education. Education is at risk due to the enormous multilevel damage done through sexual violence, which can derail a young woman's attendance and achievement despite her best efforts.

Education provides both concrete benefits (e.g., literacy, skills training, credentials, etc.) and also offers the possibility of intangible expanded social networks, less rigid gender systems, lowered adolescent pregnancy rates, and so on (cf. LeVine 2010). Juana, her family, her cohort, and her community provide a vivid example of the transformative power of female education coupled with economic opportunity in reducing gender-based violence and improving family mental health (cf. Anderson-Fye 2010b).

It is difficult to achieve policies, services, and practices around the world aimed at reducing sexual exploitation of children and adolescents and increasing educational opportunity. But given the opportunities at every level of well-being —physical, psychological/emotional, social, and economic—and the impact at levels from individuals to families to communities to societies, the importance of realizing these goals cannot be overestimated (e.g., Anderson-Fye 2010b; LeVine, LeVine, and Schnell 2001). Young women like Juana bring incredible energy and promise to the goal of well-being for themselves, their communities, and beyond. However, they need actual opportunities and pathways as well as legal and services support. While this community is unique in its constraints and possibilities, it also raises the larger questions of multilevel interventions into female adolescent mental health, which centrally includes educational opportunities and achievement.

## Notes

[1] The town name is a pseudonym.
[2] Mayan and mestizo were distinct in the local categorizations.

3 Field notes. LI refers to Longitudinal Interview. LI1 was the first year of comprehensive longitudinal interview, LI2 was the second year, and so on.
4 While some are not currently employed, they have the skills and connections to forge concrete employment opportunities.

*References*

Anderson-Fye, E. (2002). Never leave yourself: Belizean schoolgirls' psychological development in cultural context. Doctoral dissertation, Harvard University.

———. (2003). Never leave yourself: ethnopsychology as mediator of psychological globalization among Belizean schoolgirls. *Ethos*, 31 (1): 77–112.

———. (2004). A Coca-Cola shape: cultural change, body image, and eating disorders in San Andrés, Belize. *Culture, Medicine, and Psychiatry*, 28 (4): 561–595.

———. (2010a). The case of Maria: culture and trauma in a Belizean adolescent girl. In C. Worthman, D. Schechter, and P. Plotsky (eds.), *Formative Experiences: The Interaction of Caregiving, Culture, and Developmental Psychology*, pp. 331–343. Cambridge: Cambridge University Press.

———. (2010b). The role of subjective motivation in girls' secondary schooling: the case of avoidance of abuse in Belize. *Harvard Educational Review*, 80 (2): 174–202.

Annitto, M. (2011). Consent, coercion, and compassion: emerging legal responses to the commercial sexual exploitation of minors. *Yale Law and Policy Review*, 30 (1): 1–70.

Ben-Arieh, A., Casas, F., Frønes, I., and Kobin, J. E. (eds.). (2014). *Handbook of Child Well-Being: Theories, Methods and Policies in Global Perspective*. Dordrecht: Springer.

Birdsall, N., LeVine, R., and Ibrahim, A. (2005). Towards universal primary education: investments, incentives, and institutions. *European Journal of Education*, 40 (3): 337–349.

Cameron, S. (1997). *From Girls to Women: Growing Up Healthy in Belize*. Belize City: Government of Belize.

Ganju, D., Jejeebhoy, S., Nidadavolu, V., Santhya, K. G., Finger, W., Thapa, S., Shah, I., and Warriner, I. (2004). *The Adverse Health and Social Outcomes of Sexual Coercion: Experiences of Young Women in Developing Countries*. New York: Population Council.

Gerver, M. (2013). "Sinigurisha! (you are not for sale!)": exploring the relationship between access to school, school fees, and sexual abuse in Rwanda. *Gender and Education*, 25 (2): 220–235.

Gutmann, M. C. (2006). *The Meanings of Macho: Being a Man in Mexico City*. Berkeley: University of California Press.

Herman, J. (1997). *Trauma and Recovery: The Aftermath of Violence—From Domestic Abuse to Political Terror*. New York: BasicBooks.

IRIN. (2011, August 1). Madagascar: sex for school fees. *IRIN*. http://www.irinnews.org/fr/report/93390/madagascar-sex-for-school-fees.

LeVine, R. A. (ed.). (2010). *Psychological Anthropology: A Reader on Self in Culture*. Chichester, UK: Wiley Blackwell.

LeVine, R. A., LeVine, S., and Schnell, B. (2001). "Improve the women": mass schooling, female literacy, and worldwide social change. *Harvard Educational Review*, 71 (1): 1–50.

Rafferty, Y. (2013). Child trafficking and commercial sexual exploitation: a review of promising prevention policies and programs. *American Journal of Orthopsychiatry*, 83 (4): 559–575.

Roberts, R., Jones, A., and Sanders, T. (2013). Students and sex work in the UK: providers and purchasers. *Sex Education*, 13 (2): 349–363.

Rupapa, T. (2013). Gumbura's "sex for school fees project". *The Herald*, December 17. http://www.herald.co.zw/gumburas-sex-for-school-fees-project/.

Sutherland, A. (1998). *The Making of Belize: Globalization in the Margins*. Westport, Connecticut: Bergin and Garvey.

van der Kolk, B. A., McFarlane, A. C., and Weisaeth, L. (2006). *Traumatic Stress: The Effects of Overwhelming Experience on Mind, Body, and Society*. New York: Guilford Press.

Williams, T. P., Binagwaho, A., and Betancourt, T. S. (2012). Transactional sex as a form of child sexual exploitation and abuse in Rwanda: implications for child security and protection. *Child Abuse and Neglect*, 36 (4): 354–361.

World Health Organization (WHO). (2013a). Violence against women: intimate partner and sexual violence against women (Fact Sheet No. 239). http://www.who.int/mediacentre/factsheets/fs239/en/.

——. (2013b). *Global and Regional Estimates of Violence against Women: Prevalence and Health Effects of Intimate Partner Violence and Non-Partner Sexual Violence*. WHO Department of Reproductive Health and Research, London School of Hygiene and Tropical Medicine, and South African Medical Research Council. http://www.who.int/reproductivehealth/publications/violence/9789241564625/en/.

Chapter 7

# Grandmothers, Children, and Intergenerational Distress in Nicaraguan Transnational Families

Kristin Yarris

> She had to go, there was no work for her here. But of course I felt sad . . . when she left I felt like, as they say, I am living "with one less hand." Even though she is supporting us economically, I've lost her company and still, I miss her presence.
>
> Marbeya

## INTRODUCTION

IN SUMMARIZING THE IMPACTS OF HER ADULT daughter's outmigration on her own health and well-being, 52-year-old grandmother Marbeya told me, with resignation in her voice, "*me pongo a pensar mucho*" ("I get to thinking too much"). During my year of field research (2009–2010) with Nicaraguan transnational families who had a mother or father migrant living abroad, I heard this idiom of distress expressed repeatedly by grandmothers and children and came to realize it had cultural significance that I needed to attend to. My study, research for my doctorate in sociocultural anthropology, was designed to explore the lived experiences of grandmothers, women of the "third age" (*tercera edad*), who had assumed caregiving responsibilities for children following parent outmigration. This interest in grandmother caregiving within transnational families had emerged from previous research and fieldwork I had conducted as part of my master's in public health, which had explored the social determinants of health among rural Nicaraguan women. I stumbled upon outmigration in that earlier fieldwork, as I found it to be one of the most significant, culturally disruptive forces impacting the lives of women of the grandmother generation in rural Nicaragua.

Several months into my dissertation fieldwork, after hearing the complaint expressed on numerous occasions by different family members, I realized that *pensando mucho* ("thinking too much") was a culturally significant form of expressing,

*Global Mental Health: Anthropological Perspectives*, edited by Brandon A. Kohrt and Emily Mendenhall, 117–133. © 2015 Left Coast Press, Inc. All rights reserved.

to use Arthur Kleinman's (2006) words, "what really matters" for grandmother caregivers in transnational families. In this chapter, I use the story of one Nicaraguan family to show how *pensando mucho* and other embodied idioms are meaningful ways for family members to express their emotional responses to transnational life across generations and even across national borders. I explore the meanings and phenomenology of Marbeya's thinking too much by presenting excerpts of her story, which is also the story of her migrant daughter, Azucena, and her two grandchildren (Azucena's children)—14-year-old Vanessa and 8-year-old Selso. I conclude by commenting on the implications of this transnational and transgenerational approach for mental health promotion and intervention, particularly in communities with high rates of parental outmigration.

## GRANDMOTHER CAREGIVING, THINKING TOO MUCH, AND COPING

Marbeya has been the primary caregiver for Vanessa and Selso ever since their mother, Azucena, first left for Costa Rica over 12 years prior to my research, when Vanessa was just over two years old. Azucena had held various jobs in Managua but, upon hearing from other Nicaraguan women who had migrated that she might earn four to five times the salary for similar work in Costa Rica, she was encouraged to try her luck in the neighboring country. The fact that her relationship with Vanessa's father was impermanent and that he was of little help in supporting their daughter further contributed to Azucena's decision to migrate. While Azucena didn't want to leave Vanessa behind or to endure the risks of illicit border crossing and the uncertainty of migrant life abroad, she felt she had little choice but to leave her daughter with her mother. Prior to Azucena's migration, she and Vanessa had lived with Marbeya, and so for Marbeya, assuming full responsibility for her granddaughter was less a choice and more an expression of support for her daughter. Marbeya viewed caregiving as "what we have to do because there is no one else to do it."

Like other grandmothers I worked with in Nicaragua, Marbeya experienced an episode of self-diagnosed *depresión* (depression) following Azucena's migration. Marbeya recalled that her initial concerns immediately after Azucena left Managua were centered on her daughter's physical safety and security. Once Azucena had telephoned to say she had safely arrived in San José, Marbeya's thoughts turned to the impact of her daughter's absence on her life and her family's relationships. As Marbeya recounts, the realization set in that her eldest daughter was no longer present to share daily routines, conversations, and confidences, explaining, "[N]ow she wouldn't be with me and I would miss her by my side." Marbeya also began to realize how the assumption of caregiving for her grandchildren meant taking on all the responsibilities of mothering for another generation of children: "[N]ow I was mother once more all over again."

Marbeya recalled her feelings during this period this way: "Nearly a year I spent like this, depressed. I frequently closed myself in with sadness. With depression I felt like . . . with nothing, nothing they [her family members] said made it better. I was crying . . . nearly one year I threw myself away like this." Marbeya's recollection is of an all-encompassing episode of depression that even the loving support of her co-resident husband, children, and grandchildren couldn't help her escape. Elsewhere, Marbeya described her feelings during this period immediately after Azucena's departure this way: "It was as if they'd pulled out a little piece of my heart, like they'd taken half my heart when she left." Despite its severity, Marbeya did not seek help from medical providers for her depression. She told me she avoided doctors, who just thought depression "is all in my head." Gradually, Marbeya's depression faded, and she found that the daily routines of caring for her grandchildren helped her overcome her sadness and focus on the exigencies of the present. Like other grandmother caregivers in transnational families, Marbeya experiences caregiving as a set of daily responsibilities requiring a good deal of effort and energy as well as a source of resilience and a means of coping with the emotional impacts of her adult daughter's ongoing absence from family life. Marbeya also considers herself a Christian, and, along with her children and grandchildren, she regularly attends services and social activities at a neighborhood evangelical church. Marbeya views her church as a source of social support, and her religious beliefs, such as her faith that "God has a plan for our lives," help her cope with the disruption that migration has provoked in her life.

With time, Marbeya's emotional response to her daughter's migration shifted from depression to a form of chronic worry expressed through the idiom "thinking too much." In the 12 years that she lived in Costa Rica, Azucena was able to stabilize her status, secure steady employment, and obtain legal residency, enabling her to send remittances to her family in Managua every month and also to make regular visits home. Over this period, Marbeya remained Vanessa's primary caregiver and assumed care of Azucena's son, Selso. Eight years old at the time of this study, Selso was born in Costa Rica and lived there until he was five years old, when Azucena sent him back to Managua to be raised by his grandmother. During this time, Marbeya's emotional experience shifted from depression to thinking too much, which, as I discuss here, is an expression of both cognition (the *content* of thoughts) and of emotion (the way these thoughts *feel*).

Primary among the content of Marbeya's thinking too much are thoughts of her household's precarious economic status. Even with the regular remittances sent by Azucena, Marbeya had to carefully budget to ensure she had enough money to pay for Vanessa's and Selso's private school tuition, school supplies, food, clothing, and other incidental costs associated with her grandchildren's care. Thus, when I asked Marbeya what she thought about when she "thinks too much," she explained: "I become despairing (*desesperada*) when I see that the deadline to pay for their school is approaching. And sometimes when it's exam time, the children ask me for things, they ask me for this or that. This is upsetting (*desesperante*) to me, when they are asking me for things and the money [remittances] hasn't yet arrived."

Thinking too much has a specific temporal dimension, which is associated with the ongoing experience of transnational family life and the implications of migration for family relationships. Whereas Marbeya's depression was acute and episodic, thinking too much is a form of chronic worrying without apparent resolution. For Marbeya, thinking too much is also more common at night than during the day. Marbeya explained to me that during the day, her mind is occupied by household chores and the everyday labors of caregiving, whereas at night, as she lies awake awaiting sleep, her mind becomes consumed by her thoughts. She explained further that in daytime:

> You are more distracted; maybe I'm making the rice, I'm washing dishes, I'm cleaning the house. So you forget about certain things. At night, when we're lying down, that's when the cassette rewinds and you begin to think, "Oh, my god, I had to pay that bill and I forgot or I couldn't pay it!" Or, "Oh, god, I said I was going to buy that and I couldn't." Or, "I was supposed to go to the doctor and I couldn't afford to go."

In her description of thinking too much, Marbeya referred to a "cassette," a metaphor for her thoughts playing over and over in her mind like a cassette tape. Marbeya even told me these thoughts have a sound, which she vocalizes as "*riqui, riqui, riqui.*" In her description of thinking too much, we also see how the content of her thoughts focuses on economic constraints and their impacts on her household. In the wake of Azucena's migration, Marbeya assumed responsibility for household finances, receiving remittances and allocating them toward bills, school tuition, food costs, and health care expenses. This responsibility causes her ongoing worry, as remittances fall short and she is unable to make ends meet the needs of her household and the grandchildren in her care.

Important in Marbeya's descriptions of thinking too much is differentiating it from more common, less chronic, and less intense forms of worry. Thus, when I asked Marbeya about the difference between thinking too much (*pensar mucho*) and worrying (*preocuparse*), she was insistent that I understood the differences between these two distinct mental and emotional states. According to Marbeya:

> Worrying is, you know, when you have money, well then, poof!, you stop worrying. But to be thinking too much, you are thinking: "How is the money going to

last me? What am I going to use it for? If the boy gets sick today, well then I'm not going to buy a pair of shoes, I'm going to take him to the doctor." So there you have the mind (*cerebro*) going along, there's your mind (*mente*) and your brain (*cerebro*) and everything's working. That's when I am super-worried (*súper preocupada*).

Being worried, in other words, is less troubling than thinking too much, because the worries concern things with solutions, while thoughts are about problems without apparent or easy remedy. Marbeya goes on to explain: "There are things that you can resolve, at least you can solve some material things. But, internally, about your inner state of sickness or your inner health, well then that is a little more difficult." Thinking too much focuses on these "internal" things, which are more difficult to resolve than external things of the "material" sort. Even though Marbeya often thought too much about her household's economic affairs, for her these thoughts are chronic and relentless because she does not see a way to resolve the economic precariousness of her family's situation. Thus, economic thoughts can become internalized and move beyond the realm of the mere material in Marbeya's explanatory model of thinking too much.

Thinking too much also has particular significance for Marbeya as a caregiver within a transnational family. Marbeya had trouble accepting that Azucena's migration may be permanent, that her daughter may not return to Nicaragua and may remain permanently separated from her children by national borders. She said, "To me, it's not really okay that she's over there; to me, it would be better if she were here with her children." After more than a decade, what was to be a temporary absence as Azucena worked abroad and sent money home for her children has become a permanent reconfiguration of family relationships, and Marbeya participates in this reconfiguration by maintaining primary caregiving responsibilities for her grandchildren. This reconfiguration troubled Marbeya, for it upset a culturally idealized vision of family life, which is that families should remain "*toda unida*" (all united)—in other words, physically living together in Nicaragua. Marbeya talks about thinking too much in relation to a nostalgia or longing for this sort of family unity, saying, "There are moments when a nostalgia grabs me and I tell myself, 'Ay, if my daughter were here with me,' then maybe I would feel healthier, or I would feel calm because I would be relieved of this responsibility of caring for her children, I would pass it on to her. With her being here, I wouldn't have this obligation, I would hand it over to her. And that would be less thoughts for my mind." Marbeya's narrative clearly indicates her mental and emotional well-being are reflective of her caregiving responsibilities. While she wished to be relieved of her obligations to care for her grandchildren, her longing for family reunification remains figurative and imaginative, what Marbeya "would" be able to do, given the unlikely return of her migrant daughter. Marbeya also clearly connects this uncertain future of her family life to thinking too much.

In addition to the content of her thinking, or what she thinks about, I asked Marbeya how thinking feels. She responded by describing the experience of thinking too much as a feeling of being worn out (*desgastada*) or tired (*cansada*). Marbeya senses both feelings in her brain or mind (*cerebro*), and associates these feelings with sensations of pain in the back of her head and neck. She says, "I feel my mind is tired (*me siento yo el cerebro cansado*). Like worn out (*desgastada*) is how I feel, without energy (*sin energia*).... This is *dolor de cerebro* (mindache)." Thinking too much can thus involve sufferers like Marbeya in a cycle of distress, wherein she feels tired but is unable to get adequate sleep because her thoughts keep her up at night; sleeplessness in turn contributes to feelings of being "worn out" and thus to the overall chronicity of thinking too much as a significant source of mental distress.

Despite its severity and chronicity, Marbeya, like other Nicaraguan women who suffer from thinking too much, does not take this complaint into clinical settings. She tells me that, while she knows thinking too much is real, medical doctors dismiss it as a legitimate complaint: "They think it's all in our heads," she told me. Thus, thinking too much encompasses shared meanings for sufferers such as Marbeya within local, relational spaces of family and community life, where expressions of *pensando mucho* may call attention to the importance of a grandmother's caregiving roles for the maintenance of security and continuity in family life. In addition to sharing her experiences of "thinking too much" with me, Marbeya often used this expression to describe the burdens of her caregiving to her adult co-resident children, as a way to elicit their support, both emotional and material (such as their assistance in household work). Furthermore, Marbeya was a member of a network of women family members of migrants that had formed to advocate for the rights of Nicaraguan migrants in Costa Rica. While this network met infrequently, and although their work formally focused on Nicaraguan migrants abroad, Marbeya found their meetings supportive spaces to share her lived experience as a grandmother and caregiver of children of a mother migrant.

## CHILDREN, PARENT MIGRATION, AND EMOTIONAL DISTRESS

While my research with Nicaraguan transnational families focused on grandmothers like Marbeya, I also explored the lived experiences of the grandchildren in their care, the children of parent migrants. Through informal interviews, conversations, and just hanging out with children over the year of my fieldwork, I came to know children like Vanessa and Selso quite well. While I anticipated that mother migration would be unsettling for children's emotional well-being, I did not expect to find that children use culturally significant idioms to express their emotional distress. However, children like Vanessa and Selso draw on similar idioms as their grandmothers to make sense of their emotional experiences of mother migration. This finding parallels that of other medical anthropologists who have found children respond in embodied ways to the emotional impacts of parent migration (Pribilsky 2001).

Half-siblings and five and a half years apart in age, Vanessa and Selso have had somewhat distinct experiences of their mother's migration. Vanessa appears a smart, confident 14-year-old; she does well in school, earns good grades, is a teacher's favorite, and has good friends. Vanessa attends a neighborhood Christian church regularly (with her grandmother, aunts, and cousins) and was planning a religiously themed party for her much-anticipated quinceañera celebration. Like her grandmother, Vanessa identifies as a Christian and plans her party to be "Christian," with what she views is appropriate music and dress. Additionally, Vanessa takes English as part of her school coursework, and enjoys learning this second language; helping her with English homework was a good way for me to spend time with her after school. In describing her mother's migration and its impact on her life, Vanessa often compared herself favorably to her half-brother, in part because she felt she did better at school than he and enjoyed participating in church activities, whereas Selso found little interest in church.

Vanessa also told me that Azucena's absence was harder on Selso because he had lived with his mother in Costa Rica until he was five and then had the abrupt change of moving to Managua into his grandmother's household. According to Vanessa, whereas "my mother left me since I was little, I didn't know anything," Selso, meanwhile, "was raised by her, he was with her; she even breastfed him." Vanessa, Marbeya, and other members of the family agree that Selso struggled to adapt to the change in his life that coming to Managua at age four entailed. His troubles were apparent through his problematic behavior and poor performance at school, and he ultimately had to repeat the first grade, a fact that caused his mother and grandmother a good deal of worry. However, by the end of my fieldwork year, Selso seemed to be doing better, his school grades and behavior had improved, and Marbeya felt as though he was respecting her more and helping out around the house. Still, Selso seemed to me to be a reserved and somewhat withdrawn little boy. His grandmother and aunts referred to him as "*necio*" (bothersome); Vanessa called him "*hiperactivo*" (hyperactive). When I sat down to help Selso with homework, I saw how difficult it was for him to maintain his attention on the task at hand. When I asked Selso about his mother's migration, his family life, or his feelings, he would usually answer with yes-no responses delivered without visible emotion.

In April 2010, Azucena visited her mother, Vanessa, and Selso during Semana Santa (Holy Week), a visit that overlapped with Vanessa's 14th birthday. I talked with Azucena during her visit, and she told me of her plans to save money and return the following year for a large celebration for Vanessa's "quince" (15th birthday). During her visit, Azucena spent her time shopping with her mother, visiting with friends and extended family, and generally catching up on "things of the day" at home. Soon, the visit was over, and Azucena returned by bus to Costa Rica. Several days after she left, I visited the family home and asked Marbeya for permission to take Vanessa and Selso out to the mall to eat *pollo* (fried chicken, one of the children's favorite treats). We spent about two hours in the food court of the local mall, enjoying the time inside the air-conditioned space to talk at more length than we ever had before about the children's experiences and feelings of their mother's migration. Selso told me that when his mother left after her recent visit, he "felt sad because she was going to go," but in his next sentence, he shared that he also "felt happy" as he hugged her goodbye. The ambivalence of transnational family life is a common characteristic of children's emotional experience of parental migration. Children feel at once rooted to their surrogate caregivers and extended families in Nicaragua and, at the same time, they experience a longing to live with their mothers abroad (for further discussion, see Yarris 2014). Selso told me that what he most missed about his mother was a feeling of happiness—"I miss her in happiness"—and I interpreted a sense of longing in this response, a desire to be physically close to his mother once again, which Selso confirmed by saying that every time his mother leaves after a visit, he asks her "when are you coming again?" Marbeya and Vanessa had also told me that Selso had fallen ill after Azucena left days before, and I asked Selso about this. He said it was true, that he usually got sick (*enfermarse*) and felt bad (*sentirse mal*) after his mother's visits. When I asked him, "How, bad?" he responded, "Sadness; like I'm not going to have happiness." Selso went on to tell me that he missed his mother a good deal, and I asked him if he felt this longing to be with her in any specific location; his response was "in my heart." According to Selso, the only remedy for his sickness and heartache is returning to live with his mother in Costa Rica, which he says will help him "feel happy, not get sick, and not feel so much sadness."

Selso draws on embodied emotional complaints to render his mother's absence meaningful in a way that partially mirrors the response of his grandmother Marbeya. Whereas Marbeya refers to a period of depression (*depresión*), Selso talks about a general sadness or malaise, using the terms sadness (*tristeza*) and sickness (*enfermedad*). Selso's expression of pain in his heart echoes how Marbeya described feeling during the depressive episode following Azucena's initial migration, when she said she felt as though someone had "taken half her heart away." Selso was not yet born when his mother first left Managua for Costa Rica, and so his understandings of his grandmother's response to Azucena's migration have been formed through the shared stories and remembrances of his grandmother and other family members. Becoming sick (*enfermo*) or complaining of heartache might be a way for Selso to draw the concerned attention of his grandmother and co-resident aunts when his mother leaves after a visit; in a crowded household of 21 people and 11 other children, he may feel the need for individualized attention at times. Selso does not talk about thinking too much but uses instead the general complaints of feeling sad and sick, which are outwardly displayed by his unwillingness or inability to eat in the days following his mother's visits (a behavior described to me by Marbeya, Vanessa, and Selso's co-resident aunts). Finally, we may understand Selso's heartache in light of his longing to live reunited with his mother once again, a longing for family reunification that Marbeya expresses as well.

The alterations in appetite and eating that Selso experienced following his mother's visits home were also a form of shared emotional distress in this family. In one of my first conversations with Azucena about her migration, she told me that after initially migrating to Costa Rica and leaving Vanessa behind, she was unable to eat for weeks. Azucena said, "Of course, it was really difficult for me. At first when I left I got really skinny. Being over there, I didn't eat because I was thinking about her [Vanessa]." While I didn't explore the meaning of "thinking" further with Azucena, it might be that for her, as for her mother, thinking too much was a chronic state associated with the distance and despair of transnational family life. What is apparent in Azucena's recollection is that disordered eating (specifically, her loss of appetite and reduced food intake) was the way that her emotional distress manifested through her body and her behavior. Further, given that years later Selso is suffering similar changes in appetite following his mother's departures (returns to migration after visits home), loss of appetite may be another shared form of emotional distress in this transnational family.

While Selso and Vanessa are generally aware of the economic constraints facing their family, the broader political and economic factors shaping their mother's migration remain largely outside of their control. For her part, Vanessa cites as a central motivation for Azucena's work in Costa Rica the fact that "she sends money home to us so that we can be well here." Marbeya often tells her grandchildren that they must study hard in school because their mother "works two jobs over there so that you can have these opportunities here." In this way, through discourses of mother sacrifice and through the materiality of the remittances that Azucena sends home on a regular basis, Vanessa and Selso feel tied to their mother across national borders. And yet, neither the children nor their mother or grandmother can do much to influence the possibilities of Azucena's return to Nicaragua, which is shaped by a limited job market at home and relatively greater income-earning opportunities in Costa Rica. Furthermore, Azucena's ability to visit home is impacted by shifting Costa Rican immigration policy, where recent reforms have made both return visits and the possibility of obtaining legal residency for migrants and their children more difficult.[1] These broader political and economic contexts contribute to children's ambivalent emotional experiences of parent migration as they increase the uncertainty surrounding the future of family life.

Vanessa too felt a combination of sadness and ambivalence after her mother's recent visit, just as she feels after every one of Azucena's visits home. On the one hand, Vanessa was happy for the time she spent with her mother and enjoyed the small birthday present that Azucena brought from Costa Rica. Yet for Vanessa, her mother's visits have become occasions where she feels emotionally suspended between the joy of seeing her mother and the sadness of realizing it is only a fleeting few days before she leaves again. Visits contain this dialectic of presence and absence or closeness and distance, as children are reminded through a mother's temporary stay of a more permanent departure. In Vanessa's words, despite their many long-distance phone calls, there are things she can't tell her mother "because we can't talk face-to-face; it's just not the same."

During our conversation after Azucena's birthday visit, I asked Vanessa specifically to reflect on how her mother's trips back to Managua made her feel. Here I excerpt at length the exchange that followed:

> Vanessa: When it's my birthday and—where I don't see my mom and she doesn't hug me, when it's only my mamita (grandmother) hugging me, that's where I miss her so much [eyes well with tears].
> Kristin: Yeah—
> Vanessa: Yeah.
> Kristin: On your birthday!
> Vanessa: Yes. Even though she has just come, and she congratulated me, she brought me something—small, but it's something. [Smiles] A little perf- perfume. Yeah. But, yeah, it's those times when I most miss her.
> Kristin: Hmm mm. And what do you feel when she's not with you in these moments?
> Vanessa: Sadness. Sometimes I don't feel like doing anything. Thinking.
> Kristin: Thinking?
> Vanessa: Yes.
> Kristin: About what?
> Vanessa: That she's not with me. About why she left. But, sure, my grandma is always with me, and she gives me these explanations, about why she left, what she left for. (My grandma) is always with me.

In this excerpt, we have access to the troublesome and complicated emotional realities of children in transnational families, who feel torn between mothers who have left Nicaragua and grandmothers who have assumed their care at home. Vanessa refers to her ambivalence about her mother's temporary presence during visits, such as that for her recent birthday. For Vanessa, the small gift of perfume she receives stands in as a symbol of her mother's love for a fleeting moment, before her mother leaves again and Vanessa is reminded of her more permanent absence. When Vanessa tells me how this ambivalent "here but really there" (Hondagneu-Sotelo and Avila 1997) feels, she uses the phrases *tristeza* (sadness), *sin ganas de hacer nada* (disinterested or without desire to do anything), and *pensando* (thinking). Here, the texture and quality of Vanessa's lived emotional experience much resembles that of her grandmother Marbeya. Like Marbeya, Vanessa is "thinking" about the reasons for—and consequences of—her mother's absence from her life. For grandmother and granddaughter, thinking or thinking too much is not a description of a cognitive process so much as it is of a textured emotional experience, a state of distress, and a form of chronic worry that indexes the consequences of transnational migration for their individual and family lives.

## INTERGENERATIONAL DISTRESS: IMPLICATIONS FOR GLOBAL MENTAL HEALTH

In this chapter, I have described the cultural meaning and social circumstances surrounding *pensando mucho,* or thinking too much, for one Nicaraguan transnational family. This family's story shares much in common with the other 23 families of parent migrants with whom I conducted ethnographic fieldwork in Nicaragua and, I believe, with other family members living in origin communities of transnational migrant parents. By presenting the experience of one Nicaraguan grandmother and the grandchildren in her care, I have used this chapter to emphasize how an idiom of distress is shared across generations and even beyond national borders. This discussion is significant for global mental health practice and policy in three specific ways.

First, the evidence presented here points to the importance of considering culturally meaningful forms of mental distress as not only socially learned but also shared and shaped within the intersubjective space of family relationships. Here, I share with Sarah Horton (2009) the use of a phenomenological approach to reveal how emotional distress in the context of transnational migration has meaning within and across family relationships. In other words, children and their grandmother caregivers experience transnational migration as a personally and culturally significant experience, even though they themselves have not crossed national borders. These members of transnational families make sense of the disruption and uncertainty of migration by drawing on shared idioms to express their emotional distress within the intersubjective space of family life. In this way, the narrative presented here is further evidence of the ways emotions can be both embodied and also transpersonal, meaning shared across individuals within microcultural settings such as the family (Boellstorff and Lindquist 2004).

This discussion of locally meaningful forms of emotional distress in Nicaragua, whether "thinking too much" or "heartache," extends anthropological thinking about emotions as cultural and agentive, or as operating within cultural worlds to do certain things (Jenkins 1988; Lutz 1988). One of the main functions of thinking too much within transnational families is as a source of significant, shared emotional experience that can connect members of transnational families together across generations and even across national borders. In other words, even as they struggle to cope with the disruption that parent outmigration signifies for their individual and family lives, children and their grandmother caregivers may use embodied idioms such as thinking too much as a way of working through the emotional implications of transnational family life.

To be clear, I am arguing that thinking too much should be regarded as a significant idiom of emotional distress in its own right, even as it may overlap uncomfortably with biomedical or psychiatric categories such as stress and depression (see also Keys et al. 2012). By staking a claim to the emotional impact of migration on their lives as family members left behind in sending countries such as Nicaragua, children and their grandmother caregivers are expressing their incorporation into global migration processes, even as they are usually left out of migration-related policy or scholarly discourse. Finally, further research might explore whether parent migrants abroad share similar emotional complaints as family members back home, a finding that would have additional implications for transcultural and transborder mental health care.

One implication of the discussion presented in this chapter is that mental health providers, social workers, and other community leaders working with children of parent migrants and their caregivers might apply a socio-developmental approach to prevention and health promotion within this population. This means considering various social factors that impact children's emotional experiences of parental outmigration, including their age, family support networks, social and economic status, and other resources that may help foster children's well-being as they cope with the impacts of parent migration over time. Additionally, mental health interventions, whether delivered through clinical, school, or other community settings, ought to target not just individual children or children and their biological parents but instead should broaden the frame of intervention to include surrogate caregivers and other extended family members, particularly in cultural settings where family networks and relationships are central to an individual's sense of self and social belonging. Multilevel health-promotion interventions that consider personal and social environments in interaction have been shown to support the mental health of children exposed to war, violence, and other traumas by including cultural, religious, neighborhood, and family-level supports (Tol et al. 2013). Furthermore, family-based interventions to promote emotional resilience and well-being align with the Grand Challenges in Global Mental Health Initiative, by attending to the reality that "suffering related to mental disorders extends to families and communities, with the consequence that health system-wide changes are essential" to early intervention and increased social inclusion (Patel 2012: 9).

Of course, expanding psychosocially based mental health interventions through primary care systems in low-income countries such as Nicaragua requires financial resources that may not readily be available. The current Nicaraguan government has prioritized health care and spent an increasing percentage of GDP on its public health system (MINSA)—approaching 10% in 2009, according to government figures.[2] Nonetheless, MINSA has not prioritized mental health care or health promotion among families of migrants, despite the fact that an estimated one in four Nicaraguans has a family member living outside the country (Rocha Gómez 2006). I argue, given the importance of local, community-based social supports to families such as Marbeya's, that preventive, psychosocial interventions for children of parent migrants and their caregivers are best implemented by involving non-medical sectors such as education (specifically, school teachers and staff) and urban planning (specifically, Nicaragua's citizen councils), who may be best able to identify emotional distress among families of migrants and to support coping and resilience through community-based social programs (such as conversation groups, art therapy, and so on).

Second, the narrative of Marbeya's family presented here shows that parental migration impacts children's mental and behavioral health in ways that are not easily predictable. As the stories of siblings Vanessa and Selso show, a number of varying and complex circumstances shape children's responses to parent migration, including, but not limited to, children's age at parent migration, caregiving configurations prior and subsequent to parent migration, stability of caregiving following parent migration, and frequency of communication and visits with parent migrants. Thus, fully understanding the impacts of parent migration on children's mental and emotional health requires a good deal more cross-cultural research that can assess these and other variables relevant to children's experiences in larger, comparative, and longitudinal samples. Further, as Suárez-Orozco and Suárez-Orozco (2001) suggest, children of parent migrants experience migration as more traumatic when the trajectory of family life is uncertain. Thus, it is even more important for mental health providers to encourage families of migrants and migrant parents themselves to talk openly and honestly about migration with children and to foster opportunities for children to express their concerns, fears, and uncertainties about migration and family life. This may be an opportunity for a mobile-phone-based intervention of the sort that has been recently applied to health-promotion efforts among adolescents in the United States (e.g., see Vyas et al. 2012). Mobile-phone- or Internet-mediated communication with migrant parents might also be implemented in schools in communities with high rates of outmigration as a way to connect parents with children's school progress. However, it is important to keep in mind that, for children like Vanessa and Selso, mobile phones and other forms of transnational communication are inadequate substitutes for their mothers' physical presence.

Finally, idioms of distress are important ways for members of transnational families to express their emotional responses to migration in a context where they may feel they have few other ways to register their complaints. Medical anthropologists have demonstrated that idioms of distress function as modes of expression, particularly for women who may have few other means to express their discontent about social circumstances that otherwise seem largely beyond their control (Mendenhall et al. 2010; Nichter 1981; Oths 1999). Psychological anthropologists have argued that one role for ethnographic research within global mental health is to advance culturally grounded understandings of idioms of psychological distress in order to foster more holistic approaches to well-being (Keys et al. 2012). For example, community-based health-promotion interventions might build on the ties that families such as Marbeya's have to church-based groups, schools, and other social networks and use those to build social support and possibly even as resources for advocacy.

In this chapter, I have shown how, while they themselves have not crossed national borders, family members in migrant-sending communities, such as Marbeya and her grandchildren, are impacted nonetheless by transnational migration. Nicaraguan migration is increasingly feminized, meaning that over 50% of contemporary migrants are women (Torres and Barahona 2004). The reasons that women leave children behind in Nicaragua when they migrate are complex and have to do with the dangers of illicit border crossing, the costs of child care in destination countries, and mothers' desire to provide continuity in their children's lives. In these families, migrant mothers sacrifice by working abroad and sending remittances back home for their children's well-being, and grandmothers assume care for children, providing cultural continuity and social support for children and by extension for transnational families. And yet, while migrant-sending families may be relatively better off, economically speaking, due to the household impact of remittances, in Nicaragua there is little public discussion of, and even less political response to, the social and emotional needs of children of migrant mothers and their caregivers. The network of women family members of migrants to which Marbeya belongs is an exception; though this group meets infrequently and Marbeya views it more as a form of social support than political advocacy, the network was founded to bring family members together to support the rights of undocumented Nicaraguan migrants in Costa Rica. Such groups should be pushed to consider the needs and rights of family members back home in sending countries as well.

Certainly, existing legal instruments may provide a framework to advance the protection of children and family members of migrants. For example, the United Nations' Convention for the Protection of the Rights of Migrant Workers and Their Families (hereafter, the "1990 Convention") elaborates the many rights that countries should uphold for documented and undocumented migrants alike. However, the 1990 Convention often assumes that families remain together in a host country, not divided across national borders, as is the case of thousands of Nicaraguan transnational families. Additionally, a familiar problem with such multilateral human rights frameworks is that they remain largely elective and without adequate enforcement mechanisms. In this case, Costa Rica, the major destination country for contemporary Nicaraguan migrants, has opted not to sign on to the 1990 Convention.[4] Thus, the legal protections that these frameworks provide remain unenforced and far removed from the lived realities of grandmothers like Marbeya who, as surrogate caregivers in families of migrants, have few—if any—legal rights. Furthermore, given the bias in Nicaraguan law toward biological parentage, surrogate caregivers such as Marbeya find it difficult, if not impossible, to obtain legal guardianship for the grandchildren in their care, even as they maintain primary responsibility for their grandchildren's care for years or even decades in migrant parents' absence. This legal insecurity exacerbates the complex issues of possible reunification with migrant parents abroad in destination countries by adding to it the uncertainty facing children and their caregivers in sending countries such as Nicaragua. In the face of such uncertainty and families' apparent lack of control over the circumstances surrounding migration, idioms of distress such as thinking too much take on a significant social function, as they serve to express shared emotional distress across generations and across borders.

## ACKNOWLEDGMENTS

My deepest gratitude is extended to Marbeya, Vanessa, Selso, Azucena, and the rest of their family for welcoming me into their lives and for our ongoing communication via Facebook and holiday visits.

### Notes

1  Costa Rica's immigration reform legislation that went into effect in March 2010 raised to $100 (USD) the fine that migrants must pay for every month that tourist visas are expired. Since many Nicaraguans enter Costa Rica with tourist visas but then overstay them, this legislative "reform" essentially traps many migrants into illegality.

[2] See www.minsa.gob.ni. The current president, Daniel Ortega, was re-elected in 2006, bringing an end to a 16-year period of neoliberal policy in Nicaragua. Ortega has reinvented "Sandinismo" in controversial ways, shaping the Sandinista Party so it aligns with "Socialism for the 21st Century." Investment in public health, along with education and housing for the poor, is a key element of this political strategy, as is the use of Venezuela-inspired "Committees of Citizen Power," which are supposed to promote participatory democracy.

[3] Remembering that intersectoral action for health is one of the principles of the 1978 Alma Ata Declaration and one of the priorities of the World Health Organization (see http://www.who.int/publications/almaata_declaration_en.pdf).

[4] Estimates are that between 500,000 and 1,000,000 Nicaraguan migrants live in Costa Rica, a number that is probably an underestimate given their high rate of indocumentation and the discrimination Nicaraguans encounter in Costa Rica (Rocha Gómez 2006).

## References

Boellstorff, T., and Lindquist, J. (2004). Bodies of emotion: rethinking culture and emotion through Southeast Asia. *Ethnos*, 69 (4): 437–444.

Hondagneu-Sotelo, P., and Avila, E. (1997). "I'm here, but I'm there": the meanings of Latina transnational motherhood. *Gender and Society*, 11 (5): 548–571.

Horton, S. (2009). A mother's heart is weighted down with stones: a phenomenological approach to the experience of transnational motherhood. *Culture, Medicine, and Psychiatry*, 33: 21–40.

Jenkins, J. (1988). Ethnopsychiatric interpretations of schizophrenic illness: the problem of *nervios* within Mexican-American families. *Culture, Medicine, and Psychiatry*, 12 (3): 303–331.

Keys, H. M., Kaiser, B. N., Kohrt, B. A., Khoury, N. M., and Brewster, A.-R. T. (2012). Idioms of distress, ethnopsychology, and the clinical encounter in Haiti's Central Plateau. *Social Science and Medicine*, 75: 555–564.

Kleinman, A. (2006). *What Really Matters: Living a Moral Life amidst Uncertainty and Fear*. New York: Oxford University Press.

Lutz, C. (1988). *Unnatural Emotions: Everyday Sentiments on a Micronesian Atoll and Their Challenge to Western Theory*. Chicago: University of Chicago Press.

Mendenhall, E., Seligman, R., Fernandez, A., and Jacobs, E. (2010). Speaking through diabetes: rethinking the significance of lay discourses on diabetes. *Medical Anthropology Quarterly*, 24 (2): 220–239.

Nichter, M. (1981). Idioms of distress: alternatives in the expression of psychosocial distress: a case study from South India. *Culture, Medicine, and Psychiatry*, 5: 379–408.

Oths, K. (1999). *Debilidad*: a biocultural assessment of an embodied Andean illness. *Medical Anthropology Quarterly*, 13 (3): 286–315.

Patel, V. (2012). Global mental health: from science to action. *Harvard Review of Psychiatry*, 20 (1): 6–12.

Pribilsky, J. (2001). Nervios and "modern childhood": migration and shifting contexts of child life in the Ecuadorian Andes. *Childhood*, 8 (2): 252–273.

Rocha Gómez, J. L. (2006). *Una región desgarrada: dinámicas migratorias en Centroamérica*. San José, Costa Rica: Servicio Jesuita para Migrantes Centroamérica.

Suárez-Orozco, C., and Suárez-Orozco, M. M. (2001). *Children of Immigration*. Cambridge, Massachusetts: Harvard University Press.

Tol, W. A., Jordans, M. J. D., Kohrt, B. A., Betancourt, T. S., and Komproe, I. H. (2013). Promoting mental health and psychosocial well-being in children affected by political violence: Part I—current evidence for an ecological resilience approach. In C. Fernando and M. Ferrari (eds.), *Handbook of Resilience in Children of War*, pp. 11–27. New York: Springer.

Torres, O., and Barahona, M. (2004). *Las migraciones de Nicaragüenses al exterior: un análisis desde la perspectiva de género*. Managua: United Nations Population Fund.

Vyas, A. N., Landry, M., Schnider, M., Rojas, A., and Wood, S. F. (2012). Public health interventions: reaching Latino adolescents via short message service and social media. *Journal of Medical Internet Research*, 14 (4): e99.

Yarris, Kristin E. (2014). "Quiero ir y no quiero ir" (I want to go and I don't want to go): Nicaraguan children's ambivalent experiences of transnational family life. *The Journal of Latin American and Caribbean Anthropology*, 19 (2): 284–309.

Chapter 8

# Addiction in Colombia: Local Lives, Broader Lessons

Daniel H. Lende and Sarah Fishleder

## OMAR AND JOSÉ

I SAT ON A BENCH WITH A 16-YEAR-OLD BOY, and we talked about drugs. The patio of the drug treatment center surrounded us, a verdant carpet of grass topped by small trees and awkwardly trimmed bushes. We were just outside Bogotá, Colombia, a short bus trip into the high-mountain savannah dotted by flower greenhouses and the occasional factory and private school. The treatment center lay back from the main road, its own encapsulated world, where the 40 boys got good meals, played soccer, and went through a daily regimen of psychosocial therapy. The boy Omar was in the midst of telling me how bad drugs were.

"They're the worst," he said. "They damage your health and kill your brain cells. They damage the whole person." His words sounded practiced, almost bored but with a hint that this truly was something he'd like to believe. I had heard similar words many times from other kids at the treatment center.

"I know there are other alternatives now," he continued. "Other ways to have fun with friends, or to go do exercise when I feel anxious about using." Teaching the boys that there were *alternativas*, or alternatives, was one technique practiced at the center. Omar, well along in his therapy, knew them well. Drugs were bad, and there were other ways to handle *malas amistades* and *situaciones negativas*, bad friendships and negative situations.

As a medical anthropologist researching drug use in Colombia, I knew Omar well from previous conversations; there was more complexity behind what he was saying. He had a mischievous side and often got in trouble with the treatment staff for his pranks and pointed jokes about the center. It sounded like he was feeding me the lines that he thought I wanted to hear. But I wanted to know what he really thought about drugs, not just now but from before.

*Global Mental Health: Anthropological Perspectives*, edited by Brandon A. Kohrt and Emily Mendenhall, 135–149. © 2015 Left Coast Press, Inc. All rights reserved.

"*Y antes?*" And before? I asked. "What did you think about drugs in the past?"

"*En el pasado?*" He glanced at me, knew I wasn't there to judge him. A smile crept onto his lips and his eyes lit up. "*La droga era lo máximo!*" Drugs were the greatest.

This dilemma—that drugs were at once the greatest and the worst—was something every boy dealt with when he left treatment and returned to living with his family. The treatment center ran an outreach center in the middle of Bogotá, where the boys came for once-a-week sessions during the "reinsertion" phase of the overall program. They went back to often difficult family lives and to the same neighborhoods where they had once used. What had been "past" in the program was suddenly powerfully present again.

I sat on a chair with another 16-year-old boy, José, this time in a small room used for therapy sessions. We were just outside Popayán, a small city in the southwestern part of Colombia, not far from Cali. I quickly learned that José was quite different from Omar. Omar had come from a tough background. José came from a good family. I had met his loving parents earlier, and he told me that he had been in a Catholic school before he started to use drugs, first marijuana, then cocaine, and finally basuco, the Colombian version of crack cocaine. He had ended up in *la calle*, the street, but only briefly.

Omar had a long involvement with the street, mostly through other boys who acted as a makeshift gang that stole and fought and used drugs. José was the sort of kid who was never supposed to fall that low. Now he was in treatment to see if he could get that past life back.

I asked José about drugs in the past, too. Omar had been playful, telling me stories, laughing about the stupid thrills and how drugs were *un vicio*, a vice that just caught you up. For José, it wasn't a story.

As we spoke, I realized that he was growing anxious. Drugs were still present right there in his head. He wanted them. Even talking about them was bringing up *ansiedades*, or cravings. In Colombia, addiction was often defined as *querer más y más*, to want more and more, and José seemed gripped by that as he sat in a whitewashed room in another rural setting.

I stopped the interview, the only time I ever did because just talking about drugs looked to be too much. José was well along in his therapy at the treatment center, and he had seemed stable on the outside. But he was, as the counselors would say, entering *en crisis*. He didn't want to continue in treatment. He wanted out. He wanted away. Back to his family, back to his old life, and not losing any more time in this place in the middle of nowhere.

And he wanted drugs, almost desperately so.

José was calmer later in the day. The desire to use could feel overwhelming in a certain moment, something that just had to be done. But that potent urge could also pass. He hadn't left treatment, hadn't followed that desire all the way back to town and back to using drugs. But it was a close thing. If he had been at home, I was sure he would have been out the door and searching for the closest dealer he knew. With drugs as the "greatest," and the stresses of life bouncing the boys around, desire often turned into use during reinsertion.

## ALCOHOL AND DRUG USE IN COLOMBIA

Alcohol use was palpable in Colombia. Advertisements for beer filled the television and billboards. Men gathered around outdoor tables at local beer halls on Friday nights, converting paychecks into a stack of empty bottles. Party zones, filled with music and bright lights, flowed with local rum and aguardiente as well as imported whisky and vodka.

Drug use was less visible but had a visceral presence. Reports on trafficking filled the news, but these were crimes, committed in rural zones or on planes headed to the United States. Drug use itself happened at the margins of neighborhoods. Street kids sniffed glue, young gangs smoked basuco or marijuana in parks at night, and in party zones, certain bars or street vendors were known to provision what people wanted.

This ethnographic view of alcohol and drug use matches Colombia's history. Since the 1960s, Colombia has gone through rapid urbanization and moved from a closed domestic economy to an open economy integrated into global markets. Over the same period, drug trafficking became a major economic force within Colombia, first with marijuana and then cocaine and, finally, though to a lesser degree, heroin (Perez Gómez 1994). Alcohol and tobacco had become an industrialized commodity much earlier in Colombian history, early in the 1900s. Finally, with the opening economy from the 1980s onward, pharmaceutically derived drugs like Ecstasy began to enter into the Colombian market (Perez Gómez 1994). This pattern of rapid urbanization and globalization, in conjunction with the emergence of drug trafficking against an older background of alcohol and tobacco commerce, helps explain the unique patterns of substance use and abuse in Colombia.

Patterns of substance use in Colombia lie at an intermediate point between high-use countries like the United States and low-use countries in Latin America like Bolivia (UNODC 2012: 2; Degenhardt 2008). Colombia has patterns of alcohol and tobacco use similar to the United States; among youths, 70% in the U.S. and 74.2% in Colombia have tried alcohol by the last year of high school, and 31.5% of U.S. high school students and 33.4% of Colombian students reported being current smokers (CDC 2007, 2012a, 2012b; Pardo et al. 2010). The results from a nine-country survey in South America indicate that Colombian youth have higher rates of legal and illegal drug use as compared with other countries that participated in the survey (Inter-American Drug Abuse Commission 2004). Yet statistics also show that rates of drug use in Colombia are significantly lower than in the United States (UNODC 2012: 2; Degenhardt 2008). Comparative rates are displayed in the table below.

The most abundantly used drug among Colombian youth is marijuana, with lifetime prevalence rates of approximately 9.6%, and 8.4% of youth having used in the past year. In the United States, by comparison, 33.4% of youth had ever used, and 27.5% had used in the last year (UNODC 2012). In contrast, other South American countries have lower rates, from Ecuador at 6.4% lifetime prevalence of marijuana among youth, down to a 1.7% reported rate in Venezuela (UNODC 2012). For Ecstasy use in Colombia, 4.3% of youth reported having ever used, 3.7% in the past year. The U.S. statistics showed 6.4% had ever used, and 4.7% had used in the last year, while Peru reported 1.2%, Ecuador 1.3%, and Venezuela 0.53% (UNODC 2012). International surveys exploring drug use rates among youth worldwide show that in Colombia, 2.0% of youth had ever used cocaine. Comparatively, in the United States, 3.7% had ever used cocaine, while rates in Peru were 1.0%, Ecuador 2.2%, and Venezuela 0.6% (UNODC 2012).

Epidemiological research has shown that drug availability is an ecological risk factor for drug use in Colombia but also that availability itself does not account for the actual pathways by which the user comes into contact with these drugs (Brook et al. 1998; Brook et al. 2002). Brook and colleagues' research also indicates that alcohol and tobacco use act as significant predictors of marijuana use (Brook et al. 2002; Siqueira and Brook 2003). But this risk factor is similar to availability. Prior alcohol and tobacco use can form part of a developmental trajectory that leads to illegal drug use, but by itself does not explain how individuals end up using marijuana.

Lifetime and 12-Month Prevalence for Percentage of Total Population by Country and Substance

| | Marijuana | | Ecstasy | | Cocaine | | Heroin | |
|---|---|---|---|---|---|---|---|---|
| | Lifetime | 12-month | Lifetime | 12-month | Lifetime | 12-month | Lifetime | 12-month |
| USA | 33.4 | 27.5 | 6.4 | 4.7 | 3.7 | 2.2 | 1.3 | 0.8 |
| Colombia | 9.6 | 8.4 | 4.3 | 3.7 | 2.0 | 1.7 | 1.3 | 1.2 |
| Bolivia | 6.2 | 3.6 | 1.6 | – | 3.1 | 1.9 | 1.0 | 0.5 |
| Peru | 2.0 | 1.2 | 1.2 | 0.6 | 1.0 | .05 | 1.0 | – |
| Argentina | 10.9 | 7.6 | 2.0 | – | 4.1 | 2.5 | 0.9 | – |
| Ecuador | 6.4 | 4.2 | 1.3 | 0.7 | 2.2 | 1.3 | 0.9 | .05 |
| Venezuela | 1.7 | .09 | 0.5 | 0.3 | 0.6 | 0.3 | 0.4 | .02 |

Source: 2012 United Nations Office of Drugs and Crime (UNODC) World Report.

Omar and José illustrate these dynamics. Omar's family engaged in small-time drug selling in Bogotá. Omar participated in his family business as well as in petty crime with other young toughs in his poor neighborhood. He had ready access to drugs, and started first with marijuana with his friends and then moved on to basuco, or Colombian crack, which he easily obtained through his family contacts. Drugs surrounded him, and he slipped into using more and more. José, in contrast, had to seek out drugs. His family lived in a middle-class neighborhood, and most of his friends at the local school had little interest in drugs. But some of his friends liked drinking and smoking cigarettes, and José found that he did too. When a friend proposed trying marijuana, José went along. He found marijuana helped distract him from the difficulties at home and at school, and he started to use more. Then he tried cocaine when out at a local club with his friends, and that he liked even more. He began to use more and more.

Thus, in Colombia, as elsewhere, more proximate risk factors help explain who becomes involved in illegal drug use, and these factors may differ between users like Omar and José. For example, most new users become exposed through peer-to-peer interaction (Beyers et al. 2004; Kandel 1991), and peer marijuana use is one of the best predictors of marijuana use in Colombia (Brook et al. 2002). In conjunction with peer marijuana use, individual delinquency, such as stealing something in the past year, also predicted individual marijuana use. In other words, involvement with activities and people that amplify exposure to marijuana use are core proximate risk factors. In contrast, factors linked to other social contexts, such as strong family ties, religiosity, and attending church, act as strong predictors against marijuana use in Colombia (Brook et al. 2002). This pattern plays itself out as illegal drug use increases, with greater association and involvement in social contexts that are risky and where people use on a regular basis, such as the environment in which Omar grew up. For example, street living and violence have repeatedly been shown to correlate with drug use (Brook et al. 1998; Brook et al. 2002; Ross 2001), and in Bogotá, violence from peers and police was even perceived to be more dangerous than the threat of HIV among injection drug users (Ross 2001). By contrast, José had to distance himself from his family, hanging out more with friends than at home, and his potential for recovery seemed higher to many of the therapists because he already had good family ties and a home in a less risky neighborhood.

## NEUROANTHROPOLOGY AND ADDICTION

Research on the role of peer drug use on individual substance use shows dual effects: peer drug use increases the likelihood that someone else in that group will use drugs; at the same time, individuals tend to search out peers who hold similar beliefs and approve of their actions (Burk et al. 2012; Poulin et al. 2011). In other words, both peer selection and peer socialization play a role in individual drug use. Similarly, understanding addiction requires a focus on how external and internal factors come together to shape the dynamics of substance abuse. The ethnographic vignettes that opened this chapter point to how situational factors, such as the excitement and escape associated with using drugs, motivated adolescents; yet at the same time, something internal also prompted powerful urges to return to drug use. As Lende (2005) showed, excessive desire for drugs (mediated by the dopamine system) combined with individuals giving meaningful interpretations—that is, their own personal justification—to their addictive behavior. As one girl reported, she felt powerful sensations that helped compel her use, but it was also that these sensations put her into "a video" that helped her escape her difficult home life.

Central diagnostic criteria for substance dependence in the World Health Organization's International Classification of Diseases (2010) illustrate the combined individual and social dynamics of addiction. Substance dependence can be diagnosed by (1) a strong desire or sense of compulsion to take the substance; (2) difficulties in controlling substance-taking behavior; and (3) progressive neglect of alternative pleasures or interests because of psychoactive substance use. Other criteria focus on tolerance and withdrawal, as well as continued substance use despite "clear evidence of overtly harmful consequences." In other words, addiction inevitably brings together social and cultural dynamics with individual vulnerabilities, shifts in decision-making, and the impact of substances of the brain.

*Neuroanthropology* offers a framework to understand how social and cultural processes interact with human development, biology, and behavior (Downey and Lende 2012; Roepstorff, Niewöhner, and Beck 2010). Neuroanthropology is a field science that tests both neurobiological and anthropological ideas in naturalistic settings. Results are used to interrogate conclusions drawn from laboratory, clinical, and university-based research as well as to advance novel explanations based on data coming from community-based sources. Neuroanthropology has an explicit applied side, recognizing that applied practice and theory cannot be reduced to academic knowledge but require "how to" knowledge and a strong understanding of local communities and social contexts to be effective (Lende and Downey 2012b).

Neuroanthropology provides a means both to understand core dimensions of addictive behavior (Lende 2005, 2012; Schüll 2012; Snodgrass et al. 2013; Stromberg 2012) and to critique dominant medical and societal discourses that distort our understanding of addiction as well as our efforts at effective treatment and prevention (Campbell 2010; Garriott 2013; Hansen and Skinner 2012; Raikhel 2010). Neuroanthropology's critique posits, for example, that the reduction of addiction to a biological disease blamed on faulty brain circuits and bad genes is not backed up by the science of addiction, but does serve important sociopolitical ends, such as the control of funding and policy by powerful institutional players. Moreover, an emphasis on addiction as an individual problem disregards the social roots of addiction, particularly ignoring how addictive behavior runs along those social divisions that reinforce inequality. The premises of neuroanthropology, which emphasizes both social and biological dimensions of addiction, can be seen through combining scientific and anthropological literature. At the same time, the ethnographic roots of this combination are also important. Conducting research in Colombia, where neither the moral model nor the disease model (the latter prevalent in the United States) was predominant, opened up other views of addiction. Colombian treatment professionals often emphasized a social rehabilitation approach to young addicts. In addition, Colombian discourse defined addiction as *querer más y más*, to want more and more, which matched up with emerging theories in neurobiology (Lende 2005). In this way, ethnographic involvement can help to produce more holistic views of addiction, overcoming the present overemphasis on biomedical approaches seen in many countries.

Framing addiction as solely a biological problem lodged in individuals means an overemphasis on both clinical and criminal approaches that punish and regulate the behavior of people judged to engage in deviant or "wrong" behavior, and can ironically lead to worsening the consequences that result from chronic alcohol and drug consumption (Campbell 2010; Garriott 2013; Hansen and Skinner 2012; Raikhel 2010). For example, for decades in the United States, "crack addicts"—more likely to be black and poor—have been treated differently than heavy cocaine users, who are often white and wealthy. In the *Diagnostic and Statistical Manual* widely used in the United States, one of the main criteria for substance abuse has long been "frequent legal problems (e.g., arrests, disorderly conduct) for substance abuse." Not surprisingly, crack users often had many more legal problems than cocaine users, thus heightening their chances of getting diagnosed as having a problem.

Turning to addictive behavior itself, work drawing on both neuroscience and anthropology highlights how the loss of positive personal and institutional relationships often leads to a worsening in alcohol and drug use. In effect, these social relations can be seen as down-regulating addictive impulses; when they are taken away, addictive behavior can spike (Hofer 1994). As the vignettes showed, in treatment—surrounded by positive social relations—addictive impulses were generally more muted. Back in old neighborhoods, without the positive impact of daily interaction with therapists, problems could readily arise. Omar, for example, struggled early on in rehabilitation. He was surrounded by his old friends, and selling drugs offered easy money. However, his family moved away from augmenting their income through local trafficking, and Omar returned to his schooling, where his bright mind found other problems to solve. In school, he also developed new peer networks, which offered him the ability to do different things—such as skateboarding—while hanging out with friends. Nonetheless, he relapsed several times; old friends and old situations brought the fun and ease of drug use to the fore, whereas such things remained in the background while in a treatment setting.

But "fun and ease" is not enough to explain excessive drug use. Ethnographic research on addiction has consistently highlighted how absorption and immersion into addictive experiences can be very compelling (Lende 2005; Schüll 2012; Stromberg 2012). Often times, being in "the zone" or "on a trip" is a pleasant contrast to difficult social lives, thus reinforcing addictive patterns. In other words, heavy users are interpreting their substance use in both functional and meaningful ways (Lende et al. 2007), and thus the effects of drugs cannot be reduced to pharmacology. Instead, addictive experiences need to be understood as having been formed within particular social lives and within the framework of what drugs are perceived as being able to do.

At the center of addiction lies the conjunction of heightened wanting and involvement with drugs and the overlearned and habitual repetition of a behavior (Lende 2012). Wanting drugs more and more can be linked to altered dopamine processing in the brain; at the same time, what is often wanted is to feel engaged through the experience of seeking out and using drugs. That engagement can be compelling and may stand in stark contrast with lives that may feel boring or without a future or marginalized. As with many overlearned behaviors, parts of addiction become highly routine over time, something that the brain executes without much conscious effort or even control (Lende 2012). This transition to a chunked sequence of behaviors often means that an initial craving or desire can lead directly into habitual use of drugs. This combination of wanting and habit is something that can lead to enormous excess in alcohol and other drug use, particularly if there are few positive social controls present in the social contexts where use happens. Neuroanthropology offers the ability to better understand what was happening to José when he became gripped by an urge to use during an interview. His urge wasn't simply desire, but also the present sense of wanting to do a specific set of things—find the drugs, prepare them for use, use them, and then experience that sense of pleasure, release, and satisfaction that many informants spoke of about the moment of use itself.

## GLOBAL PATTERNS OF SUBSTANCE USE AND ABUSE

The World Health Organization estimates total worldwide substance use to consist of 2 billion consumers of alcohol, 1.3 billion smokers, and 185 million users of other drugs (WHO 2014). Most people who try substances, however, do not end up with problems. Only some shows signs of substance abuse, defined as harmful or hazardous use of psychoactive substances. Even fewer develop dependence (or addiction) (WHO 2013). The potential harms of abuse and dependence are varied and often depend on the drug in question (Newton 2010). Measurements of harm are generally classified in three realms: physical harm to the individual caused by the drug (inclusive of both psychological and somatic conditions); the tendency of the drug to induce dependence; and the effect of the drug on the family, community, and social aspects of the user's life (Nutt et al. 2007).

Research in school settings in Colombia amply illustrated these dynamics. Some students tried drugs, though in Colombia this occurred in lower proportions than in the United States. Only a small number of these students became more deeply involved with alcohol, tobacco, and drug use. Overall, students recognized that alcohol caused more bodily effects than drugs like cocaine; hangovers and headaches and liver problems were all issues that students mentioned. But cocaine was seen as more likely to get a person "hooked" and to cause greater damage to students' social and family life than alcohol. Many students thus stayed away from harder drugs like cocaine, whose social costs were much greater than legal substances like alcohol.

The WHO estimates that alcohol, tobacco, and illicit drugs collectively contributed to 12.4% of all deaths in 2000, and 8.9% of total years of lost life (WHO 2013). The burden generally impacts men at higher rates. For example, men made up about 80% of the tobacco- and drug-related deaths, and about 90% of alcohol-related deaths. About 65% of alcohol-related deaths generally take place before age 60, and deaths related to illicit drugs strike mostly earlier in life (WHO 2013). The burden of substance abuse does not fall neatly, however. Rather, it generally increases as countries become more developed and integrated into global markets. In a systematic review, Schmidt and Room (2012) discuss how the alcohol industry, which marks developing countries as up-and-coming pools of profit, expands the market, including aggressive pushes in advertising that place higher prestige on the globally produced drinks. This economic shift often means the loss of home-made alcohol, often made by women (in Colombia, industrial beer displaced the local *chicha*). As a result, local actors, particularly women, can lose control of an economic resource even as men increase their overall alcohol use, with accompanying social problems (Schmidt and Room 2012).

Risk factors that are seen to impact substance use and abuse in developed countries often play out in different ways in developing countries. Certainly, adverse conditions for children in developing countries include less access to education and the impact of poor nutrition and greater incidence of infectious disease (Panter-Brick, Lende, and Kohrt 2012). But these same circumstances can also lead to less availability of substances and exposure to social domains where alcohol and drug use is a common, approved behavior. Thus, interactions among markets, common risk factors associated with drug use in developed countries, and adverse experiences in early childhood bring into play developmental dynamics that no one model of substance use and abuse adequately captures. In Colombia, the pattern has been that as markets for alcohol and other drugs developed locally, the accompanying social costs of substance abuse also increased (Perez Gómez 1994). Often these costs fell along social lines, as risk factors disproportionally affected youth in adverse circumstances. For example, boys like Omar—coming from a more difficult background—often struggled more in recovery than boys like José, who had in-built social buffering given his family and social circumstances.

## GLOBAL HEALTH APPROACHES FOR SUBSTANCE USE AND ABUSE

Because addiction has social, medical, public health, economic, and political dimensions, there is no "one-size-fits-all" strategy. For example, debates over legalization too narrowly frame what can and should be done about other aspects of addiction. At the other end of the spectrum, the "drug war" approach, focusing on criminalization and repression, has failed (Global Commission on Drug Policy 2011). A better approach is to target consequences as key to an overall intervention approach. Five strategies can jointly address consequences related to substance abuse: (1) risk reduction, (2) therapy, (3) harm reduction, (4) imposition of higher social costs, and (5) a focus on harm to others.

Targeting proximate risk factors that can lead from substance use to dependence and abuse is one approach to reducing consequences. Within societies, immediate pathways to alcohol and drug abuse often fall along social faultlines (e.g., adolescents with less involvement in families and increased involvement in deviance and with peers who use drugs). However, direct targeting of "delinquency" often produces a backlash that can reinforce behavior, leaving youth with fewer options. A better approach is to broadly target social forces that lead to unequal outcomes, such as supporting families and increasing employment opportunities, and to produce more targeted interventions that offer youth viable alternatives that lead away from increasing involvement in alcohol and other drug use (Toumbourou et al. 2007).

For therapy, one of the most effective therapeutic approaches for addiction is *motivational interviewing*, a clinically effective approach to short-term treatment that can be undertaken in outpatient settings by health or social services professionals (Miller and Rollnick 2012). Motivational interviewing focuses on getting clients to consider the costs and benefits of continued substance use based on their own experiences, rather than having the health professional lecture the client on why they should change. By using a nonjudgmental approach centered on the reasons why the client wants to change, motivational interviewing helps foster long-term client-driven change in behavior.

For harm reduction, it is important to focus on approaches that minimize harm to both the individual and society (Marlatt and Witkiewitz 2010; Weatherburn 2009). Damage from addiction is cumulative and reaches beyond the person using. Addiction is manifest not only in increased amounts of substance use and spending too much time drinking or using. Rather, social and health consequences can rebound on the user, creating a more serious problem than just the drinking or using itself. For example, injection drug use can lead to HIV exposure if syringes are not easily available. Similarly, sentencing guidelines that punish certain types of substance users more than others, or that target personal possession for significant jail time rather than for fines and/or short-term sentencing, generally worsen the consequences of drug use but do little to change addictive behavior in the long run. Additionally, exposure to long prison terms does not generally make a nonviolent user a better person, and the resulting barriers to employment and opportunity do not allow for a substantial change of lifestyle. If trapped in minimum-wage jobs, adverse economic conditions could be worsened rather than alleviated. A problem-focused approach to harm reduction is one that targets preventable local consequences to users (Lende 2011).

Fourth, increasing the social costs of the everyday transactions of substance use can be an effective strategy. For example, increased taxation is known to lead to reductions in alcohol and tobacco use (Strang et al. 2012). For a broad-based behavior like smoking, exclusion from public spaces (while keeping smoking legal) increases the social costs of continued smoking: smokers have to leave a building to smoke and often have to stand in a place where such behavior is visible. This approach focuses on increasing the social costs of the behavior at a small scale, and thus provides understandable and immediate reasons to change. Rather than overboard punishments, approaches that focus on one-day intervention sessions for drug users and word-of-mouth community campaigns that get people talking about social costs offer ways to interrupt a behavior that can too often be run on habitual autopilot.

Finally, alcohol, tobacco, and drug policy needs to focus on harm to others. Rather than punishing substance use per se (making the user into a "bad person"), effective policy can target the realistic and relatable negative consequences of substance use for other people (Rhodes 2009; Strang et al. 2012). For example, drunk driving is a primary cause of traffic accidents and fatalities, and represents a robust area for interventions. Similarly, the effects of secondhand smoke on the public health of others is another area where interventions can successfully target the consequences of the behavior but not prohibit or excessively penalize smoking.

Overall, these five strategies offer ways to approach substance use and abuse, particularly addictive behavior at its most destructive, and to bolster policies that promote behavioral change and minimize consequences to self and others from the bouts of repetitive, compulsive behavior that typify addiction at its worst. Many of these strategies are in place in Colombia, either through direct governmental policy or because of long-standing social approaches to dealing with drug use. For example, family interactions among students who avoid drugs in school settings emphasize "reasons to say no," with accompanying social costs and known examples. Colombia has also increasingly taxed legal substances like alcohol and tobacco, while at the same time avoiding excessive criminalization of small-scale drug possession and use. That said, among people who become more deeply involved in drug use, heavy social costs and stigmatization often follow, particularly among poorer families who cannot pay for treatment. This often leads to risk amplification among youth who do become increasingly involved in drug use, leading in turn to increasing marginalization from families and very heavy social costs. Such social dynamics make rehabilitative approaches more difficult, since these individuals and groups have often suffered serious consequences and have little incentive to try to return to a mainstream social life that ostracized them in the first place.

Omar and José both represent individuals who had a chance to return to their families and school. They also had opportunities to develop alternative peer networks. Other boys and girls in Colombia, however, have spent years on the street and were considered *desechables*, or throwaway people. Effective drug policy requires strategies that reduce the burden of drug use on society without neglecting or further marginalizing the people most in need of care and services.

## References

Beyers, J. M., Toumbourou, J. W., Catalano, R. F., Arthur,M. W., and Hawkins, J. D. (2004). A cross-national comparison of risk and protective factors for adolescent substance use: the United States and Australia. *Journal of Adolescent Health*, 35 (1): 3–16.

Brook, J. S., Brook, D. W., de la Rosa, M., Duque, L. F., Rodriguez, E., Montoya, I. D., and Whiteman, M. (1998). Pathways to marijuana use among adolescents: cultural/ecological, family, peer, and personality influences. *Journal of the American Academy of Child and Adolescent Psychiatry*, 37 (7): 759–766.

Brook, D., Brook, J., Rosen, Z., and Montoya, I. (2002). Correlates of marijuana use in Colombian adolescents: a focus on the impact of the ecological/cultural domain. *Journal of Adolescent Health*, 31 (3): 286–298.

Burk, W. J., van der Vorst, H., Kerr, M., and Stattin, H. (2012). Alcohol use and friendship dynamics: selection and socialization in early-, middle-, and late-adolescent peer networks. *Journal of Studies on Alcohol and Drugs*, 73 (1): 89.

Campbell, N. (2010). Toward a critical neuroscience of "addiction." *BioSocieties*, 2010 (5): 89–104.

Centers for Disease Control and Prevention (CDC). (2007). Global youth tobacco survey. Country reports: Pan American Health Organization [online] 2007. http://www.cdc.gov/tobacco/global/.

——. (2012a). Fact Sheets. Underage Drinking. Center for Disease Control and Prevention. http://www.cdc.gov/alcohol/fact-sheets/underage-drinking.htm.

——. (2012b). Current tobacco use among middle and high school students—United States, 2011. *Morbidity and Mortality Weekly Report*, 16, no. 31.

Degenhardt, L., Chiu, W. T., Sampson, N., Kessler, R. C., Anthony, J. C., Angermeyer, M., Bruffaerts, R., de Girolamo, G., Gureje, O., Huang, Y., Karam, A., Kostyuchenko, S., Lepine, J. P., Mora, M. E., Neumark, Y., Ormel, J. H., Pinto-Meza, A., Posada-Villa, J., Stein, D. J., Takeshima, T., and Wells, J. E. (2008). Toward a global view of alcohol, tobacco, cannabis, and cocaine use: findings from the WHO World Mental Health Surveys. *PLoS Medicine* 5: e141.

Downey, G., and Lende, D. H. (2012). Neuroanthropology and the encultured brain. In D. H. Lende and G. Downey (eds.), *The Encultured Brain: An Introduction to Neuroanthropology*, pp. 23–66. Cambridge, Massachusetts: MIT Press.

Garriott, W. (2013). "You can always tell who is using meth": methamphetamine addiction and the semiotics of criminal difference. In E. Raikel and W. Garriott (eds.), *Addiction Trajectories*. Durham, North Carolina/London: Duke University Press.

Global Commission on Drug Policy. (2011). War on drugs: report of the Global Commission on Drug Policy. http://www.globalcommissionondrugs.org/wp-content/themes/gcdp_v1/pdf/Global_Commission_Report_English.pdf.

Hansen, H., and Skinner, M. E. (2012). From white bullets to black markets and greened medicine: the neuroeconomics and neuroracial politics of opioid pharmaceuticals. *Annals for Applied Anthropology*, 36 (1): 167–182.

Hofer, M. A. (1994). Hidden regulators in attachment, separation, and loss. *Monographs of the Society for Research in Child Development*, 59: 192–207.

Inter-American Drug Abuse Control Commission. (2004). First comparative study of drug use in the secondary school student population in Argentina, Bolivia, Brazil, Colombia, Chile, Ecuador, Paraguay, Peru and Uruguay. The Inter-American Observatory on Drugs/Organization of American States, Lima. http://www.cicad.oas.org/oid/.

Kandel, D. B. (1991). The social demography of drug use. *The Milbank Quarterly*, 69 (3): 365–414.

Lende, D. H. (2005). Wanting and drug use: a biocultural approach to the analysis of addiction. *Ethos*, 33: 100–124.

——. (2011). Beyond the drug war: drug policy, social interventions, and the future. *Neuroanthropology PLoS*; http://blogs.plos.org/neuroanthropology/2011/06/05/beyond-the-drug-war-drug-policy-social-interventions-and-the-future/ (accessed February 24, 2014).

——. (2012). Addiction and neuroanthropology. In D. H. Lende and G. Downey (eds.), *The Encultured Brain: An Introduction to Neuroanthropology*, pp. 339–362. Cambridge, Massachusetts: MIT Press.

Lende, D. H., and Downey, G. (2012). Neuroanthropology and its applications: an introduction. *Annals of Anthropological Practice*, 36 (1): 1–25.

Lende, D.H., Leonard, T., Sterk, C., and Elifson, K. (2007). Functional methamphetamine use: the insider's perspective. *Addiction Research and Theory*, 15 (5): 465–477.

Marlatt, G. A., and Witkiewitz, K. A. (2010). Update on harm-reduction policy and intervention research. *Annual Review of Clinical Psychology*, 6: 591–606.

Miller, W. and Rollnick, S. (2012). *Motivational Interviewing, Helping People Change* (Applications of Motivational Interviewing). 3rd ed. New York/London: Guilford Press.

Newton, D. E. (2010). *Substance Abuse: A Reference Handbook*. Santa Barbara: ABC-CLIO.

Nutt, D., King, L. A., Saulsbury, W., and Blakemore, C. (2007). Development of a rational scale to assess the harm of drugs of potential misuse. *The Lancet*, 369 (9566): 1047–1053.

Panter-Brick, C., Lende, D., and Kohrt, B. (2012). Children in global adversity: physical, mental behavioral and symbolic dimensions of health. In *Oxford Handbook of Poverty and Child Development*. Oxford Handbooks online.

Pardo, C., Piñeros, M., Jones, N., and Warren, C. (2010). Results of global youth tobacco surveys in public schools in Bogotá, Colombia. *Journal of School Health*, 80 (3): 141–145.

Perez Gómez, A. (1994). *Sustancias psicoactivas. Historia del consumo en Colombia*. Bogotá: Editorial Presencia.

Poulin, F., Kiesner, J., Pedersen, S., and Dishion, T. (2011). A short-term longitudinal analysis of friendship selection on early adolescent substance use (English). *Journal of Adolescence*, 34 (2): 249–256.

Raikhel, E. (2010). Post-Soviet placebos: epistemology and authority in Russian treatments for alcoholism. *Culture, Medicine, and Psychiatry*, 34 (1): 132–168.

Roepstorff, A., Niewöhner, J., and Beck, S. (2010). Enculturing brains through patterned practices. *Neural Networks: The Official Journal of the International Neural Network Society*, 23 (8–9): 1051–1059.

Rhodes, T. (2009). Risk environments and drug harms: a social science for harm reduction approach. *International Journal of Drug Policy*, 20 (3): 193–201.

Ross, T. (2001). Using and dealing on Calle 19: a high risk street community in central Bogotá. *International Journal of Drug Policy*, 13 (1): 45–56.

Toumbourou, J. W., Hemphill S. A., Tresidder J., Humphreys C., et al. (2007). Mental health promotion and socio-economic disadvantage: lessons from substance abuse, violence and crime prevention and child health. *Health Promotion Journal of Australia*, 18: 184–190.

Schüll, N. (2012). *Addiction by Design: Machine Gambling in Las Vegas*. Princeton, New Jersey: Princeton University Press.

Siqueira, L. M., and Brook, J. S. (2003). Tobacco use as a predictor of illicit drug use and drug-related problems in Colombian youth. *Journal of Adolescent Health*, 32 (1): 50–57.

Schmidt, L. A., and Room, R. (2012) Alcohol and inequity in the process of development: contributions from ethnographic research. *International Journal of Alcohol and Drug Research*, 1 (1): 41–55.

Snodgrass, J. G., Dengah, H. J. F., Lacy, M. G., and Fagan, J. (2013). A formal anthropological view of motivation models of problematic MMO play: achievement, social, and immersion factors in the context of culture. *Transcultural Psychiatry*, 50 (2): 235–262.

Stromberg, P. (2012). Collective excitement and lapse in agency: fostering an appetite for cigarettes. In D. H. Lende and G. Downey (eds.), *The Encultured Brain: An Introduction to Neuroanthropology*. Cambridge, Massachusetts: The MIT Press.

Strang, J., Babor, T., Caulkins, J., Fischer, B., Foxcroft, D., and Humphreys, K. (2012). Drug policy and the public good: evidence for effective interventions. *The Lancet*, (9810): 71.

United Nations Office on Drugs and Crime (UNODC). (2012). World Drug Report 2012. Vienna: United Nations Publications. www.unodc.org.

Weatherburn, D. J. (2009). Dilemmas in harm minimization. *Addiction*, 104 (3): 335–339.

World Health Organization. (2014). *Management of Substance Abuse: Alcohol.* WHO 2014. http://www.who.int/substance_abuse/facts/alcohol/en/index.html#.

——. (2013). *Health Topics: Substance Abuse.* WHO 2014. http://www.who.int/substance_ abuse/facts/alcohol/en/index.html#.

——. (2010). *International Classification of Diseases.* 10th revision (ICD-10). http://www.who.int/classifications/icd/en/.

## Part II

### Treatment Approaches and Access to Care in Low- and High-Resource Settings

## Brandon A. Kohrt, Emily Mendenhall, and Peter J. Brown

Since the beginning of the 20th century, anthropology has concerned itself with the study of healing approaches, the social, political, and economic forces that shape healing practices, and the role of traditional and biomedical practices in the alleviation of psychological suffering. In 1915, physician and anthropologist W. H. R. Rivers presented a series of papers to the Royal College of Physicians of London in which he outlined a theory of healing at the intersection of medicine, magic, and religion (1924). Basing his theories on fieldwork conducted in the Torres Straits between Papua New Guinea and Australia, Rivers suggested that healing is an attempt to correct moral infractions thought to incite illness. Rivers characterizes healing practices as targeting the mind, with success attributable to faith and the power of suggestion: "remedies acting through the mind were probably the earliest to be employed by Man" (1924: 122). Since this pioneering research, anthropologists have asked if there are central underlying processes in healing that are common among non-Western traditional healing, rituals in general, and psychiatric treatments such as psychotherapy.

This research inspired anthropologists to consider the power of the mind in healing the body, including the comparison of traditional healing to psychotherapy. One powerful example comes from Claude Lévi-Strauss's (1949) research comparing Cuna shamanic healing ritual for obstetric complications with the process of psychotherapy. He identified symbolism and mythic transformation as central to both practices. Anthropologists Victor Turner, James Dow, and later Melford Spiro similarly examined how emotions were manipulated to address life transitions and psychic conflict through ritual transformation. For example, Dow (1986) suggested that rather than psychotherapy being seen as the foundation for all healing, it is instead likely that there is a universal symbolic healing process that is reflected in both shamanism and psychotherapy. Dow's framework of universal symbolic healing has four steps: (1) the healing begins with a set of generalized

*Global Mental Health: Anthropological Perspectives*, edited by Brandon A. Kohrt and Emily Mendenhall, 151–154. © 2015 Left Coast Press, Inc. All rights reserved.

symbols in a cultural myth salient to healer and sufferer; (2) the healer persuades the attendant sufferer that a cultural myth defines the affliction; (3) the healer particularizes the myth to the sufferer, whose affliction becomes attached to transactional symbols; and (4) through the manipulation of transactional symbols, the sufferer's emotions are transformed to produce healing. Dow's work builds upon Lévi-Strauss's and further develops the interpersonal element by describing both the interpersonal healer–sufferer interaction and changes induced in the social environment. Dow's model echoes aspects of the psychotherapy process and relates to contemporary approaches to healing outlined in the chapters in this section.

Anthropologists have been critical of assumptions made within biomedicine, such as the development of the *DSM*'s psychiatric categories and the notion that such categories of symptoms are universal. Anthropological critiques of Western psychiatry grew out of postmodern studies and the anti-psychiatry movement. For example, the French philosopher Michel Foucault (1965) used the historical asylum system to critique how psychiatry was a form of social control for political and economic benefit. While Foucault was critiquing psychiatric care of centuries earlier, his contemporaries, the Hungarian psychiatrist Thomas Szasz and British psychiatrist R. D. Laing, attacked conceptualizations of mental illness in the 20th century (Laing 1970, 1985; Szasz 1961). As the anti-psychiatry movement burgeoned, the asylum movement was beginning to wane in the United States following President Kennedy's 1963 Community Mental Health Centers Act. With this act, institutions were closed and individuals went to live with families or back in the community; but the majority of the people released went either to nursing homes, board and care centers, jails, or became homeless, as few resources were provided for deinstitutionalization (Shorter 1997).

These social and conceptual movements led to a new group of anthropologists turning their gaze to conduct ethnographies of persons with mental illness in Western settings. For example, in the late 1970s, Sue Estroff (1981) conducted ethnographic research with persons with mental illness who had been deinstitutionalized from mental hospitals to community settings, including persons living in halfway homes and persons who were homeless. She experienced firsthand the lack of resources and support for persons with mental illness who went from locked wards to living on the streets. Tanya Luhrmann's (2000) ethnography of a psychiatry training residency program portrays the death of psychodynamic psychiatry at the hands of managed care. Luhrmann suggests that pharmacology reifies the categorical approach to psychiatry and that the pharmaceutical industry controls academic training, including residency curricula and professional society meetings. There is increasing attention toward the power of managed care in the United States and pharmaceutical companies throughout the world in providing under- and over-access to care, including the role of pharmaceutical companies in framing concepts of distress and recovery (Kirmayer 2006; Luhrmann 2000).

This section explores how treatment approaches and access to health care can shape individual experiences with mental health. Mental health care in low- and high-resources settings across the globe requires innovative strategies that attend to both social and biological underpinnings of mental disorders. We open this section with Hunter Key's "Life 'Under the Wire'" (Chapter 9), which describes how poor access to mental health care is a reflection of broader deprivation of social resources for socially and economically marginalized populations, such as Haitian migrants residing in the Dominican Republic. Jeffrey Snodgrass's "Festive Fighting and Forgiving" (Chapter 10) demonstrates that community-based practices, such as India's Holi, may serve as a coping mechanism for mental distress associated with broader political and social problems, such as geopolitical displacement. In contrast, Jack Friedman's "Who Belongs in a Psychiatric Hospital?" (Chapter 11) demonstrates how mental health is institutionalized in post-Soviet Romania, with people becoming lifelong institutionalized patients when community-based interventions and support might be more effective. Emily Mendenhall's "The 'Cost' of Health Care" (Chapter 12) then emphasizes how psychiatric intervention for psychological distress rooted in extreme social suffering can, in some cases, do more harm than good. In "The Few, The Proud" (Chapter 13), Erin Finley eloquently describes how crucial mental health services are for female veterans who experience social and combat-related trauma differently than men while in combat and once they return home. Finally, Sarah Willen and Anne Kohler's "Cultural Competence and Its Discontents" (Chapter 14) deals with personal biases that psychiatrists themselves hold, about both themselves and their patients, which can affect how they deliver psychiatric care, emphasizing how biomedical training itself constructs such biases.

## References

Dow, J. (1986). Universal aspects of symbolic healing—a theoretical synthesis. *American Anthropologist*, 88 (1): 56–69.

Estroff, S. E. (1981). *Making It Crazy: An Ethnography of Psychiatric Clients in an American Community*. Berkeley: University of California Press.

Foucault, M. (1965). *Madness and Civilization; A History of Insanity in the Age of Reason*. New York: Pantheon Books.

Kirmayer, L. J. (2006). Beyond the new cross-cultural psychiatry: cultural biology, discursive psychology and the ironies of globalization. *Transcultural Psychiatry*, 43 (1): 126–144.

Laing, R. D. (1970). *Self and Others*. 2d rev. ed. New York: Pantheon Books.

———. (1985). *Wisdom, Madness, and Folly: The Making of a Psychiatrist*. New York: Mc-Graw-Hill.

Lévi-Strauss, C. (2000 [1949]). The effectiveness of symbols. In R. Littlewood and S. Dein (eds.), *Cultural Psychiatry and Medical Anthropology: An Introduction and Reader*, pp. 162–178. New Brunswick, New Jersey: Athlone Press.

Luhrmann, T. M. (2000). *Of Two Minds: The Growing Disorder in American Psychiatry*. New York: Knopf.

Rivers, W. H. R. (1924). *Medicine, Magic, and Religion: The Fitz Patrick Lectures*. New York: Harcourt, Brace, and Company, Inc.

Shorter, E. (1997). *A History of Psychiatry: From the Era of the Asylum to the Age of Prozac*. New York: John Wiley and Sons.

Szasz, T. S. (1961). *The Myth of Mental Illness: Foundations of a Theory of Personal Conduct*. New York: Dell.

Chapter 9

# Life "Under the Wire": Perceived Discrimination and Mental Health of Haitian Migrants in the Dominican Republic

## Hunter Keys

> My uncle and aunt died from cholera. My little brother died in the earthquake. That's why we come to live here. Despite suffering humiliation, we are obligated to look for life here because there is no life in Haiti.
>
> Jhon, Haitian migrant in the Dominican Republic

> *M'ap reflechi ak dlo a* (I am thinking with tears). Dominicans humiliate you. "You're from another country," they shout. Their words strike you and fill your eyes with water.
>
> Sylvie, Haitian migrant in the Dominican Republic

### INTRODUCTION: SYLVIE AND HUMILIATION

SYLVIE HAD LEFT HAITI A DECADE AGO, when she was 18 and pregnant with her first child. Her boyfriend had been beating her, and her mother decided that the best thing for her was to move to the neighboring Dominican Republic. Her mother said that, at least over there, she might find security and more job prospects. She crossed the border *anba fil*, or "under the wire," a Haitian Kreyòl phrase for crossing without authorized documents. Eventually she found her way to a large city in the Cibao Valley. Living with extended relatives in a barrio of mostly Haitian migrants and poor Dominicans, she found a life for herself selling clothes in the market.

Sylvie was one of several participants in a mixed-methods research project investigating the mental health of Haitian migrants in the Dominican Republic

*Global Mental Health: Anthropological Perspectives,* edited by Brandon A. Kohrt and Emily Mendenhall, 155–171. © 2015 Left Coast Press, Inc. All rights reserved.

(Keys et al. 2014). When we first met, Sylvie, like many other Haitian women in the country, was selling clothes in a large, urban street market. The market was a cacophony of noise, smells, and sights. Street vendors were selling giant heaps of plantains and coconuts, slaughtering chickens, and yelling out their prices to passers-by. Pick-up trucks bearing enormous speakers were blasting bachata and merengue music. Motorcycles zipped around pedestrians. In the market, Haitian women sit on plastic buckets on the sidewalks selling clothes while Haitian men tote cell phone chargers and CDs for sale. Nearby construction sites are the other major economic opportunity for migrant Haitian men in this region of the Dominican Republic.

In the market, Sylvie described the positive gains she had made since leaving Haiti, but then she delved into the social difficulties of migrant Haitians. Dominicans sometimes "humiliate you because you're Haitian," she explained. Following the recent spread of cholera across the border, humiliation—or in Haitian Kreyòl, *imilyasyon*—had become particularly intense. Now, Dominicans "won't buy clothes from us because they think cholera is in the clothes we sell." Cholera, it seemed, had thrust an otherwise invisible population into the public eye, where they quickly became associated with, and blamed for, the dreaded disease. Our fieldwork revealed that *imilyasyon* entails belittlement, powerlessness, and inferiority in light of acute and chronic stressors, such as stigma due to epidemic cholera or the everyday struggles amid long-standing discrimination (Keys et al. 2014). Overall, *imilyasyon* is an intensely personal experience situated within large-scale, structural obstacles and a complex sociocultural and historical legacy.

## BACKGROUND: HAITIAN MIGRATION TO THE DOMINICAN REPUBLIC AND ANTI-HAITIANISMO

Sylvie's accounts must be contextualized within the sociocultural history of Haitian migration to the Dominican Republic, a history that has involved dynamic (re)conceptualizations of racial, cultural, and national identities.

Originally recruited to work on Dominican sugar plantations in the early 20th century, Haitian migrants now work in many other sectors, especially construction, rice production, and informal services such as Sylvie's sidewalk clothes sales (Ministerio de Trabajo 2011). Most migrate on the periphery of development, moving between poor, typically rural sending communities in Haiti and marginally improved receiving communities in the Dominican Republic (Martinez 1995). At present, there is no official estimate of the Haitian and Haitian-descended population in the Dominican Republic, but it is thought to be between 500,000 and 1.5 million people (Canales, Vargas Becerra, and Montiel Armas 2009), the vast majority undocumented (Ferguson 2006).

Anti-Haitian discrimination (Spanish: *anti-haitianismo*) plays a major role in their marginalized status. The roots of anti-Haitianism go back to European colonialism, when wealthy Spanish elites sought to exploit poor black and mulatto classes (Sagas 2000). The Trujillo dictatorship in the Dominican Republic (1930–1961) officially promulgated anti-Haitianism as a means to consolidate a Dominican identity (Derby 1994), culminating in the massacre of thousands of Haitians and Dominico-Haitians along the border in 1937 (Turits 2002). Anti-Haitianism construes Haitians as superstitious Vodou believers, more African and less civilized than their Dominican counterparts, and bent on conquest (Tavernier 2008). In this way, anti-Haitianism constructs a Dominican identity vis-à-vis Haiti (Howard 2007), differentiating the Dominican citizen from the migrant non-citizen, an "othering" process (Barth 1969) that attributes greater moral worth to Dominicans (Bartlett, Jayaram, and Bonhomme 2011). However, race remains a complex construct for Dominicans, as most share some degree of African descent (Sagas and Inoa 2003). Nonetheless, while anti-Haitianism is no longer an officially sanctioned institutional practice, its effects remain pervasive: routinely denied authorized status and citizenship, access to education and health care, and workplace safety and employment opportunities (United Nations 2008), Haitian migrants and their descendants live amid widespread material and social deprivation.

## "WE DON'T HAVE PAPERS": INSTITUTIONAL-LEVEL DISCRIMINATION AND DOWNSTREAM EFFECTS

"*Ou met chita*—please sit, sit," said Sylvie as we conversed in Kreyòl. She placed a plastic chair in front of me. I joined her on the sidewalk along one of the central thoroughfares in the market. As a nursing and public health student, I had come to the Dominican Republic after conducting research in Haiti's Central Plateau. In Haiti, we had explored how rural Haitians conceptualize, experience, and seek care for common mental disorders, such as depression and anxiety. Our research efforts focused on recognizing everyday language that communicates mental distress (Keys et al. 2012), characterizing the relationship between Vodou explanatory models of mental illness and treatment-seeking (Khoury et al. 2012), and culturally adapting mental illness screening instruments for use among Haitians (Kaiser et al. 2013). Prior to this experience in Haiti, I had participated in a brief service project in the neighboring Dominican Republic, where my university's School of Nursing had long partnered with a Dominican university and public hospital. After our project in Haiti, I felt a strong pull to understand the mental health of Haitian migrants, a largely neglected population in anthropological, health, and human rights literature. A year after our project in Haiti, I returned to the Dominican Republic and met Sylvie during my first week there.

Sitting in the market together, our conversation began with introductions and a discussion of Sylvie's work, which quickly led to the challenges of living without legal documentation from the Dominican government. "We don't have papers, so we sell clothing, because there's nothing else for us to do," she explained. Women, she said, work in the market. Haitian men work construction jobs in cities or as laborers on rice farms in rural areas. "Even if you have a certain level of education, [the Dominicans] don't allow you to work. . . . If you try to go to an office, they say no." I found that Haitian participants placed a high value on being documented. "If you respect yourself," continued Sylvie, "you will do anything to earn your work permit." The problem, she said, was that the work permit, or *cédula*, was simply unaffordable. Sylvie's voice started to rise, and she went on: "Listen, I'm not trying to go to Miami or New York. But, they make us pay the same amount as if we're going to the USA [over $200 USD]. It's impossible for us." Sylvie concluded that this was an intentional arrangement to keep them in low-paying jobs: "It's a way for them not to give the job to you, asking about the *cédula*." Sylvie's sentiments were echoed by a group of Haitian men working on a nearby rice farm, who remarked on the constraints faced by those living without documents and the perpetual nature of poverty: "Where can you put a day's work for 400 gourdes [approximately $10 USD]? You can't send your kids to school. They all have to bend down right there in the dirt. They do the same thing that the father is doing; once the child is grown, that's what the child will end up doing too."

Haitian rice farm laborers, Cibao Valley, Dominican Republic. Photo by author, 2011.

Still, for those who can afford documents, a better life is not always guaranteed. Later in our conversation, Sylvie described the arbitrary harassment that Haitians experience at the hands of immigration officials: "If [immigration officials] come for you, you must show them your passport. Sometimes they will treat a Haitian like a little toy, and they will make you spend what you have to get it back. . . . They will take your passport and visa from you and sell it to a Haitian that looks like you, and it's the same immigration person that will give you problems for not having your passport later." The analogy of being treated "like a toy" was echoed by other interviewed migrants. Conversations with Sylvie and others were suffused with feelings of belittlement and powerlessness, stemming from their limited standard of living and everyday dealings with immigration authorities, street-level agents charged with carrying out the "dirty work" of unfair institutional norms (Fassin 2011: 218).

## "They Humiliate Us": *Imilyasyon*, the Language of Suffering, and Common Mental Disorders

In a later conversation, Sylvie recited a list of ailments that afflict migrants: "Haitians may have accidents, headaches, body pain, [or] problems with pregnancy." From earlier work in Haiti, I was familiar with some common expressions that Haitians use when they express their suffering. Idioms of distress centered on the head, heart, or stomach. We found that these idioms can convey mental distress, particularly idioms pertaining to the head and heart (Keys et al. 2012). For example, *tèt pati* (Kreyòl) literally means "a head that has left." *Tèt cho* (Kreyòl) is literally "a hot head." These idioms are sometimes used in stressful situations that affect concentration, problem-solving, memory, or otherwise normal behavior and functioning.

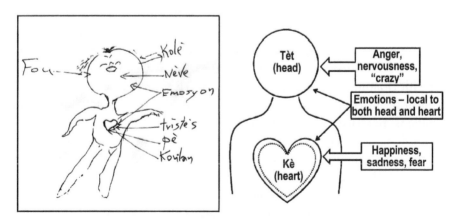

Conceptual and emotional map of the self made by focus group participants, Central Plateau, Haiti, summer 2010. Image from Keys et al. 2012.

Idioms of distress have long been recognized as an important window into local worlds, allowing outsiders to ascertain how people in other cultural settings experience, communicate, and assign meaning to their mental and physical health (Guarnaccia, Lewis-Fernández, and Marano 2003; Hinton and Lewis-Fernández 2010; Kohrt and Hruschka 2010; Mendenhall et al. 2010; Nichter 1981, 2010). Ethnographic and epidemiologic methods are useful for determining how idioms overlap or diverge from standard psychiatric categories, such as depression and anxiety. For example, in the Haitian context, head- and heart-based Kreyòl idioms of distress, such as *kè bat fò* (racing heart), *kè fè mal* (heart hurts), and *tèt fè mal* (headache), seem to correspond to symptoms that suggest autonomic arousal arising from anxiety. The idiom *reflechi twòp* (thinking too much) conveys intense rumination and sadness (Kaiser et al. 2014) and associates strongly with depression and, to a lesser degree, anxiety symptoms.

I probed the issue of headaches further with Sylvie, asking about causes of head pain. She explained that working in the sun can cause headaches, in which case pain medicine helps. Then, she said, "If someone has done something to you, you can be reflecting, and wondering what else is going to befall you. Like if mean people are going to come do bad things to you, it can make you reflect a lot and give you a headache." In Haiti, causes of "reflecting or thinking too much" (Kreyòl: *reflechi twòp*) include food and financial insecurity, trauma, and failing to realize one's goals. Here, Sylvie described "thinking too much" in the context of her interpersonal relationships with Dominicans: "[The Dominicans] may call us bad names, say 'cursed Haitian.' These words can make you reflect. . . . After a series of humiliations, this reflection can make your head hurt." When asked what relief can be found for those who think too much, she said, "They just stay at home, they don't even eat, they are just reflecting. They will stay in private, just bathe and then get back into bed and lie down. There will be people who think that their time to die has come."

In this example, Sylvie's description of "thinking too much" includes important core symptoms of depression such as social isolation and suicidal ideation. As an undocumented migrant in the street market, Sylvie comes into close contact with Dominican immigration officials as well as everyday Dominicans who frequent the market. She and many other Haitian migrants report emotions and sensations associated with depression, which they attribute to daily insults, name-calling, belittlement from Dominicans, and fear of "mean people who do bad things to you," that is, Dominican employers and government workers. In our cross-sectional survey of Haitian migrants in the area, the mean score on the Kreyòl version of the Beck Depression Inventory score was 27.11, which is in the range for clinical depression and is 30% higher than the average score among rural Haitians across the border in their home country (Wagenaar et al. 2012). While cross-sectional studies like these cannot establish causal pathways, they shed light on potential risk factors for those who may become migrants and on the psychological effects of harsh social conditions, including negative interactions with Dominicans, not found in Haiti. Thinking and reflecting too much over "a series of humiliations" exemplifies how the language of suffering is infused with meaning and communicates important aspects of psychological distress that might otherwise go undetected.

Notably, humiliation also appears connected to socioeconomic class. Another participant, an older Haitian man working as a rice farm laborer, said that humiliation was not something limited to interactions with Dominican employers and government workers, but rather it was largely experienced at the hands of poor Dominicans: "The big men [landowners], we help them in their work. The Dominicans who don't have opportunities, who don't have money like the big men, they don't want to see us around." In a separate discussion, one Haitian woman recalled how poor Dominicans threaten and steal from Haitians. She explained: a poor Dominican may "know a Haitian working in a wealthy area, [so] when payroll day arrives, they know you got your money, [so] they come at night with a gun to rob you, even if they are your friend." Many Haitian participants felt resigned to accept humiliation as inevitable, communicating feelings of disempowerment in their daily lives:

> Even if the Dominicans embarrass us, you must humble yourself before them [Kreyòl: *mete'w pti devan yo*—"to make yourself small before them"], because you are not in your country when they are humiliating you. . . . You have to be calm and accept humiliation from their hands. (Haitian man, Dominican Republic, 2012)

As these examples show, a locally meaningful term like *imilyasyon* can embody the broader social imbalances among economic classes (Rechtman 2006), including disenfranchised Dominicans, who may feel empowered by an anti-Haitian ideology (Martinez 2003). Furthermore, contrasting metaphors of feeling like "little toys" while the "big men" wield authority and power illustrate the social inequality and disempowerment borne by these individuals. For Sylvie, there is unfairness to it all, because "If you as a Haitian weren't humiliated, you would stay at home, comfortable like a Dominican. They don't have *tèt pati* (a head that has left, i.e., forgetfulness and worry), they don't have *tèt cho* (a hot head, i.e., unusual/psychotic behavior), they don't have anyone giving them problems." Contextualized within the social and class struggle from which it originates, humiliation (*imilyasyon*) can be thought of as a "label of distress" among those who suffer at the hands of others and are shut out from social and economic gains (Kohrt et al. 2004).

Institutional and personally mediated, anti-Haitian discrimination generates psychosocial stress for many Haitian migrants. Important idioms such as "thinking too much" and the locally meaningful experience of humiliation can reveal how local constructs can communicate the stress of common mental health disorders, such as depression and anxiety, while pointing to larger social inequalities among groups. For those concerned with addressing mental health disparities in low- and middle-income countries, examining the language of suffering used by marginalized groups facilitates recognition of clusters of symptoms associated with those disorders. This in turn can open up pathways for treatment and advocacy, implications that we consider below.

## "WE HAVE NO WORTH": SELF-DEVALUATION AND INTERNALIZED RACISM

A recurrent finding in interviews with Sylvie was the concept of *vale*, meaning worth or value in Haitian Kreyòl. *Vale* can refer to both the material worth of money and the feeling of self-worth held by an individual. In their use of *vale*, migrants connected these concrete and symbolic meanings. For example, one Haitian woman connected material poverty to feelings of worthlessness, saying bluntly, "In life, when you have nothing, you're worth nothing. You're poor." The poverty that many Haitian migrants experience in the Dominican Republic appeared to carry its own significance: "It's because I'm not in my country that I feel like I am worth nothing," said one community member. Feelings of worthlessness are another core symptom of depression. In our survey, 69% ($n$ = 88) of participants endorsed feelings of worthlessness on the adapted Kreyòl Beck Depression Inventory, indicating how pervasive this experience is for many migrants. What is particularly interesting is that feelings of worthlessness were attributed not just to poverty itself but also to the experience of living in poverty in the Dominican Republic as a second-class group. Sylvie said, "If a Dominican does something bad to you, it is no different than doing something bad to a dog. Because you're a Haitian, to him you are just like a dog, and you don't have any *vale* (value). It's like you're more animal than person." One Haitian man went further to say that in the Dominican Republic, not only do Haitians hold less value than street dogs, they are "faceless" (Kreyòl: *san visaj*) in the eyes of their Dominican neighbors.

Finally, in multiple retellings, when a Haitian inflicts some transgression against a Dominican, the Haitian community as a whole must expect retaliation. Sylvie explained, "If a Haitian does something bad to a Dominican, we will all pay for the other Haitian that has done bad things." Such reprisals against Haitians have been well cataloged (Paulino 2006). Participants in our study recalled stories in which Haitians were murdered in retribution for some supposed wrongdoing. One group of Haitian rice farmers recounted a chilling story of a Dominican who suspected a Haitian had stolen his cow. In turn, a handful of Haitians were murdered in revenge, individuals who presumably had nothing to do with the incident.

At the end of story, the cow was discovered to have simply wandered off—it had never been stolen. The story concludes with the cow—oblivious to the carnage in its name—meandering back to its corral. This narrative, regardless of its veracity, reveals the general state of fear and uncertainty within the migrant community. Stories of anti-Haitian violence exemplify what David Howard (2007: 726), an expert in Caribbean development studies, describes as a "fear induced . . . pre-emptive attempt to defend a racialized space or boundary." Routine violence, whether actual or implied, further contributes to perceived worthlessness, and ultimately impedes the economic growth and security desperately sought after by Sylvie and her fellow migrants.

## ANTI-HAITIANISM AS A SOCIAL DETERMINANT OF MENTAL HEALTH

Poverty and social discrimination in combination reinforce each other and together are a major threat to mental health. Discrimination is widely recognized as a social determinant of health because it systematically disadvantages certain groups (Williams and Mohammed 2009). There is ample evidence of the negative effect discrimination has on both mental and physical health (for a good review article on this subject, see Pascoe and Smart Richman 2009). As Sylvie's narrative and other examples demonstrate, anti-Haitianism operates through institutional, personally mediated, and internalized pathways (Jones 2000). In the Dominican Republic, institutional practices discriminate against Haitians by obstructing their access to authorized documents, in turn limiting access to education, health care, political rights, and other "common goods" (Leventhal 2013). In addition, discrimination can be personally mediated by one individual against another. Sylvie and others described hurtful social interactions between themselves and Dominicans, including arbitrary street-level harassment, name-calling, and belittling. Finally, discrimination can be internalized. Here, an individual accepts the devaluing attitudes and beliefs held by the dominant group, generating feelings of self-doubt, dislike, or contempt for oneself or one's group (Ahmed et al. 2007). Confronted by routine, devaluing street-level interactions as well as seemingly insurmountable structural obstacles, Sylvie and others like her expressed personal feelings of worthlessness and the notion that, as a collective body, Haitians *pa gen vale*—have no worth.

## MEETING MENTAL HEALTH NEEDS OF HAITIAN MIGRANTS

The sociocultural context of Haitian migrants contributes to the increased need for physical and mental health services, and the context simultaneously predicts a system in which care will also be delivered in a discriminatory and woefully inadequate manner. This manifests as multiple obstacles encountered by Haitian migrants as they try to access health care. First, there are financial hurdles in accessing and paying for care. Second, due to economic constraints or fear of being apprehended by authorities, many migrants delay care until their condition is unbearable. Third, many migrants feel belittled in the eyes of Dominican clinicians, who are said to favor those with legal status and insurance, which leads sick Haitians to forgo care. Fourth, in Haiti, mental health needs are often tended to by traditional healers or spiritual figures in the community rather than by biomedical providers, because of the poor care and discriminatory experiences within the biomedical care system (Wagenaar et al. 2013). Thus, for Sylvie and other Haitian migrants in the Dominican Republic, special considerations must be taken to meet their mental health needs. Our work in Haiti found that many rural Haitians prefer community-based supports for mental health concerns (Wagenaar et al. 2013), a preference likely maintained by migrants in the Dominican Republic.

Dominican health care workers in emergency rooms and rural health clinics are likely the only individuals that migrants may encounter who could address mental health in a biomedical context. There are severe shortages of trained psychiatrists and psychologists for Dominican patients, and mental health speciality services are nonexistent for migrant Haitians. Ideally, the background and life experiences of many Haitian patients deserve special attention by Dominican clinicians, particularly those who work in settings where migrants seek care, such as emergency rooms and primary care clinics. As a form of task-sharing in mental health services, emergency and primary care clinicians potentially could develop therapeutic relationships with Haitian patients by incorporating brief, migration-related items into the history-taking, which grants a global sense of the individual's life story and reveals potential sources of psychosocial stress. These items include asking about their life circumstances in Haiti, what compelled an individual to leave Haiti, if he or she came alone or with others, and how long ago. The clinician can also inquire about post-migration issues such as expectation-reality discrepancy, support networks, and daily functioning. For example, a therapeutic relationship between a Dominican provider and Sylvie might inform the provider of her past abusive relationship and economic insecurity in Haiti, potential trauma or exploitation faced during migration, and experience of hurtful interactions in the street market. This information helps formulate a picture of the patient's "local world" (Kleinman and Benson 2006), or how that person views his or her life and environment, based on the understanding that Haitian migrants face unique stressors prior to, during, and after migration. Though training Dominican clinicians to develop a more psychosocial perspective of Haitian migrant patients is not going to transform the structural violence experienced by migrants, the process of Dominican clinician engagement might facilitate broader social attention to the needs of migrants.

Of course, linguistic differences between Dominican clinicians and Haitian patients pose a challenge. Although using trained medical interpreters is ideal, this is often not possible. Hospital and clinical staff could instead recruit bilingual "culture brokers" from migrant communities. These could be Haitians who have already lived for some time in the country, speak fluent Spanish, and are familiar with issues faced by migrants. Most importantly, they should be interested in serving not only as interpreters but also as advocates.

Inquiring into the everyday lives of migrants gets at the heart of acknowledgment—"the first ethical task" in the face of someone's suffering (Kleinman and Benson 2006: 1675). Culturally sensitive approaches toward Haitian patients can help the clinician understand illness explanations, patterns of coping and seeking help, emotional expression and communication, and relationships with care providers (Berkman and Glass 2000). As we have seen, complaints of head, heart, or stomach pain can be used by Haitians to communicate psychosocial distress (Keys et al. 2012). In addition to taking psychosocially focused migration histories, Dominican clinicians can investigate medically unexplained symptoms such as vague pain, fatigue, and gastrointestinal complaints with an inquiry into possible links with impaired daily functioning, migration-related stressors, and strained interpersonal relationships (Kirmayer et al. 2011). Doing so allows clinicians to assess adaptation to the host society and provides an opportunity to promote mental health and well-being.

## COMMUNITY-LEVEL INTERVENTIONS

As Sylvie's account illustrated, anti-Haitian discrimination occurs at an interpersonal level among community members. In addition, poor social integration and lack of social support within communities increase risk for common mental health disorders like depression and anxiety (Berkman and Glass 2000). With the extremely low numbers of formally trained mental health specialists available in the Dominican Republic, and given that Haitians are unlikely to seek mental health care from general practitioners and health care workers, community-level interventions are imperative in order to reach this population. A practical step to address mental health at the community level is through increasing positive social contact between Haitians and Dominicans.

First, this approach enhances the "social capital" of a community. Social capital refers to cohesiveness and trust among community members, leads to positive social engagement, fosters a sense of control over life circumstances, and consequently has strong effects on health (Berkman and Glass 2000; Marmot 2006). Stigma and prevailing attitudes toward Haitians impede mutual trust and social cohesion. One way of reducing these barriers is through increased positive social contact, such as through community meetings, workshops, leisure activities, and other events shown to reduce prejudicial attitudes (Pettigrew and Tropp 2006; Walker et al. 2005).

In this context, community gatherings may gain more acceptance if they are based on forms of social organization that have culture-specific meaning and historical precedence. In the Dominican Republic, the *convite* (Spanish) is a form of cooperation among farmers who band together to accomplish tasks (Domínguez, Castillo, and Tejeda 1978). In Haiti, an identical structure is the *konbit* (Kreyòl) (Métraux 1951). The similar purpose and etymological root of this social structure reveal how customs and values of the two countries overlap. Through collaborative activities modeled on the *convite / konbit*, Haitian migrants and their Dominican neighbors may discover that they share similar obstacles and common goals. For example, in Sylvie's community, both Haitian and Dominican market vendors could organize a cooperative *convite / konbit* to engage with one another outside their routine occupational roles. Key community leaders could collaborate with local public health authorities and community health workers already "on the ground" to develop cooperative *convite / konbit* activities that focus on shared values and customs between Haitians and Dominicans, while educating community members about the harmful effects of anti-Haitian discrimination.

While the cooperative *convite / konbit* approach is basic in its outline, it emphasizes social cohesion among Haitian and Dominican community members. Anti-Haitian discrimination thrives where social cohesion is weak, yet it is through social networks that the stigmatized and the dominant population interact. For example, Sylvie lives in a dense urban enclave of fellow migrants and poor Dominicans. Her job in the street market brings her into a web of relationships with Dominican passers-by, immigration authorities, and other Haitian migrants. In rural areas, Haitian migrants interact with Dominican agricultural employers—the *gran neg*, or "big men" for whom they work—and poor Dominican neighbors, who themselves may feel threatened by Haitians for displacing them from jobs. It is in this context, within the lived worlds of both Haitians and Dominicans, that the stigma of being an undocumented Haitian is defined and perpetuated. Understanding the social and cultural processes that create stigma within these local worlds should be the starting point for reducing stigma (Kleinman and Hall-Clifford 2009). Positive contact events modeled on the *convite / konbit* build on this premise by opening the way for constructive relationships.

## INSTITUTIONAL-LEVEL STRATEGIES

Anti-Haitian discrimination remains embedded in such institutional practices as access to health care, education, and citizenship as well as upward mobility in the job market. Ultimately, addressing social determinants of mental health becomes as much a "political project as a health project" (Mittelmark 2003: 10). For Sylvie, this means creating social and political conditions that foster a sense of control and self-determination in her life. Thus, reform of unfair social conditions must involve community members, civil society, and policy makers. To accomplish positive change, two fundamental steps are (1) raising public awareness of social determinants of health and (2) taking legislative and policy action.

First, educating the public on social determinants of mental health can empower communities with knowledge about unjust social structures and in turn galvanize action. Concepts of dignity, opportunity, empowerment, and security resonate strongly across cultures and among populations beset by poverty (Narayan et al. 2000). These themes could form the basis of nationwide communication strategies that emphasize the two countries' shared history and cultures, counter the idea that individual decisions and behavior alone lead to mental illness, explain the central role of social determinants in producing chronic mental disorders in marginalized groups like Haitian migrants, and discuss the negative impact of mental illness on well-being (Niederdeppe et al. 2008).

Public education should link health inequalities and human rights together so that they assume a more prominent place in the public domain. For example, in the Dominican Republic, a rights-based approach could connect discrimination and xenophobia with consequent impacts on mental health and well-being. There must be concomitant legal and civil society involvement, chiefly in the areas of documentation, labor rights, and health benefits. For Sylvie, being undocumented, lacking employment rights, and being unable to access, afford, or receive quality health care dramatically affect her mental health. Legislative health policy reform can address these systemic, institutional-level problems, through such initiatives as a unified immigration policy and strengthened mental health services.

There is already an avenue to strengthen existing mental health services through reform of health policy. While the Dominican Republic has no explicit, national-level mental health policy, Law No. 12-06, passed in 2006, updated standards for mental health services and stipulated the individual right to receive mental health care (WHO/PAHO 2008). Drawing on evidence that shows how mental health interventions are associated with improved economic outcomes in resource-poor settings (Lund et al. 2011) and on human rights principles that the country articulated in its Constitution, strong arguments can be made to increase support of mental health systems nationwide, which would carry population-level benefits for both Haitian migrants and Dominicans.

Ultimately, positive change at the societal level hinges on empowerment, or the ability to chart one's own course, have control over life circumstances, and be an active partner in the change process (WHO 2005). For Haitian migrants in the

Dominican Republic, positive change encompasses the ability to participate more fully in Dominican society through access to education, employment, safe physical and social environments, health care, legal rights, and social support. For Sylvie, empowerment would entail a heightened sense of self-determination and control in her life course and a feeling of being capable of making decisions in her life. Attaining these fundamental aspects of well-being can be accomplished through individual and community-level empowerment supported by broad-based legislative reform to reduce mental health disparities.

## References

Ahmed, A., Mohammed, S. A., and Williams, D. R. (2007). Racial discrimination and health: pathways and evidence. *Indian Journal of Medical Research*, 126: 318–327.

Barth, F. (1969). *Ethnic Groups and Boundaries: The Social Organization of Culture Difference*. Boston: Little, Brown, and Company.

Bartlett, L., Jayaram, K., and Bonhomme, G. (2011). State literacies and inequalities: managing Haitian immigrants in the Dominican Republic. *International Journal of Education and Development*, 31.

Berkman, L., and Glass, T. (2000). Social integration, social networks, social support, and health. In L. Berkman, and I. Kawachi (eds.), *Social Epidemiology*, pp. 137–173. New York: Oxford University Press.

Canales, A., Vargas Becerra, P., and Montiel Armas, I. (2009). *Migración y salud en zonas fronterizas: Haití y República Dominicana*. Población y desarrollo. Santiago de Chile: United Nations Population Fund.

Derby, L. (1994). Haitians, magic and money: *raza* and society in the Haitian–Dominican borderlands, 1900–1937. *Comparative Studies in Society and History*, 36 (3): 488–526.

Domínguez, I., Castillo, J., and Tejeda, D. (1978). *Almanaque folklórico dominicano*. Santo Domingo: Museo del Hombre Dominicano.

Fassin, D. (2011). Policing borders, producing boundaries: the governmentality of immigration in dark times. *Annual Review of Anthropology*, 40: 213–226.

Ferguson, J. (2006). The Haitian migrant minority in the Dominican Republic. In T. Lesser, B. Fernandez-Alfaro, L. Cowie, and N. Bruni (eds.), *Intra-Caribbean Migration and the Conflict Nexus*. Ottawa: Tri-Graphic Printing, Ltd.

Guarnaccia, P. J., Lewis-Fernández, R., and Marano, M. R. (2003). Toward a Puerto Rican popular nosology: *nervios* and *ataque de nervios*. *Culture, Medicine, and Psychiatry*, 27: 339–366.

Hinton, D. E., and Lewis-Fernández, R. (2010). Idioms of distress among trauma survivors: subtypes and clinical utility. *Culture, Medicine, and Psychiatry*, 34: 209–218.

Howard, D. (2007). Development, racism, and discrimination in the Dominican Republic. *Development in Practice*, 17: 725–738.

Jones, C. P. (2000). Levels of racism: a theoretic framework and a gardener's tale. *American Journal of Public Health*, 90: 1212–1215.

Kaiser, B., Kohrt, B., Keys, H., Khoury, N., and Brewster, A.-R. (2013). Strategies for assessing mental health in rural Haiti: comparing local instrument development and transcultural translation. *Transcultural Psychiatry*, 50 (4): 532–558.

Kaiser, B., McLean, K., Kohrt, B., Hagaman, A., Wagenaar, B., Khoury, N., and Keys, H. (2014). *Reflechi twòp*—Thinking too much: description of a cultural syndrome in Haiti's Central Plateau. *Culture, Medicine, and Psychiatry*, 38 (3): 448–472.

Keys, H., Kaiser, B., Kohrt, B., Khoury, N., and Brewster, A.-R. (2012). Idioms of distress, ethnopsychology, and the clinical encounter in Haiti's Central Plateau. *Social Science and Medicine*, 75: 555–564.

Keys, H. M., Kaiser, B. N., Foster, J. W., Burgos Minaya, R. Y., and Kohrt, B. A. (2014). Perceived discrimination, humiliation, and mental health: a mixed-methods study among Haitian migrants in the Dominican Republic. *Ethnicity and Health*. doi: 10.1080/13557858.2014.907389.

Khoury, N., Kaiser, B., Keys, H., Brewster, A.-R., and Kohrt, B. (2012). Explanatory models and mental health treatment: is vodou an obstacle to mental health treatment in rural Haiti? *Culture, Medicine, and Psychiatry*, 36: 514–534.

Kirmayer, L., Narasiah, L., Munoz, M., Rashid, M., Ryder, A., Guzder, J., et al. (2011). Common mental health problems in immigrants and refugees: general approach in primary care. *Canadian Medical Association Journal*, 183: e959–e967.

Kleinman, A., and Benson, P. (2006). Anthropology in the clinic: the problem of cultural competency and how to fix it. *PLoS Medicine*, 3: 1673–1676.

Kleinman, A., and Hall-Clifford, A. (2009). Stigma: a social, cultural, and moral process. *Journal of Epidemiology and Community Health*, 63: 418–419.

Kohrt, B. A., and Hruschka, D. J. (2010). Nepali concepts of psychological trauma: the role of idioms of distress, ethnopsychology and ethnophysiology in alleviating suffering and preventing stigma. *Culture, Medicine, and Psychiatry*, 34: 322–352.

Kohrt, B., Hruschka, D., Kohrt, H. E., Panebianco, N. L., and Tsagaankhuu, G. (2004). Distribution of distress in post-socialist Mongolia: a cultural epidemiology of *yadargaa*. *Social Science and Medicine*, 58: 471–485.

Leventhal, S. (2013). A gap between ideals and reality: the right to health and the inaccessibility of healthcare for Haitian migrant workers in the Dominican Republic. *Emory International Law Review*, 27 (2): 1249.

Lund, C., De Silva, M., Plagerson, S., Cooper, S., Chisholm, D., Das, J., et al. (2011). Poverty and mental disorders: breaking the cycle in low-income and middle-income countries. *The Lancet*, 378: 1502–1514.

Marmot, M. (2006). Health in an unequal world: social circumstances, biology, and disease. *Clinical Medicine*, 6: 559–572.

Martinez, S. (1995). *Peripheral Migrants: Haitians and Dominican Sugar Cane Plantations*. Knoxville: University of Tennessee Press.

——. (2003). Not a cockfight: re-thinking Haitian–Dominican relations. *Latin American Perspectives*, 30: 80–101.

Mendenhall, M., Seligman, R., Fernandez, A., and Jacobs, E. (2010). Speaking through diabetes: rethinking the significance of lay discourses on diabetes. *Medical Anthropology Quarterly*, 24: 220–239.

Métraux, A. (1951). *Making a Living in the Maribal Valley, Haiti*. Paris: UNESCO.

Ministerio de Trabajo. (2011). *Inmigrantes haitianos y mercado laboral: estudio sobre los trabajadores de la construcción y de la producción del Guineo en la Republica Dominicana*. Dominican Republic: Editora Mediabyte SA.

Mittelmark, M. (2003). Mental health + inequalities = broad strategy. *VicHealth Letter*, 21 (Spring): 10–11.

Narayan, D., Patel, R., Schafft, K., Rademacher, A., and Koch-Schulte, S. (2000). *Voices of the Poor: Can Anyone Hear Us?* New York: Oxford University Press for the World Bank.

Nichter, M. (1981). Idioms of distress: alternatives in the expression of psychosocial distress: a case study from South India. *Culture, Medicine, and Psychiatry*, 5: 379–408.

——. (2010). Idioms of distress revisited. *Culture, Medicine, and Psychiatry*, 34: 401–416.

Niederdeppe, J., Bu, Q. L., Borah, P., Kindig, D., and Robert, S. (2008). Message design strategies to raise public awareness of social determinants of health and population health disparities. *The Milbank Quarterly*, 86: 481–513.

Pascoe, E., and Smart Richman, L. (2009). Perceived discrimination and health: a meta-analytic review. *Psychological Bulletin*, 135: 531–554.

Paulino, E. (2006). Anti-Haitianism, historical memory, and the potential for genocidal violence in the Dominican Republic. *Genocide Studies and Prevention*, 1: 265–288.

Pettigrew, T., and Tropp, L. (2006). A meta-analytic test of intergroup contact theory. *Journal of Personality and Social Psychology*, 90: 751–783.

Rechtman, R. (2006). Cultural standards, power and subversion in cross-cultural psychotherapy. *Transcultural Psychiatry*, 43: 169–180.

Sagas, E. (2000). *Race and Politics in the Dominican Republic*. Gainesville: University Press of Florida.

Sagas, E., and Inoa, O. (2003). *The Dominican People: A Documentary History*. Princeton, New Jersey: Markus Wiener Publishers.

Tavernier, L. A. (2008). The stigma of blackness: anti-Haitianism in the Dominican Republic. *Socialism and Democracy*, 22: 96–104.

Turits, R. (2002). A world destroyed, a nation imposed: the 1937 Haitian massacre in the Dominican Republic. *Hispanic American Historical Review*, 82 (3): 589–636.

United Nations. (2008). Mission to Dominican Republic. In *Report of the Special Rapporteur on Contemporary Forms of Racism, Xenophobia and Related Intolerance*. New York: United Nations Human Rights Council.

Wagenaar, B., Hagaman, A., Kaiser, B., McLean, K., and Kohrt, B. (2012). Depression, suicidal ideation, and associated factors: a cross-sectional study in rural Haiti. *BMC Psychiatry*, 12: 149.

Wagenaar, B., Kohrt, B., Hagaman, A., McLean, K., and Kaiser, B. (2013). Determinants of care seeking for mental health problems in rural Haiti: culture, cost, or competency. *Psychiatric Services*, 64: 366–372.

Walker, L., Verins, I., Moodie, R., and Webster, K. (2005). Responding to the social and economic determinants of mental health: a conceptual framework for action. In H. Herrman, S. Saxena, and R. Moodie (eds.), *Promoting Mental Health: Concepts, Emerging Evidence, Practice*. Geneva: World Health Organization.

World Health Organization (WHO). (2005). *Promoting Mental Health: Concepts, Emerging Evidence, Practice*. In H. Herrman, S. Saxena, and R. Moodie (eds.). Geneva: World Health Organization.

World Health Organization (WHO)/Pan American Health Organization (PAHO). (2008). *Report on Mental Health Systems in the Dominican Republic*. Santo Domingo, Dominican Republic: WHO.

Williams, D. R., and Mohammed, S. A. (2009). Discrimination and racial disparities in health: evidence and needed research. *Journal of Behavioral Medicine*, 32: 20–47.

Chapter 10

# Festive Fighting and Forgiving: Ritual and Resilience among Indigenous Indian "Conservation Refugees"

Jeffrey G. Snodgrass

**March 27, 2013: Dhuleti (day of license)**

6–8 AM: Villagers rise around 6 AM, their typical morning rhythm not broken for the first few hours (tea, toilet, washing the face, breakfast, women's sweeping of the home). At 8 AM, men visit each other's homes, sit, smoke *bidi* cigarettes and chew tobacco, followed by a calmly affectionate and lightly playful smearing of color into each other's faces, all laughing good-naturedly.

9–11 AM: Children parade through the village, flinging color on anyone who dares venture out of their homes. I remember in particular a young boy in my adopted family, about six years old, relishing his newfound power. All adults, myself included, flinch at his colorful assaults. He is relentless! Adolescents and young men and women join in as well, flirtation and typically "inappropriate" touching of members of the opposite sex, who are wrestled to the ground and bathed with color.

11 AM–2 PM: Men install a stereo with speakers and microphone on a bicycle that becomes a mobile boom-box. A percussion band forms, which visits each household, men dancing vigorously and singing enthusiastically for a few minutes before each home, not leaving until they receive their gifts of alcohol, cash, and food, their music a form of festive labor. Men also dress as women and flirt with other men, with frequent mock sexual thrusting. There is lots of energetic hugging, which often leads to the men, stumbling drunk, tumbling onto the ground into the dirt, clothes ripping. By the end, the men are sweating, dehydrated, exhausted, drunk beyond imagining, but still laughing, smiling, dirty, intertwined in each other's arms.

*Global Mental Health: Anthropological Perspectives*, edited by Brandon A. Kohrt and Emily Mendenhall, 173–190. © 2015 Left Coast Press, Inc. All rights reserved.

2 PM: The dancing ends and the calculation begins. Men count the collected money, scribbling hurriedly with pen on paper to figure out how to divvy up the spoils. Disputes break out, with particularly energetic dancers and music makers claiming larger shares of the haul.

2:45 PM: At the peak of their drunkenness, men air grievances with each other. This is when an incident between Jayanth and his son took place. Fulfilling what he perceives as his traditional headman role, Jayanth tries to step in and stop the fighting between some village men, only to be chastised by his son, with whom he then aggresses and is aggressed. Observing the incident, one woman tells me: "During Holi, no one thinks in terms of 'big or little.' Sons don't respect fathers, women don't respect husbands. Everyone is equal!"

2:45–4:30 PM: Women now make the same house-to-house tour as the men. Their dancing is equally vigorous, the singing as spirited. The mobile sound system has been abandoned, but the performance is lifted by the harmony and synergy of the women's singing. The women's fabrics are made doubly colorful with the buckets of color-infused water dumped over one another's heads. Again, hugging and public displays of affection are plentiful. Money and food are exchanged. Women force-feed each other shots of alcohol, always tit for tat, a shot for a shot. This is interesting, as women do not normally drink and certainly not publicly in this manner. Women aggressively flirt with men who are not their husbands. There is also sexually suggestive dancing and bawdy singing.

4:30–6 PM: Everyone is drunk, either hugging or fighting. (My field notes: "Oh my god, emotional chaos!") The men's fighting had continued relatively unabated since the early afternoon, but now the women have joined in as well, with frequent bouts of almost ritualized crying more common among them than fisticuffs. Around 5 PM I witness a dusty wrestling match between Jamma Singh and his family, followed by this man's disappearance into the night (more below).

7–9 PM: The fighting has ended, all is calm! Villagers dine placidly or rest calmly on their cots in front of their homes, talking in subdued tones, preparing for sleep.

### Epilogue: March 28 (the day after dhuleti)

No one eats in their own homes on this day! All are required to eat in the home of relatives or neighbors. I am told this is important, as this is a day of forgiveness. All the fights of the previous day must be forgiven and forgotten. One man tells me: "If anyone participated in any 'fighting' [larai-jhagra] the previous day, then they must hug and place a tilak [mark of blessing] on the other's forehead, asking forgiveness [*mafi*]." The next day is filled with communal feasting, solidarity, punctuated by few if any fights. Everyone is smiling, laughing, calm, *happy*. "How can we not be happy after having eaten so well?" one woman asks me rhetorically. The festival seems to have had its effect, mental states healthfully recalibrated!

THE ABOVE IS AN EXCERPT FROM my ethnographic field notes of *dhuleti*, a day of license during the Hindu festival Holi, where individuals break rules that hold the rest of the year. Every year, Mamuli villagers in central India practice this ritual, defying everyday norms, behaviors, and expectations. The *dhuleti* ritual provides an opportunity to explore how non-biomedical practices influence mental health. Anthropologists, psychosocial practitioners, and other interventionists have increasingly called for the study of so-called traditional rituals as alternatives—or complementary—to biomedical forms of mental health treatment. Below I provide the sociocultural and mental health context in which the *dhuleti* ritual was enacted and then discuss broader implications for the anthropological study of global mental health.

## THE MENTAL HEALTH OF DISPLACED SAHARIYA

My observation of the *dhuleti* ritual occurred in the context of a long-term anthropological study of mental health in India. Beginning in 2006, I began anthropological research investigating the lives of Sahariya "tribal" indigenous persons living in and near the Kuno-Palpur Wildlife Sanctuary ("Kuno" for short) in the central Indian state of Madhya Pradesh. I was interested to learn how Sahariyas' new position as "conservation refugees" might be accompanied by compromised mental health.[1] This refugee label captures the experience of about 8,000 Sahariya villagers who were moved out of Kuno between 1998 and 2002 in order to make way for Asiatic lions to be transplanted from Gujarat's Gir National Park.[2] I hoped to understand how relocation impacted the lives of displaced Sahariyas, not only immediately after displacement but also long afterward. I also wanted to understand the effects of the displacement on those Sahariya who remained behind in Kuno, as did the villagers of Mamuli,[3] whose lives are considered in this chapter.

Though remaining in their ancestral home, Mamuli's villagers are also considered by the World Bank and other international bodies to be displaced peoples, as they have lost access to natural resources such as wild game and plants, whose hunting and harvesting are now forbidden in many areas, such as Kuno's ecological core.[4] Post-displacement, Mamuli villagers also found themselves more isolated than before, which further compromised their physical security and also their livelihoods, as they are now more vulnerable to depredations from outsider communities and less able to access material goods and labor markets. Mamuli inhabitants' needs for water, schools, hospitals, and other services go largely unheard, as the Indian state focuses more fully on relocated Sahariya, who suffer more visibly because of their loss of homeland. Overall, like their physically relocated kin, the villagers of Mamuli can be said to have experienced a form of policy-generated "disaster," in the sense of collectively experienced traumatic events that are acute and time-delimited in their initial impact and followed by sustained and more chronic problems and stressors (Cernea and McDowell 2000; Fischer 2008; McFarlane and Norris 2006: 4).

The mental health problems among the world's poor has been recognized as a global mental health crisis, with some labeling it a "failure of humanity" not to extend Western expertise and resources to developing nations in an attempt to comprehend and alleviate such problems (Kleinman 2009; see also Collins et al. 2011; Patel 2012; Patel and Kleinman 2003). With this call from within the global mental health service community in mind, the aim of my research was to document stress and other forms of mental suffering in the lives of Kuno's displaced populations. However, as an anthropologist attuned to local ways of being, I wanted to do this in a way that respected cultural "idioms of distress" (Nichter 1981)—in this case, Hindu and tribal ways of framing, expressing, and minimizing mental illness and suffering. Anthropologists and others speak of the dangers of relying solely on Western mental health categories, be it "PTSD" or some other label, as this risks "medicalizing" and thus universalizing mental distress as underlying biological "disease" rather than an "illness" experience inflected by cultural conditions (Kleinman 1980, 1988; Nichter 1981; Rosen, Spitzer, and McHugh 2008; Summerfield 2008, 2012; Watters 2010; Young 1997). Instead of relying on descriptions of mental disorders in Western medical texts such as the *Diagnostic and Statistical Manual* (*DSM*), these scholars suggest framing understandings in dialogue with local systems of meaning (Almedon and Glandon 2007; Kirmayer et al. 2009; Nichter 1981; Panter-Brick and Eggerman 2012; Summerfield 2008, 2012; Watters 2010).

Indeed, many humanitarian and health organizations, such the Inter-Agency Standing Committee (IASC), the World Health Organization (WHO), and the Sphere Project, have established new guidelines recommending that relief projects addressing displacement, disasters, political violence, and grinding Third World poverty take into account local standards in regard to mental distress and its treatment (Batniji et al. 2006; Kohrt et al. 2008; Mollica et al. 2004; Van Ommeren, Saxena, and Saraceno 2005; Weine et al. 2002). Respect for local mental health practices can result in more "culturally competent" and thus also more effective psychiatric practice by outsiders trained in alternate scientific traditions (Kirmayer 2012; Kleinman 1980, 1988). It could also mean promoting collaboration between non-Western healers and Western-trained psychiatrists (Incayawar 2009; Kleinman 1980, 1988; Ngoma, Prince, and Mann 2003; Robertson 2006). Or, as in this Sahariya case, it could entail understanding how the local "work of culture"

(Obeyesekere 1990)—as in participation in religious rituals—might function as a folk psychiatry that potentially betters local mental well-being.

Though my research addresses a range of issues related to Sahariya well-being, this chapter more narrowly explores local sources of mental health *resilience*—that is, beliefs and practices that might keep Sahariya mentally tough in the face of adversity (Almedon and Glandon 2007; Kirmayer et al. 2009; Panter-Brick and Eggerman 2012). In particular, I examine how participation in *dhuleti* and the broader Hinduism's spring "festival of color"—called Holi—might provide such resiliency. The laughter and raucous sociality of Holi, in the way such celebration might relieve stress and promote positive emotions, I reason, just might be good preventive medicine, which would be particularly valuable for Kuno's chronically stressed denizens.

To explore these issues, I relied on a mix of research methods. Specifically, years of conducting ethnographic participant observation and interviews in the area were combined with structured psychiatric self-reported measures that documented differences in Sahariya mental health over nine days in spring 2012, including periods just before and after Mamuli's Holi celebrations.[5] I first present the psychiatric self-reported results, which demonstrate that participation in Holi improves subjective well-being. Then, to contextualize and explain these results, I return to ethnography and the description presented at the beginning of this chapter to explore how the puzzling and pervasive theme of conflict, and even violent conflict, might actually contribute to this festival's healing force. Overall, I hope that this investigation and approach might contribute to developing new mental health and well-being metrics and perspectives—beyond narrow livelihood and material wealth measures—for assessing the cost of human displacement. I also hope that this research might stimulate novel mental health treatment regimes in non-Western development contexts such as Kuno, a theme to which I return in this chapter's conclusion.

## HOLI IS GOOD MEDICINE: PSYCHIATRIC SURVEY RESULTS

Over nine days that included Holi, I had Sahariyas self-assess their anxiety, depression, balance of positive and negative emotion, and stress. The following table shows results from questionnaires administered by my research team in 2012 just before and after the celebration. The table's first two results show changes in anxiety and depression, as assessed via the translated 10-item Hopkins Symptoms Checklist (HSCL-10, with four anxiety and six depression items), an instrument commonly used in non-Western contexts to assess the mental health of refugees and other distressed populations (Derogatis et al. 1974). Note that both anxiety and depression fall to lower levels after celebrating Holi. Next reported are changes in a

40-item Positive and Negative Affect Scale (PANAS), a local Sahariya version of a scale more commonly used in Western contexts (Watson, Clark, and Tellegen 1988), which my team and I developed in a 2008 phase of research. There, in the context of a larger survey, we had asked 202 individuals from eight Sahariya villages in neighboring Rajasthan, "Tell us how you feel when everything is going well/poorly." The 20 most commonly recurring positive and 20 most common negative emotion items were placed in this scale, used here to assess the balance of positive and negative affect experienced that day by Mamuli's villagers. In this locally meaningful measure of emotional balance, we find a post-ritual higher balance of positive as compared with negative emotions, further suggesting improved mental well-being after having celebrated Holi. Finally, we asked informants the extent to which they felt stress that day

## Psychiatric Scale Results: Post-Ritual vs. Pre-Ritual

| Hopkins Anxiety Scale | Mamuli Villagers (n = 29) |
|---|---|
| (4 items, total 0–12, alpha = 0.70) | |
| Pre-ritual (baseline) | 3.13 (0.52) |
| Post-ritual (endline) | 2.17 (0.41) |
| Post vs. Pre | −0.97 (0.44)** |
| **Hopkins Depression Scale** | |
| (6 items, total 0–18, alpha = 0.82) | |
| Pre-ritual (baseline) | 4.59 (0.67) |
| Post-ritual (endline) | 2.26 (0.36) |
| Post vs. Pre | −2.32 (0.49)*** |
| **Positive/Negative Affect Scale** | |
| (20 positive items −20 negative items, total −40 to +40, alpha = 0.91) | |
| Pre-ritual (baseline) | 9.25 (2.30) |
| Post-ritual (endline) | 18.80 (2.22) |
| Post vs. Pre | +9.54 (2.61)*** |
| **Stress Scale** | |
| (4 items, total 0–8, alpha = 0.62) | |
| Pre-ritual (baseline) | 3.31 (0.34) |
| Post-ritual (endline) | 2.62 (0.27) |
| Post vs. Pre | −0.69 (0.40)* |

Notes: Standard errors in parentheses; * $p < 0.10$ ; **$p < 0.05$ ; ***$p < 0.01$.

from household problems, community/social strains, health, and finances. Here, too, we see that respondents reported lower stress just after celebrating Holi.

This structured data tells a clear story: scores on each of these psychiatric scales improve markedly—in both statistically and substantively significant manners—after having participated in Holi festivities. Still, this raises the question: Exactly *how* might celebrating Holi improve one's psychological state? To address this issue, I turn to ethnography, first describing the Holi festivities in some detail and then interpreting the celebration's therapeutic dynamics.

## THE PRACTICE OF HOLI: SOCIAL DIVISION AND SOLIDARITY

Like many Hindus, Sahariyas celebrate Holi over two principal days: first, the burning of Holika symbolizing the victory of good over evil (called "little Holi"), followed by a colorful second day (known as *dhuleti*, described at the beginning of this chapter).[6] The burning of Holika, a triumph of good over evil, is celebrated throughout India and the world, but Sahariyas in the village of Mamuli rework the ritual in their own manner. Over the weeks preceding Holi, they construct an effigy of Holika about 10 feet tall from tree branches, sticks, shrubs, and dry grasses gathered from nearby forests. They then burn the effigy late at night on the last full moon (*purnima*) of the Hindu lunar month of Phalgun (which usually falls in late February or March). When the torch ignites Holika, children encircle the "demoness" (*raksas*), sprinting, flinging firecrackers, and screaming in excitement. Men fire shotguns in the air (the guns were given to them by the Indian state as protection from bandits), dance, and sing raucously, intermittently crying out, "Holiye!" in joyful testimony to God's triumph over evil. Farther back from the fire, women sing bawdily in the night's flickering shadows, alternately taunting and admiring this woman who, from certain male points of view, in particular, rose too high.[7] The following day, on *dhuleti*, villagers attack each other with now store-bought synthetic powdered colors (originally they mixed natural colors with earth and ash), either flung dry through the air or infused in containers of water that are dumped over others' heads and rubbed forcefully into the hair and eyes. Spring has arrived and winter is dead. God lives, and demons have been defeated, to which the torching of Holika, the mock color battles, the song and dance, the laughter, the drinking, and the joy amply testify.

This rule-breaking is evidenced in the quote below, where an agitated Jayanth, Mamuli's headman, chastises me for allowing his son, Prathu, to take my jeep to fetch more alcohol on Holi's raucous second day:

> Let me give you some advice. You shouldn't have sent out my son on this day. Or, at the least you should have consulted with me first. This is a day when anything

can happen. Who knows, he could get grabbed by some unscrupulous types, beat up, kidnapped, hurt, killed. Or they might destroy your car. It happens on this day even to "big people"—to the collector [chief district administrative officer], the SP [superintendent of police], the DFO [district forest officer]—so why not to my son?

This illustrates the extremes of the day of license, which is followed by a day of reconcilation and feasting. As suggested by the mental health questionnaire results, this process appears to be psychologically beneficial for the participants. Below I explore the paradox of how participation in ritualized social conflict relieves rather than exacerbates stress.

## MIGHT HOLI CREATE RATHER THAN RELIEVE STRESS?

A persistent theme of conflict, even violence, pervades this festival. We see this in the assault on the demon Holika, in headman Jayanth's warning to me, and also in *dhuleti's* aggressive play. Even Holi's foundation myth, recounted to me by Mamuli villagers, tells of conflict between the mythic king Hiranyakashipu and his son Prahlada. In this story, Hiranyakashipu had been granted a divine boon as a result of his penances, which made him almost impossible to kill. Hiranyakashipu grew arrogant, demanding that his subjects stop worshipping the gods, whom he now believed to be his inferiors. He demanded the same of his son, but Prahlada, a devotee of Vishnu, refused. This infuriated Hiranyakashipu, who tried to break Prahlada in body and spirit, but to no avail. He attempted to poison his son, but the poison turned to nectar in Prahlada's mouth. He locked Prahlada in an iron tower, denying him food and water, but Prahlada survived. Prahlada even proved immune to his father's venomous snakes and trampling elephants. None of the king's efforts were successful. Finally, Hiranyakashipu ordered Prahlada to sit on a burning pyre in the lap of his aunt (the king's sister), Holika, who also had been granted a boon by the gods, which rendered her immune to fire. Prahlada prayed to Vishnu for protection, and to the king's surprise, Holika, not Prahlada, perished in the flames.

Interestingly, this myth's theme of conflict between fathers and sons was echoed in actual *dhuleti* events I witnessed in Mamuli. In one incident, alluded to above in my field notes, a group of Sahariya men, who had been singing and dancing together the entire day, began that afternoon to bicker, with one group supporting a jealous husband and the other a supposed suitor of the husband's wife. The alcohol flowed, as did the insults, and some in the group turned to fisticuffs. The village headman, Jayanth, who had been watching silently on the sidelines, intervened and struggled to restrain the now flailing male bodies. At this point,

Jayanth's son, Prathu, himself got involved: "Hey Dad, this is none of your business, step off!" "None of my business?" Jayanth retorted, "Who are you to speak to me like that? Shut your trap!" More harsh words were exchanged, with Prathu eventually calling his father a "mother's uterus" (*bosari*)—a common term of insult, which sounded odd to my ear in this context, given the paternal relationship between Jayanth and Prathu. "How dare you speak to me like that—I'll mess you up!" Jayanth screamed in return, leading Prathu to lunge at his father, grabbing his shirt collar roughly and striking him (somewhat ineffectually) a few quick blows to the chest. Villagers struggled to restrain the angry son and father—both, like most everyone else, staggeringly drunk—who were the new focus of attention.

The second incident occurred around 5 PM. As noted, central to *dhuleti's* festivities, first the men and then the women tour the village, singing and dancing in a group before every home (about 80 of them), receiving gifts of Indian rupees—typically between 10 and 50, depending on the performers' vigor—as well as food and alcohol. The men had completed their musical parade and divided the spoils. One young man in his early twenties, Jamma Singh, had received 100 Rs. (about $2 USD), with which he planned to buy more alcohol. His wife, Sonu, disagreed, saying he had drunk enough, encouraging him instead to sit and eat peacefully and spend the cash on something beneficial to the family. An argument ensued. Jamma Singh's older brother, Beniya, who was the head and symbolic father of the extended family (given that the brothers' actual father had passed away), took Sonu's side. Offended, Jamma Singh unexpectedly lunged at his older brother, and Beniya subsequently slapped his younger brother sharply across the face, leading Jamma Singh to go mad, flinging himself to the ground and rolling in the muck, screaming, "I'll go to jail! I'll go to jail!" The entire family struggled to restrain Jamma Singh in a now all-out brawl that seemed to extend five minutes or more. Jamma Singh appeared defeated, but then he suddenly leapt to his feet and escaped, sprinting full tilt on the road heading north out of the village into the jungle, barefoot, sweating, shirt ripped, screaming madly his "I'll go to jail!" mantra. His wife, children, and a stream of village children trailed behind him, but they were unable to match Jamma Singh's pace. Jamma Singh eventually disappeared in the distance, appearing as a small jerky dot. Evening approached and still there was no sign of Jamma Singh. "Maybe he'll end his life by flinging himself in a well?!" Sonu worried out loud, breaking into tears, prompting me and a bevy of relatives to take my jeep north, scanning the darkening woods with the headlights, hoping to spot Jamma Singh somewhere along the forest road, but imagining the worst, like death by exposure or leopard, risks magnified in our minds given Jamma Singh's drunken, desperate state.[8]

I could see how laughter and joyous sociality, which are abundant during Holi, might be good medicine, relieving stress and promoting positive emotions. But why the conflict, which seemed to create rather than relieve stress? And why the insistent theme of sons challenging their fathers, youth their elders, with women, be they demon aunts or human wives, playing key supporting roles? I had never in my years in India seen a son strike a father, which, to my mind, demonstrated the potential enormity of this action in this patriarchal context, given Hindus' normative reverence for parents. How exactly might violence such as that be good medicine?

## FIGHTING AND FORGIVING: EXPLAINING HOLI'S THERAPEUTICS

Holi provides an occasion for festive play. As such, it is the source of laughter and excitement, providing a joyous escape from everyday reality. As an inversion of everyday reality, Holi provides a particularly effective "magic circle" escape, redrawing everyday social rules and reality (Huizinga 1949). On this day, Holi's players have license to invert normal social rules of age, gender, and sexuality: the young threaten the old, women aggressively flirt with men, and men dress, dance, and flirt as if they were women. The drinking, too, magnifies Holi's escape function, with many villagers slipping into alcohol-induced stupors and, in their own words, forgetting about their problems. It is not difficult to understand how such temporary escape provides for a therapeutic mix of positive stimulation alternating with relaxation, lowering levels of stress, anxiety, and depression.

Further, Holi's players express themselves in ways not possible during other times of the year. We might think of Holi as a temporary inversion, where the young, female, and otherwise subordinated challenge their "betters" and thus momentarily erase social hierarchies. The excitement of Holi's newfound freedom was clear, as when village children mischievously attacked the hapless anthropologist with their bags, buckets, and water guns filled with color, channeling the same fervor they used to pummel the "evil" Holika with stones, firecrackers, and insults. Holi's rebellious air was also clear in the manner Prathu chose this festival to publicly challenge his father's authority. Interestingly, Prathu had recently left his father's house for another village quarter, where he had opened a store, selling goods (including alcohol, thus explaining that car trip of his) to a rival and more politically powerful branch of his lineage. It was within this branch that the conflict unfolded in which Jayanth intervened. Prathu thus used this occasion and more generally Holi's license, perhaps largely unconsciously, to upend his father's authority over him and instead position himself in a more advantageous way in relation to these kin. Holi, then, provides the socially subordinate with a powerful form of emotional catharsis, an idea we are continuing to examine further, and we anticipate seeing more positive post-ritual positive "bumps" in subjective well-being among, for example, young women.

Holi also allows participants to "signal" messages about themselves, magnifying this feast's positive health impact.[9] To begin, participants demonstrate their commitment to play and thus also to the group. It is not easy to release oneself from normal reality and leap into Holi's magical world of faux conflict and simulated violence.[10] I learned this in interviews, where I was told, "Holi is scary, there is no telling what will happen on this day." The threat of physical harm is at times real and present, with social others potentially using the occasion to act on a past social grudge or to develop a new one. For this reason, members of my research team, educated-caste Hindus from the neighboring state of Rajasthan and thus outsiders to this community, locked themselves inside the village school, not emerging until evening when the *dhuleti* festivities had ended. It takes a certain degree of trust to engage in Holi's frolicking, given that the license to attack can turn dark, as when one man, in festivities leading up to Holi, had his arm broken, snapped clean at the wrist, by his brother, following a day of drinking, airing of grievances, and eventual actual physical fighting over money and women. By contrast, I was told, those who do leap at the chance to play in this manner reveal something about themselves: their courageous spirit, certainly, but more importantly, the fact that they *trust* those with whom they play. That is, they show that they are insiders to the group, willing to risk bodily integrity at the hands of others. And Holi's actual risk of violence, not to mention the conspicuous consumption and intense emotional involvement, render this ritual play signal "hard to fake" and thus even more deeply revealing of one's character and trust in the group (Irons 2001).

Overall, Holi's participants come to appreciate through their play the fact that they are surrounded by and dependent upon something bigger than themselves, feelings in fact common to many religious rituals (Durkheim 1912; Turner 1982). Through rebellion and self-assertion that wipes away social distinctions, participants come to appreciate that they are surrounded by a community of others who, despite appearances, are not that different from themselves. Rebellion and violence are thus not ends for their own sake. Rather, they serve to temporarily eliminate social niceties and divisions, revealing the base desire and sometimes less than appealing common humanity behind the social facade that unites all Holi's players. Here, conflict seems necessary on this ritual occasion precisely because it leads to disagreements that can then be forgiven and overcome on the day following *dhuleti* (as described above), revealed so that it can be pushed from sight, ultimately promoting rather than compromising social solidarity. Further, the festive community is divinely sanctioned and thus righteous, in the way that Holi's serious play is ultimately an act of worship, a moment in which divinity incarnates on earth in order to defeat evil. And coming to appreciate and trust in such a community, feeling deep togetherness rather than loneliness, gets to the heart of how this rite promotes positive mental and physical well-being. The inculcation of deep faith in others, and ultimately in God him/herself, seeing that one is not alone, makes people feel safe, supported, and protected. And these experiences and feelings provide a powerful psychic balm, as was clear on the day following Holi when anxiety, depression, negative emotions, and stress dropped, calm and peace prevailing over the prior excitement and emotional chaos.

Of course, Holi's airing of grievances and (typically only feigned) conflict can be experienced as stressful by some. I am still exploring how participating in this ritual differentially impacts the young and the old, women and men, and the more or less healthy or highly socially positioned. But we need to temper the idea that stress is necessarily bad. Chronic stress that doesn't subside negatively impacts human mental and physical health (Sapolsky 1998). But stress itself is merely psychological and physiological arousal in response to environmental challenges, which, depending on context, can be experienced as either negative *distress* or as highly stimulating and pleasurable positive stress or *eustress* (Selye 1975; Csikszentmihalyi 2008). Vulnerable persons, especially when they are outside a known social circle that protects them (like members of my research team who hid on this day), can find *dhuleti* play distressful, as can those who are the victim of actual, rather than feigned, violence. But more typically, Holi celebrations lead to stimulating, enjoyable, *safe*, and only temporary challenges of normality rather than total social destruction and incapacitating fear. The "this is play" frame (Bateson 1972) renders *dhuleti's* conflict less distressful, exciting rather than overwhelming, and thus more likely therapeutic than harmful. Surrounded by trusted kin, Mamuli villagers learn, ironically often through simulated battle with others, to affirm and trust in the social and divine support that surrounds them while risks remain invisible throughout the year.

## CONCLUSION: IMPLICATIONS FOR GLOBAL MENTAL HEALTH

Psychiatric scale data suggest that ritual participation in Holi relieves anxiety, depression, and stress, promoting positive over negative emotional experience. In this chapter, I have relied on ethnographic interviews and observations to propose mechanisms for the positive mental health benefits of participating in this rite. Holi is exciting, even liberating, which leads to improved mental state. More subtly, Holi play allows participants to signal group belonging and insiderness, demonstrating to select others that they trust and can be trusted. If played with the proper verve and enthusiasm, Holi theatrically reveals the strength of community, and Sahariyas come to appreciate the depth of their connection to others. They realize that they are supported and not alone, protected by community and by God.

Long after the drama and even conflict fade, such perceptions promote peaceful states of calm relaxation, and thus positive mental well-being.

In India alone, an estimated 60 million people have been displaced since Indian independence in 1947 (Mathur 2011: 1). This includes those displaced from their homes to make way for development projects like dams, mines, or transportation corridors, as well as "conservation refugees" like the Sahariyas, whose homes have been converted to national parks, wildlife reserves, and other protected natural areas. Such policy-generated "disasters" are equivalent to refugee crises involving persons displaced for reasons of war, religious persecution, political trouble, and natural disaster (Cernea and McDowell 2000; Fischer 2008; McFarlane and Norris 2006: 4). Promoters of a top-down global mental health agenda might propose exporting Western therapists and psychiatric medications to displaced persons in disaster-hit areas such as Kuno (Collins et al. 2011; Patel 2012). However, this agenda ignores the fact that local peoples have their own mechanisms for alleviating stress, trauma, and mental disorder, which could serve as alternatives to importing standard Western "manualized" psychiatric approaches (Batniji, Van Ommeren, and Saraceno 2006; Mollica et al. 2004; Panter-Brick and Eggerman 2012; Van Ommeren, Saxena, and Saraceno 2005; Watters 2010; Weine et al. 2002). Examining ritual festivity and religious faith as sources of mental health resiliency, as I have done in this chapter, pushes us to consider cultural processes that instill in individuals and communities the strength to not only resist and recover more quickly from stress and its related negative health outcomes but also reach and maintain more positive states of being (Kirmayer et al. 2009).

To put this another way, I have explored in this chapter how culture might also be the source of how things can go *right* with the mind and body, with cultural practices like Holi leading individuals to cultivate the strength to resist or recover quickly and effectively from stress and trauma (Kirmayer et al. 2009). This analysis is consistent with views that humans are equipped with individual and social mechanisms to experience even traumatic and stressful events in ways that result in social development and growth (Konner 2007; Panter-Brick and Eggerman 2012; Tedeschi et al. 1998). Holi thus resembles the "work of culture" proposed by Obeyesekere (1990) to understand how rituals can ameliorate depression, anxiety, and distress in the context of everyday sociocultural practices. As such, communal events like these deserve more attention as a strategy for improving global mental health, be it in disaster-stricken areas like Kuno or in the context of the daily grinding poverty and hardship faced by billions of people around the world.

Methodologically, this chapter illustrates how psychiatric symptom documentation coupled with ethnography can inform discussions in global mental health and cultural psychiatry about existing social healing mechanisms in crisis contexts demanding humanitarian aid (Summerfield 1999; Tol et al. 2011). In fact, this description of Holi provides an interesting comparison with interpersonal therapy that has been used for psychological treatment in humanitarian settings (Bolton et al. 2003; Verdeli et al. 2003). The practice of Holi itself becomes a pathway for healing and expressing internalized negativity and expressing it to someone in a religious idiom. As in interpersonal therapy, Holi serves the function of reestablishing social relationships by allowing grievances and distress to be expressed to family members and neighbors.

Overall, this research demonstrates how using local rituals as a form of healing can become a fundamental source of promoting mental health among refugees, minimally complementing and enhancing other psychiatric services offered by local and Western healers in similar disaster-stricken areas. The focus of this chapter has been on conservation refugees in one central Indian wildlife sanctuary. However, all societies display some form of religion, possessing beliefs in so-called supernatural agents, forces, and realities, which cannot be directly affirmed by human senses (Spiro 1971). Further, classic anthropological theorizing suggests that ritual performances both promote communal feelings and lessen stress and anxiety across a range of contexts and communities (Durkheim 1912; Evans-Pritchard 1976; Malinowski 1978; Sosis and Handwerker 2011). This implies that people hit by other kinds of disasters, be they hurricanes, earthquakes, or even wars, might also benefit by mobilizing the resilience-promoting capacity of communally based religions, a proposition that as of yet has not been fully considered, much less implemented.

## Notes

[1] This research was funded by the National Science Foundation: SBE Award #1062787, 2011–14, "Environmental Displacement and Human Resilience: New Explanations Using Data from Central India."

[2] Due to legal wrangling in India's courts, the lions have still not arrived.

[3] This is a pseudonym, as are all respondent names used in this chapter.

[4] The World Bank expanded its definition of "displaced peoples" in 2002 to include those experiencing "restriction of access" to park or protected area resources, even when a physical change of place does not occur (Cernea 2006, 2011; Mathur 2011: 8).

[5] I also collected saliva and tracked changes in the stress hormones cortisol and alpha amylase over the same nine-day period, which is the focus of other writing and analysis.

[6] I witnessed the festival twice in Mamuli, first in the spring of 2012 and then in 2013.

[7] On Holika as a vehicle of gendered resistance, see Raheja and Gold 1994.

[8] A contrite Jamma Singh reappeared later that night.

[9] For representative works in the ritual "signaling" literature, see for example: Cronk 2005; Irons 2001; Sosis 2005.

10 Many similar rituals and festivals around the world are at once joyous and also conflictual and violent (Bakhtin 1984). Palmer and Pomianek (2007) argue that rituals in which participants risk harm at the hands of others build trust in a particularly powerful manner.

## References

Almedon, A. M., and Glandon, D. (2007). Resilience is not the absence of PTSD any more than health is the absence of disease. *Journal of Loss and Trauma*, 12 (2): 127–143.

Bakhtin, M. (1984). *Rabelais and His World. 1965*. Trans. Helene Iswolsky. Bloomington: Indiana University Press.

Bateson, G. (1972). A theory of play and fantasy. In *Steps to an Ecology of Mind*, pp. 177–193. New York: Ballantine Books.

Batniji, R., Van Ommeren, M., and Saraceno, B. (2006). Mental and social health in disasters: relating qualitative social science research and the sphere standard. *Social Science and Medicine*, 62 (8): 1853–1864.

Bolton, P., Bass, J., Neugebauer, R., Verdeli, H., Clougherty, K. F., Wickramaratne, P., and Weissman, M. (2003). Group interpersonal psychotherapy for depression in rural Uganda. *JAMA*, 289 (23): 3117–3124.

Cernea, M. M. (2006). Re-examining "displacement": a redefinition of concepts in development and conservation policies. *Social Change*, 36 (1): 8–35.

——. (2011). Broadening the definition of "population displacement": geography and economics in conservation policy. In H. H. Mathur (ed.), *Resettling Displaced People: Policy and Practice in India*, pp. 85–119. London/New Delhi: Routledge.

Cernea, M. M., and C. McDowell (eds.) (2000). *Risks and Reconstruction: Experiences of Resettlers and Refugees*. Washington, DC: The World Bank.

Collins, P. Y., Patel, V., Joestl, S. S., March, D., Insel, T. R., Daar, A. S., and Fairburn, C. (2011). Grand challenges in global mental health. *Nature*, 475 (7354): 27–30.

Cronk, L. (2005). The application of animal signaling theory to human phenomena: some thoughts and clarifications. *Social Science Information*, 44 (4): 603–620.

Csikszentmihalyi, M. (2008) *Flow: The Psychology of Optimal Experience*. New York: Harper and Row.

Derogatis, L. R., Lipman, R. S., Rickels, K., Uhlenhuth, E. H., and Covi, L. (1974). The Hopkins symptom checklist (HSCL): a self-report symptom inventory. *Behavioral Science*, 19 (1): 1–15.

Durkheim, É. (1912). *Les formes élémentaires de la vie religieuse* [The Elementary Forms of Religious Life]. Paris: Alcan.

Evans-Pritchard, E. E. (1976). *Witchcraft, Oracles and Magic among the Azande*. Oxford: Clarendon Press.

Fischer, H. W. III. (2008). *Response to Disaster: Fact versus Fiction and Its Perpetuation*. Lanham, Maryland: University Press of America.

Huizinga, J. (1949). *Homo Ludens: A Study of the Play Element in Culture*, Vol. 3. London: Taylor and Francis.

Incayawar, M., Wintrob, R., Bouchard, L., and Bartocci, G. (2009). *Psychiatrists and Traditional Healers: Unwitting Partners in Global Mental Health*, Vol. 9. New York: John Wiley and Sons.

Irons, W. (2001). Religion as a hard-to-fake sign of commitment. In R. Nesse (ed.), *Evolution and the Capacity for Commitment*, pp. 292–309. New York: Russell Sage Foundation.

Kirmayer, L. J. (2012). Cultural competence and evidence-based practice in mental health: epistemic communities and the politics of pluralism. *Social Science and Medicine*, 75 (2): 249–256.

Kirmayer, L. J., Sehdev, M., Whitley, R., Dandeneau, S. F., and Isaac, C. (2009). Community resilience: models, metaphors and measures. *International Journal of Indigenous Health*, 5 (1): 62–117.

Kleinman, A. (1980). *Patients and Healers in the Context of Culture: An Exploration of the Borderland between Anthropology, Medicine and Psychiatry*, Vol. 3. Berkeley: University of California Press.

——. (1988). *Rethinking Psychiatry: From Cultural Category to Personal Experience*. New York: Free Press.

——. (2009). Global mental health: a failure of humanity. *The Lancet*, 374 (9690): 603–604.

Kohrt, B. A., Jordans, M. J., Tol, W. A., Speckman, R. A., Maharjan, S. M., Worthman, C. M., and Komproe, I. H. (2008). Comparison of mental health between former child soldiers and children never conscripted by armed groups in Nepal. *JAMA*, 300 (6): 691–702.

Konner, M. (2007). Trauma, adaptation and resilience: a cross-cultural and evolutionary perspective. In L. Kirmayer, R. Lemelson, and M. Barad (eds.), *Understanding Trauma: Biological, Psychological and Cultural Perspectives*, pp. 300–338. Cambridge: Cambridge University Press.

Malinowski, B. (1978). *Coral Gardens and Their Magic*. New York: Dover Publications.

Mathur, H. H. (2011). Introduction and overview. In H. H. Mathur (ed.), *Resettling Displaced People: Policy and Practice in India*, pp. 1–21. London/New Delhi: Routledge.

McFarlane, A. C., and Norris, F. H. (2006). Definitions and concepts in disaster research. In F. H. Norris, S. Galea, M. J. Friedman, and P. J. Watson (eds.), *Methods for Disaster Mental Health Research*, pp. 3–19. New York: Guilford Press.

Mollica, R. F., Cardozo, B. L., Osofsky, H. J., Raphael, B., Ager, A., and Salama, P. (2004). Mental health in complex emergencies. *The Lancet*, 364 (9450): 2058–2067.

Ngoma, M. C., Prince, M., and Mann, A. (2003). Common mental disorders among those attending primary health clinics and traditional healers in urban Tanzania. *British Journal of Psychiatry*, 183 (4): 349–355.

Nichter, M. (1981). Idioms of distress: alternatives in the expression of psychosocial distress: a case study from South India. *Culture, Medicine, and Psychiatry*, 5 (4): 379–408.

Obeyesekere, G. (1990). *The Work of Culture: Symbolic Transformation in Psychoanalysis and Anthropology*. Chicago: University of Chicago Press.

Palmer, C. T., and Pomianek, C. N. (2007). Applying signaling theory to traditional cultural rituals. *Human Nature*, 18 (4): 295–312.

Panter-Brick, C., and Eggerman, M. (2012). Understanding culture, resilience, and mental health: the production of hope. In M. Ungar (ed.), *The Social Ecology of Resilience: A Handbook of Theory and Practice*, pp. 369–386. New York: Springer.

Patel, V. (2012). Global mental health: from science to action. *Harvard Review of Psychiatry*, 20 (1): 6–12.

Patel, V., and Kleinman, A. (2003). Poverty and common mental disorders in developing countries. *Bulletin of the World Health Organization*, 81 (8): 609–615.

Raheja, G. G., and Gold, A. G. (1994). *Listen to the Heron's Words: Reimagining Gender and Kinship in North India*. Berkeley: University of California Press.

Robertson, B. A. (2006). Does the evidence support collaboration between psychiatry and traditional healers? Findings from three South African studies. *African Journal of Psychiatry*, 9 (2): 87–90.

Rosen, G. M., Spitzer, R. L., and McHugh, P. R. (2008). Problems with the post-traumatic stress disorder diagnosis and its future in DSM–V. *British Journal of Psychiatry*, 192 (1): 3–4.

Sapolsky, R. M. (1998). *Why Zebras Don't Get Ulcers—A Guide to Stress, Stress-Related Disorders and Coping*. New York: W. H. Freeman Publishers.

Selye, H. (1975). Confusion and controversy in the stress field. *Journal of Human Stress*, 1 (2): 37–44.

Sosis, R. (2005). Does religion promote trust? The role of signaling, reputation, and punishment. *Interdisciplinary Journal of Research on Religion*, 1 (7): 1–30.

Sosis, R., and Handwerker, W. P. (2011). Psalms and coping with uncertainty: religious Israeli women's responses to the 2006 Lebanon war. *American Anthropologist*, 113 (1): 40–55.

Spiro, M. E. (1971). Religion: problems of definition and explanation. In M. Banton (ed.), *Anthropological Approaches to the Study of Religion*, pp. 85–126. London: Tavistock Publications.

Summerfield, D. (1999). A critique of seven assumptions behind psychological trauma programmes in war-affected areas. *Social Science and Medicine*, 48 (10): 1449–1462.

——. (2008). How scientifically valid is the knowledge base of global mental health? *BMJ: British Medical Journal*, 336 (7651): 992.

——. (2012). Afterword: against "global mental health." *Transcultural Psychiatry*, 49 (3): 1–12.

Tedeschi, R. G., Park, C. L., and Calhoun, L. G. (1998). *Posttraumatic Growth: Positive Changes in the Aftermath of Crisis*. Oxford: Psychology Press.

Tol, W. A., Patel, V., Tomlinson, M., Baingana, F., Galappatti, A., Panter-Brick, C., and Van Ommeren, M. (2011). Research priorities for mental health and psychosocial support in humanitarian settings. *PLoS Medicine*, 8 (9): e1001096.

Turner, V. W. (1982). *From Ritual to Theatre: The Human Seriousness of Play*. New York: Performing Arts Journal Publications.

Van Ommeren, M., Saxena, S., and Saraceno, B. (2005). Mental and social health during and after acute emergencies: emerging consensus? *Bulletin of the World Health Organization*, 83 (1): 71–75.

Verdeli, H., Clougherty, K., Bolton, P., Speelman, L., Lincoln, N., Bass, J., and Weissman, M. M. (2003). Adapting group interpersonal psychotherapy for a developing country: experience in rural Uganda. *World Psychiatry*, 2 (2): 114.

Watson, D., Clark, L. A., and Tellegen, A. (1988.) Development and validation of brief measures of positive and negative affect: the PANAS scale. *Journal of Personality and Social Psychology*, 54: 1063–1070.

Watters, E. (2010). *Crazy Like Us: The Globalization of the American Psyche*. New York: Simon and Schuster.

Weine, S., Danieli, Y., Silove, D., Van Ommeren, M., Fairbank, J. A., and Saul, J. (2002). Guidelines for international training in mental health and psychosocial interventions for trauma exposed populations in clinical and community settings. *Psychiatry-New York*, 65 (2): 156–164.

Young, A. (1997). *The Harmony of Illusions: Inventing Post-Traumatic Stress Disorder*. Princeton, New Jersey: Princeton University Press.

Chapter 11

# Who Belongs in a Psychiatric Hospital? Post-Socialist Romania in the Age of Globalizing Psychiatry

Jack R. Friedman

IT WAS A HOT, HUMID SUMMER DAY IN ROMANIA when I met Mona.[1] We sat in the empty cafeteria of the psychiatric hospital to discuss her experiences with mental illness and mental health care. I had spent several weeks at the hospital, so I was familiar with Mona and the hospital. The hospital itself was a collection of large, 19th-century, open-bay asylum structures standing next to more modern buildings erected during the state socialist era (1948–1989). In the shadow of this history, I worked with Mona's psychiatrist to identify people to participate in my research. I had already interviewed several dozen patients, both male and female, suffering from many of the same disorders one would find in the United States, including major depression, generalized anxiety, bipolar disorder, and psychotic disorders. My Romanian psychiatrist colleague suggested that I speak with Mona because she was "different." When I asked what made her different, he suggested that I make my own assessment.

The hospital served a diverse population, including a major city in the north of Romania as well as the surrounding counties that were primarily composed of small, rural, agricultural villages. Mona had come from one of these villages and had been seen off and on for a decade. Her problems were associated with a congenital disorder that left her with cognitive dysfunctions expressed in physical ticks, uncontrollable eye twitches, and an unspecified language disorder that resembled *palilalia* (the repetition of words, phrases, or sentences, without signs of other disorders like echolalia, stuttering, etc.). Mona also had experienced severe and frequent epileptic seizures since childhood.

Despite a relatively large vocabulary and verbose style of speaking, Mona regularly repeated words and referred to the advice that her parents had given her— to "keep smiling" through her hardships. Mona was a thoughtful woman and showed deep religious faith, talking warmly about the local village priest with whom her parents had first consulted when, at the age of ten, Mona had started to

*Global Mental Health: Anthropological Perspectives*, edited by Brandon A. Kohrt and Emily Mendenhall, 191–204. © 2015 Left Coast Press, Inc. All rights reserved.

have headaches, dizzy spells, and her first epileptic seizures. She worried that she was a burden on her family and said that she had increasing difficulty caring for her own daughter since her husband abandoned her several years before. Mona cared deeply for her family and had insight into her neuropsychiatric condition.

When I discussed with Mona the care she received in the hospital, she brightened up and enthusiastically described positive interactions with her psychiatrist. I probed her on how she felt about her treatment. She said that she was getting "pills," and said that they were helping her, although she was unable to detail *how* these pills were helping her. She instead compared her experience to the experience of others in the hospital:

> I saw this other person who was crying all of the time because she wanted to go home and I told her, I said to her and to others: "There is no way for you to go home until the doctor sees you well. You'll see that you will feel better than the way you were when you came to the hospital!" I would be like them, too, except that I had someone to talk to, to have some peace and quiet, to think about other things. . . . I have to keep thinking: "Well, I received treatment with some pills." My treatment has been changed to some other drugs. However, I have [pause] even the doctor, today, told me that I am more "smiling" now. I don't accept [that] there are some people here who are more disturbed [than me].

From the perspective of Mona's psychiatrist, she suffered from a disorder of the brain. Therefore, he wished to chemically "fix" her brain. Mona's psychiatrist treated her with valproic acid (also known as Depakote), which is used to treat bipolar disorder and is an anticonvulsant to prevent epileptic seizures, which was the primary reason Mona received the medication. He also advocated that "resting" in the hospital would help her get away from stress in her life; therefore, he prescribed benzodiazepines—a class of psychiatric medications with sedative and anti-anxiety qualities—to produce a calming effect and a rest away from her life (cf. Friedman 2012).

Throughout my research in Romanian psychiatric institutions between 2005 and 2007, I found many people like Mona who would not be living in a psychiatric hospital if they were receiving care in countries outside of Eastern Europe. The institutionalization of Mona represents a trend in Romanian psychiatry in which people are placed in a hospital setting as opposed to a community-based setting. This contributes to the over-medicalization of mental illness, both through the (mis)use of pharmaceuticals and the pathologizing of social problems.

Romanian psychiatric hospitals have functioned as places where families or the state have dumped people with developmental, intellectual, and cognitive disabilities. Many of these people—suffering from disorders ranging from global developmental delays to Down's syndrome to various other intellectual disabilities—

are relegated to living in remote psychiatric facilities, often out of sight from the general public. These psychiatric hospitals are often poorly equipped to care for these people because they offer very limited social and/or rehabilitative support. Psychosocial rehabilitation services, such as provided by clinical social workers and occupational therapists, are absent from the care of most institutionalized patients. Instead, treatment in these psychiatric institutions is dominated by the use of psychiatric medications.[2]

Based on my interactions with Romanian psychiatrists, these clinicians differentiate among people with developmental, intellectual, and cognitive disabilities, and people who are suffering from the mental illnesses traditionally treated in psychiatric hospitals in other countries (e.g., psychotic disorders, mood disorders, and so on). However, in the context of a country that lacks psychosocial services for the former group, both groups come under the purview of psychiatrists, given that both categories can be framed as brain disorders. In the absence of specialized care for people with developmental or brain-based disorders, the psychiatric hospital becomes the setting of care.[3]

## ROMANIAN PSYCHIATRY: A BRIEF OVERVIEW

My interests in Romanian psychiatry arose a decade after I had started research in the country. The research I did at the beginning of my career was conducted in a declining coal-mining region during a period when mines were being closed and unemployment became a problem, a predicament largely avoided for the first decade after the fall of the Communist Party. It was not until 2000, when I returned from my dissertation fieldwork, that I began to consider that some of what I observed as the psychological consequences of mine closures and other economic problems went beyond everyday anxiety or sadness, and bordered on clinical forms of distress. I returned in 2005 for 14 months of new research examining mental illness in psychiatric and mental health settings in five regions of Romania.

Through this research I sought to understand how people made sense of mental distress and how they accessed care for their psychological problems. I considered several questions: When do people who are facing downward mobility and the collapse of their previously secure lives begin to understand their distress as "mental illness"? How has Romanian mental health care changed throughout the years, from the fall of communism in 1989 through the major market reforms in 1998 and then after the country joined the European Union in 2007? How do psychiatrists apply mental illness categories in a population heavily impacted by downward socioeconomic mobility? How do people with severe and persistent mental illnesses—for instance, people diagnosed with severe forms of schizophrenia—fit within the broader universe of people designated as "mentally ill"? Does severe and persistent mental illness act as a profoundly "other" category, or do all mental illnesses carry similar stigma in Romania?

Romania's mental health system is dramatically different from what I was familiar with in the United States. In Romania, mental health care is almost exclusively provided in large, state-run hospitals.[4] This heavy reliance on institutionalized care in the Romanian system was inherited, with few major changes, from the state socialist era. Compared with the United States, Romania currently has nearly twice as many beds in psychiatric hospitals and over two and a half times as many psychiatric beds in general hospitals (see table below). In Romania, admissions to psychiatric hospitals and admissions to psychiatric beds in general hospitals were both about 1.65 times higher than in the United States. In contrast, the United States has over 4.6 times the available facilities for outpatient care compared with Romania. Tellingly, while outpatient services in the United States outpaced hospital admissions, Romania failed to report the number of persons treated in mental health outpatient facilities (WHO 2011).

The lack of outpatient services in Romania may be a reflection of the role of psychiatrists in mental health care. Though primary care physicians occasionally prescribe antidepressants or benzodiazepines in Romania, inpatient psychiatric hospitals—composed of anywhere from a few hundred to over a thousand beds—provide most of the care for people in emotional crisis or suffering from severe and/or persistent mental illnesses, such as severe depression. Romania offers no specialized training in psychiatric nursing, and there are few social workers working in psychiatric settings. Psychologists play only a minor, supportive role through providing assistance in testing and psychoeducation. Psychiatric hospitals rarely provide any form of psychotherapy or occupational therapy. Instead, with few exceptions, psychiatrists rely almost exclusively on psychopharmaceutical treatment.

Conditions in Romanian psychiatric hospitals vary widely. Due to the often antiquated physical layout of hospitals—many of which date from the late 19th and early 20th centuries—patients rarely have privacy. Patients are routinely re-

Comparison of Mental Health Care System Admissions and Capacities (WHO 2011)

| Per 100,000 Population | Romania | United States |
|---|---|---|
| Psychiatric hospital beds | 38.26 | 19.44 |
| Psychiatric beds in general hospitals | 36.38 | 14.36 |
| Outpatient psychiatric facilities | 0.42 | 1.95 |
| Admissions to psychiatric hospitals | 422.36 | 256.89 |
| Admission to psychiatric beds in general hospitals | 789.03 | 479.78 |

strained physically or through psychiatric medications with sedative properties. In understaffed Romanian psychiatric hospitals, medications are used to control behavior in conditions of excessive crowding. In the best university hospitals in the country, such as the University of Bucharest's Alexandru Obregia Hospital or the University of Iaşi's Socola Hospital, systemic conditions are adequate, with regular meals, heat in the winter, mostly reliable access to medications, and sufficient staffing, thus likely reducing conditions contributing to patient agitation and use of sedating medications. In some of the more remote (often rural) hospitals, conditions can be terrible. For instance, several hospitals identified in an Amnesty International report (2004) on conditions in Romanian psychiatric hospitals revealed over a dozen deaths by exposure to winter cold, regular neglect of patients' biopsychosocial needs, and poor management of violent patients.

Though the Romanian state officially offers universal health care coverage, there are large unmet needs for mental health care, including inconsistent and unreliable access to appropriate medications and laboratory evaluations. The shortage of psychiatrists in Romania further compromises the provision of mental health care. Prompted not only by the low prestige and pay in psychiatry but also by the brain drain of top talent moving out of Romania in pursuit of higher-wage positions in high-income countries,[5] this shortage has led to a situation where many physicians rely on covert payments from patients, and thus the poorest patients, being unable to pay the necessary bribes (*bacşiş*), rarely seek mental health care.

With the exception of a few of the largest, elite university hospitals, few places are able to provide comprehensive outpatient care, and many health care institutions function as dumping grounds to warehouse people who have been socially abandoned (cf. Biehl 2005), or who should be in a different, more appropriate kind of care facility, or who are being "transinstitutionalized"—that is, shuffled between institutions (Mundt et al. 2012). In the United States and many other countries, transinstitutionalization of people with psychiatric disorders has traditionally involved moving people between psychiatric hospitals and prison. In Romania, by contrast, transinstitutionalization encompasses many other institutional settings. For example, Romanian psychiatric hospitals have become the destination for many children who "age out" of state-run orphanages (cf. Stillo 2010). This problem is largely rooted in historical practices of treating medical and social problems in large institutionalized settings throughout socialist Europe. Part of this can be explained by assumptions about economies of scale: institutionalizing more patients or orphans in one place was viewed as efficient. However, since the fall of Communist Party rule, many of the worst state-run orphanages have been closed or improved, and the Romanian state has endeavored to place more children in foster families. While there continue to be significant problems with the treatment of orphans in Romania, the efforts to deinstitutionalize their care differ greatly from the continued reliance on institutionalization for adults receiving mental health care.

Ultimately, the major cause of the extensive institutionalization of people who are sub-threshold for hospitalization is that outpatient social and mental health care services are largely nonexistent in Romania (for more on this topic, see Friedman 2006, 2007, 2009, 2012; Sorel and Prelipceanu 2004). Indeed, most of the people institutionalized whom I met throughout the course of my research would not normally be cared for in a psychiatric hospital, and many of them would never be seen by a psychiatrist at all. Rather, they would be treated by a neurologist, a specialist in developmental or cognitive disabilities, a substance abuse counselor, or a psychologist. The remainder of this chapter addresses the social experiences of these "non-psychiatric" patients in the Romanian psychiatric hospital system, how they understand their own illnesses, and how psychiatrists understand them as "psychiatric cases."

## ILINCA: FROM GRIEF AND SADNESS TO INSTITUTIONALIZED MADNESS

The current problematic situation in Romania represents the intersection of institutionalized rather than community-based care combined with increasing socioeconomic instability in the context of post-socialist economic changes. The economic changes have especially burdened women, such as Ilinca. I met Ilinca, a woman in her mid-thirties, in the psychiatric ward of a mid-sized hospital in a declining, industrial region of Romania. She was haggard, her eyes sunken, dressed in a bed robe and wearing slippers—the standard dress of most people in hospitals in Romania. She was admitted six weeks previously and received a diagnosis of major depression after she complained of headaches, insomnia, and recurring nightmares. Ilinca said her problems had started three months prior when she had a miscarriage and lost twins six and a half months into her pregnancy. Her husband was an unemployed laborer who had been diagnosed with tuberculosis nine years earlier and was being treated in a sanatorium in the mountains. Ilinca also had been diagnosed with tuberculosis and spent time in the same sanatorium. To augment the meager pension and medical disability payments that her husband received— the equivalent of just over $50 per month—Ilinca had worked as a part-time cleaning woman at the local city hall, earning $45 per month. This salary brought their total household income to less than $100 per month for a family of three.

Ilinca told me that prior to her miscarriage, she had had no feelings of clinical depression—she felt "depression" from her economic troubles, but she was not *depressed* in the way she felt after her miscarriage. She explained that she had been active and regularly took walks around town and into the mountains with her mother and daughter to exercise and to enjoy nature. It seemed, though, that the miscarriage, in addition to years of living in economic uncertainty, led Ilinca to be hospitalized.

No, no, [I wasn't clinically depressed prior to the miscarriage] but I had quite a [feeling of] depression because of the woeful state of things, because what could I do tomorrow, where could I go to be able to have something today when I didn't have money or anything, and I thought about this one day after the next. [pause] Because how could I get food for tomorrow and [pause] no, that is the way it is for any woman, for any woman. And, when things stay that way I think "no, how am I going to get by [Romanian: *mă descurc*]" [pause] so I *did* have more depression, I had more, but not like this now. I got by and I got by, I went to my parents, because my mother [pause] my parents told me that when I am without something to come to them and I opened their refrigerator and that was it [pause] I took from their home. It wasn't really that we were dying of hunger—that would be an exaggeration. . . . And, maybe that's the way it was [pause] from one day to the next, a little bit of suffering, constricting, that's what I think and [pause] then I arrived at this state [being hospitalized], and it was [the result of] the stress of decades.

Ilinca's words are not especially surprising, as depression in women, particularly those women who are poor, is common across the globe. Most Romanian psychiatrists reported that the biggest change they observed over the last two decades is the sudden and dramatic increase in adult women—particularly, those 30 to 55 years of age—seeking care for problems related to depression.

Most psychiatrists explained that women composed a relatively small proportion of the mental health burden in the years before 1989, and that the proportion was even fairly small until the late 1990s. Beginning with the post-socialist economic changes throughout the 1990s, though, there has been a steady increase of depressed women. I heard this epidemiological trend repeated in every mental health setting where I conducted research—from large urban hospitals to smaller, remote rural hospitals to psychiatric wards in general hospitals, and even in the few outpatient clinics.

In general, psychiatrists share a common explanation for this trend: the economy. Women, particularly those raising children, have increasingly borne the greatest emotional and financial burden in households following the increasingly difficult economic transformations that occurred in Romania beginning in the late 1990s. These findings resemble those on a global scale, where there is a strong association of depression and poverty in low- and middle-income countries, particularly among women (Lund et al. 2010).

This upswing in women's depression may have resulted from a transforming society in which the blame for economic hardship has shifted from the political to private spheres. Macroeconomic policies following the 1989 Romanian Revolution (see Ibrahim and Galt 2002) that overthrew the Communist Party contributed to real problems of mass unemployment and dramatic downward mobility among the working class. Men previously had relied on employment in state-owned industries, so when those industries were abandoned by the state, unemployment skyrocketed. Women often became the sole source of income in the family, relying on underpaid and highly exploitative work in the service sector or in private manufacturing jobs. Women, however, also continued their roles in the domestic sphere, tending the home and childrearing with shrinking household budgets.

Psychiatrists interpreted the upswing of depressed women as a function of new pressures that women faced in working-class families. However, from the standpoint of Western medical understandings of mental illness, the "depression" that these women suffered likely reflects an "adjustment disorder" (Snyder, Strain, and Wolf 1990). Why does this matter? On the one hand, adjustment disorders are seen as "situational" disorders, wherein the sufferer shows signs of a mood disorder (for instance, depression or anxiety) due to some life stressor such as the break-up of a marriage, a child leaving home, or a financial difficulty caused by the failure of a business, the loss of a job, or a demotion at work. What makes an adjustment disorder different from major depression is that its symptoms are expected to resolve once the stressor goes away. On the other hand, "major depression" is understood to persist even when stressors improve. In most countries, unless a person with a situational depression or adjustment disorder with depressed mood shows signs of being a risk to self (e.g., is suicidal) or others, there is little reason for her or him to be hospitalized. For instance, an American psychiatrist would possibly provide Ilinca an antidepressant as a short-term measure but would also refer her to psychotherapy, grief counseling, and case management to help her address those life stressors seen as the underlying causes of her illness (cf. Schatzberg 1990).

Because Romanian psychiatry has so fully embraced organic explanations of mental illness, Ilinca's psychiatrist believed her symptoms *must* originate from some brain-based disorder. This meant that she should be carefully and liberally medicated to address an assumed, underlying chemical imbalance. In essence, Ilinca's psychiatrist's commitment to organic explanations of mental illness could be interpreted as a rationalization of the only treatments available to him. He had tools to treat a "broken brain" but worked in a system without partnerships and services to address socioeconomic and political economic conditions.

## LUCIAN: ALCOHOLISM AND THE PROBLEM OF DEPENDENCY

At 60 years of age, Lucian had become nostalgic, with much self-conscious reflection, looking back at people and events in his life through poetry. This was surprising to me, because so much of Lucian's life had been so hard for him, so filled with struggles and heartbreak and feelings of loss—lost opportunities, lost relationships, lost time, lost people—that it would seem that reviewing his life would only compound his distress. But, he did not seem overly saddened in his reflections. He told me about his "two wives"—two women with whom he spent much of his life but never married. Both of them had died three years prior, within six months of each other, and at that time Lucian found himself homeless and penniless. It was at that time that Lucian was diagnosed with tuberculosis and became a long-term patient at a TB sanitorium in the far northeast of the country near where I was conducting research. I met him as an inpatient at the psychiatric hospital, not far from the sanitorium where he lived for two years. It was not until almost 45 minutes into our first meeting that he talked about his history of alcoholism.

Lucian's alcohol use began when he was very young, as a result of a detached childhood. He was born into a world undergoing rapid sociopolitical changes following World War II. His birth mother was largely absent from his life, and Lucian was raised by a nurse in a hospital, a woman whom Lucian referred to as one of his "two mothers." He described those early years as a wild child—he was both a "mascot" in the hospital and a terror, stealing food from the canteen, befriending wild dogs that he brought into the hospital, causing all sorts of mischief while still achieving his general education and moving on to higher, technical education. He began drinking alcohol at an early age, and as he entered adulthood, his alcohol consumption caused him to lose jobs as a technician at a furniture factory, a fireman, and a stagehand in a local theater. Lucian's alcoholism resulted in his incarceration in the 1970s and 1980s and to subsequent forced labor on the infamous Danube–Black Sea Canal project—a project that, in the 1950s in Communist Romania, was known for its brutal conditions and workforce of political prisoners, comparable to the Soviet exile of prisoners to Siberia.

It was his alcohol consumption that, after his long-term stay in the tuberculosis sanitorium, brought him to the Secția Dependență—the "Dependency Ward"—of the psychiatric hospital. He had been in the psychiatric hospital for over six months when I met him, and, given his energy and his stories of a playful-if-tragic life, I asked him what plans he had for the future when he left the hospital. His mood changed dramatically:

> Mister Jack, I no longer have any future. But, it's not that I can't achieve things, because I can't say that. Do you understand me? With thought, yes, you can think— I've said that before. You can take back your soul, take it back from the start, like in your youth. . . . [Before my wife died] we had plans because she had hectares of land from her sister. It was strange that, when she died, I wasn't a beneficiary, but

it was her land, and she was the owner. . . . And, so, this left me in pieces. But, when I look at what happened, it mocks me. I can't think of a future because I have no way to express it. Mister Jack, I can't tell you about [the future] because you don't know what will happen today, you don't know about tomorrow. And, if you don't have anything, how will you think about the future from the courtyard of a hospital? How, if I don't have a home, I don't have food, I don't have anything? Do you understand? Here is the problem.

With no imaginable future—his sole source of income was $45 per month from a state disability payment—he said that he could always return to the tuberculosis sanitorium whenever he had to leave the psychiatric hospital.

Alcohol dependence is one of the most common problems attributed to patients in psychiatric settings in Romania. Often, this is a co-occurring disorder alongside some other mental illness. But in Romania, there is also a tradition of viewing alcoholism as a primary mental illness that warrants intensive, long-term psychiatric hospitalization even without a co-occurring mental illness. In an article published in the online edition of the Romanian national newspaper, *Adevărul* (Zgimbau 2010), the staff at the central hospital in Suceava County described the scope of alcoholism in that county: In 2009, they treated 700 people for alcohol-related problems, which costs on average 250 lei ($83) per day. Each person, after being stabilized, was sent to a county psychiatric hospital for a minimum of 10 days. In addition, the head of Suceava's Burdujeni hospital noted: "If, before, the majority of those with these problems were between 30 and 40 years of age, now the dynamic has changed. More of those who abused alcohol are now between 25 and 30" (Zgimbau 2010). The real cost of institutionalizing alcoholism and the social cost of the younger generation's increasing alcoholism present major challenges to society as well as to health care in Romania.

Alcoholism in the West has often been perceived as a problem of dependency, addressed through 12-step programs and other therapies that focus on changing cognition and behavior. Such programs rely more heavily on addressing participants' "willingness" to change behaviors and on their "working the steps" of a 12-step program than it is about addressing organic disorders of the brain. Some 12-step programs advocate abstinence from all substances, which might include psychiatric medications thought to lead to dependency.

In contrast, psychiatrists in Romania typically rely upon the tools at their disposal for treatment: institutionalization and psychopharmaceuticals. This is why it is common to treat those suffering from alcoholism by institutionalizing them in a psychiatric hospital, with the primary mode of treatment being psychopharmaceuticals that address "chemical imbalances" (cf. Moldovan 2013a). For a person like Lucian, then, the psychiatric hospital is used to physically constrain him, with the idea that close monitoring of behavior, movement, and access to alcohol will lead to the "drying out" of an alcoholic in a safe environment in which the symptoms of detoxification—such as delirium tremens (DTs)—can be monitored and treated.[6] Because of the focus on the biology of alcoholism in Romanian psychiatry, Lucian is restricted to a psychiatric hospital, and there is a dearth of social and behavioral treatments to offer him.

## WHAT IS TO BE DONE?

People like Mona, Ilinca, and Lucian suffer from disorders that would, in many regions of the world, be treated without resorting to psychiatric hospitalization. This would include brain-based cognitive disabilities like Mona's that could be treated with rehabilitative therapies, "situational" depression or "adjustment disorders" like Ilinca's that could be treated with psychotherapeutic talk-therapy, or alcoholism like Lucian's, elsewhere treated in 12-step programs and sober-living rehabilitative settings. Instead, in Romania, such people endure months or years in psychiatric hospitals that primarily treat them with psychiatric medications designed for the treatment of more severe mental disorders such as major depressive disorder, bipolar disorder, or schizophrenia.

I must stress that the reliance on biological explanations and psychopharmaceutical treatments for psychiatric disorders in Romania does not explain institutionalization. Actually, the explanation for Romania's heavy reliance on institutionalization is fairly mundane (though not unimportant): the Romanian state simply has not invested in ending the institutionalization that lingers from its socialist past. Institutionalization was inherited in all of the former state socialist countries of Eastern Europe and the former USSR. Those countries in Central Europe that have received more support from Western Europe have made greater strides in shifting to community mental health care. Even in those cases, though, the core of their system still relies on large psychiatric hospitals inherited from the state socialist period. What has lingered in Romanian psychiatry, though, is the complicated marriage of biological understandings of mental illness with an inherited institutional infrastructure, lack of public interest in community mental health care, and a poorly funded mental health and social services system. The synergy of these problems *together* can explain why institutionalization is still the dominant therapeutic option in Romania.

It would, perhaps, be easy to recommend the dismantling of the institutionalized system of care in Romania as a way of addressing the problems. However, to be successful in tackling the issues of poor infrastructure, inappropriate care for certain diagnoses, and the warehousing of people with acute or situational disorders such as alcoholism or depression, a deinstitutionalized mental health care system would have to build (1) a comprehensive and fully staffed network of community mental health clinics to treat people who do not need intensive hospitalization; (2) a network of rehabilitative services for people with developmental, intellectual, and other neurocognitive disabilities; and (3) a network of outpatient substance abuse treatment and rehabilitation services.

Limited efforts to provide these services have been made, but, to date, the scope of these reforms has been concentrated in smaller, boutique facilities often serving a small number of people in the major cities where the best care was already available. These new service providers are held up as "progress," but their impact on the broad failings of Romania's mental health system has been minor. Perhaps most problematic in the reform efforts is the fact that many of these new service providers rely on unstable funding sources—often NGO funding through international grants—without a full commitment from the state. As such, state-run care providers rarely see these new service providers as part of state systems of care, and these new service providers often view their own existence as transitory.

Though deinstitutionalization might be an ambitious, long-term goal, a more realistic, immediate, and sustainable change could come from improved integration of social work into the mental health system. Social work was entirely absent in Romania under late state socialism, and a decade was needed to produce a new generation of social work graduates. Unfortunately, Romanian social work has remained distant from the adult mental health care populations. One reason for this is that there is no career pathway for social workers to enter mental health care. The perception of mental illness as primarily an organic problem—again, a perspective reinforced by the centrality of psychiatrists—has limited the role that can be envisioned for clinical social workers. Yet, the majority of patients facing acute and situational mental and behavioral disorders, like Mona, Ilinca, and Lucian, would benefit from the case management and psychotherapy that clinical social workers could provide.

Finally, there are conceptual changes that would need to be addressed to make these and other structural and professional changes effective. Specifically, there must be an alternative to the overemphasis on biological explanations of mental illness, which reinforces a vicious cycle where the only options for treatment are medication and institutionalization. The central, driving principle that has most influenced Western psychiatry over the last 20 or more years has been the move to link all aspects of mental health care—from diagnosis, to treatment, to research, to the structure of health care systems—to the biological origins of mental illness. This has led to a deemphasis of psychotherapy among most Western psychiatrists, with psychotherapy shifting into the domain of clinical social workers, marriage and family therapists, pastoral counselors, and some psychologists. Psychiatrists have sought to redefine themselves as "scientists of the brain" who help disturbed individuals through a subtle dance of "chemical retuning." The irony of Romanian psychiatry is that it has adopted the biological focus of Western psychiatry more literally than practicitioners have elsewhere. In light of this, Romanian psychiatry might prove to be a cautionary tale for the future of global psychiatry.

## Notes

1 All names have been replaced with pseudonyms.

2 Such treatmeents include liberal use of first-generation antipsychotics (notably, haloperidol); liberal use of benzodiazepines (for both anti-anxiety and soporific indications) with significantly less concern about problems of dependence; and more off-label usage of antipsychotics as a "chemical restraint."

3 For a summary of the ways in which people with intellectual disabilities have been perceived by the Romanian health system, see the Romania Country Report written for the EU's Pomona Project (2002–2004, 2005–2008), which assessed the state of care for people with intellectual disabilities throughout Europe/the European Union.

4 There are no private, inpatient options in Romania, though some psychiatrists have opened private, outpatient practices targeting the wealthiest Romanians.

5 See the WHO's most recent country report in their *Mental Health Atlas* (2011) to get a sense of the scale of these problems.

6 See Moldovan (2013b) for an overview of the services available for treatment of alcoholism in Romania.

## References

Amnesty International (2004). *Romania: Memorandum to the Government Concerning Inpatient Psychiatric Treatment*. AI Index: EUR 39/003/2004. Electronic document, http://www.amnesty.org/en/library/info/EUR39/003/2004/en (accessed August 18, 2009).

Biehl, J. (2005). *Vita: Life in a Zone of Social Abandonment*. Berkeley: University of California Press.

Friedman, J. (2006). The challenges facing mental health reform in Romania. *Eurohealth*, 12 (3): 36–39.

——. (2007). Mapping the terrain of mental illness and psychiatry: anthropological observations on Romania's mental health reforms as it enters the European Union. *Revista romana de psihiatrie* (The Romanian Journal of Psychiatry), series 3, 9 (2–3): 73–77.

——. (2009). The "social case": illness, psychiatry, and deinstitutionalization in post-socialist Romania. *Medical Anthropology Quarterly*, 23 (4): 375–396.

——. (2012). Thoughts on inactivity and an ethnography of "nothing": comparing meanings of "inactivity" in Romanian and American mental health care. *North American Dialogues*, 15 (1): 1–8.

Ibrahim, G., and Galt, V. (2002). Bye-bye central planning, hello market hiccups: institutional transition in Romania. *Cambridge Journal of Economics*, 26: 105–118.

Lund, C., Breen, A., Flisher, A. J., Kakuma, R., Corrigall, J., Joska, J. A., Swartz, L., and Patel, V. (2010). Poverty and common mental disorders in low and middle income countries: a systematic review. *Social Science and Medicine*, 71: 517–528.

Moldovan, S. (2013a). Centrarea pe persoană în programele pentru recuperarea din adicție ale bisericii ortodoxe Române. *Revista română de bioetică*, 11 (1): 65–78.

——. (2013b). An elusive partnership: the Orthodox Church and the substance abuse health care system in Romania. *Social Research Reports*, 23: 39–56.

Mundt, A. P., Frančišković, T., Gurovich, I., Heinz, A., Ignatyev, Y., Ismayilov, F., and Priebe, S. (2012). Changes in the provision of institutionalized mental health care in post-communist countries. *PloS One*, 7 (6): e38490.

Pomona Project. (2006). *Pomona II, Annex VIII, Part 10: Romania Report*. Electronic document: http://www.pomonaproject.org/Annex_VIII10_Romania_Report.pdf (accessed June 9, 2013).

Schatzberg, A. F. (1990). Anxiety and adjustment disorder: a treatment approach. *Journal of Clinical Psychiatry*, 51 (11 Supplement): 20–24.

Snyder, S., Strain, J. J., and Wolf, D. (1990). Differentiating major depression from adjustment disorder with depressed mood in the medical setting. *General Hospital Psychiatry*, 12: 159–165.

Sorel, E., and Prelipceanu, D. (2004). *Images of Psychiatry, Romania: 21st Century Romanian Psychiatry*. Bucharest: Editura Infomedica.

Stillo, J. (2010). The changing role of TB sanatoria: from Sarnac New York to Romania's magic mountains. *East-West Cultural Passage*, 9: 101–114.

World Health Organization (WHO). 2011. *Mental Health Atlas, 2011. Country Profile, Romania.* http://www.who.int/mental_health/evidence/atlas/profiles/rou_mh_profile.pdf (accessed June 9, 2013).

Zgimbau, I. 2010. Alcoolicii au aglomerat secția de psihiatrie. *Adevărul.* March 10, 2010. http://neamt.adevarul.ro/locale/suceava/Alcoolicii_au_aglomerat_Sectia_de_Psihiatrie_0_222578038.html (accessed June 9 2013).

Chapter 12

# The "Cost" of Health Care: Poverty, Depression, and Diabetes among Mexican Immigrants in the United States

Emily Mendenhall

SLOUCHED OVER A MAGAZINE IN THE General Medicine Clinic (GMC) of the largest public hospital in Chicago, Beatriz[1] passed the time waiting to meet with her doctor. She was seeking routine medical care at the GMC for Type 2 diabetes (hereafter, "diabetes"), as were all of the 121 first- and second-generation Mexican immigrant women I interviewed in Chicago for a study of how social and health problems emerge and intersect in everyday life. I approached Beatriz and apologized for interrupting her reading; she smiled and indicated that I should sit down. We chatted about the lengthy time she generally must wait for medical care at the clinic and the frequency with which she attended the clinic for her diabetes care. I was familiar with the GMC because I had spent many hours recruiting patients to participate in studies over a four-year period while I worked at the hospital clinic as a research associate and then as a graduate student conducting my dissertation research. Beatriz recognized me from her previous visits and became curious about my research when I mentioned it was a study of stress and diabetes.

We sat together in a private room adjacent to the GMC, where Beatriz shared her life history with me. I began the interview by asking her, "Can you tell me about your childhood?" In most cases, women responded to this question by launching into evocative tales about their life histories—spanning regions of Mexico, the U.S. border region, and Chicago—and Beatriz was no different. I probed sparingly when my interlocutor went very far off topic, but mostly I listened to women's stories and let them lead our narrative interaction.

Beatriz's narrative reveals the complexities and cyclical nature of conditions in which poverty, stressful experiences, and access to affordable health care can contribute to, exacerbate, and complicate mental and physical health problems. This chapter shows how in fact it was the medical intervention itself that worsened

---

*Global Mental Health: Anthropological Perspectives*, edited by Brandon A. Kohrt and Emily Mendenhall, 205–219. © 2015 Left Coast Press, Inc. All rights reserved.

Beatriz's health. However, structural inequalities—such as a system where the working poor must pay for health care—and social problems, including gun violence, challenged Beatriz's capability to live a healthy life. This chapter, therefore, emphasizes how psychiatric intervention for psychological distress rooted in extreme social suffering can, in some cases, do more harm than good.

## BEATRIZ'S STORY

Beatriz described a bicultural childhood, as she was born in El Paso, Texas, and frequently crossed the border into Cuidad Juarez, where her grandmother lived. Although she maintained a close relationship with her grandmother in Juarez, Beatriz's home life in El Paso was strained after her father abandoned the family. Beatriz's mother became very abusive toward her, and, as Beatriz explained, "every time she had a chance, she'd tell me she hates me—that I have the blood of my father." She explained that her mother's verbal abuse, which was often coupled with physical battering, caused her to leave home to marry at 17 years of age. She soon became a mother and had four children with her first husband, before she left him because of his drinking and related physical abuse. She explained, "I don't know what's wrong with him. One day he pushed me against the wall [with his boot] and my head opened, like, this big." (Beatriz gestured to indicate the gash in her head.) It was at this severe point that Beatriz decided to leave her husband. She married again, for a short period, and had two more children before she left her second husband for similar grievances of physical violence.

In her third marriage, Beatriz found her life partner, with whom she spent more than 28 years and raised two more children (for a total of eight children in their household) in Chicago. Beatriz and her husband were employed in stable jobs in the service industry throughout their adult lives. However, their jobs were not well paid, and therefore they struggled to support their large family financially, living just above the poverty line. Although they often had food on the table, Beatriz and her family had limited disposable income. In addition, because of social factors in and around their neighborhood—drug use, gangs, barriers to finishing school, keeping jobs, and persistent gun violence on the streets of Chicago—Beatriz faced further challenges in supporting her children's futures. Some of these experiences touched her family in ways Beatriz never could have imagined and afflicted deep pain and mental distress. These experiences were central to how she viewed the world and understood her own health and well-being.

Beatriz's son was shot in December, a few years before the interview, during gang-related activity in her neighborhood and was injured so severely that he was expected to die. Beatriz's grief was so intense that she attempted to commit suicide by overdosing on sleeping pills and was admitted to the psychiatric unit of an urban hospital for 32 days. She calls this episode "going blank" and associates her hospitalization with the onset of diabetes. She said, "[it was the] stress that I created with that shooting of my son that got me diabetic."

Beatriz went on to explain, "After I lost the memory, they [in the psychiatric unit] almost kept me sleepy because they didn't want me to go back to that stage [of grief]. So they were feeding me, and I was going to bed, and feeding, and I gained up to 300 pounds. Right now I can say that I am skinny. [Laughter.] And I'm still like, 215, 214 [pounds] I think." Weight gain is not uncommon for people who take antipsychotic medications like the ones Beatriz was most likely receiving during her hospitalization. Beatriz was then diagnosed with diabetes four months later when she returned to the hospital as a result of a work accident. She said, "They asked me how long I was a diabetic [when I was in the hospital] and I say I'm not a diabetic. The doctor said, 'yes you have diabetes.' "

But Beatriz's stress did not end with her son's incident. Beatriz went on to explain, "My baby of the boys, Arturo, he was killed in a crossfire, too." I quietly asked her, "So you've lost two boys?" She continued, "No, the first one—he's alive, but he's in a wheelchair. But Artie . . . was the lucky one. I don't know how to see it. But, my son died, [he did not live] to 15 [years old]. Some guys were shooting and my little boy was cut through the window [sic] by a crazy bullet." Beatriz fell into her hands sobbing. Between cries she communicated, "It's been very hard for me."

Beatriz connected these two incidents not only through the actual physical act of gun violence but also in her own response to it. She went on, "I didn't lose my memory at that time," referring to the period during which she went completely "blank," when her first son was shot and she was committed to a psychiatric ward of a hospital, "but I went crazy because I have a lot of [stress] at the present moment. Because of the other—what happened with my other son." Indeed, Beatriz was also afflicted by the emotional strife that her older, recuperating son felt in the wake of his brother's death. After Beatriz lost this younger son, her elder son, while was still recuperating from his shooting, fell into drinking and other drugs precipitated by the loss of his brother. Since then, Beatriz has been taking 300 mg a day of bupropion (also known as Wellbutrin), a depression medication. Beatriz continued, "I had a lot of counseling and the counseling helps you, but you don't forget the situation, right? You just cope with it, you know. You just learn how to live with it."

Like many women I interviewed, Beatriz linked the stress of her life with her physical and psychological illness and pain. In the years after her son's death, Beatriz developed physical pain that was difficult to overcome through massage, rest, or other treatments. After numerous doctor visits, including a diagnosis of multiple sclerosis (MS),[2] her doctor diagnosed her with fibromyalgia. Fibromyalgia is a biomedical term for widespread musculoskeletal pain, often accompanied by exhaustion, memory loss, and mood swings or alterations, which has no clear cause or origin. Beatriz went on to explain:

> I just know that I was in a lot of pain. And I think they [the doctors] think [my fibromyalgia] was a psychological thing because they blame it on my depression. [Pause] They said that it was a stress, even my doctor said, well, it's what you are going through. . . . [O]ne day I felt even my heart tighten and I went to see the doctor again after two days and she told me that it was my depression, my stress, when I was feeling those pains. And at the same time I was taking Lipitor [a lipid-lowering medication], samples of Lipitor, for my cholesterol.

Despite the personal and health problems in her life, Beatriz described financial insecurity as one of the key stressors, underscoring the strong interconnections between her health and poverty. Beatriz explained, "The worst part happening right now is that I'm trying to get my house [mortgage refinanced] or we're gonna lose it. . . . It's been difficult for us, especially with my medicines. I spend [out of pocket] like $400 with medicines every two months." Because most of the women in my study lived well below the poverty line, I had not anticipated the fact that Beatriz's income status made her ineligible for Medicaid.[3] For example, those who qualify for Medicaid must make less than $22,050 annually for a family of four, and most women in my study made well below $10,000. I asked if she received her medicines through the county hospital system where she had currently come to seek diabetes care. Beatriz explained, "No, I don't [regularly] come here because I have insurance. My husband has insurance at work. In the private [insurance plan], the doctor gave me two [prescriptions for medicines] every month. But if I have to buy it, it was out of my pocket. 'Cause the insurance doesn't pay for it. It costs $250. That's what it cost and they don't cover it."

## THE "COST" OF HEALTH CARE

What is complicated about Beatriz's health conditions is the interwoven web through which the structural, social, psychological, and physical aspects of her life shape her health and play a role in the co-occurring conditions for which she has been diagnosed, including depression, diabetes, fibromyalgia, and high cholesterol. She identifies the stress of her life as a main cause of these conditions, as well as these conditions as causal to more stress leading to social and economic problems. Beatriz also demonstrates how the "cost" of health care has contributed to further social "cost" that compromises her family's security (e.g., losing their home). In this way, Beatriz's story illustrates how the cycle of poverty and stressful experiences can contribute to, exacerbate, and complicate psychiatric and physical health problems.

The interactive relationship of concurrent diabetes and depression has received a great deal of attention in the biomedical literature. Specifically, many researchers have documented and further argued that an epidemiological and biological relationship exists between depression and diabetes, and that this relationship is bidirectional (Golden et al. 2008; Knol et al. 2006; Mezuk et al. 2008). Diabetes is a common health concern for women across socioeconomic groups in the United States, but it disproportionately affects those who are poor (Cowie et al. 2010). In addition, there is a strong association between poverty and mental health globally (Lund et al. 2010), and depression afflicts women more than men, as it is closely linked with women's social roles and economic disadvantage (Kessler and Bromet 2013). Diabetes and depression become *syndemic* with poverty and other social problems as a result of their interaction in socially disadvantaged populations. The *syndemics* construct is built upon the belief that the epidemiology of health conditions is a corollary of social context, and that social conditions contribute significantly to a biosocial negative feedback loop wherein social and economic inequalities are both a cause and consequence of disease interactions and associated morbidities and mortalities (Mendenhall 2012). In my work with Mexican women in Chicago, social and economic inequalities increase the likelihood of developing depression and diabetes and their co-occurrence, a congruence that cultivates further disability, thus compounding socioeconomic inequalities (Mendenhall 2012).

Beatriz's narrative illustrates one of the key pathways through which depression contributes to the onset of diabetes: when the use of psychopharmaceuticals contributes to rapid weight gain (Schwartz et al. 2004) and increases risk for insulin resistance (Golden et al. 2008). The cumulative stresses evidenced in Beatriz's story contributed to extreme psychiatric distress, which fostered her stay in the psychiatric unit of a hospital in Chicago and the administration of antipsychotic medication. Beatriz's weight began to rise after she was treated pharmacologically during her hospitalization. To attend to her ongoing grief and distress, Beatriz continues to take a daily dose of 300 mg of bupropion—a common depression medication. She has received some counseling following the traumatic loss of her son, but psychotherapy was never mentioned as part of her treatment.

Notably, there is a "cost" of medicalizing Beatriz's suffering. Beatriz's story demonstrates how physical health problems can result when pharmacological interventions are prioritized over psychotherapeutic treatment of mental health problems. Without the loss of her son from street-level violence, Beatriz would not have gone "completely blank" and fallen into psychiatric care. It is important to recognize that depression presents differently among Latinos; for example, hearing voices is common among Latino patients outside the context of a psychotic illness. This leads to a common misdiagnosis of depression among Latinos as schizophrenia or depression with psychotic features, resulting in prescription of antipsychotic medications when they are unnecessary (cf. Alcantara, Casement, and Lewis-Fernández 2013). Without psychiatric hospitalization, Beatriz would not have taken pharmaceuticals that contributed to her rapid weight gain. These medications increase the risk for diabetes even in people who are not obese (and maintain lower body mass index), so even if she were able to lose weight later in life, Beatriz's risk for diabetes was raised as a result of the medication (Wu, Gau, and Lai 2014).

Thus, the psychiatric medication used to treat Beatriz increased her risk of developing diabetes. Because most psychiatric medications can worsen diabetes, health care providers wishing to attend to the long-term consequences of living with co-occurring depression and diabetes would do well to recognize how affordable and culturally appropriate psychotherapy can influence mental as well as physical health (Hinton et al. 2011). An example of an alternative psychotherapeutic intervention is behavioral activation, which would not only help ameliorate depression but, through behaviors increasing physical activity, would improve diabetes.

The absence of psychotherapeutic remedies had consequences for Beatriz and her family. Her consequent poor health wreaked havoc on Beatriz's family's financial situation. Although Beatriz was fortunate to be employed for much of her adult life, once she became sick she was unable to work. She depended on her husband's health insurance to treat her myriad health problems. Unfortunately, her health insurance plan did not cover all expenses of her chronic conditions, and she did not qualify for Medicaid, leaving her family to pay for her expensive medication, as opposed to psychotherapy, which could have been covered through the $200–250 she was spending per month on psychiatric medications. Psychotherapy could have also supported behavioral change and increased physical activity, thus also improving her diabetes control. Many high-deductible insurance plans in the United States leave the working poor like Beatriz and her family with medical bills that can become unmanageable, forcing them further into poverty (Sommers and Cunningham 2011). In fact, the burden of high medical costs is a major cause of bankruptcy in the United States (Himmelstein et al. 2009). This is because most underinsured families make too much money to qualify for Medicaid but too little to pay high deductibles for their health insurance plans, leaving them to pay for a large portion of their medical expenses. Thus, Beatriz's story exemplifies how medical conditions can cause further socioeconomic deprivation.[4]

## SPEAKING THROUGH DIABETES

Diabetes is one of the most common diseases treated in the GMC and in many clinical spaces across the United States. The term "diabetes" describes the biological measure of insulin resistance, which is rooted in genetics and unhealthy lifestyles that contribute to obesity, and such a definition is well understood by doctors and their patients in routine medical care (Montoya 2007). As such, clinicians often treat diabetes through recommendations of weight loss via diet and exercise and medicine adherence. In most cases, these clinical recommendations focus on "fixing" elevated glucose levels, underscoring how biomedical treatment views diabetes as a disease of the body—as opposed to one physical manifestation of a stressful life that may interact syndemically with other social and health problems. Such an approach places focus for diabetes treatment exclusively on diet and exercise, therefore overlooking the social, economic, and psychological factors that make up the "black box" of precipitating factors (which also affect one's ability to stick to diabetes management regimens). Therefore, the clinical gaze upon this very common disease overlooks myriad forces that both precipitate its onset and affect one's ability to manage the disease.

In many cases, the prescription for chronic diseases focuses heavily on compliance and "self-care" that places the responsibility of caring for or managing the disease on the patient (Ferzacca 2000). The clinician focuses only on measuring blood pressure, body mass index, glucose, and cholesterol, and adjusting medicines accordingly. For example, a clinician's response to a worsening of diabetes is to advocate dietary changes, increase exercise regimens, and introduce insulin supplementation. However, within this (mis)perception of self-care as the primary means of treating a biomedically framed disease, rarely are the social and emotional worlds of the patients considered, despite the fact that these factors can become a central part of the self-care paradigm (Mendenhall et al. 2014). Sometimes the economic barrier to treatment is considered, especially when it prevents a patient from reaching a medical center for routine care. But the experience of prolonged social suffering or past traumatic events that continue to persist in one's memory are rarely considered to be part of the diagnosis or disease. Instead, the disease is a biomedically defined problem with standard protocols for adjusting biological measures (e.g., insulin resistance). Thus, integrating a biopsychosocial approach to caring for an uncontrolled diabetic is usually excluded as an option, due to time and financial constraints, on the one hand, and the routine of treatment protocols, on the other.

In *Speaking through Diabetes*, my coauthors and I (2010) argued that Mexican immigrants navigating the U.S. medical system use diabetes as an idiom of distress in order to communicate their social and psychological problems. This argument was based on the notion that many women like Beatriz associated social and psychological suffering, from domestic violence to traumatic border crossings and social detachment, with their diabetes. This might be because the diabetes epidemic is becoming a part of the social fabric of Mexican immigrant communities: 15.6% of Mexican-Americans have diabetes (Cowie et al. 2010), and Mexican-Americans have almost a 50% lifetime risk of developing the disorder (the percentage is higher for women) (Narayan et al. 2003). Indeed, it may be that diabetes has become a more acceptable idiom of distress than depression, indicating that women are using diabetes to describe distress not only in the clinical world but also in their social worlds.[5] Moreover, women may be using diabetes strategically to access medical treatment, discovering that using the idiom of diabetes is more effective at promoting an ongoing care relationship with the GMC, as opposed to seeking ongoing depression treatment. In contrast, this finding may be a reflection of the fact that all the individuals in my studies have been previously diagnosed with diabetes and therefore may use diabetes (or their "diagnosis") as an entry point, or even a call for help, when social services and psychological support are limited, and often unbeknownst to them.

This is one of the benefits of conducting interviews in the clinical sphere, where individuals may use certain words and communicate certain messages with specific goals. While the goal may be to receive medical, social, or psychological support, it could be just a matter of being heard. As reported by many anthropologists who work with populations who have suffered from structural and interpersonal violence, some of their interlocutors believe that in-depth narrative interviews could be cathartic.[6] While this is a common trend in medical and psychological anthropology, the location of the interview itself, such as the clinic, may shape the idioms that patients use to communicate their distress. Indeed, women I have interviewed in urban settings in the United States—as well as in urban India and South Africa—link stressful and sometimes traumatic experiences with their diabetes, making evident their firm belief in the interconnections between social worlds and biomedical diseases.[7] Thus, the Mexican immigrant women from my studies may have linked social stress with diabetes in order to find space to discuss their social and psychological suffering. This diagnosis might be, therefore, their entry point into the medical system, thereby being a critical idiom to use in biomedical discourse, in this case, with me, an interviewer associated with the clinic in which they received their care.

The opportunity to strategically navigate the biomedical system, however, is not the privilege of all people with diabetes in the United States. Those who can pay for medical care, and those who qualify for publically funded insurance programs (Medicaid or Medicare), may have an advantage for navigating the biomedical system due to their association with a public program (although, this, too, is not always the case). But there is a significant portion of the U.S. population who, like Beatriz, maintain a liminal space in the system, who, in other words, are the "underinsured" and fall through the cracks, because either (1) they make too much money to qualify for government aid but too little to afford the medical costs of an insurance plan, or (2) they have a privately managed insurance plan with large deductibles and copays that leaves patients and their families to cover the majority of their medical bills. Even more problematic, undocumented immigrants often are left outside of the medical scheme altogether (born in El Paso, this was not part of Beatriz's narrative, although it was for many women in my study). Because the market-driven health care system in the United States distinctly divides people who have health insurance, either through employers or personal plans, and those who do not, there are still many who receive no health care, let alone holistic health care that attends to biopsychosocial dimensions of human suffering.[8]

## ATTENDING TO SOCIAL DETERMINANTS OF DEPRESSION IN DIABETES CARE[9]

Beatriz's story brings forth three critical questions integral to mitigating the effects of syndemics among impoverished populations in the United States. First, what can biomedicine do to address the social causes of multiple, clustered health problems among the poor? Second, for patients who are suffering from multiple interacting diseases, what is the best course of medical treatment? Third, how can biomedicine avoid iatrogenic syndemics (i.e., health problems caused by biomedical treatment regimens)? Below, I address each question in turn within the context of Beatriz's narrative.

The first question points to the inherently social aspect of disease interactions or syndemics, which is self-evident in many women's narratives and must be addressed in medical care and treatment. Like Beatriz, many women in my study expressed that discord in their social lives was intrinsic to their lack of well-being. When Beatriz explained the causes of her mental health problems, as well as her diabetes, she described them in terms of social strife she encountered from childhood, culminating with the loss of her children to gun violence in the streets of Chicago. By bringing these personal and family problems with her into the medical clinic, Beatriz demonstrated that she understood this social discord to be central to her illness experience and therefore situated within the stress–diabetes interface. In this way, Beatriz indicated that her social world could not be dissociated from her diabetes care. This finding suggests that clinicians must address the social and psychological dimensions of their patients' lives in order to understand and effectively communicate with their patients about diabetes management (Loewe and Freeman 2000).

Yet, traditional biomedicine has been slow to acknowledge that social factors play an important role in disease (Farmer et al. 2006; Good 1994; Singer 2009). By conceding that social factors contribute to people's personal beliefs about disease onset and shape how they care for their illnesses, physicians can make a larger, more effective impact in communicating with and caring for patients. For example, through a holistic approach, a physician may decide to treat a patient's comorbid depression not with medications but by enrolling the patient in a social support group; such an approach would provide an emotional outlet for that individual and an opportunity to attend to social problems that may be the root of both emotional distress and barriers to diabetes care. The women in my research repeatedly noted that primary care physicians compartmentalized their social and psychological struggles, either overlooking them completely or referring them to a psychiatrist or social worker to address these "non-medical" problems (Mendenhall 2012). Of course, many doctors may simply believe that structural and social interventions are "not our job" (Farmer et al. 2006). This belief suggests that clinicians are trained to think of their job as entailing the diagnosis and treatment of physical ill-ness (as opposed to solving social problems, which in most cases seem out of reach of the clinical sphere). Alternatively, they may simply be ignoring women's social and psychological needs because the constraints on their time prevent the in-depth dialogue necessary to understand patients' social and emotional problems. Elevat-ing the pay and role of social workers in the biomedical system may rectify this problem, making their work central to improving health outcomes.

The second question brings forth the issue of medical treatment, including the potential effect of treating diabetes and depression simultaneously. Beatriz's narra-tive exemplifies how psychiatric medication in the context of ongoing social and economic problems fails to address the underlying factors contributing to common mental disorders, such as depression, anxiety, and post-traumatic stress disorder (PTSD). Beatriz's family problems were evident in her life story, and increased her risk of depression. Moreover, Beatriz probably has experienced episodic depression and comorbid PTSD, for which she received treatment in the wake of her suicide attempt. However, using medication to address Beatriz's psychological issues did not get to the source of the problem, as she was still extremely distressed with fam-ily issues at the time of the interview. Additionally, it is concerning that despite ev-idence that family discord plays a powerful role in diabetes management among Latinos (Fisher et al. 2000), clinicians rarely attend to family stress in clinical care.

Thus, there is an obvious need for treatments that address the negative feed-back loop among structural and social problems, depression, and diabetes. While this approach may seem outside the purview of clinical medicine, there is prece-dent for such an approach. Perhaps the most famous model of this kind was de-signed by Partners in Health (PIH), an organization co-founded by medical an-thropologists and physicians Paul Farmer and Jim Yong Kim, and others (Farmer et al. 2006). This model recognizes that addressing structural and social problems is central to mitigating the effects of structural violence and improving community and individual health. For example, they argue that instead of focusing on behav-ioral or lifestyle factors for HIV prevention (the standard in clinical treatment in the United States), attention should be given to the aspects that make HIV a "so-cial" disease, such as poverty, gender inequality, and racism (Farmer et al. 2001).

Their projects in Boston, as well as in Peru, Rwanda, Russia, and Haiti, have proven to improve health among some of the poorest communities, with a particular focus on the interactions of HIV and tuberculosis. Atul Gawande described in a *New Yorker* article entitled "The Hot Spotters" how such a community-focused program that attends to ameliorating the social contributors to disease can be more cost-effective in the long run (Gawande 2011), setting precedent for the concurrent treatments of social, mental, and physical health problems. Such an integrative approach is essential for patients whose needs extend beyond the physical domain.

The final question concerns the problem of biomedicine actually worsening disease interaction(s). I have argued that focus on the physical aspects of disease, as opposed to a multidimensional framework of disease and suffering, can actually contribute to poorer health. This problem has escalated within the current U.S. political context, as Congress continues to dismantle the social safety net and to drastically reduce critical mental health and social services. For example, when I worked at a large public hospital as a research associate (2006–2007), hundreds of health-related jobs were lost because of the financial downturn, and at one point almost half of the outlying county clinics were closed. During this time, I attended a speech by the interim director of the hospital, who stated that hiring an additional cardiologist and gynecological oncologist should enable them to meet the needs of the community in lieu of shutting down these established clinics nestled in the center of needy communities. At the same time, there was discussion of shutting down prevention programs that focused on screening for breast and cervical cancers, to save money. There was no mention at all of psychotherapy or task-sharing mental health support to nonspecialists as an approach to save costs, despite their proven health benefits and low cost. These actions are self-evident of the fact that safety-net systems in the United States struggle to find adequate financing and, as a result, may focus on curative services as opposed to preventive ones, despite well-established research that such an approach is not a solution for chronic disease. Unfortunately, many of these financial decisions are made from the view through biomedical goggles, as opposed to a public health lens that might consider meeting the critical health needs of the poor. When this is the case, the traditional biomedical approach is even more compromised by reductions of critical services that provide opportunities to address the social and psychological factors interacting syndemically with diabetes among the poor.

## A CALL TO ACTION

Clinicians cannot address this issue without the proper support and resources. To improve the care of diabetes and the lives of low-income patients, we need to make mental health care integral to diabetes care (Prince et al. 2007). Direct one-on-one counseling must be more available and affordable for people who have experienced severe trauma, extreme poverty, and diabetes complications. Moreover, group psychotherapy interventions hold promise for select populations even in extremely low-resource settings with high burdens of both political violence and poverty (Bolton et al. 2003, 2007). Gender-specific support groups must become routine for diabetes care and should be available for all patients, especially for those with poor and/or worsening diabetes control. Clerks, nursing staff, and physicians should all be required to inform high-risk patients of the services available and to encourage their attendance.

In addition, language barriers must be addressed for the large majority of Spanish-only speakers seeking health care in the United States (as well as for many other-language-only speakers). More effort needs to be made to match Spanish-language patients with Spanish-speaking physicians. Although in some cases there are insufficient numbers of Spanish-speaking physicians, logistical barriers to matching Spanish-speaking physicians and patients must be overcome to ensure a higher quality of care. This is particularly important due to the high rates of depression-related disability and poor diabetes management among Mexican-Americans (deGroot et al. 2006; Fisher et al. 2000). With the great need of Spanish-speaking patients within safety-net clinics in the United States, it is a serious disservice to overlook matching Spanish-only speaking patients with available Spanish-speaking physicians.

Biopsychosocial models of care are cost-effective. After years of budget cuts, political power in the United States is building for increasing primary care for low-income populations. More recently, there has been an effort to remediate these cuts by reorienting the remaining community clinics to focus solely on primary care, which may have a positive impact on long-term health as well as repercussions for county hospitals which must absorb more of the serious health concerns that were once triaged at outlying clinics (Lydersen 2010). Within a context of severe budget cuts, it is difficult to convince policy makers to incorporate more clinical psychologists and social workers into these primary care centers. However, the Affordable Care Act has transformed health care access in Illinois, expanding access to health insurance for the working poor whose income is under $45,000 (previously $30,000) for a family of four. Yet, undocumented immigrants remain uncovered. With budget concerns at the center of many medical decisions within the United States, it is clear that a more rigorous biopsychosocial model is pertinent and would be beneficial in addressing the increasing burden of diabetes, depression, and their overlap among low-income groups.

In conclusion, there is an urgent need to implement approaches such as those of Partners in Health in Boston, Massachusetts (Farmer et al. 2006), and Jeffrey

Brenner in Camden, New Jersey (Gawande 2011), into primary care protocols for diabetes care in the United States. Not only are these proven to be effective approaches to addressing the multidimensional aspects of poor health among the poor in the United States, but they are also cost-effective in the long term. By acknowledging the social and psychological aspects of people's diabetes, integrated primary care can help to mitigate the upward trends of diabetes onset and depression-related morbidity and mortality among socially disadvantaged people in this country.

## Notes

[1] All names have been replaced with pseudonyms.

[2] Multiple sclerosis is an intense, chronic, and disabling disease that attacks the central nervous system.

[3] Beatriz's income level would make her eligible for Medicaid under the Affordable Care Act, although she was not eligible for Medicaid in 2010 when the study was conducted.

[4] Under the Affordable Care Act, which became effective in 2014, documented working poor women ineligible for Medicaid in 2010 would now have access to health care.

[5] For a more extensive discussion about how women may narratively make sense of suffering through their chronic illness, see Mendenhall 2012: chap. 2.

[6] See "Synthesizing the Syndemic" (Mendenhall 2012: chap. 1) for a more extensive discussion.

[7] Also see Mendenhall et al. 2012; and Mendenhall and Norris in press.

[8] The Affordable Care Act increases health insurance access to the working poor; however, the undocumented remain outside of this framework.

[9] This section is adapted from the conclusion of "Syndemic Suffering: Social Distress, Depression, and Diabetes among Mexican Immigrant Women in Chicago" (Mendenhall 2012).

## References

Alcantara, C., Casement, M. D., and Lewis-Fernández, R. (2013). Conditional risk for PTSD among Latinos: a systematic review of racial/ethnic differences and socio - cultural explanations. *Clinical Psychology Review*, 33 (1): 107–119.

Bolton, P., Bass, J., Betancourt, T., Speelman, L., Onyango, G., Clougherty, K. F., Neugebauer, R., Murray, L., and Verdeli, H. (2007). Interventions for depression symptoms among adolescent survivors of war and displacement in northern Uganda: a randomized controlled trial. *JAMA*, 298 (5): 519–527.

Bolton, P., Bass, J., Neugebauer, R., Verdeli, H., Clougherty, K. F., Wickramaratne, P., Speelman, L., Ndogoni, L., and Weissman, M. (2003). Group interpersonal psycho - therapy for depression in rural Uganda: a randomized controlled trial. *JAMA*, 289 (23): 3117–3124.

Cowie, C. C., Rust, K., Byrd-Holt, D. D., Gregg, E. W., Ford, E. S., Geiss, L., Bainbridge, K. E., and Fradkin, J. E. (2010). Prevalence of diabetes and high risk for diabetes using A1C criteria in the U.S. population in 1988–2006. *Diabetes Care*, 33 (3): 562–568.

deGroot, M., Pinkerman, B., Wagner, J., and Hockman, E. (2006). Depression treatment and satisfaction in a multicultural sample of Type 1 and Type 2 diabetic patients. *Diabetes Care*, 29: 549–553.

Farmer, P., Léandre, F., Mukherjee, J. S., Claude, M., Nevil, P., Smith-Fawzi, M. C., and Kim, J. Y. (2001). Community-based approaches to HIV treatment in resource-poor settings. *The Lancet*, 358: 404–409.

Farmer, P., Nizeye, B., Stulac, S., and Keshavjee, S. (2006). Structural violence and clinical medicine. *PLoS Medicine*, 3 (10): e449.

Ferzacca, S. (2000). "Actually, I don't feel that bad": managing diabetes and the clinical encounter. *Medical Anthropology Quarterly*, 14 (1): 28–50.

Fisher, L., Chesla, C. A., Skaff, M. M., Gilliss, C., Mullan, J. T., Bartz, R. J., and Lutz, C. P. (2000). The family and disease management in Hispanic and European-American patients with Type 2 diabetes. *Diabetes Care*, 23 (3): 267–272.

Gawande, A. (2011). The hot spotters: can we lower medical costs by giving the neediest patients better care? *The New Yorker*, January 24.

Golden, S. H., Lazo, M., Carnethon, M., Bertoni, A. G., Schreiner, P. J., Roux, A. V., and Lyketsos, C. (2008). Examining a bidirectional association between depressive symptoms and diabetes. *Journal of the American Medical Association*, 299 (23): 2751–2759.

Good, B. (1994). *Medicine, Rationality, and Experience: An Anthropological Perspective.* Cambridge: Cambridge University Press.

Himmelstein, D., Thorne, D., Warren, E., and Woolhandler, S. (2009). Medical bankruptcy in the United States, 2007: results of a national study. *The American Journal of Medicine*, 122 (8): 741–746.

Hinton, D. E., Hofmann, S. G., Rivera, E., Otto, M. W., and Pollack, M. H. (2011). Culturally adapted CBT (CA-CBT) for Latino women with treatment-resistant PTSD: a pilot study comparing CA-CBT to applied muscle relaxation. *Behavioral Research and Therapy*, 49 (4): 275–280.

Kessler, R. C., and Bromet, E. J. (2013). The epidemiology of depression across cultures. *Annual Review of Public Health*, 34: 119–138.

Knol, M. J., Twisk, J. W., Beekman, A. T., Heine, R. J., Snoek, F. J., and Pouwer, F. (2006). Depression as a risk factor for the onset of Type 2 diabetes mellitus. A meta-analysis. *Diabetologia*, 49 (5): 837–845.

Loewe, R., and Freeman, J. (2000). Interpreting diabetes mellitus: differences between patient and provider models of disease and their implications for clinical practice. *Culture, Medicine, and Psychiatry*, 24 (4): 379–401.

Lund, C., Breen, A., Flisher, A. J., Kakuma, R., Corrigall, J., Joska, J. A., Swartz, L., and Patel, V. (2010). Poverty and common mental disorders in low and middle income countries: a systematic review. *Social Science and Medicine*, 71: 517–528.

Lydersen, K. L. (2010). Staff worry about shifts in county health system. *The New York Times*, December 11.

Mendenhall, E. (2012). *Syndemic Suffering: Social Distress, Depression, and Diabetes among Mexican Immigrant Women.* Walnut Creek, CA: Left Coast Press, Inc.

Mendenhall, E., and Norris, S. (in press). HIV is ordinary, diabetes new: remaking suffering in a South African township. *Global Public Health*.

Mendenhall, M., Seligman, R., Fernandez, A., and Jacobs, E. (2010). Speaking through diabetes: rethinking the significance of lay discourses on diabetes. *Medical Anthropology Quarterly*, 24 (2): 220–239.

Mendenhall, E., Shivashankar, R., Tandon, N., Ali, M. K., Venkat Narayan, K. M., and Prabhakaran, D. (2012). Stress and diabetes in socioeconomic context: a qualitative study of urban Indians. *Social Science and Medicine* 75: 2522–2529.

Mezuk, B., Eaton, W. W., Albrecht, S., and Golden, S. H. (2008). Depression and Type 2 diabetes over the lifespan: a meta-analysis. *Diabetes Care*, 31 (12): 2383–2390.

Montoya, M. J. (2007). Bioethnic conscription: genes, race, and Mexicana/o ethnicity in diabetes research. *Cultural Anthropology*, 22 (1): 94–128.

Narayan, K. M. Venkat, Boyle, J. P., Thompson, T. J., Sorenson, S. W., and Williamson, D. F. (2003). Lifetime risk for diabetes mellitus in the United States. *Journal of the American Medical Association*, 290 (14): 1884–1890.

Prince, M., Patel, V., Saxena, S., Maj, M., Maselko, J., Phillips, M. R, and Rahman, A. (2007). No health without mental health. *The Lancet*, 370 (9590): 859–877.

Schwartz, T. L., Nihalani, N., Jindal, S., Virk, S., and Jones, N. (2004). Psychiatric medication–induced obesity: a review. *Obesity Reviews*, 5 (2): 115–121.

Singer, M. (2009). *Introduction to Syndemics: A Systems Approach to Public and Community Health.* San Francisco: Jossey-Bass.

Sommers, A., and Cunningham, P. J. (2011). Medical bill problems steady for U.S. families, 2007–2010. *Track Reporting*, 28: 1–5.

Wu, C.-S., Gau, S. S.-F., and Lai, M.-S. (2014). Long-term antidepressant use and the risk of Type 2 diabetes mellitus: a population-based, nested case-control study in Taiwan. *Journal of Clinical Psychiatry*, 75 (1): 31–38.

## Chapter 13
# The Few, the Proud: Women Combat Veterans and Post-Traumatic Stress Disorder in the United States

Erin P. Finley

LAURA ESPOSITO[1] JOINED THE U.S. ARMY shortly after September 11, 2001, and for her it was the culmination of a long-held dream. At 29, she was older than most new recruits, with a well-established career. She had always wanted to join the military but held off because her mother thought the military was for people "who had nothing else to fall back on." When the terror attacks of 9/11 occurred, she had been working with veterans through a local service organization for more than a decade, and suddenly her mother's objections were no longer compelling. She signed up for the Army Reserves, and two months after completing basic training, she deployed to Kuwait.

This was 2003, at the time of the initial U.S. invasion of Iraq, and little of the vast military infrastructure that would soon spread across the region was yet in place. Laura was assigned to a transportation unit that was primarily male, with very few women, and found it "kind of hard to get along." There were no cots to sleep on and no showers or latrines, so the unit slept on the ground, built their own showers, and burned their own waste. When the unit's vehicles arrived, they found they had been stripped of all the spare parts that other units needed. "It's all about surviving; even within the unit, people were taking things from each other's vehicles because you have to have everything when you go out on missions."

Once the first missions began coming in, Laura volunteered for everything, "even though I was terrified of what was out there. I was like, I'm going, I'm going, cuz it was like a sense of freedom for me." Laura drove a heavy equipment transport System (HET) designed to transport tanks and weighing somewhere in the range of 40,000 pounds, an almost unimaginable behemoth to navigate through the sands of the Persian Gulf, with tires that alone weighed upward of 500 pounds each. After four months of moving military equipment around Kuwait, their unit was sent into Iraq. They were assigned to Taji, an old Iraqi military facility that had

*Global Mental Health: Anthropological Perspectives*, edited by Brandon A. Kohrt and Emily Mendenhall, 221–238. © 2015 Left Coast Press, Inc. All rights reserved.

been blown to pieces but retained its airfield, making it valuable as a staging point for Apache helicopters and other flight operations. The barracks had been inhabited by Iraqi soldiers and were decorated with graffiti of American buildings with Iraqi planes flying into them and pictures of the American flag upside down. Relations with the Iraqi support personnel allowed on base were strained, and there were multiple instances in which Iraqis were intercepted bringing weapons or explosives onto the base, none of which left members of Laura's unit feeling safe in their beds. Meanwhile, weather conditions went from intense heat to extreme cold, which Laura coped with by continuing to volunteer for every mission she could.

One of these missions, a 30-vehicle convoy to a camp in northern Iraq, ended up stretching from days into weeks. The camp was taking regular fire and, after several military police were killed, the situation became so tenuous that the convoy wasn't allowed to leave. When the convoy finally departed, it was hit by an ambush, rescued by other convoys in the region, and then one of the vehicles ran over an improvised explosive device (IED) on the way home. Laura says of the experience, "None of us were killed, so we were all very fortunate."

But she goes on to say, "I was in hell. I would tell my mom every time I talked to her that I was in hell." As time went on, she witnessed more and more Iraqi casualties, and wondered at her own reaction. "I had some people on my unit that cried and I felt like maybe I was sick because I didn't. 'Why are you crying because they got killed? It was either them or us.' That's what I'd say—I felt like I was numb after a while."

Then her unit returned stateside, and she was, she says now, "an emotional wreck when I got home—I could not get back into things." As a reservist, she was released from active duty and returned to her pre-war life and her old job. "Then I was expected just to live a normal life. . . . It was hard." She missed the camaraderie and closeness her unit had shared while deployed. "The president of the organization is a—he was in the Air Force—so he pulled me into his office and he talked to me and I cried, and he told me, 'I think you're going to have to get some help.' "

On his advice, she went to the local Vet Center, one of the Veteran Administration's network of community-based clinics intended to provide mental health care for combat veterans. She received a diagnosis of post-traumatic stress disorder (PTSD) related to her combat experiences, which came as no surprise, given what she had heard from other veterans about PTSD. But she did not feel as though the Vet Center staff were prepared to deal with veterans of her generation, so newly back from war. Even the language of their standard clinical questions seemed aimed at Vietnam veterans. She felt uncomfortable and quickly stopped going.

She tried taking a civilian job working on base, thinking she would be more comfortable being around soldiers, but that wasn't enough, and she ultimately requested to go back on active orders. "I belong in uniform. That's where I feel good." Some months later, she received a call from the main VA hospital and agreed to see one of the psychologists there for a few months, but when the pace of her work picked up, she left treatment again.

Another year passed. She became pregnant and, lacking health insurance, spent the first few months receiving care in a local clinic for low-income mothers, not aware that the VA could provide her with prenatal care. At the next visit with her VA provider, she learned that the VA would pay for her care at the local military outpatient care facility, which, she said, was "awesome." After her son was born, she found herself a single mother living back at home with her mother and disabled older brother. When the VA called again more recently to follow up, Laura told the social worker that she was having trouble with anger. She says she gets too angry about things like political debates over immigration and food stamps, and sometimes finds herself overwhelmed by her 16-month-old son. "I yell at him and I have to step back and I'm like, 'what are you doing?!'" She ended up joining a group class in anger management and feels now that she is learning how to manage her anger more effectively. She also leans heavily on her Catholic faith, attending church at least weekly and relying on prayer to see her through. "I'm glad I have my faith, because I don't know what I'd do if I didn't."

Both her spirituality and her involvement in behavioral health care have played an important role in her help-seeking decisions. When she was initially put on a medication that left her feeling emotionally numb, she asked herself, "Do I want to be like this?" and ultimately stopped the medication and increased her time at church. "I always knew—let go and let God, that's my antidepressant. He helps a lot." Even so, she has continued to struggle with anger and says, "I hate that it gets really bad with my family. The people that you love the most—the people that were there for you the whole time, and I turn around and I'm like a monster with them."

She sees this as an important reason to attend the PTSD psychoeducation classes offered by the VA, which she continues to find helpful. "It's weird—there's a lot of stuff that I'm going through that I don't realize—because a lot of stuff that I feel and think I don't associate with the fact that I was over there. Then when [her provider] paints the picture, it's like, oh wow."

She believes now that PTSD is "something that can be overcome if you apply yourself to it. It's an emotional, I think, disorder. And it can affect you and your lifestyle immensely if you don't try and resolve it in some way." She points to the example of a Vietnam veteran who is in her group at the VA, and says, "I don't want to be here 30 years from now still fighting this."

## WOMEN IN THE MILITARY

Laura is one of some 180,000 American women who have deployed to the wars in Iraq (Operation Iraqi Freedom [OIF] and Operation New Dawn [OND]) and Afghanistan (Operation Enduring Freedom [OEF]) since 2001 (Street, Vogt, and Dutra 2009). We first met in 2007, when I was conducting an ethnographic study of PTSD among OEF/OIF veterans in south Texas, research that had grown out of my prior work with former combatants in Northern Ireland and East African refugees living in the Atlanta area. Laura was one of the first female OEF/OIF veterans I met, but there have been many more in the intervening years. For the first time in history, women make up approximately 14% of the U.S. Armed Forces, and, while forbidden until recently to serve in what were formally defined as "combat roles," have served on the ground and under fire in every sense, including as combat medics, pilots, transport personnel like Laura, military police, and intelligence officers (Street, Vogt, and Dutra 2009). Moreover, the conflicts in Iraq and Afghanistan have had no clear front lines and thus few relatively "safe" areas (Hoge, Clark, and Castro 2007; Street, Vogt, and Dutra 2009). With women's growing presence have come rapid shifts within the military, with forward operating bases in Iraq and Afghanistan now offering women's health care and separate barracks for female service members—even establishing living quarters for married couples deployed simultaneously (Myers 2009). What many have seen as the last frontier for female service members, the formal restriction against women serving in combat roles (such as infantry), was lifted in early 2013 and is expected to open up some 200,000 new positions for women in the military (Peralta 2013).

Although women have served in every U.S. conflict since the Revolutionary War (Street, Vogt, and Dutra 2009), no other era has seen women serving in uniform in a combat zone in such numbers, raising myriad questions about the physical and mental health consequences of such service, and about women's experiences of combat PTSD, in particular. An official diagnosis of PTSD is predicated on an individual having experienced at least one event in which he or she is exposed to a serious threat of harm to self or others, having symptoms of intrusive thoughts or dreams, avoids reminders of the trauma(s), re-experiencing feelings or thoughts associated with the event(s), and having an exaggerated startle response, an inability to sleep or concentrate, or difficulty in controlling one's anger lasting for longer than 30 days afterward (APA 2000, 2013; Keane, Marshall, and Taft 2006). Although combat PTSD has been the focus of intense research and clinical attention for decades, the relative infrequency of combat-deployed women has meant that this attention has focused almost exclusively on men, as have the services that have evolved to provide post-combat care. The new ubiquity of women in combat, and the understanding that these women are likely to have post-combat needs of their own, was greeted in the early 2000s with recognition that critical information on women's unique risks and needs was lacking, as was a comprehensive network of services.

The research and clinical understanding that have emerged over the past decade, therefore, have been deeply informed by the experiences of women like Laura. Although the questions are still emerging far faster than the answers, there is an unprecedented new understanding of what these years of conflict have meant for female American service members.

## STRESSORS ACROSS THE DEPLOYMENT CYCLE

To begin to consider what has been learned, it is helpful to think in terms of what is called the *deployment cycle*, or the *emotional cycle* that service members and their families pass through over the course of the period leading up to a long-term assignment away from home (pre-deployment), through the actual leave-taking (deployment), sustainment (establishing new routines and new sources of support), preparing for the return home (redeployment), and post-deployment (Pincus et al.

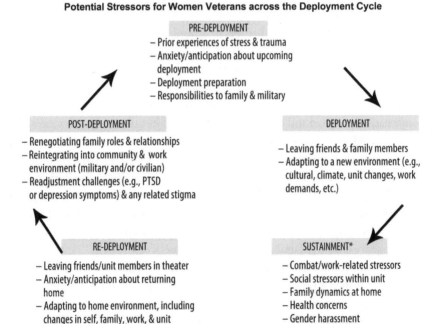

**Potential Stressors for Women Veterans across the Deployment Cycle**

**PRE-DEPLOYMENT**
- Prior experiences of stress & trauma
- Anxiety/anticipation about upcoming deployment
- Deployment preparation
- Responsibilities to family & military

**POST-DEPLOYMENT**
- Renegotiating family roles & relationships
- Reintegrating into community & work environment (military and/or civilian)
- Readjustment challenges (e.g., PTSD or depression symptoms) & any related stigma

**DEPLOYMENT**
- Leaving friends & family members
- Adapting to a new environment (e.g., cultural, climate, unit changes, work demands, etc.)

**RE-DEPLOYMENT**
- Leaving friends/unit members in theater
- Anxiety/anticipation about returning home
- Adapting to home environment, including changes in self, family, work, & unit

**SUSTAINMENT\***
- Combat/work-related stressors
- Social stressors within unit
- Family dynamics at home
- Health concerns
- Gender harassment
- Military sexual trauma

\* Most of the potential stressors attributed to the sustainment phase (e.g., military sexual trauma) may also occur at other stages of the deployment cycle, although women veterans may be particularly vulnerable during this period.

2004). Each of these stages is associated with its own emotions and challenges (Faber et al. 2008).

Laura's story illustrates a number of stressors that occur across the deployment cycle, all of which have relevance for understanding PTSD among this new generation of female warriors. The most obvious of these is combat itself, conflict-related violence that is inexorably a part of war. Like Laura, who witnessed the killing and wounding of Iraqis, lived on bases that were continually mortared, narrowly missed her vehicle being blown apart by an IED, and was caught in an ambush on the return from northern Iraq, 73.4% of women in one recent study of OEF/OIF veterans reported combat experiences during their deployments, as did 81.7% of men (King et al. 2013). More than 150 female service members were killed in Iraq or Afghanistan between 2001 and 2013, and another 965 were wounded in action (U.S. Department of Defense 2009). As Laura's story reveals, such violence also occurs in settings that may seem unfamiliar and hostile, heightening the sense of perceived threat.

Whereas women's risk for combat exposure in recent years has nearly equaled men's, women have proven to be at much greater risk than men for sexual assault, both prior to their time in the military (as children or as young adults) (Carter-Visscher et al. 2010; Koola et al. 2013) and during military service (Kimerling et al. 2010). Military sexual trauma, which includes sexual assault as well as threatening sexual harassment, has been found to occur among 15% to 42% of female service members, compared with 0.7% to 12.5% of men (Katz et al. 2012; Kimerling et al. 2010; Suris et al. 2013). Survivors of sexual assault, one of the most intimate and proximal of traumas, are at elevated risk of going on to develop PTSD (Keane et al. 2006), and as the negative effects of trauma are often cumulative (Keane et al. 2006), the combination of sexual and combat traumas may place affected female veterans at particular risk. Moreover, the emerging research literature on military sexual trauma seems to suggest that it is associated with higher rates of PTSD than either civilian sexual assault (Suris et al. 2007; Yaeger et al. 2006) or even "high" levels of combat exposure (Kang et al. 2005). Those who experience military sexual trauma and go on to develop PTSD are also more likely to experience depression or anxiety and to cope with symptoms using unhealthy behaviors such as disordered eating, substance misuse, or excessive exercise (Maguen et al. 2012; Mattocks et al. 2012).

A number of explanations have been proposed to explain why military sexual trauma can have such a powerful impact, all of which point to the importance of context in shaping experiences of trauma. Service members who experience military sexual trauma may feel trapped in a military or deployed environment, with little possibility for escape or avoiding the perpetrator(s) (Street et al. 2011). They may feel betrayed by leadership or peers who have violated the close bonds forged among those who serve together; Laura, for instance, said the unit members she served with in Iraq became "family" (Street et al. 2011). And those who dare to report sexual trauma during deployment have too often been silenced, ignored, or penalized by military leadership (Street et al. 2011). The social structures and cultural ethos of the military environment may itself put female service members at increased risk for sexual harassment and assault, given that these "sexual stressors" have been found to occur more commonly in settings that are male-dominated and characterized by large power differentials (Ilies et al. 2003; Lafontaine and Tredeau 1986; Street, Vogt, and Dutra 2009).

Street and colleagues (2009) have also pointed out that gender harassment—or hostile or degrading behaviors focusing on biological sex—is more commonly experienced by women than by men, and may represent an ongoing and significant stressor for women in the military, particularly during combat deployments when positive unit relationships are essential to ensuring safety and security. Although Laura was fortunate to have had a good male friend during deployment whom she describes as a kind of ally, she still felt it was "hard because you still have a lot of men who don't want you to be part of it because this is a man's world. I had to prove myself. Changing [500 pound] tires like a man. I mean doing, no kidding, what you would think a man would do. And I . . . if I needed help, I was like, 'No, get away, it's my job just like it's yours.'"

Even now, home again and working in uniform in a military office, she still encounters such attitudes. A representative from one of the veterans' service organizations came in recently and began railing against a female Vietnam veteran who had approached him, disgusted that she would even consider herself a veteran. Laura was furious, but shrugs and says, "So you get it still, and I don't think that's ever going to end." Although she remains proud that she "wasn't seen as a woman who couldn't do her job," she says, "I suffer like crazy now—my body feels like crap—because of some of the things I did."

More generally, it is not at all clear that female veterans are seen in American society as "real veterans" who have faced real risks and made a real contribution, and some women may be left feeling as though their service remains unacknowledged or even unwelcomed (Street, Vogt, and Dutra 2009). To underscore the importance of this sense of homecoming, one study found that the perception of an unsupportive homecoming reception among female Vietnam veterans played a significant role in mediating the relationship between trauma experiences and subsequent PTSD (Fontana, Schwartz, and Rosenheck 1997). Multiple studies have found that female service members perceive lower levels of social support across all phases of the deployment cycle than do their male colleagues, with implications for depression and PTSD symptoms (Carter-Visscher et al. 2010; Vogt et al. 2005).

Deeply ingrained cultural models for gender roles in American life also affect the impact of family-related stressors on both male and female service members.

Given that roughly 56% of active duty service members are married and 44% have children (U.S. Department of Defense 2010), a growing number of families have been faced with long-term deployments. Over more than a decade of war, extended (3–15 months) and often multiple deployments have taken their toll on military families, with divorces among enlisted couples rising and studies showing that children in the families of deployed service members are at greater risk for emotional difficulties (Chandra et al. 2010) as well as for abuse and neglect (Gibbs et al. 2007). Since women frequently remain the primary caregivers within families, and female service members are more likely to be single parents than their male counterparts (U.S. Department of Defense 2010), female service members may face additional challenges in planning for and coping with deployment. One study conducted among a National Guard unit facing deployment a month later found that both men and women were deeply concerned about how family members would manage in their absence (Carter-Visscher et al. 2010). Even so, women felt less prepared for the deployment than did men and were more than twice as likely to be depressed; PTSD symptoms among women were more likely than among men to be associated with concerns about family disruptions that might occur during their absence (Carter-Visscher et al. 2010). Upon the return home, women may also face particular challenges in renegotiating social roles and relationships that may have changed substantially in their absence (Faber et al. 2008; Mattocks et al. 2012).

Although Laura did not become a mother until after her deployment, her struggles with PTSD and with reintegrating into post-deployment life have continued to affect her life with her son. Not only does she continue to try to make sense of her experiences and her lingering anger, but also she says she feels more vulnerable than ever before. "When I was out there [in Iraq], I felt very safe, just because I thought, nobody's going to mess with me. . . . I thought I was a badass. . . . It was different when I came back. . . . I feel like I need to carry a gun with me when I'm putting my child in his car seat at night, you know. . . . [A] woman with a child is vulnerable, and I'm sure thieves or whatever see it as that."

## Gender and PTSD Risk among Recent Veterans

In summary, women veterans of the conflicts in Iraq and Afghanistan are commonly exposed to a variety of stressors, including combat, sexual harassment or assault, gender harassment, a lack of social support within units and American society more broadly, and family-related stressors, all of which may place them at risk for developing PTSD during or after their deployments. Although not all of these stressors are themselves traumas, each of them can contribute to a cumulative level of stress that increases the likelihood of developing mental and/or physical health concerns over time. In fact, research has consistently shown the importance of both peri-traumatic (Ozer et al. 2003) and post-traumatic (Brewin, Andrews, and Valentine 2000) factors in shaping PTSD risk, including social support and pivotal post-deployment life events such as divorce, unemployment, or loss and bereavement (Vogt 2011).

And yet, perhaps the most striking finding to emerge out of the past 30 years of research on combat PTSD is that, while most veterans who return from combat deployments go through a period of what may be called "reintegration" or "readjustment," taking some months to adjust to civilian life after long months in a highly stressful and almost exclusively military environment, only a minority go on to develop PTSD. This has proven to be the case for women veterans as well. Although many women go through a period of readjustment, experiencing problems with sleeping, struggling to feel comfortable among family and friends, re-engaging with partners or children, and reacquainting themselves with the norms of daily life (such as driving, grocery shopping, and so on), most go on to achieve a "new normal" and often a sense of gratitude and personal growth for their experiences (Finley 2011).

Nonetheless, because combat exposure among American women has been relatively rare until recently, and because the literature on non-combat trauma has shown that women are somewhat more likely to develop PTSD after traumatic experiences than are men (Breslau et al. 1997; Tolin and Foa 2006), it was widely expected that female veterans would exhibit higher rates of PTSD following OEF/OIF deployments.

The research to date does not support this hypothesis. Vogt, Vaughn, and colleagues (2011) conducted a survey among a nationally representative sample of 595 OEF/OIF veterans and found that although men did report greater levels of exposure to combat, the aftermath of battle, and perceived threat than did women, the differences were relatively small, consistent with reports from the field. Most surprisingly, however, the authors found no difference in the association between combat-related stressors and post-deployment mental health for men and women—in other words, men and women exposed to similar levels of stressors developed similar levels of mental health symptoms post-deployment—suggesting comparable levels of resilience. Although more research is required, consensus appears to be emerging that combat PTSD among military populations is much more similar than different across men and women, perhaps due to increasingly similar training, roles, and stress exposures across the deployment cycle (Hoge et al. 2007; King et al. 2013), as well as to the shared cultural environment of the military (Finley 2011).

It is worth noting that additional research examining the pathways by which stressors across the deployment cycle contribute to PTSD has indicated one important gender difference. Although risk for developing PTSD among all combat veterans appears to be shaped by warfare exposure, relationship concerns, and social support during and after deployment, women who indicate more severe relationship concerns while deployed have been found to report more life stressors and less social support after deployment. This suggests that relationship concerns may have greater implications for women's adjustment after returning home (Vogt, Smith, et al. 2011). These findings resonate with what I heard in 2007 from one Army chaplain, whose summary of the key difference in PTSD between male and female soldiers can be paraphrased as follows: "The wives [of soldiers] stay. The husbands leave." In some cases, the difference between men's and women's experiences of PTSD may be less dramatic than the difference in the support they receive once back at home.

## THE CARE ENVIRONMENT FOR WOMEN VETERANS

An additional factor shaping women veterans' experiences of combat PTSD in the aftermath of recent deployments is the mental health care environment available to them. All OEF/OIF/OND veterans are eligible for free care from the U.S. Department of Veterans Affairs (VA) for five years following their separation from the military if they were active duty or were National Guard or reservists activated for more than 180 days, with lifetime care continuing for any condition related to their military service. And yet the VA had spent much of the 20th century developing a network of care that was primarily aimed at serving aging men. While this effort has, by most accounts, been highly successful—the VA consistently outranks most private health care in patient outcomes and satisfaction (Longman 2007)—the rapid increase in the number of women veterans seeking care since the First Gulf War left the VA unprepared to provide appropriate services. By 2003, there were some 1.1 million living female veterans, and despite a few health service initiatives for women that had begun in the 1980s, it was widely recognized that women's mental health services remained a critical gap, with particular weaknesses in care for PTSD and substance abuse (Suffoletta-Maierle et al. 2003).

The past decade has seen enormous effort by the VA to better understand and address women's health service needs, and yet difficulties remain. Women may be more likely to face logistical barriers to care-seeking, such as a lack of knowledge about VA eligibility or a lack of child care to allow them to attend appointments (Vogt et al. 2006). Women veterans are also likely to have negative perceptions of VA care and to elect to seek care in non-VA settings, although this has proven to be less true among women living close to a dedicated VA Women's Health Center (Washington et al. 2006). Women, and particularly those with PTSD related to sexual trauma, may also feel less comfortable seeking care in predominantly male

VA environments, where group therapy sessions may be made up mostly of men, waiting rooms are filled with men, and clinicians may be most experienced in providing care for men. It is also an issue of some concern that women are more likely to seek care in non-VA settings, as evidence-based treatments for PTSD are widely available within the VA and only rarely offered in community settings, meaning women may receive poorer quality care for PTSD overall. Unfortunately, at least one study suggests that women are also more likely than men to receive inappropriate medications for PTSD (benzodiazepines) within VA settings (Lund et al. 2013), although reasons for this remain unclear.

Even so, the care picture for women veterans is increasingly positive. The evidence-based psychotherapies for PTSD that have been adopted by VA providers nationwide were originally developed among female survivors of sexual assault and have proven to be effective in reducing PTSD symptom severity among both female and male combat veterans (Monson et al. 2006; Schnurr et al. 2007). Consistent with trends across the wider U.S. population (Mackenzie, Gekoski, and Knox 2006; Ojeda and Bergstresser 2008), female veterans appear to be less hesitant than males to seek out mental health care (Elbogen et al. 2013). Where women do report concerns about seeking care in VA settings, they are generally similar to men's, suggesting that system inadequacies are not primarily gender-based (Elbogen et al. 2013). Moreover, women seeking PTSD care within the VA appear to be slightly more likely than men to receive an approximation of a "full dose" of psychotherapy treatment (eight sessions within 14 weeks) within the first year of their PTSD diagnosis (Seal et al. 2010).

Ongoing efforts continue to increase understandings of female veterans' experiences and needs, and to build a VA health care network that is as patient-centered and accessible and provides as high quality care for women as it does for men. Some of these initiatives have been small, such as a recent move by one hospital facility to put up a wall of photographs recognizing the service of women veteran employees, after a hospital administrator (herself an Iraq veteran) was taken to task by a patient for the fact that there were no pictures representing women on facility walls. Others have been intensive, including development of a national VA Women's Health Research Network to conduct high-priority research, which can now boast more than 200 researchers nationwide, nine task force committees dedicated to specific issues (including PTSD), and dozens of funded research studies (Yano 2013). Clinical efforts include implementing universal screening for military sexual trauma (Hyun et al. 2012), the appointment of military sexual trauma coordinators to serve survivors at every VA facility, and ongoing efforts to identify best practices in treating PTSD related to military sexual trauma (Suris et al. 2013) and to establish whether co-morbidities and disease trajectories over time vary by gender. In fact, although there is clear room for improvement in VA care for women veterans with PTSD, the next real frontier may be conditions that commonly co-occur alongside PTSD. Female veterans remain at greater risk than men for post-combat depression (Wells et al. 2010) and continue to exhibit worrisome rates of substance abuse (Elbogen et al. 2013), suicide-related behaviors (Ilgen et al. 2012), and homelessness (Hamilton, Poza, and Washington 2011). Understanding how women's experiences of these concerns may be unique and may require unique approaches remains an ongoing challenge.

## THE EXPERIENCE OF U.S. WOMEN VETERANS: IMPLICATIONS FOR GLOBAL MENTAL HEALTH

More and more militaries around the globe (including examples from Australia, Norway, and Israel) are increasingly integrating women into a variety of operational roles, as are United Nations peacekeeping missions. As this trend continues, the behavioral health lessons of the U.S.'s wars in Iraq and Afghanistan are likely to have growing relevance. Cross-cultural research on PTSD to date has typically mirrored the findings among U.S. civilians, in the sense that women have proven to be at greater risk for developing PTSD after trauma than men, although overall prevalence rates and symptom presentation vary by country and population (Keane et al. 2006). For example, research among child soldiers in Nepal has found that girls were more likely than boys to develop PTSD, even after adjusting for trauma exposure (Kohrt et al. 2008). Betancourt and colleagues (2013) have also found that young female combatants in Sierra Leone who survived wartime rape experienced significantly increased anxiety and depression symptoms; these findings underscore the importance of understanding the impact of sexual violence on the adaptation of girls and women in the aftermath of combat.

For now, the United States remains unique both in the sheer numbers of women it has sent into combat and the quantity of the research gauging the mental health consequences. However, given the uniformity with which exposure to combat and conflict-related violence has emerged as a risk factor for PTSD, it seems reasonable to predict that combat exposure will continue to be associated with elevated PTSD risk regardless of gender. The greatest variation seems likely to occur in the impact of other social stressors on veterans' well-being and responses to trauma, particularly those related to social support and family disruptions associated with service. For example, the United States currently stands alone among Western nations in requiring service members to complete deployments as long as 12 to 15 months at a time. The British Army, by contrast, aims to limit the duration of deployments to 6 months, followed by a 24-month break, based on research showing that the length of deployments and the downtime between them is strongly associated with mental health (Fear et al. 2010). Thus, in other nations, where the social demands of service and the social roles of men and women both in the home and within the military are likely to differ, it may be that pathways of risk for PTSD themselves differ, with consequences for gender disparities, prevalence, and severity.

The U.S. military case also provides an example for understanding women's response to sexual violence, with implications for women worldwide. Over the past several years, the U.S. military has recommitted itself to the task of preventing sexual harassment and assault, but has not yet achieved a military environment that is as safe and supportive for female service members as it needs to be. It seems that, in the area of preventing military sexual trauma, the United States still has much to learn from other nations. However, the VA continues to pioneer new infrastructure and treatment efforts aimed at increasing access to best practices for PTSD resulting from military sexual trauma, and these lessons are likely to be relevant for designing programmatic responses to sexual violence in a variety of cultural and institutional settings.

On the whole, the American case suggests two key lessons for global mental health in responding to PTSD. The first is the importance of working to ensure meaningful access to the full spectrum of high-quality mental health services, from screening to treatment. This may sound lofty, given how difficult it is to offer evidence-based care for PTSD even in a nation as resource-wealthy as the United States. Yet the necessity of providing care to a population of veterans characterized by deep economic disparity and large geographic distances, particularly in rural areas, is prompting the VA to develop new strategies for delivering quality care via telehealth (using phone, Internet, or videoconference technology) and other modalities that are likely to prove useful in low-resource settings as well. Early efforts to adapt evidence-based psychotherapies for use in non-Western settings, meanwhile, show promising results (e.g., Kaysen et al. 2013).

The second lesson is that care environments themselves, beyond access and screening and treatment modalities, must be patient-centered for both men and women. Women with PTSD and other mental health concerns arising from violence must feel welcome, safe, and as though clinicians are knowledgeable and comfortable in meeting their needs. Laura left care at the Vet Center because she felt the clinicians there could not address her experience, but came back because clinicians at the VA took time to reach out. In the end, she remained engaged in treatment because she found it to be useful and meaningful in helping her recover from PTSD and to reach her goals for herself, her son, and her life. And this, after all, is a mission worth fighting for.

## Note

[1] Pseudonym.

## References

APA (2000). *Diagnostic and Statistical Manual of Mental Disorders, Text Revision (4th Edition, DMS-IV)*. Washington, DC: American Psychiatric Association.
——. (2013). *Diagnostic and Statistical Manual of Mental Disorders, 5th edition: DSM-5.* Washington, DC: American Psychiatric Association.
Betancourt, T. S., McBain, R., Newnham, E. A., and Brennan, R. T. (2013). Trajectories of internalizing problems in war-affected Sierra Leonean youth: examining conflict and postconflict factors. *Child Development*, 84 (2): 455–470.
Breslau, N., Davis, G., Peterson, E. L., and Schultz, L. (1997). Psychiatric sequelae of post-traumatic stress disorder in women. *Archives of General Psychiatry*, 54 (1): 81–87.
Brewin, C. R., Andrews, B., and Valentine, J. D. (2000). Meta-analysis of risk factors for post-traumatic stress disorder in trauma-exposed adults. *Journal of Consulting and Clinical Psychology*, 68 (5): 748–766.
Carter-Visscher, R., Polusny, M. A., Murdoch, M., Thuras, P., Erbes, C. R., and Kehle, S. M. (2010). Predeployment gender differences in stressors and mental health among U.S. National Guard troops poised for Operation Iraqi Freedom deployment. *Journal of Traumatic Stress*, 23 (1): 78–85.
Chandra, A., Lara-Cinisomo, S., Jaycox, L., Tanielian, T., Burns, R., Ruder, T., and Han, B. (2010). Children on the homefront: the experience of children from military families. *Pediatrics*, 125 (1): 13–22.
Elbogen, E. B., Wagner, H. R., Johnson, S. C., Kinneer, P., Kang, H., Vasterling, J. J., et al. (2013). Are Iraq and Afghanistan veterans using mental health services? New data from a national random-sample survey. *Psychiatric Services*, 64 (2): 134–141.
Faber, A. J., Willerton, E., Clymer, S. R., MacDermid, S. M., and Weiss, H. M. (2008). Ambiguous absence, ambiguous presence: a qualitative study of military reserve families in wartime. *Journal of Family Psychology*, 22 (2): 222–230.
Fear, N. T., Jones, M., Murphy, D., Hull, L., Iversen, A. C., Coker, B., et al. (2010). What are the consequences of deployment to Iraq and Afghanistan on the mental health of the UK armed forces? A cohort study. *The Lancet*, 375 (9728): 1783–1797.
Finley, E. P. (2011). *Fields of Combat: Understanding PTSD among Veterans of Iraq and Afghanistan*. Ithaca, New York: Cornell University Press.
Fontana, A., Schwartz, L. S., and Rosenheck, R. A. (1997). Posttraumatic stress disorder among female Vietnam veterans: a causal model of etiology. *American Journal of Public Health*, 87: 169–175.
Gibbs, D. A., Martine, S. L., Kupper, L. L., and Johnson, R. E. (2007). Child maltreatment in enlisted soldiers' families during combat-related deployments. *JAMA*, 298: 528–535.
Hamilton, A. B., Poza, I., and Washington, D. L. (2011). "Homelessness and trauma go hand-in-hand": pathways to homelessness among women veterans. *Women's Health Issues*, 21 (4): s203–s209.

Hoge, C. W., Clark, J. C., and Castro, C. A. (2007). Commentary: women in combat and the risk of post-traumatic stress disorder and depression. *International Journal of Epidemiology*, 36 (2): 327–329.

Hyun, J. K., Kimerling, R., Cronkite, R. C., McCutcheon, S., and Frayne, S. M. (2012). Organizational factors associated with screening for military sexual trauma. *Women's Health Issues*, 22 (2): e209–e215.

Ilgen, M. A., McCarthy, J. F., Ignacio, R. V., Bohnert, A. S. B., Valenstein, M., Blow, F. C., et al. (2012). Psychopathology, Iraq and Afghanistan service, and suicide among Veterans Health Administration patients. *Journal of Consulting and Clinical Psychology*, 80 (3): 323–330.

Ilies, R., Hauserman, N., Schwochau, S., and Stibal, J. (2003). Reported incidence rates of work-related sexual harassment in the United States: using meta-analysis to explain reported rate disparities. *Personnel Psychology*, 56 (3): 607–631.

Kang, H., Dalager, N., Mahan, C., and Ishii, E. (2005). The role of sexual assault on the risk of PTSD among Gulf War veterans. *Annals of Epidemiology*, 15 (3): 191–195.

Katz, L. S., Cojucar, G., Behesti, S., Nakamura, E., and Murray, M. (2012). Military sexual trauma during deployment to Iraq and Afghanistan: prevalence, readjustment and gender differences. *Violence and Victims*, 27 (4): 487–499.

Kaysen, D., Lindgren, K., Zangana, G. A. S., Murray, L., Bass, J., and Bolton, P. (2013). Adaptation of cognitive processing therapy for treatment of torture victims: experience in Kurdistan, Iraq. *Psychological Trauma: Theory, Research, Practice, and Policy*, 5 (2): 184–192.

Keane, T. M., Marshall, A. D., and Taft, C. T. (2006). Posttraumatic stress disorder: etiology, epidemiology, and treatment outcome. *Annual Review of Clinical Psychology*, 2: 161–197.

Kimerling, R., Street, A. E., Pavao, J., Smith, M. W., Cronkite, R. C., Holmes, T. H., et al. (2010). Military-related sexual trauma among Veterans Health Administration patients returning from Afghanistan and Iraq. *American Journal of Public Health*, 100: 1409–1412.

King, M. W., Street, A. E., Gradus, J. L., Vogt, D. S., and Resick, P. A. (2013). Gender differences in posttraumatic stress symptoms among OEF/OIF veterans: an item response theory analysis. *Journal of Traumatic Stress*, 26: 175–183.

Kohrt, B. A., Jordans, M. J. D., Tol, W. A., Speckman, R. A., Maharjan, S. M., Worthman, C. M., et al. (2008). Comparison of mental health between former child soldiers and children never conscripted by armed groups in Nepal. *JAMA*, 300 (6): 691–702.

Koola, M. M., Qualls, C., Kelly, D. L., Skelton, K., Bradley, B., Amar, R., et al. (2013). Prevalence of childhood physical and sexual abuse in veterans with psychiatric diagnoses. *Journal of Nervous and Mental Disease*, 201: 348–352.

Lafontaine, E., and Tredeau, L. (1986). The frequency, sources, and correlates of sexual harassment among women in traditional male occupations. *Sex Roles*, 15 (7–8): 433–442.

Longman, P. (2007). *Best Care Anywhere: Why VA Health Care is Better than Yours.* Sausalito, CA: PoliPointPress.

Lund, B. C., Bernardy, N. C., Vaughan-Sarrazin, M., Alexander, B., and Friedman, M. J. (2013). Patient and facility characteristics associated with benzodiazepine prescribing for veterans with PTSD. *Psychiatric Services,* 64: 149–155.

Mackenzie, C. S., Gekoski, W. L., and Knox, V. J. (2006). Age, gender, and the underutilization of mental health services: the influence of help-seeking attitudes. *Aging and Mental Health,* 10 (6): 574–582.

Maguen, S., Cohen, B. E., Ren, L., Bosch, J. O., Kimerling, R., and Seal, K. H. (2012). Gender differences in military sexual trauma and mental health diagnoses among Iraq and Afghanistan veterans with posttraumatic stress disorder. *Women's Health Issues,* 22 (1): e61–e66.

Mattocks, K. M., Haskell, S. G., Krebs, E. E., Justice, A. C., Yano, E. M., and Brandt, C. (2012). Women at war: understanding how women veterans cope with combat and military sexual trauma. *Social Science and Medicine,* 74 (4): 537–545.

Monson, C. M., Schnurr, P. P., Resick, P. A., Friedman, M. J., Young-Xu, Y., and Stevens, S. P. (2006). Cognitive processing therapy for veterans with military-related posttraumatic stress disorder. *Journal of Consulting and Clinical Psychology,* 74 (5): 898–907.

Myers, S. L. (2009). Living and fighting alongside men, and fitting in. *The New York Times,* August 16, 2009.

Ojeda, V. C., and Bergstresser, S. M. (2008). Gender, race-ethnicity, and psychosocial barriers to mental health care: an examination of perceptions and attitudes among adults reporting unmet need. *Journal of Health and Social Behavior,* 49 (3): 317–334.

Ozer, E. J., Best, S. R., Lipsey, T. L., and Weiss, D. S. (2003). Predictors of post-traumatic stress disorder and symptoms in adults: a meta-analysis. *Psychological Bulletin,* 129 (1): 52–73.

Peralta, E. (2013). Panetta is lifting ban on women in combat roles. National Public Radio, January 23, 2013, from www.npr.org/blogs/thetwoway/2013/01/23/170093351/panetta-is-lifting-ban-on-women-in-combat-roles.

Pincus, S. H., House, R., Christensen, J., and Adler, L. E. (2004). The emotional cycle of deployment: a military family perspective. *Journal of the Army Medical Department,* April–June: 615–623.

Schnurr, P. P., Friedman, M. J., Engel, C. C., Foa, E. B., Shea, M. T., Chow, B. K., et al. (2007). Cognitive behavioral therapy for posttraumatic stress disorder in women: a randomized controlled trial. *JAMA,* 297 (8): 820–830.

Seal, K. H., Maguen, S., Cohen, B. E., Gima, K. S., Metzler, T. J., Ren, L., et al. (2010). VA mental health services utilization in Iraq and Afghanistan veterans in the first year of receiving new mental health diagnoses. *Journal of Traumatic Stress,* 23 (1): 5–16.

Street, A. E., Kimerling, R., Bell, M. E., and Pavao, J. (2011). Sexual harassment and sexual assault during military service. In J. I. Ruzek, P. P. Schnurr, J. J. Vasterling, and M. J. Friedman (eds.), *Caring for Veterans with Deployment-Related Stress Disorders,* pp. 131–150. Washington, DC: American Psychological Association.

Street, A. E., Vogt, D. S., and Dutra, L. (2009). A new generation of women veterans: stressors faced by women deployed to Iraq and Afghanistan. *Clinical Psychology Review*, 29 (8): 685–694.

Suffoletta-Maierle, S., Grubaugh, A. L., Magruder, K. M., Monnier, J., and Frueh, B. C. (2003). Trauma-related mental health needs and service utilization among female veterans. *Journal of Psychiatric Practice*, 9: 367–375.

Suris, A., Lind, L., Kashner, T., and Borman, P. (2007). Mental health, quality of life, and health functioning in women veterans: differential outcomes associated with military and civilian sexual assault. *Journal of Interpersonal Violence*, 22 (2): 179–197.

Suris, A., Link-Malcolm, J., Chard, K. M., Ahn, C., and North, C. (2013). A randomized clinical trial of cognitive processing therapy for veterans with PTSD related to military sexual trauma. *Journal of Traumatic Stress*, 26: 28–37.

Tolin, D. F., and Foa, E. B. (2006). Sex differences in trauma and posttraumatic stress disorder: a quantitative review of 25 years of research. *Psychological Bulletin*, 132 (6): 969–992.

U.S. Department of Defense. (2009). *Military Casualty Information*. www.dmdc.osd.mil/dcas/pages/main.xhtml (accessed June 10, 2013).

——. (2010). *Demographics 2010: Profile of the Military Community*. Washington, DC: Office of the Deputy Under Secretary of Defense. http://www.militaryonesource.mil/12038/MOS/Reports/2010-Demographics-Report.pdf.

Vogt, D. S. (2011). Mental health stigma as a barrier to service use: findings and recommendations for research based on military and veteran populations. *Psychiatric Services*, 62: 135–142.

Vogt, D. S., Bergeron, A., Salgado, D., Daley, J., Ouimette, P., and Wolfe, J. (2006). Barriers to Veterans Health Administration care in a nationally representative sample of women veterans. *Journal of General Internal Medicine*, 21: s19–s25.

Vogt, D. S., Pless, A. P., King, L. A., and King, D. W. (2005). Deployment stressors, gender, and mental health outcomes among Gulf War I veterans. *Journal of Traumatic Stress*, 18 (2): 115–127.

Vogt, D. S., Smith, B., Elwy, R., Martin, J., Schultz, M., Drainoni, M.-L., et al. (2011). Predeployment, deployment, and postdeployment risk factors for posttraumatic stress symptomatology in female and male OEF/OIF veterans. *Journal of Abnormal Psychology*, 120 (4): 819–831.

Vogt, D. S., Vaughn, R., Glickman, M. E., Schultz, M., Drainoni, M.-L., Elwy, R., et al. (2011). Gender differences in combat-related stressors and their association with postdeployment mental health in a nationally representative sample of U.S. OEF/OIF veterans. *Journal of Abnormal Psychology*, 120 (4): 797–806.

Washington, D. L., Yano, E. M., Simon, B. F., and Sun, S. (2006). To use or not to use: what influences why women choose VA health care. *Journal of General Internal Medicine*, 21: S11–S18.

Wells, T. S., LeardMann, C. A., Fortuna, S. O., Smith, B., Smith, T. C., Ryan, M. A. K., et al. (2010). A prospective study of depression following combat deployment in support of the wars in Iraq and Afghanistan. *American Journal of Public Health*, 100: 90–99.

Yaeger, D., Himmelfarb, N., Cammack, A., and Mintz, J. (2006). DSM-IV diagnosed post-traumatic stress disorder in women veterans with and without military sexual trauma. *Journal of General Internal Medicine*, 21: S65–S69.

Yano, E. M. (2013). What progress have we made on the VA Women's Health Services research agenda? Paper presented at the VA Health Services Research and Development Cyberseminar.

Chapter 14

# Cultural Competence and Its Discontents: Reflections on a Mandatory Course for Psychiatry Residents

Sarah S. Willen, with Anne Kohler

A VITAL FICTION STANDS AT THE HEART of the biomedical enterprise. As medical students and residents acquire the symbols of their profession (white coats, stethoscopes, pagers) and undergo its initiation rites (cadaver lab, first physical examination, scutwork and exhaustion, rising through the ranks as a resident trainee), they learn that they are "supposed" to see their patients through a single, universalizing gaze: the gaze of biomedicine. Not only are clinicians expected to treat all patients alike regardless of distinguishing features, but the various facets of their own identity—gender, religious affiliation, racial/ethnic identity, sexual orientation, and so on—are not supposed to influence interactions with their patients. In short, doctors are to be doctors, full stop, and the culture of medicine is to trump other forms of identification and commitment.

These universalizing principles are important to Dr. Chris Graham, a third-year psychiatry resident in a prestigious residency training program in the northeastern United States. In theory, he believes patients' backgrounds—and, for that matter, physicians'—should be irrelevant in clinical encounters. Yet, as he explained in an interview, things get complicated in the real world of clinical practice. This became immediately apparent to him during his medical training in a major American city where most of his patients were both black and poor, and most struggled with one or more additional sources of disadvantage and vulnerability, such as low educational attainment, single parenthood, domestic violence, ill health, unemployment, and/or substance abuse.

Although he knows none of these problems intimately, Dr. Graham does share one feature with many of the patients he encountered as a medical student: he, too, is of African descent. He explained that as medical school wore on, he

*Global Mental Health: Anthropological Perspectives*, edited by Brandon A. Kohrt and Emily Mendenhall, 239–254. © 2015 Left Coast Press, Inc. All rights reserved.

began to notice within himself a disturbing tendency toward a kind of internal-ized racism. He encountered

> a lot of minority individuals who were using drugs and having co-morbid psychi-atric problems. And I actually decided to not stay in [that city] because I wanted to see a broader spectrum of mental illness so I could [avoid] building a negative stereotype about my own people, because that was happening . . . when I would hear "34 year-old, substance-abusing . . . young woman," I'd have a black person in my mind. . . . Why should that be?

In part after noticing this largely unconscious tendency, Dr. Graham decided he needed to pursue residency training in another city with a less homogeneous patient population. As a resident, he was pleased to see patients who upset those stereotypes; this, he said, "is what I have been seeking." He offered an example: being told he was about to see a 34-year-old, substance-abusing patient, and "a white male would sit down. I'd be like, 'Oh.' . . . That's why I came, so that I could fight that notion that mental illness or substance abuse had to be in one popula-tion."

Even in these new surroundings, however, Dr. Graham struggled with his own inclination to stereotype. For instance, he described a patient in his forties, a black man who complained of anxiety so severe it prevented him from working. Rather than approaching his patient through a "universalizing" biomedical gaze—or, for that matter, feeling any special connection to him as one black man to another—Dr. Graham was instead deeply suspicious of his patient for reasons that made him uncomfortable. In this case, however, his feelings were not about racial difference. Rather, they stemmed from *cultural* differences between his own background as a "Caribbean African-American," born in the United States to Caribbean parents, and that of his patient, whom he described as "American African-American."

Dr. Graham enumerated several significant differences between the two groups. First, he explained, Caribbean African-Americans have "an immigrant ethos, an immigrant energy that comes in and says, . . . 'If I work, I can do it. Every-one can make it.'" Like sociologist Mary Waters, who wrote an important book on this topic (1999), Dr. Graham explained that many "American African-Americans" have harbored resentment toward Caribbean African-Americans, begrudged the group's material success relative to non-immigrant black Americans, and exhibited varying degrees of inter-group racism. A primary reason for these negative feelings, he suggested, dates back several hundred years to the groups' very different experi-ences of slavery. In his experience, Caribbean-Americans will say things like, "We had slavery too, we had slaves. But we fought and overcame. . . . We kicked them out of the islands," and so forth, whereas "American African-Americans" take a more fatalistic stance, saying things like, "Oh well, you know, we didn't, we couldn't, we're helpless. Even after attaining freedom we're still kind of not free at all." The latter stance, he suggested, "is a very different legacy."

Returning to this particular patient, Dr. Graham wondered whether his own suspicions resulted from an appropriate sense of clinical intuition or, alternatively, from his own cultural background and cultural prejudices.

> Am I thinking . . . because I have this Caribbean-American sort of "just-go-to-work" perspective . . . he's just lazy and not really depressed and anxious? Am I not appreciating his anxiety, the depth of his depression? He doesn't look depressed when he comes here, he doesn't sound depressed. By my criteria, he doesn't sound depressed. His anxiety is sort of equivocal . . . he's able to function in a sense. So the tension is, is that me, or is that him? And I ultimately, I didn't fill out his disability form, because I said, "You don't look disabled to me." [laughs] And is that, how did that come about? Is that me or him?

Dr. Graham's honest and self-critical comments are striking for many reasons, above all because he gives voice to the kind of inner conversation that most of us would be too shy, or fearful, or defensive to acknowledge, let alone verbalize. For better or for worse, Dr. Graham's racial/ethnic and cultural background has a far-reaching influence on who he is and how he understands the world around him, including his professional environment and his relationship to patients who seek his care.

## CULTURAL COMPETENCE AND ITS DISCONTENTS

The tensions, conflicts, and questions that emerge in this interview with Dr. Graham would probably offer rich material for discussion in a course on "cultural sensitivity" or "cultural competence." In fact, he was involved in precisely such a course at the time we spoke—a required course that was part of his residency training program. Unfortunately, however, none of his rich and complex experiences were placed on the table for discussion, representing but one among many missed opportunities in this well-intentioned but largely unpopular course.

Taking that course as ethnographic focus, this chapter asks: why is "cultural sensitivity" or, to use the more common term, "cultural competence," such a difficult issue to engage in with clinicians-in-training? The instructors for the course we explore were both attending psychiatrists, and their students were a diverse cohort of psychiatry residents. The format involved 18 hour-long sessions scheduled in sustained blocks of four to six weeks over a single academic year. The course objective, according to the instructors, was to "[i]ncrease residents' awareness of the cultural, social, and economic factors that influence the diagnosis and treatment of mental health disorders in order to [offer] a clinical intervention that is congruent, fair, and effective to the patient's reality."

From the perspective of cultural competence pedagogy, the course can best be described as a disappointment. Dr. Graham's reflections, along with the broader findings reported below, suggest one key reason for the course's lack of success: its insufficient attention to what we can think of as "counter-transference." In the psychodynamic tradition, patients are understood to project their own emotions, fears, and desires—unconsciously—onto the clinicians who care for them. In other words, patients' perceptions of a clinical encounter are shaped and constrained by their past experiences and by emotional patterns developed in earlier relationships—for example, by what we can call "transference." Dr. Graham's observations point toward a crucial parallel insight: *clinicians do the same thing.* Attention to the biographical and emotional baggage that clinicians bring into their clinical work—their "counter-transference"—thus seems to be an important step if one's aim is to help them cultivate what's often described as cultural sensitivity or cultural competence.

What happens in a cultural sensitivity course that ignores this crucial issue? The course in which Dr. Graham participated offers some answers. Despite the instructors' good intentions and ongoing efforts to experiment with content and format from one year to the next, it failed repeatedly to meet either residents' expectations or, as the instructors bravely acknowledged, their own. One resident summed things up in blunt terms:

> I feel like this door keeps getting swung wide open, a big huge gaping wound. People with a lot of feelings because they are of the minority race, or any number of minority races, let loose a whole bunch of feelings. And . . . the majority either feel, like, horribly guilty, or accused, or criticized. Because it's not their intention to make people feel that way. And it's hard to examine what has happened.

With Dr. Graham's experience as backdrop and this quotation in mind, this chapter engages three questions: First, how and why might a cultural sensitivity course for mental health clinicians go so terribly awry? Second, what changes to the course structure, content, and dynamics might have yielded a less frustrating, more satisfying, and more clinically relevant experience for residents? Finally, what broader questions does this course raise about the larger project of "training" clinicians in cultural competence and its correlates?

A few brief reactions provide a helpful point of departure. According to the most generous assessments, the course in which Dr. Graham participated created opportunities for self-reflection and critical engagement about questions of human difference. Significantly, however, such moments of reflection took place outside of course sessions themselves. Less generous assessments described the course as "frustrating," "uncomfortable," or even an experience that left residents feeling "unheard" or "unsafe." In fact, several suggested that the course had actually

produced previously nonexistent "camps"—"the camp of, let's say, privileged individuals," one resident explained, "and then the other camp has called itself the colored people or something. Is that what it is? No, 'the brown people.' . . . Yes, this is
an actual terminology that has developed. There's the brown people, and then
there's everyone else."

After struggling to make the course work for seven years, things grew so tense
in this particular year that the clinician-educators' confidence in their ability to
teach the course was shaken, and midway through they informed the residency
program director that they would not offer it the following year.

Why are pedagogical efforts to frame culture and difference as matters of clinical concern so emotionally fraught and, potentially, so explosive?

## TWO MODELS: KNOWLEDGE OF OTHERS VERSUS KNOWLEDGE OF ONESELF

Current research on cultural competence and its correlates (such as cultural sensitivity, "cultural humility" [Tervalon and Murray Garcia 1998], or "cultural safety"
[DeSouza 2008]) suggests two main educational approaches. The first presumes
that "knowledge is power"—that providing clinicians with more knowledge about
different racial/ethnic or cultural communities will help improve health outcomes
and reduce health disparities. A key risk in such courses, however, is the danger of
speaking in overgeneralizations or even stereotypes—such as, "Haitian patients believe X" or "Latino patients do Y" (Kleinman and Benson 2006). A second approach takes a very different tack and challenges students to reflect on their own
cultural and racial/ethnic identities, address their own blind spots and anxieties,
and quite literally transform *themselves*. Whereas the first approach tends to ignore
counter-transference, the second places it at the center.

The course under examination here was largely in keeping with the first of
these two models. Five insights arose in preliminary analysis of our study findings
(Willen, Bullen, and Good 2010), all of which point toward the importance of engaging clinicians' own experiences. These preliminary insights are as follows.

First, cultural competence initiatives that ignore the powerful emotional valences associated with culture, race/ethnicity, and other forms of difference do so
at their peril—and at risk of undermining their fundamental objectives.

Second, confronting these fraught issues is no small task; given their tremendous emotional potency, opening them up for critical engagement will almost inevitably "open up a huge can of worms" (Willen, Bullen, and Good 2010).

Third, the very invitation to reflect publicly on the clinical implications of
such fraught issues is likely to engender feelings of vulnerability and risk, especially

if conversations are expected to take place among professional colleagues. Significantly, feelings of vulnerability and risk will vary, both in degree and in kind, in accordance with participants' backgrounds and lived experience. For clinicians or clinicians-in-training to accept such an invitation, instructors must be prepared to cultivate and manage this vulnerability in ways that are both educationally meaningful and respectful of personal stakes.

Fourth, it no longer makes sense to assume that physicians represent "mainstream" culture and that "otherness" is an attribute of patients. A common example in our findings involved interactions between white, U.S.-born patients and U.S.-born physicians with recent family histories of immigration (Chinese-American, Korean-American, Armenian-American, and so on).

Finally, the two course models outlined above—the knowledge-based model and the reflexive model—may seem contradictory, but the most successful courses may be precisely those that convey clinically relevant insights and skills while simultaneously engaging seriously with the counter-transferential implications of human difference.

Our research on cultural competence included 18 audio-recorded pre- and post-course interviews with a total of 11 residents of the 14 in the course; 12 instructor interviews, including 9 with the primary course instructor; and close observation of 18 course sessions. The majority of interviewees were unusually forthright in their reflections and observations, and the lead instructor was unusually open to critical feedback (and, in fact, has written about his struggles teaching the course; see Bullon 2013). One potential source of sample bias merits mention. Interviewees represented a diverse set of racial/ethnic and cultural backgrounds, as elaborated below, while the three who declined were all white. Although any explanation can only be speculative, this pattern supports the hypothesis that members of "majority" backgrounds found the course's central themes difficult to discuss.

## RESIDENTS' PERSPECTIVES: UNTAPPED RESOURCES, MISPLACED ASSUMPTIONS, AND HOT-BUTTON TERMS

### Untapped Resources

Perhaps the most striking feature of this group of residents was its internal diversity. Members of the cohort, which was roughly split between male and female residents, variously identified as white, black, Latino, Asian, and—with an exasperated grimace at the prospect of being labeled as such—"biracial." Other self-descriptors indicated either ethnic background (Indian-American, Caribbean-American, and so on) or religious affiliation. The diversity within this particular cohort, especially as compared with preceding cohorts, was no coincidence. As several sources corroborated, it was the result of a concerted effort to diversify a residency program that historically had been primarily white—an effort that generated a fair amount of ambivalence among the residents.

For many, the course's failure to employ this internal diversity as a resource was another missed opportunity. One resident reacted strongly to the course's tendency toward abstraction and intellectualization: "It's kind of like, we're just talking sort of intellectually, which is a good exercise at times but . . . I feel like a better discussion would actually engage our emotional process also, to some extent." Although residents' personal experiences did on occasion arise in course discussions, my course notes corroborate interviewees' sense that this powerful pedagogical resource remained largely "untapped." Importantly, the lead instructor also communicated to me that he felt frustrated by such missed opportunities.

## Misplaced Assumptions: Residents are Not Blank Slates

Yet insufficient attention to the cohort's internal diversity was not the most prominent source of frustration among residents. Rather, they were most troubled by the instructors' apparent assumption that they were presenting the residents with something new, something they had not previously encountered during their education and training. Most recalled with ease, and often frustration, earlier seminars and courses they had taken. One resident explained that "cultural competence was a big thing" when she was in medical school in the early 2000s, and that at the time, "80 percent of the class . . . rolled their eyes at this stuff." The importance of this point cannot be understated. Most recent graduates of U.S. medical schools have been exposed to at least some lectures, workshops, discussions, and/or experimental exercises focusing on issues of culture and human difference. As a result, residents' perception that the instructors regarded them as "blank slates" evoked strong reactions and powerful emotions ranging from frustration, to resistance, to insult.

## Hot-Button Terms

On a related note, the course evoked hot-button terms—including "political correctness," "diversity," and even "cultural competence" itself—that generated considerable anxiety and discomfort. Several residents recalled strong negative reactions when the course was first mentioned in their second year of residency. One indicated that several of her colleagues appeared "confused and frankly a little offended" when the course premise was first introduced. Another remembered a similar reaction: "[T]wo residents in the class . . . rolled their eyes. Like 'ugh.' And I remember thinking, 'What is that about? A couple of words and you get eye rolls! . . . 'Diversity class' must be a very strong two words.'"

As these comments suggest, the political and emotional connotations borne by terms like "cultural competence" and "diversity"—which may long predate participation in a course like this one—can strongly influence residents' willingness to engage or invest. Some residents clearly expressed a sense of "political correctness fatigue," or frustration with widespread, largely unspoken expectations to censor or sanitize their language to avoid any terms that might prove offensive.

I will return to the affective potency of these topics and terms below. For now, let us simply note that these residents' reactions raise challenging questions about how factors such as generational identity, sociopolitical context, and personal experience can affect the "teachability" and "learnability" of pedagogical material involving culture and human difference (Willen and Carpenter-Song 2013).

*Unclear Expectations: What is Culture Anyway?*

A fourth key issue also merits mention: persistent ambiguity about the concept of culture itself. Interviews with course instructors evinced a broad and flexible definition of "culture." Both understood culture as involving multiple dimensions of human variation—race/ethnicity, religious background, gender identity, sexual orientation, immigration status, socioeconomic class, and so on—all of which interact to shape individual and group experiences of identity and social interaction. Moreover, both instructors recognized that different facets of one's cultural identity, understood in this manner, emerge or recede in different interactive settings. The lead instructor found it equally important to consider the "culture of medicine" itself (Good 2001; Good et al. 2003). In particular, he recognized its potential for precipitating misunderstandings between health care professionals, who are "native" to biomedical culture, and patients, for whom much of that culture can be mysterious and confusing. Unfortunately, however, this nuanced understanding of what culture is and how it "works" seems to have gotten lost in translation.

*What Constitutes Clinically Useful Cultural Knowledge?*

Other residents registered a second, substantially different complaint: that the course structure, and especially its guest lectures on specific groups (such as Latinos, African-Americans, Russians, Muslims), conveyed a reductive and stereotypical understanding of culture. Nonetheless, reactions to the guest lectures varied, even among those who extended this critique. Several suggested that a (non-Muslim) social scientist's guest lectures on Muslims fell into the trap of stereotyping and reductiveness, whereas reactions to a presentation on Russian patients, delivered by two psychiatrists of Russian background, were somewhat more appreciative. Reactions to presentations focused on African-American patients by an

African-American psychiatrist and on lesbian, gay, transgender, and bisexual patients by a psychologist who did not identify her own sexual orientation were mixed. Although it is not clear what specifically accounted for these varied responses, possible factors include the guest lecturers' professional credentials and/or their personal connection, or lack of connection, to the group(s) about which they spoke.

## AN "INFLAMMATORY TRUTH"

Three insights emerge with particular clarity from these findings. First, culture and other forms of difference—especially race/ethnicity—bear powerful emotional valences, and inviting critical engagement will almost inevitably open up a proverbial "can of worms" (Willen, Bullen, and Good 2010). Second, courses that ignore these emotional valences and their counter-transferential implications do so at their own peril. Third, clinicians are unlikely to reflect meaningfully on counter-transference stirred up by cross-cultural encounters, clinical or otherwise, in the absence of an enduring "safe space" that makes them feel recognized, valued, and respected. Creating such a "safe space" requires understanding and appreciating the different perspectives participants bring to the table. It also requires *time*, a commodity in short supply in the course described here.

One especially tense course session made clear the importance of these insights: a guest lecture by an African-American psychiatrist who presented case material involving several of his African-American patients. Not only did resident responses vary dramatically, at least in part by personal background, but his presentation also elicited the most succinct and telling summary of the course: the notion that discussions of human difference, at least in the United States, revolve awkwardly around what many Americans experience as "a big huge gaping wound."

Residents were struck, albeit in very different ways, by the guest lecturer's stark analysis of race relations in the United States. His case material invoked a wide variety of historical incidents and scholarly works, including the 1954 lynching of Emmett Till, a 14-year-old African-American boy, for supposedly flirting with a white woman; the writings of scholar and civil rights activist W. E. B. DuBois; and the novels of writer Ralph Ellison. The lecture also highlighted the "horrendous disparities" in U.S. health status; the persistence of white racism and unacknowledged white privilege; and the internalization of racialized thinking by black Americans. Yet the speaker's most provocative claim, which became lodged in several residents' minds, was the straightforward assertion that "America was built on white supremacy." Although many critical social scientists would hear this as a descriptive rather than as a polemical statement, for some residents it launched a cascade of emotions that found no satisfactory resolution within the framework of the course.

In interviews, however, these emotions rose rapidly and readily to the surface. One resident, herself a person of color, was deeply moved by the presentation. She explained that their guest's assertion that "America was built on white supremacy" had not occurred to her before but, she concluded upon reflection, it was "not untrue."

> I've never heard anyone say that, I never even actually thought it as a fully formed thought, but I mean it's not untrue. I mean it's true ... this is how America came together, like the brown people were not respected . . . but that's inflammatory, this piece of truth, like we don't talk about it.

For her, the guest lecture offered an opportunity to recognize and begin to reflect on this "inflammatory piece of truth"—a truth, it is important to note, that hit close to home for personal reasons.

Some colleagues who did not identify with "the brown camp" heard this comment very differently, she recalled. In particular, several heard it as more inflammatory than truthful, including one resident who said, "Well, I don't think that's appropriate and I don't understand why he has to say that." She went on to distinguish her own reaction from those of some colleagues, especially those who are white: "I think many of the, you know, majority population, they've lived in a situation that is relatively privileged, and so the picture of America that lives in their mind is . . . [a] privileged, and, like, fairly fair place to live." Those in what she called the "brown camp," however, experienced social life very differently: "[A]s a general rule, many of us are resigned to the notion that we live in a world that is unfair, that often will not be a happy, sort of, you know, generally comfortable existence, and that difficult things may just happen to you because of how you look." This observation—a forthright recognition of invisible white privilege and enduring, if equally invisible, legacies of discrimination—strikes precisely at the heart of what's at stake in courses like this one.

Yet, little opportunity was available at the end of the presentation for discussion, nor was any opportunity to debrief offered at the next class meeting. Here we bear witness to yet another missed opportunity. A resident who also described himself as "brown" noted that discussions of race and class tended to become political very quickly and that the residents felt alternately frustrated and confused about what he described as the split between "white vs. non-white." Those who felt accused or blamed were tempted to tune out or even stop attending the course. What might have happened if the residents had been able to raise their concerns in the context of class discussion? At this point we cannot know.

What is clear, however, is that individuals' backgrounds profoundly influence their perceptions of the social and political realities in which they live, with powerful implications for all forms of social interaction—including interactions in both the classroom and clinical settings. And, of course, critical engagement with different facets of human difference will feel different depending on where one stands. In the present context, members of the "brown camp" tended to be open to public reflection on this guest speaker's hard-hitting critique of American society's purported "white supremacist" roots, while some with "mainstream" backgrounds grew upset, even indignant, at the thought that they might be held personally accountable, however indirectly, for today's inequalities.

## A Vital Fiction and a "Big Huge Gaping Wound"

What can we deduce from these divergent reactions, and what can they tell us about the "gaping wound" that was revealed? What is the nature of this wound, and what does it suggest about conceptions of culture and difference, or about biomedical training, in the contemporary United States?

One provisional conclusion is that this course, and the guest lecture described above in particular, scratched away at the vital fiction that stands at the heart of the biomedical enterprise: the notion that medicine is universal, and that neither the background of the clinician nor that of the patient matters. Given the centrality of this vital fiction to the process of biomedical socialization, it comes as no surprise that a lecture emphasizing its constructedness would evoke such different responses—or that it would tap such deep and powerful counter-transferential reactions. Some residents welcomed the opportunity to discuss their discomfort with this vital fiction, including some who felt that sharing their own experiences of otherness, discrimination, or woundedness might help colleagues who had never had such experiences gain insight into the lived experience of being "othered." Residents for whom such experiences were foreign, however, sometimes felt threatened, or accused, or held personally accountable for persistent forms of discrimination. In this course, neither group, to the extent such groups did exist, had the opportunity to speak or hear the other out.

How, then, can we understand the "gaping wound" so central to this course? In my assessment, it is not simply about racism, or xenophobia, or any other form of particularized stereotyping and discrimination. Rather, it references something much deeper, a condition that permeates U.S. society in general, and U.S. biomedical training in particular: a generalized inability to speak about the enduring chasm between widely celebrated ideologies of egalitarianism and meritocracy, on the one hand, and the obstinate persistence of stereotypes, prejudices, and, most importantly (and most embarrassingly) structural inequalities, on the other.

Under ideal circumstances, both of the gaps that emerged—between a rhetoric of equality and enduring legacies of discrimination and inequality, on the one hand, and between experiences of woundedness and blame, on the other—could have provided a launching pad for rich discussion about the subtle relationship between difference and power in clinical encounters. Instead, some residents with "unmarked" (mainstream) identities felt personally accused and attacked when a provocative guest speaker exposed the structural foundations of persistent inequalities. Similarly, they were troubled by the implications that they themselves might have benefited from what McIntosh (2003 [1988]) has famously called the "invisible knapsack of white privilege." As a result, the group missed a valuable opportunity to consider the subtle, even silent ways in which attitudes of "white supremacy" that dominated in the country's founding era persist, albeit in attenuated form, to this day. Residents who felt "like guilt is being imposed upon them or projected onto them" had no real opportunity to express or discuss these feelings.

## TAKE-HOME INSIGHTS: THE NEED FOR A "SAFE SPACE"

Regardless of personal background, residents tended to rally around several suggestions that might have made a difference in the tone, tenor, and success of the course.

First, many would have preferred a more participatory classroom dynamic. In one resident's view, "when they would let us free flow it was actually quite useful." Yet the format of the course, in which either instructors or guest lecturers tended to hold the floor, "shut a lot of people down" and left "a lot of people not feeling safe and not having the place in their mind" to consider how course material might relate to their clinical work.

Another resident noted that "people are quite unsettled" at the end of each course session—so much so that the group often had trouble focusing at the beginning of the next hour's class. Before shifting gears, she said, everyone needed to "calm down and work [things] through." "I've seen it week in and week out," she continued, "but I'm not certain . . . why." As another colleague put it, without a "safe space" for discussion, and without adequate time to process the complex emotions that emerged, "it never seems to be quite ideal, the whole setup of putting something out there and then just leaving us with it."

This 10-minute overflow into the subsequent class is an especially useful finding. It suggests that the course did, in fact, speak to the full group by tapping into significant concerns and stirring up powerful feelings. Had the available class time and the classroom atmosphere been managed differently—for instance, by cultivating a "safe space" for discussion instead of relying on a didactic, knowledge-based approach—then this emotionally charged residue could have become a springboard for illuminating and potentially transformative discussion. To be effective, such a "safe space" would need to feel safe not only for residents eager to discuss the course's core concerns but also for those who were either uninterested or, more importantly, who felt threatened and simply tuned out.

Although a majority of residents strongly supported the suggestions outlined here, others (and sometimes the same individuals at different moments) expressed a desire for material that was more scientific, empirically grounded, and/or "generalizable." In other words, they had hoped for more robust "knowledge" rather than opportunities to gain deeper insight into their patients, themselves, or the impact of broader societal factors on the relationship between the two. A more successful approach, one might conclude, would meld the two reigning course paradigms and create a "safe space" that prioritized both goals.

## CONCLUSION: LOOKING INWARD, LOOKING UPSTREAM

Putting issues of culture and difference on the table for discussion among clinicians-in-training is a challenging prospect, especially in the post–civil rights era United States, where a myth of color-blind meritocracy holds sway. Many health care institutions have recognized the need to navigate difference more effectively in clinical settings—partly in response to the recognition that "culture counts" and partly in response to growing "hyperdiversity" (Good et al. 2011). Still, many clinician-educators remain stymied in their efforts to identify viable strategies that clinicians and clinicians-in-training can apply in their everyday clinical work. For these stakeholders, and especially given the serious deficiencies identified in many contemporary cultural competence efforts, we urgently need better ways of rendering these issues teachable and learnable. The high stakes of these issues became painfully clear as this chapter went press, just weeks after waves of outrage erupted following the highly publicized deaths of several young black men, and one young boy, under suspicious circumstances at the hands of police officers in Ferguson (Missouri), Staten Island (New York), and Cleveland (Ohio).

Whether cast in the ostensibly benign idiom of culture or the more ideologically charged idiom of "diversity," classroom discussions of these topics can immediately raise hackles and ignite passions, especially when they evoke sensitive issues—either directly or indirectly—such as political correctness, affirmative action, tokenism, invisible privilege, and liberal guilt. Indeed, the cultural sensitivity course examined here touched upon, and perhaps even aggravated, what one resident described as "a big huge gaping wound" festering beneath the surface of the course and, arguably, of American society more generally. As I understand it, this "gaping wound" refers not simply to entrenched legacies of racism and discrimination, but rather to a wide-ranging inability to speak about how American ideologies of equality persist alongside harmful stereotypes, subtle forms of discrimination, and—above all—entrenched structural inequalities.

What can we conclude from this discussion? One set of conclusions relates to cultural competence pedagogy. It is no easy task to carve out space for clinicians and clinicians-in-training to broach interpersonally sensitive issues of human difference, and instructors in courses like this one face a wide variety of formidable obstacles. First, as Dr. Graham's opening remarks suggest, the *universalizing biomedical gaze* tends to ignore, or even pretend away, social and cultural differences that might influence clinical rapport. Second is the underlying *nature of medical training,* which tends to simplify and schematize, whereas thinking about culture and difference demands that we problematize and complicate. Third, *clinicians, and especially clinicians-in-training, are often reluctant to make themselves vulnerable* by publicly discussing their own experiences of discrimination and/or invisible privilege. A final matter is *the crucial challenge of crafting a safe space* in which different groups of participants are willing to confront the "gaping wound" identified here and its implications.

Still, a much larger question looms. To what extent can courses like this one truly benefit patients who face barriers, sometimes formidable ones, to the health care they need? Is culture, in fact, the most significant barrier they face—or do structural vulnerabilities and structural barriers far outweigh the more subtle cultural differences that can interfere with clinical rapport? And if culture is not the most important obstacle, then are courses like this one worth the effort?

These tough questions push in the direction of a very different sort of conclusion. According to a growing line of critique, attempts to cultivate cultural competence often serve as little more than a fig leaf for much broader systemwide—indeed, societal—failures to address "horrendous health disparities." These disparities are caused by multiple forms of structural vulnerability and structural violence, including poverty, institutionalized racism and sexism, sociopolitical disenfranchisement, limited educational attainment and scientific literacy, patterns of residential segregation, and poor transportation infrastructure, among others.

From this broader angle, we must ask: how likely are cultural sensitivity or cultural competence courses to remediate health disparities and improve health outcomes? Should cultural competence courses remain a component of clinical training, or should they perhaps be replaced by courses that examine how social, political, and economic inequalities interact and become embodied in both epidemiological (Farmer 2003; Krieger 2005) and experiential terms (Csordas 1990; Leder 1984; Willen 2012)? In other words, should cultural competence courses be replaced by courses on the social determinants of health, syndemics (Singer 2009), and/or "structural competency" (Metzl and Hansen 2014)? Or, alternatively, do we need courses that cultivate *both* forms of critical consciousness—one looking upstream, to the structural causes of clinically relevant phenomena, the other looking inward to consider the role of difference and counter-transference in face-to-face moments of clinical interaction?

These are among the most challenging, and pressing, questions that need to be considered if mental health professionals, and clinicians in other arenas, hope to play a meaningful role as individuals or as professional communities in redressing today's deep, complex, and still difficult-to-talk-about problems of structural inequality, especially in the health domain.

## ACKNOWLEDGMENTS

This chapter is a substantially revised version of an earlier piece published in 2013 as "Confronting a 'Big Huge Gaping Wound': Emotion and Anxiety in a Cultural Sensitivity Course for Psychiatry Residents," *Culture, Medicine, and Psychiatry*, 37 (2): 253–279.

## *References*

Bullon, A. (2013). Learning by teaching an unsuccessful "cultural sensitivity" course. *Culture, Medicine, and Psychiatry*, 37: 280–287.

Csordas, T. J. (1990). Embodiment as a paradigm for anthropology. *Ethos*, 18: 5–47.

DeSouza, R. (2008). Wellness for all: the possibilities of cultural safety and cultural competence in New Zealand. *Journal of Research in Nursing*, 13 (2): 125–135.

Farmer, P. (2003). *Pathologies of Power*. Berkeley: University of California Press.

Good, M.-J. D. (2001). The biotechnical embrace. *Culture, Medicine, and Psychiatry*, 25: 395–410.

Good, M.-J. D., James, C., Good, B. J., and Becker, A. E. (2003). The culture of medicine and racial, ethnic, and class disparities in healthcare. In B. D. Smedley, A. Y. Stith, and A. R. Nelson (eds.), *Unequal Treatment: Confronting Racial and Ethnic Disparities in Health Care*. Washington, DC: Institute of Medicine, National Academies Press.

Good, M.-J. D., Willen, S. S., Hannah, S., Vickery, K., and Park, L. T. (eds.) (2011). *Shattering Culture: American Medicine Responds to Cultural Diversity*. New York: Russell Sage Foundation.

Kleinman, A., and Benson, P. (2006). Anthropology in the clinic: the problem of cultural competency and how to fix it. *PLoS Medicine*, 3: e294.

Krieger, N. (2005). Embodiment: a conceptual glossary for epidemiology. *Journal of Epidemiology and Community Health*, 59: 350–355.

Leder, D. (1984). Medicine and paradigms of embodiment. *Journal of Medicine and Psychiatry*, 9: 29–43.

McIntosh, P. (2003 [1988]). White privilege: unpacking the invisible knapsack. In A. Podolefsky, and P. J. Brown (eds.), *Applying Cultural Anthropology*, pp. 125–128. Boston: McGraw-Hill.

Metzl, J. M., and Hansen, H. (2014). Structural competency: theorizing a new medical engagement with stigma and inequality. *Social Science and Medicine* 103: 126–133.

Singer, M. (2009). *Introduction to Syndemics: A Critical Systems Approach to Public and Community Health*. New York: John Wiley and Sons.

Tervalon, M., and Murray-Garcia, J. (1998). Cultural humility vs. cultural competence: a critical distinction in defining physician training outcomes in multicultural education. *Journal of Health Care for the Poor and Underserved*, 9: 117–125.

Waters, M. C. (1999). *Black Identities: West Indian Immigrant Dreams and American Realities*. New York/Cambridge, Massachusetts: Russell Sage Foundation/Harvard University Press.

Willen, S. S. (2012). Introduction: migration, "illegality," and health: mapping embodied vulnerability and debating health-related deservingness. *Social Science and Medicine*, 74: 805–811.

Willen, S. S., Bullon, A., and Good, M.-J. D. (2010). Opening up a huge can of worms: reflections on a "cultural sensitivity" course for psychiatry residents. *Harvard Review of Psychiatry*, 18: 247–253.

Willen, S. S., and Carpenter-Song, E. (2013). Cultural competence in action: "lifting the hood" on four case studies in medical education. *Culture, Medicine, and Psychiatry*, 37: 241–252.

# Part III

## TASK-SHARING AND ALTERNATIVE CARE MODELS

## Brandon A. Kohrt and Emily Mendenhall

"**N**o health without mental health!" is the rallying cry of many global mental health advocates, practitioners, and researchers (Prince et al. 2007). This political statement is meant to draw attention not only to the lack of recognition of mental illness as a social concern but also to the severe shortage of mental health services and practitioners. The term "treatment gap" emphasizes this issue by highlighting the gap between the availability and the need for mental health services, which exceeds 75% in most parts of the world (Kohn et al. 2004) and can be as high as 90% in the low-income countries, such as Ethiopia (Alem et al. 2009). A fundamental underpinning of the treatment gap is the enormous scarcity and inequality in the distribution of specialist mental health professionals, such as psychiatrists, psychologists, and psychiatric nurses (Kakuma et al. 2011). The current estimated shortage of 1.18 million specialist mental health personnel (Kakuma et al. 2011) is not equally distributed: in low-income countries, the median number of psychiatrists per 100,000 population is 0.05, in lower-middle-income countries 0.54, in upper-middle-income countries 2.03, and in high-income countries 8.59 (WHO 2011).

Even when care is available, it often does not meet the needs for the local socioeconomic context, it is not culturally appropriate, and treatment (such as medication and psychotherapy) is not evidence based; thus, in some cases, care may not only be unhelpful, it may be harmful, as discussed in Part II. Recognition of the size of this personnel deficit and of the lack of appropriate care in most settings has led to support of the concept of *task-sharing* as a mental health care delivery solution, which is the focus of many ethnographic accounts put forward in this section. Task-sharing, also referred to as *task-shifting*, is the process of training primary care and community health workers to assume some health care responsibilities traditionally delivered by specialists (WHO 2008, 2010). Global mental

*Global Mental Health: Anthropological Perspectives*, edited by Brandon A. Kohrt and Emily Mendenhall, 255–258. © 2015 Left Coast Press, Inc. All rights reserved.

health advocates argue that transforming the role of specialists from service-delivery to public mental health leadership in low- and middle-income countries provides a "rational" solution to the mental health treatment gap (Lancet Global Mental Health Group 2007). This role involves designing and managing mental health treatment programs, building clinical capacity in primary care settings, supervising and assuring quality of mental health services, and providing consultation and referral pathways (Patel 2009). Then nonspecialists—such as community health volunteers, peer helpers, social workers, midwives, auxiliary health staff, teachers, primary care workers, and persons without a professional service role—can deliver mental health care to a larger body of people struggling with mental illness.

The concept of task-sharing mental health care is not a novel development of the current global mental health movement or of infectious disease global health initiatives. In the 1970s, international efforts to improve mental health care were initiated by the World Health Organization. Immediately before the Primary Health Care (PHC) strategy adopted with the Alma-Ata Declaration in 1978, the WHO attempted to raise awareness through a major report entitled "Mental Health Collaborative Study for Strategies on Extending Mental Health Care" (Murthy and Wig 1983). This report proposed the integration of mental health activities into the duties of community health workers. Similar WHO studies proposed the incorporation of traditional medical practitioners into primary health care (Westermeyer 1976), although this idea was met with considerable critique (Singer 1977). Interestingly, in the wave of reform activities of the 1970 and 1980s, emphases were placed on narrative-based evaluation (Sriram et al. 1990), problem- rather than disease-focused algorithms (Essex and Gosling 1983), and aspects of therapeutic alliance (Murthy and Wig 1983), elements that are not as clearly articulated in the current model. With the influx of funding and support for HIV/ AIDS, task-sharing took on a central role in combating HIV/AIDS and other infectious diseases such as malaria and tuberculosis (Aggarwal and Kohrt 2013; Raviola, Becker, and Farmer 2011; WHO 2008). These approaches contributed to the design of the WHO strategic action plan, the current mental health Gap Action Programme (mhGAP) approach, which emphasizes task-shifting in global mental health (WHO 2010).

Few anthropological studies have examined the challenges and opportunities associated with task-sharing mental health services. In this final section, we explore task-sharing, based on examples from Liberia, Haiti, Ethiopia, Mozambique, and the United States. Here we will introduce some important ethnographic encounters around task-sharing and delivery of mental health services. Kohrt and Jallah's

"People, Praxis, and Power in Global Mental Health" (Chapter 15) introduces the World Health Organization's mhGAP, a global strategy for providing mental health services at the community and primary care levels. They discuss both the utility of such a program and local challenges in its implementation. In Chapter 16, "'Thinking too much' in the Central Plateau," Kaiser and McLean describe how task-sharing mental health care to people working in the community can enhance people's mental health and how an apprenticeship model for training such workers is crucial. Maes, in "Task-Shifting in Global Health" (Chapter 17), describes some of the challenges of employing community health workers who—in the Ethiopian context—are unpaid workers expected to glean only personal satisfaction from their work; in many cases, food insecurity and mental distress surface as a result of their work. Kalofonos takes this further in "We Can't Find This Spirit of Health" (Chapter 18), describing the need to attend to the mental health of community health workers in order to provide economic and food security for people working in community health; this elevates the morale not only of volunteers and other health workers but also of patients. Finally, in "Shared Humanity" (Chapter 19), Myers introduces the importance of nonspecialist mental health workers in the United States through a discussion of a peer-provider model for psychosis.

## References

Aggarwal, N. K., and Kohrt, B. A. (2013). Medical diplomacy and global mental health: from community and national institutions to regional centers of excellence. *Community Mental Health Journal*, 49 (6): 805–814.

Alem, A., Kebede, D., Fekadu, A., Shibre, T., Fekadu, D., Beyero, T., and Kullgren, G. (2009). Clinical course and outcome of schizophrenia in a predominantly treatment naïve cohort in Ethiopia. *Schizophrenia Bulletin*, 35: 646–654.

Essex, B., and Gosling, H. (1983). An algorithmic method for management of mental health problems in developing countries. *British Journal of Psychiatry*, 143: 451–459.

Kakuma, R., Minas, H., van Ginneken, N., Dal Poz, M. R., Desiraju, K., Morris, J. E., and Scheffler, R. M. (2011). Human resources for mental health care: current situation and strategies for action. *The Lancet*, 378 (9803): 1654–1663.

Kohn, R., Saxena, S., Levav, I., and Saraceno, B. (2004). The treatment gap in mental health care. *Bulletin of the World Health Organization*, 82: 858–866.

Lancet Global Mental Health Group. (2007). Scale up services for mental disorders: a call for action. *The Lancet*, 370: 1241–1252.

Murthy, R. S., and Wig, N. N. (1983). The WHO collaborative study on strategies for extending mental health care, IV: a training approach to enhancing the availability of mental health manpower in a developing country. *American Journal of Psychiatry*, 140 (11): 1486–1490.

Patel, V. (2009). The future of psychiatry in low- and middle-income countries. *Psychological Medicine*, 39 (11): 1759–1762.

Prince, M., Patel, V., Saxena, S., Maj, M., Maselko, J., Phillips, M. R., and Rahman, A. (2007). No health without mental health. *The Lancet*, 370 (9590): 859–877.

Raviola, G., Becker, A. E., and Farmer, P. (2011). A global scope for global health—including mental health. *The Lancet*, 378 (9803): 1613–1615.

Singer, P. (1977). *Traditional Healing: New Science or New Colonialism? Essays in Critique of Medical Anthropology*. Buffalo, New York: Trado-Medic Books.

Sriram, T. G., Moily, S., Kumar, G. S., Chandrashekar, C. R., Isaac, M. K., and Murthy, R. S. (1990). Training of primary health care medical officers in mental health care: errors in clinical judgment before and after training. *General Hospital Psychiatry*, 12 (6): 384–389.

Westermeyer, J. (ed.). (1976). *Anthropology and Mental Health: Setting a New Course*. The Hague: Mouton.

World Health Organization (WHO). (2008). *Task Shifting: Rational Redistribution of Tasks among Health Workforce Teams: Global Recommendations and Guidelines*. Geneva: World Health Organization.

——. (2010). *mhGAP Intervention Guide for Mental, Neurological and Substance-Use Disorders in Non-Specialized Health Settings*. Geneva: World Health Organization.

——. (2011). Mental Health Atlas. Geneva: Department of Mental Health and Substance Abuse. http://www.who.int/mental_health/publications/mental_health_atlas_2011/en/.

Chapter 15

# People, Praxis, and Power in Global Mental Health: Anthropology and the Experience Gap

Brandon A. Kohrt, with Reverend Bill Jallah

REVEREND BILL JALLAH, A LIBERIAN religious leader and agricultural social entrepreneur in his late fifties, and I, an American anthropologist and psychiatrist, stood in front of a room of 34 community health volunteers, nurses, midwives, and persons living with mental illness in a hospital annex in Greenville, the headquarters of Sinoe County, Liberia. We were part of a team training these nonspecialist health workers to deliver mental health services in a *task-sharing* initiative.

In February 2014, a few months before the Ebola virus disease outbreak consumed the country's health system, Reverend Bill and I had traveled with other mental health trainers for 10 hours on a dirt road from the capital, Monrovia, to Greenville, a town of 20,000 people on the southeastern coast of Liberia. In Greenville, we saw the remnants of a planned city with wide, paved streets, grassy median divides, and a city-wide water system as evidenced by fire hydrants on the sidewalks. It was a beautiful coastal town in the 1970s. From the 1980s through the early 2000s, the infrastructure of Greenville and the rest of the country was devastated by years of civil war during the presidencies of Samuel Doe and Charles Taylor. Now, a decade after the political violence and Taylor's departure, many of the houses still have not been rebuilt. The roads have not been repaired. Water no longer runs to houses, let alone to the fire hydrants. Electricity is limited to businesses and houses that can afford gasoline-powered generators that hum intermittently throughout the city.

The health system and mental health services also were ravaged by the years of political violence and subsequent economic deprivation. Prior to the war, there had been functional but limited mental health services in Liberia. In 1980, there was one psychiatric facility outside of Monrovia, the Catherine Mills Rehabilitation Hospital, which was staffed by three psychiatrists. By the time of Charles Taylor's

*Global Mental Health: Anthropological Perspectives*, edited by Brandon A. Kohrt and Emily Mendenhall, 259–276. © 2015 Left Coast Press, Inc. All rights reserved.

departure in 2003, Catherine Mills was destroyed and there was only one psychiatrist for the population of 4 million.

Our objective in Greenville was to conduct a five-day mental health training for primary care workers. The training was based in part on the curriculum of the World Health Organization's Mental Health Gap Action Programme (mhGAP) (WHO 2010), which includes an implementation guide (*mhGAP-IG*), a 121-page manual for a 35- to 40-hour training curriculum. WHO designed mhGAP to facilitate delivery of mental health services in primary care and other settings by utilizing health workers who are not mental health specialists. This is one example of task-shifting, or task-sharing, in global health, wherein primary care workers, community health workers, and community members who are not health workers deliver services traditionally performed by experts in health care systems in high-income countries. Our goal of the training was to raise awareness about detecting and managing some aspects of mental illness within the context of primary care using mhGAP and other tools.

This endeavor in Sinoe County is one example of a growing global movement to train nonspecialist health workers to share responsibilities for mental health care in low-resource settings. WHO previously attempted task-sharing-type programs, such as the WHO Collaborative Study on Strategies for Extending Mental Health Care in the 1970s and 1980s (Murthy and Wig 1983). However, it was only after touted success of task-shifting to address service needs for HIV/AIDS and other infectious disease (WHO 2008) and attention to the economic burden of mental illness (Murray and Lopez 1996) that mental health care began to receive much needed attention. The second decade of the 21st century has witnessed a burgeoning of these programs in sub-Saharan Africa, South Asia, Southeast Asia, Latin America. and the Caribbean. This represents the confluence of new tools such as WHO mhGAP, increased funding for mental health from development agencies such as the United Kingdom's Department for International Development (DfID), the European Union, and the Canadian government, and the research prioritization and funding from foundations such as the Wellcome Trust and the U.S. National Institute of Mental Health (NIMH).

This moment in the history of mental health care presents hope for people living with mental illness, and their families, throughout the world. This global mental health movement is also the site of both internal reflection and external criticism from clinicians, development workers, and academics. In this chapter, we explore debates in global mental health grounded within the context of our experiences in Liberia. We argue that only through firsthand experiences is it possible to progress beyond rhetoric into praxis to minimize potential harm and maximize potential benefit of the global mental health movement. We begin with Reverend

Bill's personal account and then connect this with current critiques in the field of global mental health.

## LIVING WITH MENTAL ILLNESS IN LIBERIA

Reverend Bill and I had traveled to Greenville with government mental health clinicians and staff from The Carter Center Mental Health Program Liberia Initiative. Beginning in 2010, The Carter Center, founded by former President Jimmy Carter and his wife, Rosalynn, an advocate for persons living with mental illness, partnered with the Liberia Ministry of Health and Social Welfare (MoHSW) to facilitate capacity building in government mental health services. The program was developed and implemented in accord with Liberia's National Mental Health Policy and National Mental Health Strategic Plan. The goal was to develop the capacity of mid-level government health workers (nurses and physicians' assistants) to assume responsibilities for mental health services. Throughout the years of political violence and in the decade following, the majority of mental health care had been deliverered through nongovernmental organizations (NGOs) rather than incorporated into government services.

The Carter Center program was intended to be different from these NGO programs both in its incorporation into government facilities and in the development of a training program and educators who would sustain the program after The Carter Center's departure. In addition, there was focus on promoting mental health policy and multi-tiered anti-stigma reduction to facilitate positive collaborations with religious leaders, journalists, and police (Kohrt et al. 2015). Unlike the mhGAP trainings, which are based on a one-week curriculum for primary care workers, The Carter Center mental health training program was a six-month didactic and clinical program, supplemented with ongoing supervision and continuing educational opportunities after graduation.

The presence of these mid-level mental health clinicians was crucial for the mhGAP-based task-sharing. Without these clinicians, there would have been inadequate supervision to safely and effectively implement the contents of brief mhGAP-style trainings. In Liberia, only after four years of training mid-level mental health clinicians, which resulted in 150 mental health experts throughout the country, did brief mental health trainings begin. At that time, mid-level mental health clinicians were available in Sinoe County to supervise the mhGAP trainees at a ratio of two to four new trainees to one mental health clinician. The process in Liberia demonstrates that considerable work is needed in some contexts to prepare for types of task-sharing such as mhGAP.

Supervision by clinicians with expertise in mental health care was not the only prerequisite for an mhGAP-based training. There was also a need to address the stigma against mental illness that is so pervasive throughout the world. Reverend Bill's participation in the training was part of an anti-stigma component that we had added to the mhGAP curriculum. In addition to his identity as a religious leader and person who used agriculture to advance human rights, Bill also has an identity as a person living with mental illness and a consumer of mental health services. Reverend Bill became involved in this project and other activities with The Carter Center Mental Health Program through his activism and work with people in disadvantaged situations. The Liberian National Mental Health Strategic Plan called for supporting advocacy groups of persons with mental illness (also known as "mental health service consumers") and their family members. As a person living with mental illness working with The Carter Center, Bill actively participated in trainings such as this one in Sinoe County, as well as trainings with journalists, pharmacists, and other health workers. Through interactions with Bill and other mental health consumers, trainees came to see the human side of living with mental illness.

After a day of training the Sinoe County health workers, Reverend Bill and I returned to the concrete building that had recently been turned into a six-room hotel. Bill and I sat outside on plastic chairs and talked as boys driving motorcycle taxis sped up and down the street. Bill described how different his life had been nine years earlier. He gave me an extended version of the story he had told the trainees earlier that day.

> From 2005 . . . , there was a little stability [in my life]. My wife was convinced that I could try to go into work for other people. So I accepted this job with Save the Children for their school trainer in poultry management [for war-affected youth], I did that successfully for one year [in Monrovia]. Then, they were looking for a trainer to go to Lofa County. Then I accepted it. My wife and children said, "Let's give dad a chance." It was just a one-year contract. So I went for this one. All was fine as it relates to work. My wife was not there; my children were not there. So I just overworked, overworked, overworked. Sometimes it was stressful. I got too caught up in what I was doing and I stopped taking my medication. I went for one month and nothing happened, then two months and nothing happened.

> But there was a lot of competition [among the workers]. There was a little bit of jealousy because of the rapport I had with the kids. I had a project plan to grow peanuts, and when the boys came, we asked for land for this. The people gave us land. I was doing poultry management, I was doing swamp development, and then I engaged even in extra activities. The other guys were not getting cooperation from their kids. They were talking about me, "What is this guy doing?" To hurt me, they did this thing—we only had one motorbike, so they restricted the motorbike from my usage. Then, the lady who was cooking for the children that

I employed . . . [t]hey threatened to remove the lady and bring another lady from Fuya, a Kisi girl. When I found out, I told her, "If they will take you from me just because you are not Kisi, then I might as well just pack and go home. I came here not principally to fight about things like this. I came to help the kids." She said, "Don't go. If you go, who will help these kids?" So then, I got into a confused state. Just imagine, I am not taking my medicine for two, now three months.

Then I started experiencing that progression of mood disorder. But for some reason, I did not catch myself to go back on the medicine. When I am experiencing mood disorder, then what happens is that my mind opens up a lot. My mind opens up to be more intellectual, my understanding goes wide, so I was enjoying this, and I forgot that this was a road—a path—to danger. So then, the very day that a UN [United Nations] team was coming to evaluate our work, I went into crisis. Early in the morning, I got up. I had organized a drama for our kids. I had a lot of stuff for them. I had them lined up the days before. I had practiced this and practiced this. I was so excited about. That morning—guess what? I was standing at the entrance to the poultry farm—in my briefs! Can you imagine that? With my pesticide here, with my spray can here, with other stuff, valuable effects, everything for the project! These strange ideas started coming, "Oh, what would be an impressive reception for these people?" And, that is how when people got up in the morning, they saw all this strange, strange stuff that I had done when I got up at 5:00 in the morning.

They came and suddenly said, "Oh no! The spirit has captured this guy! You see? He is crazy now!" They kept saying, "Crazy! Crazy! Crazy!" They started making things worse in my own consciousness. I was standing and the people were just backing and staying away and staring and talking. The more they did that, the more they were further irritating. When I tried to go close to them to hear what they were saying, they thought that I was going to be violent with them. So they started throwing stones at me. When they started throwing stones at me, I started darting back and forth.

Bill went on to explain that the onlookers thought that he had become afflicted by spirits of people killed during the Liberian civil war.

In that area, there were many harmful things done by ULIMO-J [United Liberation Movement for Democracy in Liberia—Roosevelt Johnson faction]. The ULIMO-J had done a lot of harm there and killed a lot of people and warring factions. Most of the children we were training were all orphans from all the killing done by the ULIMO-J during the war. At this time, they thought people who killed a lot in the war—they thought that the spirits would haunt them. So, that is what they thought was happening to me.

So these people started throwing stones. Then I started getting in a violent mood. I thought I was going to fight the whole community. Then the whole community joined, by this time it was about 8:00 in the morning. . . . I was dodging these rocks and moving toward them. I would pick up something, and have a piece of stone in my hand for self-defense. Well, the town [people] and the police came. The police had me arrested. The police were arresting me and beating me. They took me and carried me to the cell and put me in jail. I stayed there the whole day. It was on a Monday. Toward the evening I think around 8:30 PM, after the [UN] guys had come to visit our field office and then left, some parents whose children I had been training, they came [to the jail]. Then I explained that I had been a mental health patient and had stopped taking my drugs. They took me to the hospital and put me through a lot of tests—malaria, etc. I was then brought home.

Everything was quiet after I started taking medicines when I got home back in Monrovia. I was very, very embarrassed. The church was embarrassed. . . . I took some time to sleep. [Then a few months later] in 2006 I made a definite decision—inasmuch as we need to drink water and to eat food every day in order to sustain, I am going to take my medicine everyday come what may. I promised my brother, I am never going to embarrass you in that way. Since that time, I have been committed from 2006 to now, eight years. We are planning to celebrate my tenth stability year. It will be in 2016, it will be my 10-year anniversary. It will be a big celebration.

Imagine, in 1972 if I had clinicians [like the ones we are training] with all of this psychoeducation that we are giving to them, I would not have gone 30 years [without regular treatment]. Every time I look at those 30 years as wasted years. One day I will pray and say God, I want you to paste those 30 years that I lost, back to my age today—from age 22 to age 52. They were all wasted years. I am now 59. I want the Lord to replenish these years with all of the vitality, strength, and influence to contribute to myself, my family, my work, and my environment.

This was Reverend Bill's account of a manic episode that was pivotal in how he perceived and managed his bipolar affective disorder. Reverend Bill's personal experiences are a starting point for an anthropological exploration of critiques and challenges in global mental health. Global mental health has been built in part on the concept of a *treatment gap*, which is the discrepancy between the putative burden of mental health problems and the availability of evidence-based treatments (Kohn et al. 2004). A problem of generalized critiques and universal strategies in global mental health is an *experience gap*. Some aspects of current critiques are too distant from the experiences of persons living with mental illness in low- and middle-income countries. Thus, the critiques are not ideally suited to improve actual lives and reduce suffering for people such as Bill. Similarly, global mental health research and intervention will be most successful when endeavors strive to narrow the experience gap among those who design policies, deliver care, and receive care.

Bill's story is one example of focusing on experiences to evaluate and disseminate the accounts and challenges of persons at different levels of health care design, delivery, and utilization. This approach reflects anthropological sensitivities that are relevant for decreasing the experience gap in global mental health. My role with The Carter Center had been to apply an anthropological lens to understand the experiences of people living with mental illness in Liberia. I conducted ethnographic and other qualitative research throughout the country. Working with Bill and others, we documented help-seeking practices, including biomedical services and traditional healing. We recorded idioms of distress and other cultural labels used to describe mental illness. We also explored the social status of persons with mental illness, including the impact of stigma, and the role of stakeholders—family, police, and community leaders—in the support of persons with mental illness. As a cultural psychiatrist, I incorporated this ethnographic research into training Liberian health care workers about mental illness and treatment.

Below, we examine three critiques of global mental health from an ethnographic perspective. The critiques are (1) appropriateness of psychiatric categories cross-culturally; (2) the reframing of social problems as medical problems; and (3) the role of psychotropic medication and pharmaceuticals in global mental health (cf. Patel 2014).

## PSYCHIATRIC DIAGNOSTIC CATEGORIES AND CULTURE

The cross-cultural relevance of psychiatric categories, such as bipolar disorder, is one of the common critiques levied against global mental health. This debate is not new. For over a century, researchers have questioned the applicability of psychiatric categories across cultures, in view of the concepts of universality, on the one hand, and cultural relativism, on the other. Moving from these conceptual poles, it is helpful to look at the specific example of Reverend Bill's experience. For Reverend Bill, the label of "bipolar disorder" was employed by a Liberian psychiatrist to frame the symptoms and treatment, in this case a psychotropic medication referred to as a "mood stabilizer." Bill adopted this term to self-describe his suffering. This is part of his illness model: he perceives medication as improving his ability to function in his occupational, familial, educational, and social activities. When he stopped taking his medication, the symptoms returned and he was unable to function in these activities. In addition, he embarrassed himself and his family. For Bill, the labels of "bipolar" and "mood disorder" helped him, as well as his relatives, to clarify what behaviors could be attributed to him and what to his illness. This guided his family—in terms of predicting behavior and deciding when it was advisable to include Bill in household activities, based on attribution of agency during periods of stabilization and relapse—and helped his clinicians to determine what type of treatment he should receive. By all accounts—Bill's, his family's, and his clinicians'—his symptoms responded to the medication.

Yet, Bill's story begs us to question if there are alternatives in Liberian cultures and languages that may better encapsulate Bill's experience. One hypothesis is that local idioms would be more appropriate in terms of Bill's social experience, his own understanding of the condition, and in guiding local treatments. In our work on idioms of distress and terms for psychological suffering in Liberian English, we did not encounter any terminology that strongly overlapped with the symptom clusters of bipolar disorder. When asking Bill what others called him, he said they called him "Crazy, *krackey*, dump pile hero, Larry, and *zepsey*." All of these are stigmatizing terms. None of them helps identify a specific treatment. In addition, these terms are applied to the individual rather than to an illness. Whereas the term "bipolar" can be used to distinguish between the person and the illness, these Liberian English terms conflate the person and illness. Therefore, the social consequences are more severe when terms such as "dump pile hero" or "*zepsey*" are applied, as compared with the term "bipolar" in this context.

Was there a better locally appropriate treatment associated with a local diagnosis that would have been as or more effective than mood stabilizer medication? Bill had pursued traditional healing with great expense on multiple occasions. After his manic episode, Bill visited a traditional healer, a *zoe* herbalist, for the last time with hopes of finding a cure:

> [After I came home] I said, I am not going to any herbalist. I know what happened in the past. It was my own fault to go to the herbalists in the past. But then my wife said, "The thing that confuses me is that there is no healing. Even though when you are on the medicine, you are doing fine, why are you taking medicine all your life? If there is someone who says they can cure you, maybe we can go for it." So she got convinced and [my family] said they would take me to this faith healer.

> They took me to the guy. He had all these talisman. I am familiar with these. He was a Loma *zoe* [traditional healer] from my ethnic group. He said, "Bill, the problems stem from your family. There is somebody in your family that really knows that you are progressive and you are successful in life. He is jealous so he bewitched you. I am going to make this solution today so you never have this problem anymore. I want you to bring home a black chicken and one red chicken. I will perform the ritual, and I will give you seven days—I will give you seven

days, and then you will bury that guy." He said that I would bury that guy. He [meant that guy] will die in seven days. He said my uncle bewitched me.

I said to him, so you are telling me to bring this black chicken and this red chicken, and you will kill my uncle! I am so confused. I told the herbalist, "So you think I will go to the extent of killing somebody! I don't want to do that." The herbalist said to my family, "You are all a part of this thing here. You are a part of this thing. The man is supposed to die then Bill will be free." We said "No." We went back home.

Bill laughed as he told me the end of this story. I had asked him if there were options other than medication that could have helped. He explained that he had tried them all. When the recommendation came to kill his uncle to cure his bipolar disorder, he knew it was time to stop looking for other options and take his medication.

Bill's experience points to a divide in cultural applicability of common mental disorders (such as depression and anxiety) versus severe and persistent mental illness (such as bipolar disorder and schizophrenia). In Summerfield's (2008) critique of the lack of an evidence base for global mental health, he argues that there is better support for the treatment of severe mental illness than for common mental disorders. However, we argue that it would be inappropriate to make this claim simply based on Bill's experience. Instead, one needs to examine the broader research and clinical issues related severe mental illness versus common mental disorders.

First, there is an important body of cross-cultural psychiatry research on the problematic diagnoses of bipolar disorder versus schizophrenia. In the United Kingdom, black Caribbean islanders were more likely to be diagnosed with schizophrenia compared with white Britons with the same symptom profile, who would be diagnosed with bipolar disorder more frequently than schizophrenia (Bell et al. 2008; Louden 1995). Similarly, in the United States, African-Americans are more likely to be diagnosed with schizophrenia, whereas European-Americans with the same symptoms are labeled with bipolar disorder (Bell et al. 2008). In the United Kingdom, this differential led to the anti-racist psychiatry movement (Fernando 2013) (for a challenge to these claims, see Selten and Hoek 2008; Singh et al. 2007). And, in the United States, one expectation for the more recent versions of the *Diagnostic and Statistical Manual of Mental Disorders* (*DSM-3* onward) was that they would help to reduce bias and increase the reliability of diagnoses across populations and among clinicians (American Psychiatric Association 1980, 2013). Even though some anthropologists consider the *DSM* a tool of cultural imperialism, it is important to consider the kinds of practices that were commonplace before symptom-based diagnostic criteria became widely used.

Therefore, a lesson learned from Bill regarding cross-cultural psychiatric categories is not that certain disorders may have more or less cultural applicability. Any label, whether for severe or mild mental illness, has potential to be misapplied or manipulated. Instead, what we should consider from Bill are the following two questions: (1) *What are the personal, familial, and professional impacts of a psychiatric label?* How does the term improve or threaten the individual's self-concept or help-seeking? How does the term affect how others interact with the person, especially family interactions? And, how does a term shape institutional response for health care providers, as well as for employment, educational institutions, and social service institutions? For Bill in Liberia, "bipolar" was advantageous over local terms on multiple levels. In contrast, in other settings, a local idiom may be more helpful for self-concept, family response, and help-seeking.

A second question is (2) *How does the label ultimately influence the type and outcome of treatment?* Does the label lead to a treatment that benefits the patient and family? In cases of misapplication of the label "bipolar," as happens with children and persons with substance abuse disorders, the label can lead to ineffective and potentially dangerous treatment. In Bill's case, the label of "bipolar" led to helpful treatment, whereas other labels did not help for social status or for guiding treatment.

## MEDICALIZATION OF SOCIAL PROBLEMS

Another critique of global mental health is that it can represent a medicalization of social problems (Kleinman 2012). Medicalization is a topic frequently studied in medical anthropology. It refers to framing a problem from a medical perspective, implying a categorical distinction between disease/disorder versus health. It also implies a need for some form of treatment (Kleinman and Desjarlais 1994; Scheper-Hughes and Lock 1987). For example, the anthropologist Margaret Lock (2001) studied menopause among Japanese women, revealing that the experience of menopause, previously considered a natural part of life and not considered particularly distressing, was reframed in the late 20th century as a medical problem requiring medical intervention.

The concerns around medicalization are that it diverts attention and resources from addressing social origins of distress and instead frames suffering at the individual level, thus removing blame from social problems. It leads to stigmatizing individuals and groups rather than drawing attention to political, economic, and other social problems. I have witnessed examples of this firsthand in high-resource settings: child psychiatric facilities in the United States. Some children subjected to prolonged hospitalizations had psychological distress and behavioral problems, but did not unequivocally meet criteria for a psychiatric disorder. For these children, there were insufficient resources to address issues such as parental drug use, community violence, and lack of appropriate services in schools—so the children were labeled as mentally ill and hospitalized. This could lead to lengthy hospitalizations while parents delayed accepting children back home or while waiting for group home placements, and these services were considerably expensive: the cost of hospitalizing a child for a week is comparable to six months of salary for a teacher's aide.

However, one needs to be cautious about interchangeably applying interpretations of medicalization that occur in high-income settings or medicalization by oppressive regimes for political control to claims for widespread problems in global mental health. A person living in poverty and receiving mental health care need not be synonymous with the medicalization of poverty. The most comprehensive studies of poverty and mental health have been conducted by South African psychiatrist Crick Lund and colleagues (Lund et al. 2010, 2011). Using techniques of meta-analysis, they have shown that poverty alleviation programs, as a group, do not have a consistent positive effect on reducing the burden of mental illness. However, it is difficult to summarize the field because there are such varied approaches to poverty alleviation. Some, such as conditional cash transfer and asset promotion programs, may be beneficial to reduce mental health problems, but current studies are inconclusive. In contrast, Lund and colleagues show that mental health interventions consistently show improvement in economic indicators. In every study they identified, mental health interventions increased economic indicators, with varying levels of magnitude and significance. Therefore, appropriate treatment of mental illness likely has a benefit on economic and other social problems.

Anthropological inquiry through ethnography and other qualitative research methods is crucial in considering the issue of medicalization. How do poverty alleviation measures actually affect daily lives and mental illness risk factors? Similarly, how does the experience of mental health treatment affect personal and family social, occupational, and economic activities? If mental health treatment facilitates social and economic engagement, then it is likely to help reduce symptoms and social risk factors. If psychiatric treatment removes individuals from opportunities for socioeconomic engagement (e.g., through hospitalization), then this type of medicalization likely threatens individual well-being and represents neglect of social problems. For Bill, his success would not be possible without appropriate psychiatric care, including medication. Simultaneously, Bill is a motivated and skilled leader and social entrepreneur. If he were unable to meet his and his family's economic needs, then his psychiatric symptoms would likely be considerably worse because of higher stress levels and reduced resources to pay for medicine and care.

## PHARMACEUTICALS IN GLOBAL MENTAL HEALTH

The next critique of global mental health concerns the role of psychiatric medication and pharmaceutical companies. Studies have repeatedly demonstrated that pharmaceutical marketing practices change the behavior of both health care providers and patients (Adair and Holmgren 2005; Chren and Landefeld 1994; Huang 2000). The use of financial incentives, expensive gifts, vacations and travel, and even providing a meal influence how physicians in the United States choose among medications in all fields of medicine, not just psychiatry. It is also clear that pharmaceutical companies are primarily profit-making institutions and have historically had the highest profit margin of any industry: the top 10 drug companies garnered profits margins of 17%, as compared with median profit margins of 3.1% for all other industries on the Fortune 500 list (Angell 2005; Pattison and Warren 2003). While the issues of influence and profit are not unique to mental health, it seems that other health fields have not had to struggle with the pressures of pharmaceutical influence to the same degree. For example, global health efforts in HIV treatment programs benefit pharmaceutical companies through mechanisms such as the U.S. President's Emergency Plan for AIDS Relief (PEPFAR), and the global health efforts are influenced by the work of pharmaceutical companies (Dietrich 2007). Nevertheless, global mental health suffers from concerns about the role of pharmaceuticals to a much larger extent.

Again, we should reflect upon the experience of Reverend Bill and others in Liberia to consider how best to engage with this critique. From Bill's personal account, the issue of over-medication, being forced to take medications, or feeling manipulated into taking medication was not part of his narrative. For Bill, the major problems have been the opposite—he has had trouble getting access to medication. This is a problem for nearly all Liberians. Less than 8% of health facilities in Liberia carry at least one type of psychiatric medication, and that includes medication for epilepsy (Clinton Health Access Initiative 2011). Most facilities are unable to treat patients with psychiatric and neurological illnesses because of the lack of medication. When medicines are available, they are often expired drugs donated by health facilities or drug companies through NGOs.

Illegal drug sellers, referred to as "black baggers," travel throughout Liberia selling everything from expired drugs to drugs of unknown quality produced in Nigeria or other nearby countries. During a trip to inland Liberia in an area without electricity and with poor roads, I went to a clinic where the only psychiatric medications available were expired anticonvulsants that could also be used to treat bipolar disorder. However, a government worker had confiscated all of these expired medications. I then learned in a nearby village that the government worker was now selling these drugs (which had been distributed from the clinic free of charge) and telling patients to take them at doses far below the level of therapeutic efficacy.

Another problem in Liberia is that most health facilities are not equipped to monitor the side effects or safety of psychiatric drugs. The most effective medication for bipolar disorder, lithium, requires regular blood monitoring to assure that an individual does not reach toxic levels, which can be fatal. Because of a lack of blood testing, many effective drugs for psychiatric care (such as lithium, divalproex acid, and clozapine) are not available through most of Liberia. Therefore, availability of medications and availability of monitoring facilities are both lacking in Liberia.

Research in middle-income countries presents a slightly different picture from what we have observed in Liberia, which is basically a population-wide gap in access. In India, for example, the medical anthropologist Stefan Ecks has shown that the so-called treatment gap between need for medicines and availability of medications is complicated (Ecks 2005, 2013; Ecks and Basu 2009). According to Ecks, in India, psychotropic medications—specifically, selective serotonin reuptake inhibitors (SSRIs) such as fluoxetine (Prozac)—to treat depression are actually widely available. Instead, he identifies gaps in terms of knowledge of those dispensing the medicines; for example, primary care workers have limited knowledge about indications for treatment and monitoring. There is also a gap between those who need and those who actually get the medicine. Ecks's work reflects the global picture, for which there are population-wide differences, some populations suffering over-treatment and others suffering under-treatment.

These issues are not limited to cross-population gaps and excesses regarding treatment. Another important concern in global mental health is intra-individual gaps and excesses. For marginalized individuals, there is a greater risk of taking too much medication at one point in an illness and then taking too few medications at other times. For example, in parts of the United States, where the community mental health infrastructure is weak, some individuals do not get appropriate care when out in the community and often lack access to medications. Then, when these same individuals end up in an emergency room or are admitted to a psychiatric hospital, they tend to be overmedicated, often ending up on three, four, or five psychiatric medications. They are then discharged, do not get medicines refilled, and go back to zero. Thus, with vulnerable populations, we need to consider not only between-group differences but also within-individual variation in excesses and absence of medication.

A final issue to consider with medications in global mental health is health care provider behavior. Universalized critiques of global mental health and pharmaceutical companies often neglect to consider the motivations of the health care provider. During our mhGAP training in Liberia, and during similar trainings I have co-facilitated in Uganda, Nepal, and elsewhere, we teach primary care workers about diagnosis and medication using the *mhGAP-IG*. This guide also contains sections on psychotherapies and psychosocial treatments. However, these often are not taught in detail, so the practitioners default to medication treatments. A key issue is how to improve the availability of psychotherapy treatments—which are often marginalized in high-income counties as well. Programs such as the Program for Effective Mental Health Interventions in Under-Resourced Health System (PREMIUM) funded by the Wellcome Trust are important means for addressing this. Similar cognitive behavior therapy programs, such as the Thinking Healthy Program delivered by female health workers in Pakistan, are also useful (Rahman 2007; Rahman et al. 2008). All told, in global mental health, it is important that medications not become the default treatment. Anthropological studies of psychotherapy trainings, provider preferences, and policy makers and funders are important to consider in analyzing the availability of psychotherapy alternatives or adjuvants to medication.

## ALTERNATIVE APPROACHES TO GLOBAL MENTAL HEALTH CRITIQUE: POWER AND THE EXPERIENCE GAP

Reverend Bill's story and other accounts of experience suggest that the current critiques of global mental health are not especially representative or helpful for the growth of the field—and they can overly simplify or mislead. All of these critiques have power differentials in common. Therefore, a focus on power and power systems and processes, rather than on decontextualized critiques of diagnostic labels, medicalization, pharmaceutical companies, and globalization, would push the field of global mental health forward. For example, the critique of diagnostic labels assumes that providers and patients lack the ability to negotiate labels and to allow for personalized interpretation of *DSM*, mhGAP, and other cultural artifacts. Concerns about medicalization also make paternalistic assumptions that patients, providers, and families will not benefit from psychiatric treatment. A focus on power can examine how medicalization is employed at policy, provider, and patient levels to identify benefits, harm, and tradeoffs. With regard to pharmaceutical companies, the issues of manipulation and profit seeking are unlikely to go away, so how can providers and patients be empowered to choose or reject medication, and what alternatives do they have? It is possible to empower providers and patients by teaching the most appropriate ways to use medication, by providing the most appropriate medicines, and by engaging the laboratory facilities needed to properly manage medications; most importantly, they can be empowered with psychotherapies and psychosocial interventions that may be equally or more effective than medicines for some patients.

In envisioning alternative frameworks to critique and improve global mental health, James Griffith, a psychiatrist and family therapist with extensive experience with refugee and immigrant populations in the United States and a collaborator in a family-based treatment program for severe mental illness in post-conflict Kosovo, and I have advocated for new praxis in global mental health that highlights four processes (Kohrt and Griffith 2015). First, the individual interactions need to be structured to facilitate dialogue. Whether between patient and provider, provider and administrator, consumer and policy maker, or researchers from high-income countries and low- and middle-income countries, how interactions are structured to facilitate dialogue rather than didactics or asymmetric monologues is important. Anthropology and philosophy can help inform this process by moving these interactions from subject–object relations to subject–subject relations.

Second, all interactions need to be considered within the context and constraints of ecological systems, such as how do macro-cultural processes influence interactions among institutions, health professionals, and other personnel (Singer 1989, 1995). This focus on ecological systems—a centerpiece of critical medical anthropology—can be used to inform how individual interactions between patients and providers—whether in Greenville, Liberia, or in New York—are shaped by the economic, political, and other cultural processes that are occurring. This highlights how interventions need to address multiple ecological levels and not just the patient–provider interaction (Kohrt 2013).

Third, the anthropological framework that approaches all tools and technologies as cultural artifacts needs to be considered. For anthropologists, the *mhGAP-IG*, *DSM*, and culturally adapted psychotherapy manuals are all cultural artifacts (Gaines 1992). How can cultural artifacts, spaces, and places be adapted to optimize dialogue as the first goal and to lead to equalization of power? For example, tools such as the *mhGAP-IG* and *DSM* do not directly include guidance on adaptation or flexibility—how could that better be incorporated?

Finally, the fourth process to observe is unintended consequences (Kleinman 2010). Studies all need to constantly monitor the unintended consequences of practices such as task-sharing, cultural adaptation of psychotherapy, prescription of psychotropic medication, professionalization of volunteer workers, and other issues raised in this volume.

Anthropology is crucial to close the experience gap in global mental health. Both practice and critique will be better served if grounded in the experience of persons living with mental illness, their family members, their health workers, other caregivers, policy makers, and other stakeholders. Reverend Bill's story is one of many possible pathways for success in global mental health. While his identity is influenced by mental illness, it is also defined by his role in the community as a social entrepreneur, which is enabled in part by appropriate mental health treatment, and by his role as advocate for others to improve mental health services and the representations of others' voices in that process.

*References*

Adair, R. F, and Holmgren, L. R. (2005). Do drug samples influence resident prescribing behavior? A randomized trial. *American Journal of Medicine*, 118 (8): 881–884.

American Psychiatric Association (1980). *Diagnostic and Statistical Manual of Mental Disorders*. 3rd ed. Washington, DC: American Psychiatric Association.

———. (2013). *Diagnostic and Statistical Manual of Mental Disorders: 5th Edition: DSM-5*. Washington, DC: American Psychiatric Association.

Angell, M. (2005). *The Truth about the Drug Companies: How They Deceive Us and What to Do about It*. New York: Random House Trade Paperbacks.

Bell, C., Williamson, J., and Chien, P. (2008). Cultural, racial and ethnic competence and psychiatric diagnosis. *Ethnicity and Inequalities in Health and Social Care*, 1 (1):34–41.

Chren, M-M., and Landefeld, C. S. (1994). Physicians' behavior and their interactions with drug companies: a controlled study of physicians who requested additions to a hospital drug formulary. *JAMA*, 271 (9): 684–689.

Clinton Health Access Initiative (2011). Health Facilities Accreditation Report. Monrovia, Liberia: Clinton Health Access Initiative.

Dietrich, J. W. (2007). The politics of PEPFAR: the president's emergency plan for AIDS relief. *Ethics and International Affairs*, 21 (3): 277–292.

Ecks, S. (2005). Pharmaceutical citizenship: antidepressant marketing and the promise of demarginalization in India. *Anthropology and Medicine*, 3 (2005): 239–254.

———. (2013). *Eating Drugs: Psychopharmaceutical Pluralism in India*. New York: NYU Press.

Ecks, S., and S. Basu (2009). The unlicensed lives of antidepressants in India: generic drugs, unqualified practitioners, and floating prescriptions. *Transcultural Psychiatry*, 46 (1): 86–106.

Fernando, S. (2013). *Cultural Diversity, Mental Health and Psychiatry: The Struggle against Racism*. New York: Routledge.

Gaines, A. D. (1992). Ethnopsychiatry: the cultural construction of psychiatries. In A. D. Gaines (ed.), *Ethnopsychiatry: The Cultural Construction of Professional and Folk Psychiatries*, pp. 3–50. SUNY Series in Medical Anthropology. Albany: State University of New York Press.

Huang, A. J. (2000). The rise of direct-to-consumer advertising of prescription drugs in the United States. *JAMA*, 284 (17): 2240.

Kleinman, A. (2010). Four social theories for global health. *The Lancet*, 375 (9725): 1518–1519.

———. (2012). Medical anthropology and mental health: five questions for the next fifty years. In M. C. Inhorn and E. A. Wentzell (eds.), *Medical Anthropology at the Intersections: Histories, Activisms, and Futures*, pp. 116–129. Durham, North Carolina: Duke University Press.

Kleinman, A., and Desjarlais, R. (1994). Neither patients nor victims—towards an ethnography of political violence. *Actes de la recherche en sciences sociales*, (104): 56– 63.

Kohn, R., Saxena, S., Levav, I., and Saraceno, B. (2004). The treatment gap in mental health care. *Bulletin of the World Health Organization*, 82 (11): 858–866.

Kohrt, B. (2013). Social ecology interventions for post-traumatic stress disorder: what can we learn from child soldiers? *British Journal of Psychiatry*, 203: 165–167.

Kohrt, B. A., and Griffith, J. L. (2015). Global mental health praxis: perspectives from cultural psychiatry on research and intervention. In L. J. Kirmayer, R. B. Lemelson, and C. Cummings (eds.), *Revisioning Psychiatry*. New York: Cambridge University Press.

Kohrt, B. A., Blasingame, E., Compton, M. T., Dakana, S. F., Dossen, B., Lang, F., Strode, P., and Cooper, J. (2015). Adapting the crisis intervention team (CIT) model of police–mental health collaboration in a low-income, post-conflict country: curriculum development in Liberia, West Africa. *American Journal of Public Health*. doi: 10.2105/AJPH.2014.302394.

Lock, M. (2001). The tempering of medical anthropology: troubling natural categories. *Medical Anthropology Quarterly*, 15(4): 478–492.

Louden, D.-M. (1995). The epidemiology of schizophrenia among Caribbean-born and first- and second-generation migrants in Britain. *Journal of Social Distress and the Homeless*, 4 (3): 237–253.

Lund, C., Breen, A., Flisher, A. J., Kakuma, R., Corrigall, J., Joska, J. A., Swartz, L., and Patel, V. (2010). Poverty and common mental disorders in low and middle income countries: a systematic review. *Social Science and Medicine*, 71 (3): 517–528.

Lund, C., De Silva, M., Plagerson, S., Cooper, S., Chisholm, D., Das, J., Knapp, M., and Patel, V. (2011). Poverty and mental disorders: breaking the cycle in low-income and middle-income countries. *The Lancet*, 378 (9801): 1502–1514.

Murray, C. J. L., and Lopez, A. D. (1996). *The Global Burden of Disease: A Comprehensive Assessment of Mortality and Disability from Diseases, Injuries, and Risk Factors in 1990 and Projected to 2020*. Cambridge, Massachusetts: Harvard University Press.

Murthy, R. S., and N. N. Wig (1983). The WHO collaborative study on strategies for extending mental health care, IV: a training approach to enhancing the availability of mental health manpower in a developing country. *American Journal of Psychiatry*, 140 (11): 1486–1490.

Patel, V. (2014). Why mental health matters to global health. *Transcultural Psychiatry*, 51 (6): 777–789.

Pattison, N., and Warren, L. (2003). 2002 Drug industry profits: hefty pharmaceutical company margins dwarf other industries. *Public Citizen Congress Watch*, June 2003. Washington, DC: Public Citizen.

Rahman, A. (2007). Challenges and opportunities in developing a psychological intervention for perinatal depression in rural Pakistan—a multi-method study. *Archives of Women's Mental Health*, 10 (5): 211–219.

Rahman, A., Malik, A., Sikander, S., Roberts, C., and Creed, F. (2008). Cognitive be-haviour therapy-based intervention by community health workers for mothers with depression and their infants in rural Pakistan: a cluster-randomised controlled trial. *The Lancet*, 372 (9642): 902–909.

Scheper-Hughes, N., and Lock, M. M. (1987). The mindful body: a prolegomenon to fu-ture work in medical anthropology. *Medical Anthropology Quarterly*, 1 (1): 6–41.

Selten, J-P., and Hoek, H. W. (2008). Does misdiagnosis explain the schizophrenia epi-demic among immigrants from developing countries to Western Europe? *Social Psy-chiatry and Psychiatric Epidemiology*, 43 (12): 937–939.

Singer, M. (1989). The coming of age of critical medical anthropology. *Social Science and Medicine*, 28 (11): 1193–1203.

——. (1995). Beyond the ivory tower—critical praxis in medical anthropology. *Medical Anthropology Quarterly*, 9 (1): 80–106.

Singh, S. P., Greenwood, N., White, S., and Churchill, R. (2007). Ethnicity and the Men-tal Health Act 1983. *British Journal of Psychiatry*, 191 (2): 99–105.

Summerfield, D.(2008). How scientifically valid is the knowledge base of global mental health? *British Medical Journal*, 336 (7651): 992–994.

United Nations (2006). United Nations Convention on the Rights of Persons with Dis-abilities. http://www.un.org/disabilities/convention/conventionfull.shtml/.

Weaver, L. J., and Hadley, C. (2011). Social pathways in the comorbidity between Type 2 diabetes and mental health concerns in a pilot study of urban middle- and upper-class Indian women. *Ethos*, 39 (2): 211–225.

World Health Organization (WHO) (2008). *Task Shifting: Rational Redistribution of Tasks among Health Workforce Teams: Global Recommendations and Guidelines.* Geneva: World Health Organization.

——. (2010). *mhGAP Intervention Guide for Mental, Neurological and Substance-Use Dis-orders in Non-Specialized Health Settings.* Geneva: World Health Organization.

Chapter 16

# "Thinking Too Much" in the Central Plateau: An Apprenticeship Approach to Treating Local Distress in Haiti

Bonnie N. Kaiser and Kristen E. McLean

## BENEATH THE MANGO TREE

MARI'S FAMILY TOOK HER TO A LOCAL hospital when she stopped eating for several days. It was the latest episode of a recurrent illness that members of her community—a small rural town in Haiti's Central Plateau—refer to as *reflechi twòp* (Kreyòl for "thinking too much"). During such episodes, Mari often sits alone beneath a mango tree for hours on end, her chin resting on one palm, seeming distracted and far away. She often experiences headaches and trouble sleeping, and more often than not the episodes of thinking distract her from eating. Mari does not think toward a solution; she merely reflects (Kreyòl: *reflechi*) on her myriad problems. Some are the same problems faced by most Haitians today: poverty, hunger, and unemployment. But for Mari, the central problem—the one that dominates her thoughts, passing through her mind repeatedly as though on a reel of film—is her husband Toma's illness.

For the past year, Toma has experienced bouts of extreme bodily pain, leaving him incapacitated, unable to work or care for his family. During a particularly bad episode, Mari and members of Toma's extended family took him to the local clinic, which consisted of a small building with one doctor and two auxiliary nurses, a laboratory, and a small pharmacy, making it one of the better-equipped facilities in the region. Normally the journey would have taken several hours, with Toma carried on a mattress in a wheelbarrow. But considering the urgency of his condition, the neighbors scraped together enough money for a motorcycle taxi. At the clinic, the family wept audibly, as though already mourning his loss, none more so than Mari.

It was at the clinic that Jak first encountered Mari. He recently completed apprenticeship training as a community mental health worker, tasked with identifying community members suffering from mental distress, providing basic psychosocial

*Global Mental Health: Anthropological Perspectives*, edited by Brandon A. Kohrt and Emily Mendenhall, 277–290. © 2015 Left Coast Press, Inc. All rights reserved.

support through follow-up visits, and referring patients to a psychologist in the region. Jak approached Mari, who appeared extremely distraught and worried, and began asking questions about her life and her husband's illness.

Mari explained that she was pregnant and her husband was extremely sick. No one could do anything to support the family, and she spent much of her time sitting and "thinking too much." She tried to send her children to school, but the director sent them back, telling them to return when they could pay their school fees. Mari was desperate. Jak invited her to attend an upcoming mobile clinic, in which members of the mental health team from Zanmi Lasante, a Partners in Health–associated NGO founded by Dr. Paul Farmer and colleagues, would be visiting the area. She agreed, and they also settled on a day for him to visit her at home.

Jak began visiting Mari twice a month in her family's *lakou* (homestead) to monitor her progress and provide ongoing support. Jak was short, with a large, beaming smile, and his patient manner and intent listening helped put Mari at ease. After an extended greeting, Jak began the visit with a screening tool, the Zanmi Lasante Depression Symptom Inventory (Rasmussen et al. 2014). This locally developed mental health screening tool assesses experience of symptoms that are known to be relevant and well understood in this region, and Mari was able to answer the questions easily. Jak inquired about local Kreyòl idioms of distress like *de la la* (fatigue/depressed mood), *kè sere* (tight heart/sadness), and *reflechi twòp* (thinking too much). To this, she answered, "*Toujou* (always), my husband can't get better." When the Zanmi Lasante mental health worker first visited Mari, the notion of mental illness was unknown to her, but the experience was familiar. To her, the distress was referred to as *reflechi twòp* (thinking too much), something she hoped would never consume her life again.

In this chapter, we return to the story of Jak and Mari as we explore two issues of central concern in current global mental health interventions: how best to identify and communicate mental distress and how to implement effective solutions for problems of health care access. First, we explore the idiom of distress "thinking too much" (*reflechi twòp*) as used in rural Haiti. In contrast to terms like "depression" and "trauma," which have no widely understood equivalents in Kreyòl, "thinking too much" is a well-understood cultural concept of distress that conveys mental distress. Through anecdotes drawn from rural Haiti and global mental health literature, we argue that precedence should be given to such locally meaningful cultural concepts of distress, rather than focusing solely on Western-defined psychiatric disorders like depression and anxiety. Second, we consider the challenges to addressing mental disorders in a resource-poor setting such as rural Haiti. We propose that task-sharing, in the form of an apprenticeship approach, offers strong potential to implement basic mental health care where few specialists are available.

This study derives from mixed-methods research conducted in the summers of 2010 and 2011 and throughout 2013, concerning mental health in Haiti's Central Plateau. The research was conducted by two multidisciplinary teams of graduate researchers, including students of public health, medicine, nursing, law, education, and anthropology. The research was embedded in a mental health training as a part of our pilot community mental health worker initiative (McLean et al., in press). Much of the information conveyed in this chapter derives from our experiences in designing, implementing, and evaluating this multi-stage, transcultural training. The process involved three phases: (1) review of the literature, plus qualitative data collection to adapt a community-based mental health training to the Haitian context; (2) implementation and qualitative process evaluation of a structured group pilot training; and (3) implementation and evaluation of an apprentice-style pilot training. The apprentice-style training built upon the classroom lectures and activities associated with didactic-style training but, additionally, incorporated observation and practice in the field. Case visits progressed from the apprentice shadowing a licensed social worker on house visits, followed by debriefing and discussion, to the apprentice conducting home visits while being observed by the licensed social worker, again followed by debriefing and discussion.

**Content Development**

1. Identify relevant content (review of literature; prior ethnographic data collection from May to June 2010)
2. Develop provisional training manual
3. Qualitative data collection (key informant interviews, participant observation)

Revise manual based on cultural adaptation

**Group Training Pilot**

1. Training of 14 community health workers using manual (6 modules over 3 days)
2. Qualitative process evaluation (participant observation during training; semi-structured interviews; focus group discussions, pre-/post-tests)

Design of alternative approach

**Apprenticeship Pilot**

1. Training of 3 apprentices using manual in addition to practical experience in the field
2. Qualitative process evaluation (participant observation during training and counseling sessions; debriefing; semi-structured interviews)

Long-term follow-up (participant observation and interviews)

Development of training and apprenticeship program for nonspecialist health workers in Haiti

## "Thinking Too Much" and Cultural Concepts of Distress

Mari's story highlights several key characteristics of the idiom "thinking too much" as we heard it used in our interviews and participant observation (Kaiser et al. 2014; see also Hunter Keys's descriptions of "thinking too much" among Haitian migrants in the Dominican Republic in Chapter 9 of this book). As the term suggests, the central feature of "thinking too much" is persistent rumination, particularly an unwavering focus on a singular problem, to the point of seeming detached or far away. The term *reflechi* (to mull over, ruminate, reflect) is particularly apt to communicate the meaning captured by the idiom, as opposed to other Kreyòl terms for thinking, with meanings closer to "believe," "calculate," or "process." Importantly, "thinking too much" is characterized by thinking that is *not* directed toward a solution, as one social worker explained to us:

> But when we say "*l'ap reflechi*" (he/she is thinking), it's not in the sense of resolving a problem. It's not that the person is in the midst of thinking in a scientific way. It's someone who has a problem that torments them. Now at each instant they're thinking of this problem.

The cultural concept of distress is also marked by social isolation, quiet, weight loss, and trouble sleeping.

Thinking too much often arises due to material deprivation, such as lack of money or food, and can be exacerbated by lack of activities. In Mari's case, her husband's inability to work due to his illness, coupled with the responsibilities of a newborn child, added to her distress. Such situations are generally brought about by external factors, such as job loss or failed crops, in addition to poor health. However, they are often internalized as failure to achieve one's goals or fulfill social expectations, which brings about shame. As one community member explained, "Bad thinking, calculating, you have work to do in front of you and you have nothing in front of you to be able to do it. You are not capable." Thinking too much can also begin as a culturally acceptable response to sad or traumatic events. Behaviors associated with thinking too much—such as isolating oneself and becoming quiet—are considered more acceptable than crying.

The primary solution that our participants suggested for thinking too much is organizing activities, such as soccer tournaments, dancing, or sewing lessons, to help people occupy their time that would otherwise be consumed with thinking. Indeed, helping others to identify relevant activities represents a central part of Jak's work with each patient. In sessions with them, he often asks about what they like to do for fun or to feel more hopeful. On the other hand, one community leader we interviewed opined that helping someone manage stress by finding social activities provides only temporary relief. After the activities are over, the sadness returns as the person reflects on the true cause of his or her "thinking too much." Indeed, structural inequalities seem to drive thinking too much, leaving people with a lack of agency to improve their lives. One man described these broader drivers of distress:

> There is no work! It is the impossibility; it's poverty that puts everyone in all these things because people are sitting down, only sitting down, eating. And the food, they don't know where it will come from, and they are thinking about how to get food. . . . You can't think of anything else.

Indeed, one of the challenges mentioned by Jak and other community mental health workers in providing treatment was that they themselves were often approached for money and other material goods. Effectively contending with "thinking too much" requires addressing these broader structural factors.

Thinking too much is one of many cultural concepts of distress that we identified in Haiti's Central Plateau (Kaiser et al. 2013; Keys et al. 2012). Idioms of distress represent culturally meaningful ways of expressing emotional and psychological distress, suffering, and vulnerability (Nichter 1981). Idioms of distress are particularly intelligible because they are embedded in culturally salient ways of making sense of personhood, emotions, values, and functioning of the body (Kohrt and Hruschka 2010). For example, Cambodians often make sense of dizziness, palpitations, and physical weakness as *khyâl* attacks, brought on by a rising of a wind-like substance through channels that guide bodily functions (Hinton et al. 2010).

Some of the most-studied idioms, such as *ataque de nervios* among Latino populations and *koro* among Southeast Asian populations, are cultural concepts of distress—groupings of symptoms recognized by a cultural group as communicating a particular form of distress (Guarnaccia, Lewis-Fernández, and Rivera Marano 2003; Hinton and Lewis-Fernández 2010). At the same time, it is important to recognize that such idioms do not exist apart from the world but are indeed situated within it. As such, cultural concepts of distress are not value-free statements about symptom presentation: they make claims about social position and power (Kohrt et al. 2014; cf. Nichter 2010). For Mari, thinking too much not only communicates a set of emotional and somatic experiences but also highlights the significant amount of free time available for thinking too much that is brought about by lack of opportunities for gaining employment, achieving one's objectives, and fulfilling socially expected roles. Jak recognizes the significance of this idiom for communicating a particular form of distress, as well as the importance of encouraging Mari to identify meaningful activities and social roles that she can pursue to avoid thinking too much.

Due to their particular cultural salience, idioms of distress can prove equally or more useful than psychiatric categories in the identification of those suffering from mental distress (Bolton 2001; Kohrt et al. 2004). For example, in Sri Lanka, idioms of distress predicted functional impairment above and beyond a PTSD scale and depression inventory (Jayawickreme, Jayawickreme, and Goonasekere 2012). Incorporation of idioms of distress can improve outcomes of standardized screening instruments when used cross-culturally and can also detect forms of mental distress that such instruments miss (Shibre, Teferra, and Morgan 2010; Van Ommeren et al. 2000). Furthermore, because idioms of distress often reflect the social imbalances between the powerful/dominating and the powerless/dominated (Rechtman 2006), incorporating local illness nosologies and healing systems within mental health interventions can potentially empower those who have long faced stigma and disenfranchisement within their societies.

## TASK-SHARING MENTAL HEALTH CARE IN LMICS

Despite appropriate identification of mental distress, referral to specialist mental health care is often not an option in low- and middle-income countries (LMICs), and many challenges exist in addressing mental health problems in resource-poor settings such as rural Haiti. For instance, worldwide there remains a scarcity of mental health professionals to deliver treatment for mental distress (Saxena et al. 2007; WHO 2011). Globally, there is a projected shortage of 1.2 million mental health professionals, with this gap being greatest in LMICs (Kakuma et al. 2011; WHO 2000). For countries like Haiti, this translates to an estimated 70% to 100% of individuals suffering from depression alone going untreated (Jacob, Sharan, and Mirza 2007).

Haiti is the poorest country in the Western Hemisphere (UNDP 2004), making meeting health care challenges particularly difficult. Medical care is insufficient in Haiti due to lack of infrastructure and trained professionals, especially in rural areas (Chatterjee 2008; WHO 2003). A Pan American Health Organization/WHO report (2003) estimated that there were only 10 psychiatric specialists working in the public sector, and most were concentrated in Port-au-Prince. Fortunately for Mari, a trained community mental health worker (Jak) was operating in her community and was able to identify her symptoms of distress. Furthermore, a local NGO employed psychologists, who took referrals for cases indicating severe distress. Unfortunately, such resources are rare in many rural areas within Haiti, as is the case in most LMICs. Researchers and public health practitioners must work to address these gaps in mental health services, though best practices for intervention are still being debated.

One of the most convincing avenues for providing mental health care in low-resource settings is through training people like Jak to work in mental health care provision. People like Jak are becoming the foundation of growing efforts aimed at task-sharing of mental health care among mid-level health care workers, community workers, and other paraprofessionals (Padmanathan and De Silva 2013; Patel et al. 2007; WHO 2006). Task-sharing refers to the redistribution of mental health services from highly qualified specialists (psychiatrists, psychologists, social workers, etc.) to nonspecialist health workers or paraprofessionals in order to make more efficient use of available human resources (WHO 2008). Task-sharing grew out of work with paraprofessional health workers providing community-based services for HIV treatment (see Maes, Chapter 17). This approach has been recommended as a practical, cost-effective way to ensure greater access to care in LMICs, which hold a large portion of the global burden of mental disorders and the lowest proportion of care providers (Somasundram 2006; WHO 2010).

This can be exemplified through the culturally adapted and community-based intervention that we proposed, based on our research, for Jak and other paraprofessionals to provide in Haiti. Based on the cultural idiom "thinking too much," we proposed an intervention focused on cognitive restructuring and behavioral activation that would promote positive thought patterns and behavioral change. As a result of this training, Jak was able to identify Mari's symptoms of distress (such as headaches, social isolation, and "thinking too much") and encourage her to pursue problem-solving activities and other coping mechanisms. This was evident during home visits when Mari complained that her husband couldn't work and was worried about the future welfare of her children, and Jak pushed her to think of sources of social support. When he asked whom she could always count on, she identified her extended family. She also noted that she could depend on her children for emotional support. After some probing, Mari conceived a solution on her own: though her family was not in a position to help her financially, she would enlist their aid in planting and cleaning the corn in her garden, an activity that her husband used to perform when he was well. While Jak was able to help Mari by drawing upon his repertoire of skills, he was also prepared to refer her to specialist care upon recognizing the severity of her case.

Jak's work with Mari exemplifies a fundamental challenge that results from task-sharing approaches: the need to adapt mental health interventions for delivery by nonspecialists (Rahman et al. 2008). Emerging research indicates that with appropriate supervision and follow-up, it is feasible to educate and train community health workers like Jak and other nonspecialist health care providers and community members to offer short-term mental health treatment (Onyut et al. 2004; Patel and Thornicroft 2009; Ventevogel et al. 2012), based on evidence developed through randomized controlled trials (RCTs) (Bolton et al. 2003; Jordans et al. 2010; Patel et al. 2010; Rahman et al. 2008). Based on our research in Haiti, we suggest that local community members may be ideal for task-sharing initiatives because they are more knowledgeable about local explanatory models and cultural concepts of distress, such as "thinking too much" (Keys et al. 2012).

Other mental health interventionists have utilized a number of different approaches for the design of mental health task-sharing initiatives, such as cognitive behavioral therapy (CBT), interpersonal therapy (IPT), basic psychoeducation, and problem solving (Patel et al. 2007). Such psychotherapeutic interventions have been shown to be effective in the treatment of mood disorders in high-income countries, and evidence is growing concerning their relevance for treating emotional distress in LMICs (Churchill, Hunot, and Corney 2001; Patel et al. 2007). For example, CBT was successfully used by community health workers like Jak in rural Pakistan to treat mothers with symptoms of depression (Rahman et al. 2008). IPT is another commonly utilized approach within mental health task-sharing initiatives in LMICs. This form of therapy helps to identify the connection between interpersonal problems and symptoms of mental distress. When adapted for groups, participants practice interpersonal problem-solving together and build skills to contain grief and manage role transitions in their lives (Verdeli et al. 2008). This approach has been employed by Bolton and colleagues (2003) to successfully treat depression and anxiety symptoms among a group of adults in southern Uganda.

The care Jak provided for Mari resulted from mental health training that utilized a combination of these approaches, in addition to basic psychoeducation. The intervention that we implemented in rural Haiti was intended to train motivated community members to identify cases of mental distress, provide basic psychosocial support, and determine when to refer individuals to specialist services. Specific skills addressed included symptom recognition, active listening, stress management, and other problem-solving techniques. The intervention was adapted using a participant-oriented approach to include local idioms of distress, including thinking too much. Incorporating idioms of distress into clinical communication and interventions in this way has been shown to improve treatment outcomes. Indeed, we found through our research and programmatic efforts that developing culturally rooted mental health programming that relies on task-sharing can be beneficial and cost-effective in rural Haiti.

## The Apprenticeship Model

We attribute the success of our pilot task-sharing intervention to three main factors: (1) the use of local idioms of distress such as "thinking too much" to frame the training content within Haitian ethnopsychology; (2) the careful selection of motivated individuals to participate in training activities; and (3) the structure of the apprenticeship model. The apprenticeship model fosters practical application of skills coupled with close supervision. This approach to building human resource capacity for mental health care has the potential to be more effective and sustainable than large, one-off trainings of community health workers (CHWs) in providing psychosocial services.

Idioms of distress such as thinking too much were largely influential in the adaptation of the training at various stages. By framing training modules and group activities using such idioms, teaching and learning became more culturally meaningful and relevant to the local context. Theoretically, training skills centered around elements of CBT, including the encouragement of positive thought patterns and behavioral activation, which were intended to counter the incessant rumination and idleness often associated with thinking too much.

Our experiences in selecting trainees for task-sharing interventions have taught us a number of lessons. First, it is important to recruit motivated, community-identified individuals for the provision of psychosocial services. The participants in our apprenticeship pilot training were ideal recruits because they were already providing emotional support to community members via informal pathways and had expressed interest in learning additional skills. In addition, we recommend predictable and consistent remuneration in order to foster the sustainability of interventions, including quality of care and low turnover rates (Maes, Kohrt, and Closser 2010). It may also be advantageous to provide further incentives, including certification or recognition by national education organizations for newly acquired skills (Necochea 2006; WHO 2003).

We also attribute the success of Jak's training to the structure utilized. The apprenticeship model served as a useful format in which Jak could learn and grow into his new role in task-sharing mental health services for community members such as Mari. This additional support, which was lacking from the structured training, is what Jak received as part of our pilot task-sharing endeavor. Qualitative process evaluation of the apprenticeship pilot demonstrated improved understanding of concepts related to the provision of mental health support and ability to put skills into practice. For example, during debriefing following the shadowing of a licensed social worker, Jak's colleague acknowledged increased understanding gained from witnessing psychosocial skills being applied in a contextualized setting: "I really appreciate the positive method you used to let the lady know that there are a lot of things that she can do. . . . When you say that you are supposed to empower a person to solve their own problem, I didn't understand it before. But I now understand." Based on our experience in rural Haiti (McLean et al. in press), we feel that practical learning coupled with supervision, in line with the traditional apprenticeship trade approach, is responsible for the success of Jak's training and his subsequent ability to identify and counsel Mari and others. In particular, Jak described that he had previously encountered cases such as Mari's during his work but felt inadequately prepared to provide appropriate support or care. However, after gaining new skills and having the opportunity to put them into practice during his apprenticeship, he felt capable of approaching Mari when she accompanied her husband to the clinic. He sought her out completely on his own in this instance. In the two years following his training, Jak has helped to identify and provide care to dozens of such patients. Partners in Health/Zanmi Lasante clinicians have noted anecdotally that patients who receive follow-up care with Jak tend to have better outcomes than those receiving only medication.

The apprenticeship model enabled problem-based learning and practical implementation of skills, with valuable feedback and guidance from skilled supervisors. The global mental health literature calls for regular supervision, as it is imperative to the success and scaling up of task-sharing models (WHO 2007, 2008). Post-training supervision has been shown to be one of the strongest predictors of behavior change (Fixsen et al. 2005), and studies from LMICs show that trainees prefer exposure to real-life experiences in applying newly learned skills (Makanjuola 2012). A study by Budosan and Jones (2009) in Indonesia, for example, found that a longer training spread out over time, with both theoretical *and* practical components coupled with supervision, was more effective for changing mental health practices. Rahman and colleagues (2008) suggest that for settings with limited access to trained supervisors, peer supervision may also be feasible. This allows trainees to meet regularly to discuss cases, share advice, and brainstorm solutions to challenges they face; doing so in a supportive environment may be a sustainable solution to supervision, given the scarcity of mental health professionals.

## BENEATH THE MANGO TREE AGAIN

At each visit, Jak and Mari sat beneath the same mango tree. But unlike when Mari sat there alone, these conversations focused on sources of hope and coping strategies. Jak asked Mari about any new activities and sources of support that have helped her to feel happier. At first, it was difficult for Mari to focus on anything but negatives, the life problems that overwhelmed her. But with Jak's urging, Mari began to focus on the hope that her family gives her, as well as solutions to cope with her "thinking too much" rather than her problems. These were not grand solutions but piecemeal changes that could help her to accomplish small goals. Jak encouraged her to create activities to occupy her time so that she would not sit idly and think too much. During one visit, Mari explained that she had recently begun to cook and clean again and that caring for her children brought her satisfaction. She had joined a local sewing class. Upon mentioning her success with turning to prayer, Jak probed as to whether there were any activities associated with the church that she enjoyed. To this, she answered affirmatively that she enjoyed attending church activities the most, explaining that this is where she found hope. Furthermore, she resolved to sell meat pies in town whenever she could, which gave her a sense of accomplishment and additional income. Jak encouraged this improvement by explaining to Mari that

> [what you suffer from] is not a terrible sickness. It can't be cured, but at any time it can get better. I know many people who have it who have gotten better. People who are sick or suffering, they can't do activities; they can't work or go to school. They are tired, lack strength. Whenever their problems resolve, they start doing all their activities again. You couldn't clean the house, but now you are getting better. You're going to have strength to start all of your activities again.

Indeed, following Jak's encouragement, Mari has experienced a decrease in depressive symptoms and an improvement in life functioning. With the support of Jak and his colleagues at Zanmi Lasante, Mari's goal of preventing *reflechi twòp* from ever again consuming her life is becoming a reality.

## References

Bolton, P. (2001). Cross-cultural validity and reliability testing of a standard psychiatric assessment instrument without a gold standard. *Journal of Nervous and Mental Disease*, 189: 238–242.

Bolton, P., Bass, J., Neugebauer, R., Verdeli, H., Clougherty, K. F., Wickramaratne, P., et al. (2003). Group interpersonal psychotherapy for depression in rural Uganda: a randomized controlled trial. *JAMA*, 289: 3117–3124.

Budosan, B., and Jones, L. (2009). Evaluation of effectiveness of mental health training program for primary health care staff in Hambantota District, Sri Lanka posttsunami. *Journal of Humanitarian Assistance*, May 2009. http://sites.tufts.edu/jha/archives/509/.

Chatterjee, S. (2008). Haiti's forgotten emergency. *The Lancet*, 372: 615–618.

Churchill, R., Hunot, V., Corney, R., Knapp, M., McGuire, H., and Tylee, A. (2001). A systematic review of controlled trials of the effectiveness and cost-effectiveness of brief psychological treatments for depression. *Health Technology Assessment*, 5: 1–173.

Fixsen, D. L., Naoom, S. F., Blase, K. A., Friedman, R. M., and Wallace, F. (2005). *Implementation Research: A Synthesis of the Literature*. Tampa: University of South Florida, Louis de la Parte Florida Mental Health Institute, The National Implementation Research Network.

Guarnaccia, P., Lewis-Fernández, R., and Rivera Marano, M. (2003). Toward a Puerto Rican popular nosology: *nervios* and *ataque de nervios*. *Culture, Medicine, and Psychiatry*, 27: 339–366.

Hinton, D. E., and Lewis-Fernández, R. (2010). Idioms of distress among trauma survivors: subtypes and clinical utility. *Culture, Medicine, and Psychiatry*, 34: 209–218.

Hinton, D. E., Pich, V., Marques, L., Nickerson, A., and Pollack, M. H. (2010). Khyâl attacks: a key idiom of distress among traumatized Cambodia refugees. *Culture, Medicine, and Psychiatry*, 34: 244–278.

Jacob, K. S., Sharan, P., Mirza, I., et al. (2007). Mental health systems in countries: where are we now? *The Lancet*, 370 (9592): 1061–1077.

Jayawickreme, E., Jayawickreme, N., and Goonasekere, M. (2012). Using focus group methodology to adapt measurement scales and explore questions of wellbeing and mental health: the case of Sri Lanka. *Intervention*, 10: 156–17.

Jordans, M. J., Komproe, I. H., Tol, W. A., Kohrt, B. A., Luitel, N. P., Macy, R. D., et al. (2010). Evaluation of a classroom-based psychosocial intervention in conflict-affected Nepal: a cluster randomized controlled trial. *Journal of Child Psychology and Psychiatry*, 51: 818–826.

Kaiser, B., Kohrt, B., Keys, H., Khoury, N., and Brewster, A.-R. (2013). Strategies for assessing mental health in Haiti: local instrument development and transcultural translation. *Transcultural Psychiatry*, 50 (4): 532–558.

Kaiser, B., McLean, K., Kohrt, B., Hagaman, A., Wagenaar, B., Khoury, N., and Keys, H. (2014). *Reflechi twòp*—thinking too much: description of a cultural syndrome in Haiti's Central Plateau. *Culture, Medicine, and Psychiatry*, 38 (3): 488–472.

Kakuma, R., Minas, H., van Ginneken, N., Dal Poz, M. R., Desiraju, K., Morris, J. E., et al. (2011). Human resources for mental health care: current situation and strategies for action. *The Lancet*, 378: 1654–1663.

Keys, H. M., Kaiser, B. N., Kohrt, B. A., Khoury, N. M., and Brewster, A. R. (2012). Idioms of distress, ethnopsychology, and the clinical encounter in Haiti's Central Plateau. *Social Science and Medicine*, 75: 555–564.

Kohrt, B. A., and Hruschka, D .J. (2010). Nepali concepts of psychological trauma: the role of idioms of distress, ethnopsychology and ethnophysiology in alleviating suffering and preventing stigma. *Culture, Medicine, and Psychiatry*, 34: 322–352.

Kohrt, B. A., Hruschka, D. J., Kohrt, H. E., Panebianco, N. L., and Tsagaankhuu, G. (2004). Distribution of distress in post-socialist Mongolia: a cultural epidemiology of *yadargaa*. *Social Science and Medicine*, 58: 471–485.

Kohrt, B., Rasmussen, A., Kaiser, B., Haroz, E., Maharjan, S., Mutamba-Byamah, B., et al. (2014). Cultural concepts of distress and psychiatric disorders: literature review and research recommendations for global mental health epidemiology. *International Journal of Epidemiology*, 43 (3): 365–406.

Maes, K. C., Kohrt, B. A., and Closser, S. (2010). Culture, status and context in community health worker pay: pitfalls and opportunities for policy research. A commentary on Glenton et al. (2010). *Social Science and Medicine*, 71: 1375–1378.

Makanjuola, V., Doku, V., Jenkins, R., and Gureje, O. (2012). Monitoring and evaluation of the activities of trainees in the "training of trainers" workshop at Ibadan, south-west Nigeria. *Mental Health in Family Medicine*, 9: 25–32.

McLean, K. E., Kaiser, B. N., Hagaman, A. K., Wagenaar, B. H., and Kohrt, B. A. (in press). Task sharing in rural Haiti: qualitative assessment of a brief, structured training with and without apprenticeship supervision for community health workers. *Intervention: Journal for Mental Health and Psychosocial Support in Conflict Affected Areas*.

Necochea, E. (2006). Building stronger human resources for health through licensure, certification and accreditation. Capacity Project: knowledge sharing—Technical Brief 3. Global Health Workforce Alliance. http://www.who.int/workforcealliance/knowledge/toolkit/37/en/.

Nichter, M. (1981). Idioms of distress: alternatives in the expression of psychosocial distress: a case study from South India. *Culture, Medicine, and Psychiatry*, 5: 379–408.

——. (2010). Idioms of distress revisited. *Culture, Medicine, and Psychiatry*, 34: 401–416.

Onyut, L. P., Neuner, F., Schauer, E., Ertl, V., Odenwald, M., Schauer, M., et al. (2004). The Nakivale Camp Mental Health Project: building local competency for psychological assistance to traumatised refugees. *Intervention*, 2: 90–107.

Padmanathan, P., and De Silva, M. J. (2013). The acceptability and feasibility of task-sharing for mental healthcare in low and middle income countries: a systematic review. *Social Science and Medicine*, 97: 82–86.

Pan American Health Organization. (2003). *Haiti: Profile of the Health Services System.* Washington, DC.

Patel, V., and Thornicroft, G. (2009). Packages of care for mental, neurological, and substance use disorders in low- and middle-income countries: PLoS Medicine Series. *PLoS Med*, 6: e1000160.

Patel, V., Araya, R., Chatterjee, S., Chisholm, D., Cohen, A., De Silva, M., et al. (2007). Treatment and prevention of mental disorders in low-income and middle-income countries. *The Lancet*, 370: 991–1005.

Patel, V., Weiss, H. A., Chowdhary, N., Naik, S., Pednekar, S., Chatterjee, S., et al. (2010). Effectiveness of an intervention led by lay health counsellors for depressive and anxiety disorders in primary care in Goa, India (MANAS): a cluster randomised controlled trial. *The Lancet*, 376: 2086–2095.

Rahman, A., Malik, A., Sikander, S., Roberts, C., and Creed, F. (2008). Cognitive behaviour therapy-based intervention by community health workers for mothers with depression and their infants in rural Pakistan: a cluster-randomised controlled trial. *The Lancet*, 372: 902–909.

Rasmussen, A., Eustache, E., Raviola, G., Kaiser, B., Grelotti, D., and Belkin, G. (2014). Development and validation of a Haitian Creole screening instrument for depression. *Transcultural Psychiatry*. 2014 Jul 30. pii: 1363461514543546 (Epub ahead of print).

Rechtman, R. (2006). Cultural standards, power and subversion in cross-cultural psychotherapy. *Transcultural Psychiatry*, 43: 169–180.

Saxena, S., Thornicroft, G., Knapp, M., and Whiteford, H. (2007). Resources for mental health: scarcity, inequity, and inefficiency. *The Lancet*, 370: 878–889.

Shibre, T., Teferra, S., and Morgan, C. A. A. (2010). Exploring the apparent absence of psychosis amongst the Borana pastoralist community of Southern Ethiopia. a mixed method follow-up study. *World Psychiatry*, 9: 98–102.

Somasundram, D. (2006). Disaster mental health care in Sri Lanka. In J. Diaz, R. Murthy, and R. Lakshminarayana (eds.), *Advances in Disaster Mental Health and Psychological Support*, pp. 36–49. New Delhi: VHAI Press.

UNDP. (2004). *La vulnérabilité en Haïti: chemin inévitable vers la pauvreté?* [Vulnerability in Haiti: The Inevitable Path toward Poverty?]. Geneva: United Nations Development Programme.

Van Ommeren, M., Sharma, B., Makaju, R., Thapa, S., and de Jong, J. (2000). Limited cultural validity of the Composite International Diagnostic Interview's probe flow chart. *Transcultural Psychiatry*, 37: 119–129.

Ventevogel, P., van de Put, W., Faiz, H., van Mierlo, B., Siddiqi, M., and Komproe, I. H. (2012). Improving access to mental health care and psychosocial support within a fragile context: a case study from Afghanistan. *PLoS Medicine*, 9: e1001225.

Verdeli, H., Clougherty, K., Onyango, G., Lewandowski, E., Speelman, L., Betancourt, T., et al. (2008). Group interpersonal psychotherapy for depressed youth in IDP camps in northern Uganda: adaptation and training. *Child and Adolescent Psychiatric Clinics of North America*, 17: 605–624.

World Health Organization (WHO) (2000). International consortium of psychiatric epidemiology. Cross-national comparisons of mental disorders. *Bulletin of the World Health Organization*, 78: 413–426.

——. (2003). *Quality and Accreditation in Health Care Services: A Global Review.* Geneva: World Health Organization.

——. (2006). *Disease Control Priorities Related to Mental, Neurological, Developmental and Substance Abuse Disorders.* Geneva: World Health Organization.

——. (2007). *Community Health Workers: What Do We Know about Them?* Geneva: World Health Organization.

——. (2008). *Task Shifting: Rational Redistribution of Tasks among Health Workforce Teams.* Geneva: World Health Organization.

——. (2010). *mhGAP Intervention Guide for Mental, Neurological and Substance Use Disorders in Non-Specified Health Settings.* Geneva: World Health Organization.

——. (2011). *Mental Health Atlas 2011.* Geneva: World Health Organization.

Chapter 17

# Task-Shifting in Global Health: Mental Health Implications for Community Health Workers and Volunteers

Kenneth Maes

THERE IS A SMALL TRAFFIC CIRCLE on the southwest portion of Addis Ababa's ring road, not far from the capital city's landfill. Unlike other new roundabouts in the city, which consist of nothing more than circular curbs filled with dirt, this one contains some cement paving stones, and at its center stands a waist-high cement pillar with a small bronze plaque, placed in 2007 by the Ethiopian government, identifying the circle as "Volunteers Square." It is miles away from the monumental squares located in Addis Ababa's city center. There are no big buildings around, and much of the immediate surroundings consist of dirt lots littered with trash. Yet on a sunny Saturday morning in May 2008, for the second annual Ethiopian Volunteers Day, the traffic circle became a ceremonial space, packed with people and temporary canopies colored red, green, and yellow, the colors of Ethiopia's flag. Traffic police were on scene to keep the unusual number of pedestrians safe from the minibuses, dump trucks, and SUVs that made their way through the roundabout. So were a few state and private news reporters, cameras in hand.

This year, the Ethiopian Volunteers Day event was planned by a local nongovernmental organization (NGO) that trained and deployed the largest group of volunteer community health workers (CHWs) in Addis Ababa—more than 600 of them. The vast majority (90%) of these were women, a gender bias that is consistent with regional and global patterns across CHW programs.[1] While many were in their late thirties and forties and married, a substantial proportion were in their twenties and thirties and unmarried, a reflection of the preponderance of young, educated, unemployed, and unmarried individuals in Addis Ababa and populations throughout the Global South.[2] The NGO expected them to serve for a period of 18 months, spending 15 to 40 hours a week visiting the homes of a

*Global Mental Health: Anthropological Perspectives*, edited by Brandon A. Kohrt and Emily Mendenhall, 291–307. © 2015 Left Coast Press, Inc. All rights reserved.

dozen or more people living with HIV/AIDS, providing them counseling, treatment support, and care, and accompanying them as they sought resources from clinics, NGOs, and government welfare offices. The NGO provided $5–$10 USD per month to reimburse the CHWs' transportation expenses but did not provide regular remuneration, and instead expected them to serve as volunteers. Before becoming CHWs, a few had held jobs as teachers or factory workers, and some had independently provided care to people with HIV/AIDS in their neighborhoods, while most were either in secondary school or scraping by as house servants, day laborers, food sellers, or parking attendants.

For the Ethiopian Volunteers Day event, the NGO mustered up at least 200 of its CHWs and provided them all with matching white t-shirts and paper visors, on which had been printed the following words (in Amharic): "Let us protect children from HIV/AIDS and spread volunteer service" and "Everyone should give volunteer service in order to improve the country and fellow people!" The t-shirts and visors also displayed the logos of the local NGO and several of its international funders, including Family Health International (FHI), a prominent U.S.-based NGO involved in HIV/AIDS care and treatment support in Ethiopia and worldwide.

In their t-shirts and visors, packed into the circle and milling about the surrounding area, the volunteer CHWs waited for the arrival of the invited guests—officials from local and international NGOs and government health offices. When the officials eventually arrived, they took their seats under the canopy that had been reserved for them. The event then unfolded with several synthesizer-accom-

Ethiopian Volunteers Day, 2008, Addis Ababa.

Children perform a song for volunteer community health workers, Addis Ababa.

panied performances by professional Ethiopian dancers and a series of speeches, jokes, and poems delivered by the invited officials.

In their speeches, the officials expressed their admiration for the volunteers' willingness to sacrifice and be humble in their pursuit of improving the lives of people with a stigmatized and life-threatening illness. They also reiterated to the assembled volunteers and onlookers that volunteering as a CHW gives one a sense of happiness and fulfillment. An Ethiopian official from FHI's country office asserted that although the volunteers' day-to-day work is full of challenges, "they are happy with what they are doing." An Ethiopian man representing another local NGO said that the benefits of volunteering "begin with mental satisfaction." A Ugandan woman representing the UN Volunteers (UNV) program, whose speech title was listed in the event's program as "The Need to Promote Voluntarism," proclaimed, "the joy that comes from volunteering is the biggest reward."[3]

These messages were not unique to Ethiopian Volunteers Day. They echoed, for instance, a CHW initiation and graduation ceremony put on by the same local NGO and FHI in 2005. At that event, an Ethiopian official from FHI assured the volunteers, "Your mind becomes satisfied from giving care and fulfilling your responsibility to the nation." A government official promised the volunteer initiates that they would be satisfied when they saw their patients improve and become healthier.

## LABORS AND LIVES

The rise of syndemics involving HIV/AIDS, other infectious and noninfectious diseases, poverty, and decrepit national health systems has led to an internationally promoted policy of shifting health-care tasks ("task-shifting" or "task-sharing") from more highly paid and highly trained health professionals to lower paid, less intensely trained, and more numerous health workers (Schneider and Lehmann 2010; Simon et al. 2009). This concept of task-shifting is now invoked for treatments ranging from infectious disease medication management to psychotherapy for mental illness. With the One Million Community Health Workers Campaign, the Frontline Health Workers Coalition, and the World Health Organization's Global Health Workforce Alliance, global health policy makers, donors, and programmers have made it very clear in recent years that they want CHWs in particular to play a big role in achieving primary health care goals (Kakuma et al. 2011; Singh 2011; Watt et al. 2011; WHO 2008).

I first visited Ethiopia in the summer of 2006, after meeting an Ethiopian physician who directed the country's largest HIV/AIDS treatment clinic, which at that time was providing free antiretroviral therapy to a rapidly expanding number of new patients. The well-respected doctor had visited Emory University earlier that year, where I was then a graduate student in search of a dissertation project. At the time, I was interested in understanding the social and clinical circumstances surrounding the deaths of people who had recently gained access to antiretroviral medications. During my first summer in Addis Ababa, I studied Amharic and worked with a translator to conduct verbal autopsies (i.e., postmortem interviews) for about 30 patients who had died during 2005 and 2006 while receiving treatment at the clinic run by my physician host. One of the first things I learned was that often times the volunteer CHW who had cared for and supported the treatment of the deceased was the person most informed and prepared to speak about both clinical and social aspects of the patient's death.

As I learned about these volunteer CHWs, my research interests drifted toward their own labors and lives. I wanted to know who they were, what motivated them to confront death and discrimination, how they formed relationships with patients, and what role they played in the internationally funded antiretroviral therapy programs that were then rolling out across Ethiopia. Whether people receive care, survive, and achieve greater well-being or face abandonment, sicken, and die depends in large part on CHWs. From my perspective, the work that these people did was the most valuable work I could imagine, and yet as volunteers, very little of the vast sums of money that were then going into global HIV/AIDS treatment programs was finding its way into their impoverished households. At the same time, employment was extremely scarce in Addis Ababa, especially for young people, as in other urban centers of the Global South. I wanted to understand why a policy of promoting volunteerism prevails and what it means for the experiences of CHWs.

Community health workers are not just another material health asset. They are social actors within the communities they serve. They are people with complex social and psychological lives that influence health policy and programmatic outcomes—both intended and unintended. The programs that recruit and deploy them, in turn, impact their lives in important ways, by altering their social networks and interpersonal relationships, shaping their desires, and sometimes presenting new economic opportunities.

A growing social science literature critically examines these dynamics, focusing on CHWs' motivations and desires; their exchanges of emotions and prestige in addition to health knowledge and technologies; their solidarities (or lack thereof) with intended beneficiaries; and their evolving positions within the global health industry and local political hierarchies. One study that stands out involved extensive ethnographic research on the social impacts of international donor-funded HIV/AIDS programs in Malawi (Swidler and Watkins 2009). In this context, the authors argue, programs offered "only years of insecure work" to local "volunteers" who actually hoped to receive secure jobs. At the same time, the programs inadvertently raised the volunteers' aspirations for salaried jobs and their associated patron-client networks, leading them to spend years in "an opportunistic, anxiety-provoking chase after an ever-receding mirage" (Swidler and Watkins 2009: 1192).

Many of the volunteer CHWs I encountered in Addis Ababa could also be described as opportunistic and anxious for improvement in their lives. As I show below, the volunteer CHWs who sat down with me for in-depth interviews frequently expressed frustration with their socioeconomic situations, and identified unemployment and lack of payment as important factors shaping their experiences of psychological distress. Furthermore, the three rounds of surveys that I conducted with a random sample of 110 of these volunteers, which included a checklist of common mental disorder (CMD) symptoms, showed that a large proportion of the volunteers had high symptom loads (see Maes et al. 2010 for more details). The survey also provided some striking statistics describing their poverty, with household per capita income levels well under $1 USD per day, and over half experiencing moderate to severe food insecurity.

This portrait of volunteer community health workers as exceedingly poor, frustrated, anxious, and distressed starkly contrasts with the picture of volunteering as a generator of happiness and well-being conveyed by health officials within the colorful volunteer initiation, graduation, and recognition ceremonies I observed in Addis Ababa. Outside of these episodic events, too, I have had many conversations with Ethiopian policy makers and officers involved in community health initiatives about the mental and spiritual satisfaction that CHWs supposedly enjoy.

Claims about the positive emotional, spiritual, and health benefits of volunteering appear to be widespread in Addis Ababa, where Orthodox Christianity dominates culturally, and in other places around the world, partly because such claims are rooted in folk knowledge and religious beliefs that are common throughout the world. In Nepal, for instance, where Hinduism and Buddhism (both Dharmic religions) account for the majority of the population, a group of researchers asked health officials and program managers about the motivations of the Female Community Health Volunteers that have been active in Nepal since the late 1980s (Glenton et al. 2010). The researchers found that the officials and managers were able to justify not paying the volunteers partly on the basis of local cultural beliefs regarding spiritual merit or *dharma*. By humbly serving others, according to the health officials, community health volunteers pursue spiritual merit, which is seen as an appropriate and sufficient reward.[4]

Without examining the perspectives and desires of the volunteers themselves, the authors of the Nepal study used the statements by health officials to argue that paying wages to community health volunteers would ruin a functioning CHW program. They argued that wages would make the volunteers more beholden to the state rather than to their intended beneficiaries, who would stop respecting and trusting the volunteers, and would corrupt or "crowd out" the volunteers' prosocial motivations and threaten their spiritual merit.[5] The authors concluded that, in the context of Nepal, it is problematic to say that adequate and sustained monetary remuneration is essential to the effectiveness and sustainability of CHW programs (cf. WHO 2008).

We should welcome concern over the social and spiritual well-being of CHWs—in Nepal or Ethiopia or anywhere. And there is a big need for research that examines the complex system of knowledge, beliefs, and economics that influence how health officials come up with, promote, implement, and defend CHW policies. But we must question policy recommendations about CHW pay that do not rigorously investigate the experiences and desires of CHWs themselves. And we should beware of the confluence of Western psychological theories and local religious beliefs when they are used by public health officials and practitioners to justify not paying poor people for their labor. The promotion of volunteerism by NGOs, governments, and donors in the global health industry, as well as attempts of managers to keep CHWs productive and happy with their unpaid positions, needs to be studied alongside volunteers' strivings for socioeconomic advancement.

During the two years that I examined the labor and lives of volunteer CHWs in Addis Ababa, I took seriously policy makers' claims about the psychosocial and spiritual benefits of volunteering, as well as CHWs' own testimonies of mental and spiritual satisfaction derived from providing compassionate care and support to others, particularly stigmatized and impoverished people who stood to gain so much. For example, Alemnesh,[6] a young woman, told me about a patient for whom she had cared. "When she was told that she had HIV, she was crying on the road. But now she accepts it, and she is peaceful. She is changed a lot now. When you see that, you will become happy. That is *aïmero ïrkata* [Amharic for "mental satisfaction"]." A volunteer named Eskinder, likewise, told of the time he reconciled a hospitalized teenage girl and her aggressive father, who wanted to withhold antiretroviral treatment from his daughter. It took him several weeks of persistent counseling, but he finally convinced the father to soften. Eskinder reflected that by reconciling people like this, he and his fellow CHWs created happiness and peace for the conflicting parties, pleased God, and generated emotional and spiritual benefits for themselves. "When you reconcile others," Eskinder affirmed, "you will give them happiness, and you will also be satisfied. You will be blessed. For me, that is big happiness."

In the next part of this chapter, I use the survey data and narratives I collected to show how CHWs' experiences of distress relate to their lack of secure employment and complement their testimonies of volunteering as a generator of positive social and emotional experiences. Through my surveys, interviews, and observations, I came to understand people's desires and needs for jobs as well as for the positive social, spiritual, and emotional aspects of humbly serving others. This has led me to ask what kinds of budgetary and social actions—at community, national, and global scales—can be taken to meet these needs. I also have come to believe that CHWs should be in leadership roles in innovative efforts to build and maintain solidarity and the positive experiences of being a CHW. I believe this has the potential to greatly improve their own and their patients' well-being.

## "There is No Happiness with Me"

Alemayehu was unmarried, 33 years old, and living with his parents while volunteering. His sisters had married and migrated to the Middle East to work as domestic servants, and sent money to their parents every few months.[7]

Alemayehu's father was a retired soldier who had served since the latter years of Emperor Haile Selassie's reign. This had important implications for Alemayehu's life, including his eventual decision to become a CHW. After the overthrow of Haile Selassie, Alemayehu's father was deployed to the Ogaden region of Ethiopia to battle Siad Barre's invading forces. Later he was deployed to Asmera to fight guerrillas seeking Eritrea's independence from Ethiopia. During his time on the front lines of these wars, he would send part of his paychecks to his wife and family. Eventually he was shot and wounded, and returned to Addis Ababa. In 1991, he retired from the military and found low-paid work as a house guard in an upscale neighborhood.

Two years later, Alemayehu dropped out of secondary school because he wanted to contribute to the family income. He began working in cotton-processing factories and construction day labor. Though these jobs are economically desirable among a population of young men facing up to 50% unemployment (Serneels 2007), for Alemayehu they were menial and meaningless. After working at them for several years, he stopped and decided to become a volunteer CHW.

Alemayehu was one of the CHWs present at Ethiopian Volunteers Day. When he sat down with me for an interview a couple of weeks after the event, the t-shirt he received that day was visible beneath his collared shirt. When asked what he thought of the event, he joked that it was a bit rushed, due to the late-arriving invited guests. But once things got started, he said, "the mood of the celebration was beautiful. It made me so happy that everyone gathered together and that the volunteers were recognized." Indeed, many of the CHWs I observed at Ethiopian Volunteers Day responded heartily to the speeches and performers, at times collectively waving their visors and ululating, laughing, and applauding.

When asked what benefits he got from volunteering, Alemayehu insisted that he did not get anything material, but affirmed that volunteering made him happy. "I also get spiritual satisfaction, thinking that I might get something good from God." In a subsequent interview, conducted with Alemayehu and his father together, it became clear that his parents encouraged his volunteer efforts. Even though he was not materially supporting the family, they believed he was meeting an important need of their country, and it resonated with their civic and religious values.

At the first and second rounds of survey data collection, however, Alemayehu reported 17 common mental disorder (CMD) symptoms. During a subsequent interview, Alemayehu explained in his own words what was behind the high level of psychological distress that he reported. He said that he had lately been experiencing a "sleeping problem."

> Now at least three times in a week, I wake up [in the middle of the night]. I think about my family . . . about supporting them with a good job. I will not sleep until the next day. There is no happiness with me. When I can't sleep, I will feel depressed all day.

Alemayehu reported moderate to severe food insecurity in surveys. He was far from unique: more than half of the survey sample reported moderate to severe food insecurity, and 80% of the sample reported at least mild food insecurity. Further, the level of food insecurity was strongly correlated with CMD symptom loads: the greater the severity of food insecurity, the greater the number of symptoms reported (Maes et al. 2010). For many CHWs in the sample—women and men—food insecurity pointed to their underlying situation of unemployment.

For Alemayehu and other unmarried men, being unemployed meant more than food insecurity or material poverty. Unemployment was stressful because it translated into an inability to become adults and get married, and to gain the respect (including self-respect) that comes with reciprocating material support with family members and others (Mains 2012). Thus, employment stunted one's ability to achieve social expectations of what it means to be a successful man in society.

For women, too, unemployment translated into food insecurity and a stressful sense of dependency. Rahel was divorced and a mother of grade-school-aged twins. Her broad smile and bright eyes had led me to invite her to participate in in-depth interviews. She reported in the survey that she was 28 years old, but she looked several years older. Perhaps poverty and stress had prematurely aged her skin and hair, or perhaps, as my research assistants warned was common among women in Addis Ababa, she had told us she was younger than she truly was.

Rahel told me she had worked previously as a house servant and occasionally sold tomatoes, onions, and green peppers on the streets of the slum where she lived. She also had provided independent voluntary care for sick people in her neighborhood for some time. She said, "in all my life, what makes me happiest is to see patients being human—being able to work and feed themselves." Having migrated to Addis Ababa with one of her sisters from the northern city of Gondar after completing only five years of schooling, her employment options were very limited.

According to Rahel, when the NGO staff learned of her helpful reputation, they recruited her to become one of the NGO's volunteers. "They said [about me], 'She will be qualified.'" The same NGO staff also arranged for her to adopt a young boy who had been orphaned by AIDS. "They gave me the child, saying, 'We trust that she will raise him properly.'"

In surveys, Rahel reported severe food insecurity. During the first round of survey data collection, she also reported several CMD symptoms, including suicidal thoughts. In a subsequent interview, she explained that she had contemplated suicide a few weeks before the first survey, on a day like any other that she had no food to feed her children. She reassured me, however, that she was not repeatedly or seriously thinking about killing herself. When asked how she managed to get by, she said that her benevolent landlord kept her rent low, that her neighbors provided her with occasional handouts, and that the NGO staff provided her and her children with food support.

Despite her thoughts of suicide, Rahel appeared psychologically resilient, focusing on her humble blessings. She was thankful, for instance, that God had given her children who were "not like children that bother a [poor] family."

They don't say, "Give me lunch. Give me breakfast." They don't say, "There is *injera* in some other house."[8] Most children come home from school and ask you for *mekses* (supper). But my children put down their bags and study. If I don't have anything for them to eat [for dinner], they simply say, "You have nothing today," and they go to sleep. This is God's gift.

Still, Rahel emphasized that she was "very much troubled" by her chronic dependency and inability to feed her children.

The distress of married women often was related to a sense of dependency on their husbands. Yet the narratives provided by Rahel and other women should not suggest that all unemployed women were stressed primarily by their roles as wives and mothers. Like men, some of the unmarried women who spoke with me played major roles in supporting their parents and siblings, and desired to escape poverty and become respected benefactors who provided material support to poor people beyond their kin networks. Lack of good jobs created stress because it meant being unable to achieve a better social position.

For instance, Alemnesh was 26 years old, unmarried, and living with her parents. She recounted her initial interest to become a volunteer as a case of "spiritual envy" (Amharic: *menfesawi qïnat*). She heard about others doing it and desired to be like them. She did not report household food insecurity, unlike the majority of volunteers in the survey sample. This was apparently because her father, an ex-soldier who served during the military Marxist regime (the *Derg*), currently worked, while her two siblings held professional jobs in Addis Ababa. Yet Alemnesh reported a high level of CMD symptoms in the first and second surveys.

The source of Alemnesh's psychological distress became clearer as she narrated her previous experiences of working abroad as a house servant—once in Saudi Arabia and once in Kuwait. By going abroad to work, she had supported her parents and helped put her brother and sister through college.

When I went [abroad], it was for them. I did whatever they needed. And thanks to God, even if I didn't do anything for myself, I [supported] my family. And [my brother and sister] have reached a good level now. They both graduated, and he is working in Ethiopian Airlines, and she is working in the Ministry of Agriculture. And when you see that, you realize that all your exhaustion was for good. I suffered a lot [abroad]. But even if it was [difficult], it is after suffering that you get something.

Alemnesh's peers and supervisors recognized her as an outstanding and reliable volunteer. But after learning that her cousin in Dubai had arranged for her to get an entry-level job with an organization—a job that was not another house servant job—Alemnesh dropped out of the volunteer program, 10 months prior to completing the 18-month commitment expected. She confidently rationalized her decision:

Let alone 150 [US] dollars, there is no job [in Addis Ababa] that will pay you 50 dollars [per month]! . . . I joined this work [volunteering]. But if it is God's will that I get some other opportunity, I will not hold myself back. I served eight months, and I am very, very close with the patients, [especially] with the children. And it is difficult [to leave . . .]—but it is life.

The satisfaction Alemnesh experienced through volunteering was evident. But so was her frustration with the lack of modestly paid jobs in Addis Ababa. She had worked abroad as a lowly house servant and had suffered untold hardships for years to raise her brothers and family to a higher level. Now back in Addis Ababa, she had not yet attained the life she envisioned, which centered on having a decent job that enabled her "to be a respected person," to continue "to fulfill what my family needs," and "to feed and clothe the poor." She stated, "If God gives me wealth, I will be happy if I can do such kind of things. My dream is like that."

Alemnesh's outlook appears very similar to that of Alemayehu. Alemayehu and other men I interviewed said that they wanted to be able to financially support their families and other community members in need. When asked how people can avoid anxiety and sadness, Alemayehu replied, "I think that if you work, then the pressure of life can decrease and you will not be worried by anything. And if you do good things for human beings, then you will not worry. You will get mental rest (Amharic: *aimero ereft*)." In the absence of secure, modestly paid work in Addis Ababa, young women like Alemnesh were compelled to seek opportunities in the Middle East.

In sum, volunteering clearly failed to alleviate the distress that comes from being unemployed and materially dependent on others, even as it allowed CHWs to experience mental and spiritual satisfaction through providing non-financial support to patients.

## "These Things Worry Me"

Unfortunately, the satisfaction that comes with closely relating to and helping patients was not always attainable. Relationships with patients, in fact, were sometimes another source of stress for volunteers. This was because many patients and their families were concerned primarily with obtaining employment and secure food access. The volunteers sometimes witnessed and played a role in uplifting cases in which patients regained their health *and* found jobs or resumed jobs they previously held. But often times, the volunteers witnessed, and felt powerless to change, their patients' experiences of chronic unemployment and food insecurity. It was not enough that they could help patients through counseling and caring, mediating conflicts, supporting drug adherence, and linking them with erratic NGO and government sources of material support.

During the time that Alemayehu was experiencing his sleeping problem, he was visiting a dozen patients, which was roughly the average patient load among his volunteer peers. He told me, "When I wake up [in the middle of the night], I also think about what [my patients] tell me in the day about their problems. . . . Yesterday there was one woman who was lying on the ground. She had nothing to eat. The [antiretroviral] medication was there in her room, unused. Now they get food aid only when their body mass [index] is less than 18.5 [kg/m$^2$]. And I can see these things. . . . So these things worry me."[9]

The witnessing and distress Alemayehu describes were shared with many volunteers, including Markos, who said, "Now I am beginning to feel awful. Almost half of [the patients who were previously receiving food aid] have been dropped from the food aid program. They are just angry. Now you will go to a care recipient's home and all you see is crying. And they start to cry when they see you." The emotions that these volunteers described was not just a feeling of pity or disappointment with the apparent capriciousness of donor aid, but a shameful feeling of not being able to provide patients with the material support they needed.

It was further emotionally distressing when volunteers became the target of patients' frustrations. This could come in the form of challenging questions posed by patients. For example, Alemayehu said that some care recipients who experienced food shortage would ask him, "With what can I take the medication? My insides are burning with medication only." Asayech explained,

> It seems [some care recipients] don't want you as a volunteer caregiver because there is no benefit they receive from you. . . . When they meet us on the road, they think there is something [food] in the backpacks we carry. But the backpack contains our [nursing] materials. "What do you carry in this bag?" they ask. "Why do you have it if it is empty?"

Beyond challenging questions like these, volunteers faced insults and even physical abuse. As one woman who volunteered explained, "There are many patients, and sometimes they will insult you. Forget the insults, but they might [physically harm] you. Volunteer caregiving is a sacrifice. It is a risk—when their stomachs are empty."

Unemployment and food insecurity generate psychological distress by introducing uncertainty and shame into people's lives and eroding meaningful forms of reciprocity (Amare 2010; Hadley et al. 2012). The experiences of the volunteers and patients I encountered in Addis Ababa provide unique support for this claim. Strife—instead of solidarity—between volunteers and patients in the context of antiretroviral treatment is not unique to Addis Ababa. Such strife reflects a broad pattern across global health interventions, including those for mental health, where sophisticated drugs and medical technologies are more accessible than basics like food and jobs (Biehl 2007; Kalofonos 2010; Maes and Kalofonos 2013).

## WHAT CAN BE DONE?

It is clear that CHWs are more than distributors or promoters of biomedical knowledge, technologies, and their associated behaviors (Nading 2013). CHWs, especially those who work with programs that address highly stigmatized illnesses like HIV/AIDS or mental health disorders like psychosis and depression, often engage in serious social and emotional labor. Further, it is clear that we must not view mental health as a service that communities need and CHWs provide. That is, CHWs do not just "work on" the mental health of others. They *share* in the mental health of their unique social networks, and their mental health is intimately connected to their social exchanges and solidarities.

Currently, while mental health services and research are growing in Ethiopia, resources are still very scarce and are concentrated in Addis Ababa.[10] Because of their roles, the CHWs I encountered, probably had access to more psychosocial support than most people. I found that supervisors were aware of their CHWs' stressful situations involving unemployment and strife with patients, and offered informal psychosocial support to help them handle these experiences as constructively as possible. Perhaps CHWs in this (and similar) situations need more formal psychosocial support, such as group interpersonal psychotherapy (cf. Bolton et al. 2003). Yet it became clear to me that what they needed most was income, in addition to the positive emotions that they were already experiencing as CHWs.

Though it is problematic to simply generalize from HIV/AIDS-focused CHWs in Addis Ababa to CHWs in the various places they operate around the world, I contend that across programs and locales, CHW jobs are potentially *good* jobs from the perspectives of many unemployed and underemployed men and women. The caveat is that this may be true only if such jobs synergistically combine regular income and job security with the emotional satisfaction and experiences of solidarity that can come with working to improve the health and well-being of others.

Anthropologist Daniel Mains, an author in this volume, argues that work is valued by youth in urban Ethiopia primarily for what it does to one's relationships and social position. Working in any occupation, or remaining unemployed, places men and women in particular relationships to others, and these relationships have important impacts on experiences of psychological distress and well-being (Mains 2012). The ethnographic work I conducted reveals that being a volunteer CHW in Addis Ababa allowed women and men to form solid relationships with others, particularly patients with a stigmatized illness, which had positive impacts on their own mental health. Yet the CHW role did not put these women and men into their ideal positions within their ideal social networks, mainly due to the fact that it was unpaid work. As unpaid volunteers, they remained overly dependent economically on others and were too often unable to give patients and others material support.

There is clearly a great need to advocate and work toward policies aimed at creating secure and fairly remunerated jobs for CHWs. In addition to carefully studying the labors and lives of CHWs, including their own perceptions of and efforts to change how their labor is bought by global health institutions, anthropologists can play an important role by "studying *up*" (Nader 1972) to understand how policy makers make CHW policies and what it might take to convince them to use scarce resources to create secure and salaried jobs. "Studying up" refers to studying people in power such as policy makers, NGO leaders, clinicians, and employers. This contrasts with the dominant thrust of anthropological research, in which patients, persons living in poverty, and marginalized groups are the primary research participants. By studying up, we can develop a clearer understanding of policy makers' competing values and goals, and how these shape the complex policy-making process, and hopefully help CHWs and other stakeholders come to agreement on job creation policies.

Yet simply creating more CHW jobs is surely not a panacea for poverty reduction and community health. CHW job creation might even lead to new inequalities and erode solidarities between CHWs and intended beneficiaries who remain unemployed, as suggested by Glenton and colleagues (2010) in regard to Nepal. The potential for envy and strife, however, may be avoided by combining the creation of CHW jobs with dedicated efforts to reinforce beliefs that community health work is morally admirable, and to enhance cooperative solidarity between CHWs, intended beneficiaries, and health institutions so that community health work actually remains psychosocially satisfying. In a global health industry that includes well-paid experts and large numbers of underpaid and unpaid CHWs, it is easy to be critical of CHW-recognition ceremonies, such as the one I described at the opening of this chapter, and of the day-to-day reinforcement of CHWs' willingness to humbly sacrifice their time and energy for the benefit of others. But, on the other hand, the genuine mental satisfaction that CHWs experience though combating discrimination, caring for patients, and reconciling interpersonal conflicts, depends in part on the efforts of NGO and government staff, in addition to local church leaders and families, to ritually and mundanely reinforce the significance of such experiences, to culturally construct the CHW role as one that should be admired as morally upright, and to pump volunteers up with positive emotions there on the spot. Ceremonies like Ethiopian Volunteers Day are not perfect, but they are important.

Thus, there is a clear need to maintain these kinds of efforts and, more importantly, to innovate and improve them. One way to go about this is to take a more critical and reflexive approach, by testing out new techniques and evaluating them according to their impacts on solidarity, motivations, and values. CHWs should become more central actors in such efforts. Many public health practitioners and health officials have plenty of experience in designing and participating in ceremonies, rituals, and communication efforts in order to shape values, motivations, and behaviors of CHWs and intended beneficiaries. But CHWs, I believe, should not just be sitting in the audience. They should be coming up with innovations and evaluating them according to their own understanding of what creates solidarity between CHWs and intended beneficiaries and what makes their work psychosocially and spiritually fulfilling.

## Notes

1  See Akintola 2008.

2  See Gurmu and Mace 2008.

3  Unlike the Ethiopian volunteer CHWs honored at the event that day, UN Volunteers, who serve in various countries around the world, are actually well remunerated. They receive a monthly allowance that is intended to cover "basic living expenses" (but often goes much further); allowances for travel, "settling-in" and "resettlement," paid at the beginning and end of the assignment; annual leave; as well as life, health, and disability insurance (see http://www.unv.org/how-to-volunteer/register-to-be-a-un-volunteer/qualifications-and-conditions-of-service.html). For many, serving as a UN Volunteer is a lucrative opportunity leading to regular (and even better-paid) employment within a UN agency.

4  Such claims may also be influenced by the global dissemination of a growing Western scientific literature in social epidemiology and the neurosciences on the positive psychological and other health impacts of volunteering, the findings and paradigms of which often resonate with local knowledge. This literature tends to focus on volunteers living in North America. See, for example, Borgonovi 2008; Poulin 2014; Schreier, Schonert-Reichl, and Chen 2013.

5  The authors cite an article on motivation crowding theory in the *Journal of Economic Surveys* to help make this point (Frey and Jegen 2001).

6  All names used in this chapter are pseudonyms.

7  Facing limited work opportunities within urban Ethiopia, many women brave the difficulties of migrating to the Middle East to gain an income as domestic servants. For some of the women CHWs I encountered in Addis Ababa, becoming CHWs happened after returning from stints in the Middle East, and for some it preceded this sort of labor migration. See the case of Alemnesh later in this chapter, and Maes (2012). Young Ethiopian men, too, often dream of migrating abroad to work and to escape their positions of economic dependency upon their families (Mains 2012).

[8] *Injera*, a pancake made from fermented *teff* and other grains, is a staple of local diets.

[9] In 2008, the World Food Programme (WFP) began to require that people living with HIV/AIDS also have a body mass index below a cutoff of 18.5 (kg/m$^2$) to be eligible for food aid that used to be distributed more generously. Food insecurity has emerged as a major problem that interacts with HIV/AIDS infection and treatment in synergistic ways. See Singer 2011 and Kalofonos 2010.

[10] See, for example, Alem et al. 2010.

## References

Akintola, O. (2008). Unpaid HIV/AIDS care in southern Africa: forms, context, and implications. *Feminist Economics*, 14 (4): 117–147.

Alem, A., Pain, C., Araya, M., and Hodges, B. D. (2010). Co-creating a psychiatric resident program with Ethiopians, for Ethiopians, in Ethiopia: the Toronto Addis Ababa Psychiatry Project (TAAPP). *Academic Psychiatry*, 34 (6): 424–432.

Amare, Y. (2010). *Urban Food Insecurity and Coping Mechanisms: A Case Study of Lideta Sub-City in Addis Ababa*. Addis Ababa: Forum for Social Studies.

Biehl, J. (2007). *Will to Live: AIDS Therapies and the Politics of Survival*. Princeton, New Jersey: Princeton University Press.

Bolton, P., Bass, J., Neugebauer, R., Verdeli, H., Clougherty, K. F., Wickramaratne, P., Speelman, L., Ndogoni, L., and Weissman, M. (2003). Group interpersonal psychotherapy for depression in rural Uganda: a randomized controlled trial. *JAMA*, 289 (23): 3117–3124.

Borgonovi, F. (2008). Doing well by doing good: the relationship between formal volunteering and self-reported health and happiness. *Social Science and Medicine*, 66 (11): 2321–2334.

Frey, B. S., and Jegen, R. (2001). Motivation crowding theory. *Journal of Economic Surveys*, 15 (5): 589–611.

Glenton, C., Scheel, I. B., Pradhan, S., Lewin, S., Hodgins, S., and Shrestha, V. (2010). The female community health volunteer programme in Nepal: decision makers' perceptions of volunteerism, payment and other incentives. *Social Science and Medicine*, 70 (12): 1920–1927.

Gurmu, E., and Mace, R. (2008). Fertility decline driven by poverty: the case of Addis Ababa, Ethiopia. *Journal of Biosocial Science*, 40 (3): 339–358.

Hadley, C., Stevenson, E. G. J., Tadesse, Y., and Belachew, T. (2012). Rapidly rising food prices and the experience of food insecurity in urban Ethiopia: impacts on health and well-being. *Social Science and Medicine*, 75 (12): 2412–2419.

Kakuma, R., Minas, H., van Ginneken, N., Dal Poz, M. R., Desiraju, K., Morris, J. E., and Scheffler, R. M. (2011). Human resources for mental health care: current situation and strategies for action. *The Lancet*, 378 (9803): 1654–1663.

Kalofonos, I. A. (2010). "All I eat is ARVs": the paradox of AIDS treatment interventions in central Mozambique. *Medical Anthropology Quarterly*, 24 (3): 363–380.

Maes, K. C. (2012). Volunteerism or labor exploitation? Harnessing the volunteer spirit to sustain AIDS treatment programs in urban Ethiopia. *Human Organization*, 71 (1): 54–64.

Maes, K., and Kalofonos, I. (2013). Becoming and remaining community health workers: perspectives from Ethiopia and Mozambique. *Social Science and Medicine*, 87: 52–59.

Maes, K. C., Hadley, C., Tesfaye, F., and Shifferaw, S. (2010). Food insecurity and mental health: surprising trends among community health volunteers in Addis Ababa, Ethiopia during the 2008 food crisis. *Social Science and Medicine*, 70 (9): 1450–1457.

Mains, D. (2012). *Hope is Cut: Youth, Unemployment, and the Future in Urban Ethiopia*. Philadelphia: Temple University Press.

Nader, L. (1972) Up the anthropologist: perspectives gained from studying up. In D. Hymes (ed.), *Reinventing Anthropology*, pp. 284–311. New York: Pantheon Books.

Nading, A. M. (2013). "Love isn't there in your stomach": a moral economy of medical citizenship among Nicaraguan community health workers. *Medical Anthropology Quarterly*, 27 (1): 84–102.

Poulin, M. J. (2014). Volunteering predicts health among those who value others: two national studies. *Health Psychology*, 33 (2): 120–129.

Schneider, H., and Lehmann, U. (2010). Lay health workers and HIV programmes: implications for health systems. *AIDS Care*, 22 (Supplement 1): 60–67.

Schreier, H., Schonert-Reichl, K., and Chen, E. (2013). Effect of volunteering on risk factors for cardiovascular disease in adolescents: a randomized controlled trial. *JAMA Pediatrics*, 167 (4): 327–332.

Serneels, Pieter. (2007). The nature of unemployment among young men in urban Ethiopia. *Review of Development Economics*, 11 (1): 170–186.

Simon, S., Chu, K., Frieden, M., Candrinho, B., Ford, N., Schneider, H., and Biot, M. (2009). An integrated approach of community health worker support for HIV/AIDS and TB care in Angonia district, Mozambique. *BMC International Health and Human Rights*, 9 (1): 13.

Singer, M. (2011). Toward a critical biosocial model of ecohealth in southern Africa: the HIV/AIDS and nutrition insecurity syndemic. *Annals of Anthropological Practice*, 35 (1): 8–37.

Singh, P. (2011). *One Million Community Health Workers Technical Task Force Report*. New York: Earth Institute at Columbia University.

Swidler, A., and Watkins, S. C. (2009). "Teach a man to fish": the sustainability doctrine and its social consequences. *World Development*, 37 (7): 1182–1196.

Watt, P., Brikci, N., Brearley, L., and Rawe, K. (2011). *No Child Out of Reach*. London: Save the Children.

World Health Organization (WHO). (2008). *Task Shifting: Rational Redistribution of Tasks among Health Workforce Teams—Global Recommendations and Guidelines*. Geneva: World Health Organization.

Chapter 18

# "We Can't Find This Spirit of Help": Mental Health, Social Issues, and Community Home-Based Care Providers in Central Mozambique

Ippolytos Kalofonos

I began visiting Beatriz five months ago. When I first arrived, Beatriz would do that thing, go to the clinic one day, make an appointment, then follow other programs, so she remained sick. Well, her baby was born with problems. I called her over and spoke with her, and had her arrange for me to meet with her and her husband. After speaking to them, I went and consulted with her father. Her father had separated from her mother, and married the mother of Lucia [another young woman who was also ill]. Well now, his daughter is sick, and his wife's daughter is sick. You see? That's our situation here. So, I asked to speak with young Lucia's husband as well, and he gave me permission to enter his house and speak with them. They were going to a traditional healer for treatments, then going to the clinic, round and round. I proposed another mechanism. I said, "Will you accept, starting today, your wife accompanies us, begins new consultations?" I also spoke about this with her father, who then spoke with his son-in-law. So we took them all to the testing center: the two young women, Beatriz and Lucia, and one of the young men, Lucia's husband. They were all positive, and the husband also had tuberculosis, which he began treatment for. Now they are all following their treatment, I keep visiting them, checking on them, but they are fine. Just Beatriz's husband, he doesn't want to test, but his wife, she is free to pursue her treatment and he has no problem with us.

Arminda

A SINGLE MOTHER OF THREE in her sixth decade of life, Arminda was a community home-based care (CHBC) volunteer participating in an ethnographic study on the local impact of the HIV/AIDS treatment scale-up in central Mozambique (Kalofonos 2008, 2010, 2014; Maes and Kalofonos 2013). This passage provides a

---

*Global Mental Health: Anthropological Perspectives*, edited by Brandon A. Kohrt and Emily Mendenhall, 309–323. © 2015 Left Coast Press, Inc. All rights reserved.

glimpse into the arduous nature of her work as she counseled ill individuals and their families, recruited them for HIV testing, monitored and accompanied them through treatment, and offered comfort-oriented care and assistance with activities of daily living as well as spiritual and emotional support. According to UNAIDS, a joint United Nations program on HIV/AIDS, volunteers such as Arminda constitute one of the "key pillars" of AIDS treatment programs and have been "one of the outstanding features of the epidemic" (UNAIDS 2002, 2010).

In practice, however, their work is not always recognized by local actors or supported by their own organizations. While medical care for AIDS in Mozambique was administered through government health clinics, a program administrator explained that "social" issues were left to "the community."

I came to this research as a medical student and anthropology doctoral candidate interested in what happened "on the ground" when global health interventions were put into action. I was particularly interested in following the scale-up of antiretroviral treatment, which had not yet been initiated when I began working in central Mozambique. I initially focused on the experiences of people living with HIV/AIDS, but I quickly encountered and became interested in community home-based care volunteers and the work they did.

This chapter presents the experiences of frontline providers such as Arminda and those for whom she cares. The complex issues they confront together emphasize the practical difficulty of separating medical from social issues in considering health issues in general. The division of medical and social is particularly shortsighted for mental health. These narratives point to the importance of addressing structural and socioeconomic issues such as livelihood and food insecurity for mental health alongside the clinical indicators of treatment. These are key concerns for the well-being not only of patients but also of the community health workers who perform vital functions of global health programs.

## ARMINDA: "I HAVE A PERSONAL SPIRIT FOR THIS"

Arminda had been a volunteer with a community-based organization in Mozambique, Together for Life, for over 10 years and was one of the leaders, overseeing the work of the other volunteers in her neighborhood. Like many of her generation, her life story was defined by the region's violent political transitions. She grew up in an *aldeia*, a colonial village liberated by Frelimo during the war of independence against the Portuguese in the latter half of the 1960s. As Frelimo ascended and supported African nationalist movements in neighboring Rhodesia and South Africa, Rhodesian forces fought back, first directly (locally known as "Smith's War," referring to the Rhodesian leader) and then by fostering a proxy war through a Mozambican insurgency called Renamo. She recalled those uncertain days of her childhood: "We suffered the war out there in the bush, the war of our neighbor, Ian Smith. He came with airplanes, dropping bombs. We ran carrying bundles in our hands, whatever we could fit on our heads. I was a girl at the time, but my mother was pregnant so I had to carry my baby brother." As Zimbabwe's war ended and the armed conflict in Mozambique escalated in the 1980s, thanks to support from South Africa and the United States, Arminda's family fled to Zimbabwe. The family moved to Beira to join a brother in 1990, before settling in Chimoio a few years later. As much as 40% of the Mozambican population was estimated to have been displaced during this period. Rural inhabitants moved to neighboring countries or urban centers along the international highway (Hanlon 1996).

Chimoio is linked to Zimbabwe by a shared Shona cultural history and an international highway. Chimoio grew from a colonial railway stop into a city around a Portuguese textile factory built in 1944. Nationalized in 1975 and privatized in the late 1980s, the factory employed 2,500 to 5,000 residents before folding in 2000 (Guerreiro 2003; Pitcher 2002). Chimoio's population has grown from 50,000 at independence in 1975 to over 250,000 in recent years (Instituto Nacional de Estatística 2008). Most residents live in shantytowns, called the "cane city," which ring the former colonial "cement city." This zone dramatically grew during the war and has continued to expand in subsequent years. Households in the cane city combine wages or income from the informal market with subsistence production on *machambas* (subsistence plots) outside the city. The dominant languages are Portuguese and Chiteve, a variant of Shona.

Arminda operated a neighborhood market stall in one of the sprawling popular neighborhoods. She lived behind the stall with her daughters and frequently hosted a visiting relative or two. She had separated from her husband many years before and never felt the need to remarry. Arminda converted to the Universal Church of the Kingdom of God, an international Pentecostal church, soon after she moved to Chimoio in the mid-1990s: "My daughter had been sick with a bronchitis that just never passed: cough, pneumonia, for seven months. Nothing I could do seemed to help, until my brother took me to his church and with prayer, it passed. I joined the church, and our family has continued to be blessed ever since." The postwar period in Chimoio has seen an explosion of locally, regionally, and internationally based Pentecostal churches that focus on healing (Pfeiffer 2002). These churches are particularly popular among women, and recruit through healing practices.

Arminda first learned about Together for Life from a colleague in the market and was recruited by a fellow church member active in the organization. She recalled hearing about "this association where many people come together from different countries and exchange opinions about religion, about civilization, about these positive diseases." It reminded her of an association of refugees she had been a part of during her years in Zimbabwe: "We had a partnership there, we made a contribution and then there was help for all in times of illness or death. We also studied ideas together, how to live with others, how to educate children. . . . I was introduced to different kinds of religion. That had been a great experience. I thought it would be good to have it again."

She was one of the first to be involved in the emerging CHBC project in the late 1990s. When the Ministry of Health began instituting formal trainings in the early 2000s, Arminda was among the first to receive the certifications, which she proudly displayed: Prevention and Care of STDs and HIV/AIDS, Basic Care of the Sick, Basic Care of Children and Vulnerable Orphans, Agriculture and Micro-enterprise. In addition to this formal training, Arminda had experience caring for a daughter and a brother with AIDS.

Arminda felt she had a spiritual calling to do this work. Her father was a *curandeiro*, a traditional healer. She assisted him and recalled what she inherited and learned from him:

> I have a personal spirit for this. My father was a *curandeiro* . . . sick people always came [to our house]. So this work was nothing new. My patients also, those who can walk, they come here and tell me their stories. Sometimes they feel isolated at home, there are things they can speak to me about that maybe they are too proud to share with their families. It's not difficult for me, because in my father's house, we always ate together [patients and family], we were all one family. I once asked "*Papá*, why is our family always so full? My uncle's house is not like this, why is ours?" He answered, "When you are accustomed to hosting guests in your home, at another moment, you will find yourself in another country, another place, and those you helped will recognize you and open their homes."

Arminda took pride in her work, particularly in the trust that her neighbors granted her by opening up about their HIV status and their personal challenges. She was well known in the neighborhood. The ill and their family members sought her out: "They tell me, *Mamá*, I can tell you my secret." Other times she would be referred by local leaders. Clinic staff referred patients to their local volunteers. Arminda would gradually approach families she did not know well, taking her time to familiarize herself with the situation and to gain trust. Volunteers were officially assigned up to five or six patients to follow, but in practice they might follow many more than that. They could routinely spend two to three days per week on their visits.

When the project began in the mid-1990s, hospitals were overwhelmed and had no treatment to offer. People died at home, and the volunteers provided palliative care, bathing the sick and helping to make them comfortable while educating and consoling families. As testing and treatment became available, their duties shifted to outreach and recruitment. Post-antiretroviral scale-up, they encouraged their patients to either test, begin treatment, or stay adherent. They documented the health status of those they visited, collecting statistics that would be pooled at the organization level and "uploaded" to the ministry of health and funders. Data collection forms used pictures for the generally illiterate volunteers and included numbers on antiretrovirals, tuberculosis treatment, prophylaxis, pregnancy, those enrolled in the clinic, those lost to follow-up, and death. There were as many as 130 volunteers in Chimoio and 240 total for the entire province.

As they counseled, educated, cleaned, recruited, monitored, and accompanied, volunteers provided emotional and psychological support. While HIV clinics employed talented, if overburdened, social workers who worked with patients and families to mobilize social support as well as peer counselors to troubleshoot adherence issues, there were no formal mental health interventions, despite the fact that mental health disorders such as depression and anxiety have a relatively high prevalence among the HIV-positive (Collins et al. 2006) and in food-insecure areas (Weaver and Hadley 2009). With clinics struggling to meet the HIV testing and treatment needs of their patients, Mozambique has few health care workers trained to assess and treat people with mental illness (WHO 2005). While mental health services are officially integrated into primary care and a comprehensive mental health plan is in place, the majority of mental health resources are concentrated in the capital of Maputo. Existing mental health services cover 0.29% of the population, and in 2007 the system was estimated as capable of offering only one mental health care visit per week in health centers outside of the capital (MISAU 2007: 51). By default, mental health was included in the vast category of "social issues" and largely left to "the community." Thus, mental health care was provided by volunteers like Arminda who labored without compensation.

## IVO: "IT IS THOSE THOUGHTS THAT KILL"

One of Arminda's former patients, Ivo, became a peer counselor in the HIV clinic. He explained that the isolation, loneliness, and hopelessness he had suffered was the deadliest aspect of the disease:

> Many die from rage, not from the disease. Rage at not having anyone that consoles them, at being shut up in the house. When I was ill, I felt alone, I thought many things, that I used to be well. Now I am like this. I will die like this. I have no more life like this. That stress starts and the stress can ruin a person. Thinking too much! It is those thoughts that kill.

Ivo recalled overhearing family and friends speaking of his imminent death. He felt his family pulling away from him as he wasted away. He himself believed he was going to die and recalled withdrawing within himself. Chronic illness frequently drained the resources and energy of households and families. In the case of AIDS, an illness with no cure and, prior to the scale-up, no viable treatment, families were faced with hard choices about where to allocate scarce resources, a form of "lifeboat ethics" where the "pragmatics of saving the savable" was evoked (Scheper-Hughes 1992). When individuals were blamed for contracting HIV through immoral behavior and their disease worsened despite the family's best efforts, families at times withdrew care in order to benefit more productive members. This attitude is frequently labeled "stigma," a term implying fear and ignorance, but that does not adequately capture the political-economic dimensions of the dynamic (Parker and Aggleton 2003). The Shona term for the phrase Ivo used, "thinking too much," is *kufungisisa*, and has been proposed as a Shona model of depression and anxiety (Patel et al. 2001).

Ivo felt immobilized by his physical illness, tortured by his thoughts, and enraged at his helplessness. He recalled Arminda's frequent visits and gentle, patient urging to get tested:

> I was at zero. I was sick and had nothing and felt I had tried everything. Arminda is a neighbor, and she would visit and see how I was. On one of her visits she asked, "Have you gone to the AIDS clinic?" I tried to get there before, but they said, "No, you first have to get tested for HIV," and I did not know where or how to get that done. So I went to get tested, but they said I had to go to the hospital first. I was confused and afraid. All these doors, papers, and places to go.... I just went home. And that was it. I thought life ended with AIDS anyways. Arminda came and picked me up the next day. She said, "Let's go [to the AIDS clinic]." And we went.

Arminda's guidance not only led to medical treatment for Ivo, but he also qualified for a supplemental food basket from the World Food Program (WFP). Arminda also referred Ivo to the association of people living with HIV/AIDS that Together for Life had founded when their patients began recovering. Many of the HIV-positive volunteers joined this group, which was an important source of peer support and education, and battled the toxic isolation Ivo described. Ivo was active in the association during the treatment scale-up, and he was recruited to work as a peer support counselor. Ivo's case illustrates the ways "thinking too much," stigma, food insecurity, poverty, and HIV/AIDS interacted syndemically (Singer and Clair 2003).

Arminda's status as a known and trusted neighbor gave her an opportunity to develop a relationship with Ivo over time. She reached out to her demoralized and overwhelmed neighbor, offered him hope, and connected him to important resources for survival. Ivo reflected on the impact Arminda had in his life: "She is my guide and my savior. I think she saved me. When I had nowhere to turn and nothing to eat, she took me to the proper place, and I received food and the treatment I needed." Not all of Arminda's patients shared Ivo's success.

## CHICA: "YES, I AM BETTER. BUT MY STOMACH HURTS!"

I accompanied Arminda on her visit to Chica, a woman whom she had recruited for testing and antiretroviral treatment. Arminda was concerned about Chica's difficulties in adhering to her medication regime amid a stressful and chaotic life. We came upon Chica's house around lunchtime. A young woman was cooking peas in front of the family hut as an elderly woman and two children ate porridge that was the characteristic beige color of USAID corn-soy blend. On the far side of the yard, another young woman and man sat selling *nipa*, a powerful brew of fermented sugar cane.

We entered the hut and, after initiating the visit with a short prayer, Arminda proudly introduced Chica, saying: "Here is my patient and I can tell you she is much better!" Chica added: "Yes, I am better. But my stomach hurts!"

In the months since Arminda had first seen her, Chica had begun antiretroviral therapy and her health and appearance had improved significantly, despite spotty adherence and clinic attendance. Antiretrovirals were commonly said to cause hunger in central Mozambique (Kalofonos 2010), and indeed Chica endorsed this: "This medicine, it bites. It's not like a normal hunger. If I don't eat when I take it, I tremble and shake. It is said this medicine will kill you if you don't eat with it. If I take my pills at night, my stomach wakes me up, and I have to eat. In the morning when I awake, I have to eat again." She had been awarded one of the precious and limited WFP ration cards, entitling her to receive 10 kilograms of corn-soy blend and 1 kilogram of legumes per month, an amount that, when shared among her three children, two grandchildren, and her elderly mother, lasted four days. She also sold *nipa* and sought odd jobs. When she did not have food to eat, Chica often skipped her antiretroviral medication. She told Arminda of her anguish:

> I have no hope of anything here. Nothing. Full of problems. My heart aches. I just try not to think too much. I'd like to find some work, or a husband who will take care of me. Living well, you don't think much. Now when you start to get sick, looking for money and not finding any, children needing things . . . doesn't that make you think too much? *That's* the disease that can kill. It invites death.

Arminda listened empathically, prayed with her, and discussed possible avenues of support. Chica disclosed that she engaged in serial short-lived sexual relationships with men who could provide her with material support and did not always use condoms. Her current stomach pain was accompanied by a foul-smelling vaginal discharge that she was ashamed to reveal, lest she be rebuked for having unprotected sex. She had been told this was gonorrhea in the past, and she occasionally treated it with antibiotics, when she could afford to seek treatment. Arminda arranged to accompany Chica to the clinic later that week to be assessed and also encouraged her to stay adherent to her antiretrovirals. Arminda would visit daily for the rest of the week to continue to support Chica's adherence. Arminda would bring food from her own home for Chica to take with her antiretroviral medications.

## Arminda's Distress

The storm of challenges Chica faced amplified her distress by causing her to "think too much," leading to hopelessness and despair. Arminda was able to offer guidance and emotional and treatment support, but she could not offer steady employment or sustenance. Arminda had mixed feelings following a visit with Chica, which she expressed as she wrinkled her brow:

> That's the difficulty of this work. When a patient doesn't have food, doesn't have soap to wash their clothes, no way of getting to the hospital when they are ill, with children who depend on her . . . I bring them things from my own home, because I can't let a patient die of hunger. You have to take a bit of whatever you have. Sometimes she'll come herself to my house, "*Mamá*, I'm hungry!" But what can I do? I'm a person too.

Arminda and her fellow volunteers were acutely aware of their limitations, and they were often overwhelmed by the needs of their patients. They were not able to transport the bedridden to hospitals due to cost and lack of transportation. Further, they were unable to offer more than symbolic amounts of food from their own homes when their patients complained of hunger. While they experienced considerable satisfaction when their patients recovered, they were distressed by their inability to address their patients' basic needs, especially for food. They also endured many losses, as more of Arminda's patients had died than were still alive: "We are used to seeing them greet us, having conversations, looking for a way forward together. That makes us proud of work done well. But when a patient dies, we feel it."

Volunteers often took setbacks personally and suffered feelings of guilt and thoughts that led to sleepless nights as well. One of Arminda's colleagues told me: "I get this nervousness, a kind of stress, and loneliness, because there is often nothing more I can do." Arminda's comment above, "I'm a person too," is a reminder that the volunteers were often in the same situations of chronic uncertainty as their patients, and were often HIV-positive themselves or caring for family members with AIDS. As frontline providers, volunteers not only suffered emotional consequences of their work but also might be blamed for setbacks. Families turned on volunteers when their loved ones died despite following the advice and counsel volunteers gave. Arminda was threatened by the husband of a woman who tested HIV-positive. At other times, volunteers were accused of actually causing illness through witchcraft so that they might be paid to visit the sick and keep the benefits meant for patients.

Despite the satisfaction and pride that Arminda derived from relationships she formed with patients like Ivo and Chica, she expressed some frustrations. She was frustrated by inconsistent and insufficient sources of support for her patients, the majority of whom complained of hunger. Together for Life lost their WFP contract, cutting off the supplemental food baskets her patients looked forward to. As the number of patients in treatment grew, the amount of food assistance broadly available did not keep pace. Volunteers were no longer asked to record data regarding food availability, a trend that concerned Arminda.

Like most volunteers, Arminda hoped her certifications and experience would translate into steady employment. She recalled, "When we were trained, we were told we would be needed one day [as salaried workers]. Well, that day has not come." Furthermore, Together for Life's incentives for volunteers were inconsistently provided and deemed inadequate. Initially, most volunteers received trainings and certificates, t-shirts, snacks and lunches, and allotments of rice, corn, oil, or soap. With the rapid treatment scale-up, the Ministry of Health set an official incentive rate of around 60% of the minimum wage (about $24 USD/month) for volunteers. This was meant to prevent NGOs from paying volunteers higher salaries than nurses and, moreover, was a *recommended* payment amount, not a requirement that volunteers be paid. For women like Arminda, the monthly incentive was usually half the amount she made through her market stall, representing a significant sum. What Arminda and her colleagues actually received depended on the flow of grant monies. After years of demands and appeals made by Together for Life volunteers, they finally began receiving the recommended amount (volunteers for another local organization received only half of this amount). After a year, however, the grant supplying this funding expired and the future of the program was in doubt. Arminda expressed her frustration:

We are expected to carry the burden of labor but not the benefits? Our organization has built a nice office. Those people who work in the office, they drive cars to work. But those of us who do the work in the neighborhoods? This is not our office, and that hurts. We built that office, we built the organization. We arrive at the homes of the sick, and they say, "Together for Life is here." We are Together for Life. But we [volunteers] are the last to receive and the first to lose. Perhaps we should discuss selling the office.

For Arminda, the "work in the neighborhoods" was the difficult work of relating to and accompanying patients and their families. From her perspective, it was unfair that officers of the organization enjoyed elite status and materially benefited from her work while her aspirations for socioeconomic advancement went unfulfilled. The issue of payment was controversial. The administrators of Together for Life's home-based care programs feared that payment of volunteers would render the programs unaffordable and therefore unsustainable. They worried that volunteers who were motivated by payment would be less effective than those motivated by altruism, compassion, and a religious calling. At one CHBC meeting, a program coordinator scolded the volunteers, telling them, "This work should come from the heart. It should not be done for payment, but to help our neighbors, our brothers and sisters. It is our work that we do. If we get paid, it is not a bad thing, but we do not do this work in order to be paid, and we do the work even when we are not being paid." Another coordinator told me that the essential qualification of a CHBC volunteer was *"Tem que ter sentimento"*; a literal translation of the Portuguese statement is, "they have to have feeling," or the capacity for compassion. While an altruistic motivation in volunteers was prioritized by the organization, the administrators and coordinators cited above did, in fact, receive salaries for their own work.

Arminda recalled her initial vision for the project, of a collective effort for communal improvement, with disappointment. We had just visited another volunteer and participant in this study who was HIV-positive and had suffered a stroke resulting in partial paralysis. Arminda reflected on the cruel irony that this long-time volunteer was now in the same position as her patients, with no protections or benefits despite her many years of service: *"Mamá* is sick, her arm is paralyzed, she can't work, what will she eat? A person who was working. Today she has stopped and what benefits does she have?" She reflected on the prosocial spirit of the volunteers and lamented the absence of this spirit in other quarters:

> We know how to help one another, and we have our patients who rely on us. . . . Who wants to work for nothing? Those of us with this spirit, we still visit the sick. You can't just call this work. . . . This isn't an enterprise or a business, it's more like a church. . . . But this spirit doesn't appear for everyone. We've got this situation amongst the volunteers. We are dying and being buried in disgrace. We lack transport, we lack coffins, nothing to cover even ourselves. Where is Together for Life? They have fallen on hard times. This spirit is needed . . . a spirit of help, support. Here in the city, we can't find this spirit of help.

Despite her frustration, Arminda maintained that she and her fellow volunteers would continue volunteering. But she noted a double standard: that while they selflessly served their patients, they could not expect the same from their organization. This may reflect the difficult reality of community-based organizations whose fortunes are tied to two- and five-year grant cycles, yet Arminda noted that as volunteers fell, the organization remained standing. Neither the burden of labor nor the chronic uncertainties that the volunteers faced were equally shared.

## MEDICAL ISSUES, SOCIAL ISSUES, AND MENTAL HEALTH

This chapter presents the experience of Arminda, a CHBC volunteer working with people living with AIDS in central Mozambique. She and her patients face syndemic HIV/AIDS, food and livelihood insecurity, stigma, and psychological distress. Food insecurity has been shown to be linked to high-risk sexual behavior among women (Weiser et al. 2007). There is a negative cycle of interaction between mental health and poverty (Lund et al. 2011) and between mental health and food insecurity (Weaver and Hadley 2009), particularly in the context of HIV/AIDS (Maes et al. 2011). Interventions targeting livelihood can decrease stigma and foster well-being among people with AIDS (Holmes and Winskell 2013). Improving food insecurity and strengthening social support may have synergistic beneficial effects on both mental health and HIV outcomes among people living with HIV/AIDS in resource-limited settings such as central Mozambique (Tsai et al. 2012).

CHBC has the potential to simultaneously address many of these issues by providing direct care, education, and support and by guiding sufferers to appropriate resources while training and supporting members of this same community. The example of the AIDS treatment scale-up is proposed as a template for the scale-up of other chronic conditions, including mental illness (Patel and Prince 2010; Rabkin and El-Sadr 2011). Paying attention to volunteer experiences may avoid reproducing flawed approaches.

This chapter shows how volunteer programs can rely on taken-for-granted ideas of "community" as a preexisting resource to be tapped by global health initiatives and as a stand-in for underfunded and undermined public health systems (Maes 2012). The justification for the creation of the CHBC program, that health care networks are weak and overwhelmed by HIV/AIDS, was in fact the result of structural adjustment policies that dismantled the public health and social service sectors in Mozambique in the 1980s. Life-saving treatment is provided to those who are HIV-positive, who are then encouraged to look to the community for support. Those enlisted to care for and support these patients are expected to do so voluntarily and altruistically, out of a neighborly duty. Volunteers themselves, however, hope that their participation in the programs will lead to employment and greater stability. A pool of trained but unemployed laborers is created and maintained, anxiously hoping for benefits to fall their way while serving as the front line of global health initiatives.

The service Arminda and her colleagues were able to provide was severely limited by material constraints and lack of support. Volunteer and peer-support networks can contribute to the success of chronic illness interventions but must be actively supported and sustained with regular training and fair compensation. Arminda's experience points to the paradoxical results of the "sustainability doctrine" characteristic of donor-funded AIDS programs: that while promising "autonomy, empowerment, self-reliance, and a coherent, rational modernity . . . [it has] created nearly its opposite" (Swidler and Watkins 2009: 1192). This approach is coming under scrutiny by some of the principal global health actors. In a 2008 report on task-shifting, the WHO recommends:

> Countries should recognize that essential health services cannot be provided by people working on a voluntary basis if they are to be sustainable. . . . Part-time volunteers have an important role to play by offering a limited scope of supplementary support services among their local community. However, if community health workers are to be properly integrated into health systems, and are trained to provide essential services, then their commitment must be sustained through a variety of measures including adequate wages and/or other appropriate and commensurate incentives. (WHO 2008: 41–42)

The report goes on to point out that lack of payment has consistently proven to be a major cause of workforce attrition in community health worker programs around the world. This is echoed by a recent Save the Children report: "[Community health workers] should not be seen as a cheap alternative or quick fix. CHWs are most effective where they are part of a 'continuum of care' that runs from the household to the hospital, and require effective training, management support, and adequate remuneration" (Watt et al. 2011: 5). Another WHO report notes there is no evidence that volunteerism can be sustained for long periods (Lehmann and Sanders 2007). Nonetheless, an analysis of proposals to the Global Fund to Fight AIDS, Tuberculosis, and Malaria indicates that countries tend to focus on short-term, in-service training rather than long-term development of human resources for health (Drager, Gedik, and Dal Poz 2006). Despite these discussions, creating jobs in health and social services remains a contested way to improve well-being in low-income countries (Ferguson 2010).

## MOVING FORWARD

To truly address mental health needs in under-resourced settings such as central Mozambique, I argue that issues that were bracketed out as "social" during the rollout of antiretroviral treatment, such as food insecurity, unemployment, and poverty, must be conceptualized as central to mental health. Supporting this assertion, Lund and colleagues (2011) cite evidence that some poverty alleviation interventions, such as conditional cash transfers and asset promotion, are clearly associated with mental health benefits. With such a reframing, it is particularly shortsighted to ignore the well-being of community volunteers, given the significant overlap between the volunteers and the target population, in this case people with HIV. Supporting the CHBC volunteers not only allows them to serve this population, but allows them to attend to their own needs and those of their family members. With the HIV prevalence in Chimoio at around 25% of the population at the time of this research, this would benefit people with HIV. Providing CHBC volunteers with steady employment and adequate support could potentially be an intervention benefiting outcomes related to both mental health and HIV/AIDS.

Tsai and colleagues (2012) found a strong association between food insecurity and depression symptom severity among people with HIV/AIDS in Uganda, particularly among women who lacked access to instrumental social support, defined as provision of tangible material assistance that is needed, as opposed to emotional, informational, or diffuse social support. Their findings indicate that addressing food insecurity and social support may have synergistic benefits to both mental health and HIV/AIDS outcomes, further demonstrating the difficulty of separating medical from social issues in practice. The CHBC volunteers' desire to bring their patients food reflects an intrinsic understanding of the dynamics that Tsai and colleagues document statistically. Emotional support and education are simply not enough to support people with complex medical and mental health issues in severely impoverished areas. CHBC is a form of instrumental social support, and directly addressing food insecurity benefits mental health.

Community-based support systems can play a critical role in addressing the mental health treatment gap, but the health workers must be consistently and adequately trained, supported, and fairly compensated to ensure their long-term effectiveness and to avoid exploitation and burnout. These policies should be clearly mandated, with accountability for implementers and a longitudinal plan that includes consideration of training, benefits, remuneration, and career advancement for community health workers. Further research is needed to establish what specific forms of intervention could have the greatest impact on community-level mental health and the role community-based caregivers could play in such interventions. The example of Arminda indicates that there are willing partners who are prepared to commit to such an engagement, but they are asking for a sustained commitment from governments, donors, and implementing organizations.

## Note

1   The names of people and organizations in this chapter are pseudonyms.

## References

Collins, P. Y., Holman, A. R., Freeman, M. C., and Patel, V. (2006). What is the relevance of mental health to HIV/AIDS care and treatment programs in developing countries? A systematic review. *AIDS*, 20 (12): 1571–1582.

Drager, S., Gedik, G., and Dal Poz, M. R. (2006). Health workforce issues and the Global Fund to Fight AIDS, Tuberculosis and Malaria: an analytical review. *Human Resources for Health*, 4: 23.

Ferguson, J. (2010). The uses of neoliberalism. *Antipode*, 41 (S1): 166–184.

Guerreiro, M. S. (2003). Textáfrica está à venda. *Moçambique*, 34: 37–38.

Hanlon, J. (1996). *Peace without Profit: How the IMF Blocks Rebuilding in Mozambique*. Oxford: Irish Mozambique Solidarity & the International African Institute in association with J. Currey.

Holmes, K., and Winskell, K. (2013). Understanding and mitigating HIV-related resource-based stigma in the era of antiretroviral therapy. *AIDS Care*, 25 (11):1349–1355.

Instituto Nacional de Estatística. (2013). *Estatísticas do Distrito Cidade de Chimoio, 2013*. http://www.ine.gov.mz/estatisticas/estatisticas-territorias-distritais/manica/novembro-de-2013/cidade-de-chimoio.pdf/view.

Kalofonos, I. (2008). "All I eat is ARVs": living with HIV/AIDS at the dawn of the treatment era in central Mozambique. PhD dissertation, Department of Anthropology. University of California, San Francisco.

——. (2010). "All I eat is ARVs": the paradox of AIDS treatment interventions in central Mozambique. *Medical Anthropology Quarterly*. 24 (3): 363–380.

——. (2014). "All they do is pray": Community labour and the narrowing of "care" during Mozambique's HIV scale-up. *Global Public Health: An International Journal for Research, Policy and Practice*. doi:10.1080/17441692.2014.881527.

Lehmann, U., and Sanders, D. (2007). *Community Health Workers: What Do We Know about Them?* Geneva: World Health Organization.

Lund, C., De Silva, M., Plagerson, S., Cooper, S., Chisholm, D., Das, J., and Patel, V. (2011). Poverty and mental disorders: breaking the cycle in low-income and middle-income countries. *The Lancet*, 378 (9801): 1502–1514.

Maes, K. (2012). Volunteerism or labor exploitation? Harnessing the volunteer spirit to sustain AIDS treatment programs in urban Ethiopia. *Human Organization*, 71 (1): 54.

Maes, K., and Kalofonos, I. (2013). Becoming and remaining community health workers: perspectives from Ethiopia and Mozambique. *Social Science and Medicine*, 87: 52–59.

Maes, K. C., Shifferaw, S., Hadley, C., and Tesfaye, F. (2011). Volunteer home-based HIV/AIDS care and food crisis in Addis Ababa, Ethiopia: sustainability in the face of chronic food insecurity. *Health Policy Plan*, 26 (1): 43–52.

MISAU. (2007). *Estratégia e plano de acção para a saúde mental*. Maputo: Ministério da Saúde, Moçambique.

Parker, R., and Aggleton, P. (2003). HIV and AIDS-related stigma and discrimination: a conceptual framework and implications for action. *Social Science and Medicine*, 57 (1): 13–24.

Patel, V, and Prince, M. (2010). Global mental health: a new global health field comes of age. *JAMA*, 303 (19): 1976–1977.

Patel, V., Abas, M., Broadhead, J., Todd, C., and Reeler, A. (2001). Depression in developing countries: lessons from Zimbabwe, *British Medical Journal*, 22: 482–484.

Pfeiffer, J. (2002). African independent churches in Mozambique: healing the afflictions of inequality. *Medical Anthropology Quarterly*, 16 (2): 176–199.

Pitcher, M. A. (2002). *Transforming Mozambique: The Politics of Privatization, 1975–2000*. African Studies Series, 104. Cambridge/New York: Cambridge University Press.

Rabkin, M., and El-Sadr, W. M. (2011). Why reinvent the wheel? Leveraging the lessons of HIV scale-up to confront non-communicable diseases. *Global Public Health*, 6 (3): 247–256.

Scheper-Hughes, N. (1992). *Death without Weeping: The Violence of Everyday Life in Brazil*. Berkeley: University of California Press.

Singer, M., and Clair, S. (2003). Syndemics and public health: reconceptualizing disease in bio-social context. *Medical Anthropology Quarterly*, 17: 423–441.

Swidler, A., and Watkins, S. C. (2009). "Teach a man to fish": the doctrine of sustainability and its effects on three strata of Malawian society. *World Development*, 37 (7): 1182–1196.

Tsai, A. C., Bangsberg, D. R., Frongillo, E. A., Hunt, P. W., Muzoora, C., Martin, J. N., and Weiser, S. D. (2012). Food insecurity, depression and the modifying role of social support among people living with HIV/AIDS in rural Uganda. *Social Science and Medicine*, 74 (12): 2012–2019.

UNAIDS. (2002). *Report on the Global HIV/AIDS Epidemic*. Geneva.

——. (2010). *Global Report: UNAIDS Report on the Global AIDS Epidemic*. Geneva.

Watt, P., Brikci, N., Brearley, L., and Rawe, K. (2011). *No Child Out of Reach*. London: Save the Children.

Weaver, L. J., and Hadley, C. (2009). Moving beyond hunger and nutrition: a systematic review of the evidence linking food insecurity and mental health in developing countries. *Ecology of Food and Nutrition*, 48: 263–284.

Weiser, S. D., Leiter, K., Bangsberg, D. R., Butler, L. M., Percy-de Korte, F., Hlanze, Z., and Heisler, M. (2007). Food insufficiency is associated with high-risk sexual behavior among women in Botswana and Swaziland. *PLoS Medicine*, 4 (10): e260–e270.

World Health Organization (WHO). (2005). *Mental Health Atlas 2005*. Geneva: World Health Organization.

Chapter 19

# "Shared Humanity" among Nonspecialist Peer Care Providers for Persons Living with Psychosis: Implications for Global Mental Health

Neely Myers

## The Fall

One summer morning in 1977, Jeremy stared out the window of his New York City apartment that he shared with his wife, Susie. The window faced east into the rising sun. Seven stories below him, the city seemed to writhe and twist. Horns sounded. Crowds surged and shifted on the sidewalks. *There are so many people out there*, he thought, staring into the shadows. It was hard to know who was watching.

His silver Zippo sat next to the ashtray. He held it up to the window and watched it glint in the piercing sunlight. He reached for a cigarette.

"Don't light that," Susie scolded him, her voice seeming far away.

"What did you say?" Jeremy asked.

Susie walked over and placed his coffee on the table with a thunk, and slumped into her chair.

"What, what?" she asked him. "I didn't say anything. What's the matter with you?"

Jeremy stared at her heavy breasts, visible through the thin fabric of her nightgown, as was her swollen belly.

Angry, he sipped his coffee, lit his cigarette, and lifted the paper to block her from view.

His wife began to pace the kitchen, clanging pots and pans as she made him eggs and toast. Jeremy was not hungry, though.

He had been up very late the night before and he was not sure if he had slept, but he must have, because he did not remember getting into this chair or when

*Global Mental Health: Anthropological Perspectives*, edited by Brandon A. Kohrt and Emily Mendenhall, 325–340. © 2015 Left Coast Press, Inc. All rights reserved.

Susie first walked into the kitchen. He felt like maybe he just woke up. Everything seemed to be glittering; maybe he was just asleep.

*What do I remember?* he asked himself.

After work the night before, he had gone out with a few of his clients to a private club. They smoked some marijuana, snorted a little cocaine, and had several gin and tonics. Somehow, he was now home, sitting up, slumped in this chair, drinking coffee. He noted that he had a different, half-empty pack of cigarettes than the one he had carried to the bar from work.

Then he felt *it* coming, the cold sweat, the wave of nausea, the tunnel vision. His heart pounded erratically. He simply could not remember if the FBI followed him home last night or not. What if they had seen Susie?

He dropped the newspaper, stood up and pressed his face to several of the windows. He looked for their watches—they signaled each other with sunlight refracting from their watches to track his activities. He was looking so hard that he forgot about Susie.

"Jeremy," she asked in a strangled voice, "where were you last night?"

*Do not look at her*, he told himself, sweating. *If you look at her, the agents will see her.*

She started to cry, walked up behind him, and wrapped her arms around his long, thin waist.

"You cannot go to work like that," she insisted.

Jeremy realized she was right. And he had to keep working, no matter what. He had a baby on the way.

"That's why you have a wife, stupid, remember?" Susie said.

But maybe she had not said it. She felt too still pressed against him. She must be putting thoughts in his head, he realized. Or maybe it was the FBI again. Maybe they had recorded her voice so they could broadcast it into his ears.

He wondered if he should try and find some help, but who would help him? The police were in cahoots with the agents. Anyone else would just tell him he was crazy. But he knew better. The agents just wanted to kill him.

He pushed her hands away and stood up. He took the coldest shower possible. He scrubbed himself hard with the washcloth. As he trimmed his mustache, he nicked his cheek.

*I feel nothing*, he mused.

He put on underwear, pants, and a shirt, and looked in the mirror. He looked like someone else. His wife came in and put on his tie, but he refused to make eye contact. He had to keep her safe.

"We need to talk later," she said in a nasty voice. "You need to come home after work!"

He ignored her and walked out the door. Halfway down the hallway, he turned back when he realized he had forgotten his Zippo lighter. He raised his hand to knock just as Susie opened the door and threw the lighter at him. They made eye contact in the instant before he missed it.

"Damn it!" he shouted. He snatched the lighter from the floor, and stormed away. *Now the agents have seen her!* He fumed.

Jeremy walked to work. Afterwards, he schmoozed clients at a bar. He decided to drink but not snort any cocaine or smoke any marijuana. His wife was waiting. She would have the table set for dinner, a little candle burning in their kitchen for two. Soon there would be three.

But if he went home, he might look at her, and then they would see her again. They had seen her this morning, but he hoped that maybe that was too brief for them to really get a good look at her. There was a camera embedded in his eye and it recorded everything he looked at, which terrified him. If they noticed her, they might hurt her. They might take the baby. Or both of them.

But he was so tired. He had been awake for too many days with the help of the cocaine, and he felt like a rotting tree. He looked at a clock on the wall and noticed it was 11 PM or so. He decided to leave. Hopefully she was in bed by now, so he would not see her.

As he walked towards his apartment, he felt strongly that someone was following him. Someone's watch glinted in the headlights of a taxi and a sword of panic sliced through his chest. He saw the person look at him as he walked past. He lit another cigarette to calm down. He was pretty sure the smoke made it harder for the agents to see him, too. Some sort of smokescreen.

Maybe, he thought, he should tell Susie that they needed to leave the city. The city could wear people out—all of the traffic, the lights, the sirens. He had tried to ask her to move to the country, but she wanted to keep working at the hospital where she was a nurse. She thought the commute would be too difficult.

Maybe he should just tell her why, he realized. He would not have to look at her. He could explain that they needed to meet outside the city to talk. He could say it was just a weekend getaway, he realized. And then he could see if anyone followed them. Maybe no one would follow them.

"That's dumb," he heard the woman passing next to him say.

The next person scowled at him. "You are so stupid," he said.

"And ugly," a voice said from behind him.

He started to run, but then realized he was going the wrong way. He tried to remember his address. And then it hit him. It was July 19th and the number for the month of July was 7, and he lived on the 7th floor. In apartment 19. And it was July 19th.

The clue had been right in front of him this whole time and he had missed it. The FBI had taken Susie.

They were going to kill her, and the only way he could save her was to die. He started to run.

Footsteps pounded behind him. People shouted. Headlights and streetlights bobbed and weaved. Cars swerved.

He unlocked the door to the building and ran up the steps, gasping as he made it to the seventh floor.

There were voices yelling at him now, it seemed like all the neighbors were in the hallway screaming as he tried to unlock the door. They told him she was gone, that he had to die, that he was so stupid. But he recognized these voices; he had heard them before. They were not his neighbors. Sometimes they sounded like Susie, or his father, or a friend growing up. He really had been trying not to hear them, though. Marijuana, cocaine, alcohol, and barbiturates—he had tried everything. But it was not reliable; he could not control them all the time.

He swung open the door.

"Shut up!" he yelled, clutching his head. "Shut up!"

He wanted so much for the voices to be wrong.

The neighbors said later that when they heard him, they thought he was arguing with Susie.

When Jeremy burst into the apartment, and there was no candle, no table for two, no dinner. He looked at the clock. It was 11:49 PM.

The voices were right. He knew what he had to do.

Jeremy flung open the door to their small balcony and jumped.

## NONSPECIALIST PEER CARE PROVIDERS

Decades later, also in the month of July, I met Jeremy in a mental health clinic in a major metropolitan area where I was conducting ethnographic research. My anthropological research aims to improve mental health services for people diagnosed with serious mental illnesses in low-resource settings in the United States, where I have been conducting research for the past decade. In this work, I have been primarily interested in a new model of mental health services—a peer-provided care model.

Peer-provided care is offered by "peers." A recent report suggested that a peer is "one who has at some time been disrupted or disabled by a psychiatric, trauma, or substance use condition ... and as a result has 'lived experience'" with such challenges as a determination by others that one lacks competency, major life disruptions such as homelessness, unemployment, extended isolation, loss of important relationships, childhood or adult trauma, abuse, problems in pursuing dreams of personal goals, arrest, and so forth (iNAPS 2013). Peers thus often claim to be "experts by experience."

Expertise by experience means that rather than—or in addition to—formal mental health training, a person has lived through the everyday experiences of managing a serious mental illness, which often includes disability and discrimination. Most of the peer staff I met over my decade of fieldwork experiences had lived through the same issues that the users of the services they provided were experiencing, which included navigating a complicated public mental health system, acquiring psychiatric disability benefits to earn a meager subsistence when one could not work, enduring prolonged periods of homelessness, and taking multiple psychiatric medications that often had serious side effects and required careful dosing and balancing. Studies suggest that well-trained peers are able not only to offer counsel and care that has similar effects on people as professionally licensed social workers (Chinman et al. 2000), but also to better understand service users' everyday experiences, and so engage in "shared humanness" with them (Davidson et al. 1999; Mead and Hilton 2003; Schutt and Rogers 2009; West 2011).

In 2011, I began to spend time in a new, peer-run mental health services center in a metropolitan area of the United States and eventually decided to undertake ethnographic fieldwork there. I am deeply invested in understanding how people recover from serious mental illnesses and go on to lead meaningful lives, which happens to some people and not to others (Bellack 2006; Harding et al. 1987; Torgalsboen 2005). Previously, the people at this peer mental health service program had been users of a more traditional mental health services program that used professional social workers to offer group therapy and skills training courses. These kinds of programs, at least in this urban area, were widely regarded to be failing. Many people became revolving-door mental health patients who never went on to lead independent lives outside of the mental health system (Estroff 1993; Hopper 2002). In contrast, a peer service program developed in the suburbs seemed to be doing very well. As a result, the state had asked the peer service providers in the suburbs to try running new programs in the city based on their model.

## BECOMING A PEER SERVICE PROVIDER

Jeremy was 27 when he jumped out of the window. He described himself as "stonewalled" in an unhappy marriage, but he was fairly happy, successful, and working hard. He was excited to become a father and hoped their unborn child might help revive his marriage.

"And then one day," he said, licking his lips and leaning forward, "I woke up and there was a conspiracy against me."

The next thing he knew, he was waking up in the hospital after jumping seven stories to his death.

"I did not even hesitate," he told me. "I did not even write a note. I knew what I had to do one minute and the next I was in the air. My belief in the conspiracy was that strong."

A tree branch broke his fall.

I met Jeremy at the clinic where they were developing the new, peer service program, and I had the pleasure of interviewing him as one of my 30 interview participants. I also spent nine months collecting the ethnographic data for this project by having myself, or one of the two other members of my research team, spend time in the clinic conducting clinical ethnography. The point of ethnography is to understand what it means to undertake the tasks of everyday life as a person in a certain social context (Luhrmann 2010). My team worked in the "border zone" of the clinic (Mattingly 2010) to examine what the tasks of everyday life were for users in a peer services context, and how those tasks helped or hindered them in their intention to recover from their illness episode and take charge of their own lives. We attended classes, ate meals with people, went to staff meetings, and spent time looking at the users' Facebook pages, listening to music, playing cards, and just chatting.

Jeremy was a prominent member of this community, but he was not the patient. He was a licensed clinical psychologist. Jeremy held a PhD and provided psychotherapy to his clients. He most enjoyed working with people who were considered to be seriously mentally ill and also had substance abuse issues. Around 50% of people diagnosed with serious mental illnesses—most often, schizophrenia, bipolar disorder, and major depression—also have a substance abuse problem (Mueser et al. 1995; Regier et al. 1990).

People seemed to think, Jeremy told me, that substances would help them control their symptoms. I had heard other people in other clinics talk about this before as well. They called it "self-medication." Some research suggests that self-medication attempts can lead people down a more difficult path. For example, some studies claim that marijuana use can exacerbate the onset of psychotic disorders and cause symptoms to occur earlier in vulnerable people (Compton et al. 2009; Kristensen and Cadenhead 2007).

Jeremy told me that he had been trying to self-medicate in the days before he jumped out the window. Cocaine helped him to think more clearly, which enabled him to overcome some of the cognitive deficits people can feel with schizophrenia, much like caffeine can boost your ability to concentrate. Marijuana helped him to calm down, he told me. It made the voices less intense. And besides, both of these drugs often came with a crowd of people who wanted to hang out together. Those people were not so judgmental about strange mental behaviors. "Odd behaviors seem more funny to people," another former crack abuser with schizophrenia once said, "when you are all high."

However, in this research project and others across the United States, most people tell stories of crisis related to their self-medication. Street drugs can be very addictive. They are expensive, and dangerous to obtain. Many also exacerbate symptoms of a psychotic disorder in vulnerable people like Jeremy.

Jeremy did not blame the drugs for his suicide attempt, though. He was sober that night. He knew it had been the voices. He had become a clinical psychologist to help other people who experience frightening voices. Only about one-third of people who use medications to quiet their voices actually stop hearing voices; another third experience a partial silencing of their voices (Shergill et al. 1998). Jeremy wanted to help the rest. But, he explained, he did not personally still hear voices. His voices stopped when he finally went into treatment after jumping out of the window, which included psychoanalysis and some periods of antipsychotic medication use when the voices became especially intense.

Jeremy was especially excited about his job because he had the opportunity to work at a *peer*-directed mental health clinic. About four-fifths of the staff there, including the director, considered themselves to be "peers." Jeremy told me that "peer services" are run by "people who have been through it, in life, and . . . who bring it to their work, the experiences that they've been through, and the help they've gotten, the compassion that they've gotten, the compassion that they have." He continued, "I'm relating to a person who is going through terrible pain, or has been through a lot of trauma, and needs not just instruction, but also a great deal of empathy and respect for their struggle, as I learned to respect my struggle."

"There should be more [peer agencies]," he suggested. "There is . . . less pretense, more comfort." He again mentioned that being a peer therapist was somehow easier on the therapist as well. "I'm confident that I know what the guy or gal is going through, so it's second nature to me to be . . . with them."

Jeremy had been through the system, and he thought the system had helped him. After jumping out the window, Jeremy spent two years as an inpatient in a mental hospital. This is very rare nowadays, as insurance companies often will not pay for any extended stay.

When he awoke in the hospital, he was "terribly, terribly depressed and feeling lousy about myself, you know, totally out of it, with—at times—delusions, and you know I was basically cared for and supported by people who didn't understand." The first place Jeremy was taken to was "very chaotic, very loud, very confusing, very condescending."

He was absolutely terrified. And then they diagnosed him. "Chronic paranoid schizophrenic was a big word; they were using it a lot," he said with frustration in his voice. "And now, they use bipolar, major depression with psychotic features, but basically it's feeling very bad about yourself, usually there has been trauma in your life, there's been abuse."

He would have preferred the kinds of explanations he tried to give his own patients, as he was always trying to remind them that "delusions are perceptual problems and they go away, they can be worked with, they are usually caused by a street drug. Depression is treatable, they have great medications today . . . you emphasize the positive part." Jeremy's claims resonate with the literature around positive approaches to mental health crises, accentuating people's strengths, and recovery-oriented literature about helping people to manage their symptoms and see them as temporary even if they are urgent (Copeland 2008; Ridgway et al. 2002).

Seeing that he was struggling, Jeremy's (now former) wife, Susie, "scoured the city" searching for a place where he would have the best chance at recovery. After two weeks, his family had him transferred to a better hospital. He liked the place where he ended up. "I was basically saved," he said, even if it was a very difficult and demeaning process.

"I had a great insurance policy at the time," Jeremy told me, and he had received the best private care in the best private facilities as the patient of some very famous psychiatrists.

Jeremy was lucky that his wife and family advocated for him to receive the best treatment and was also fortunate to have an insurance policy that would pay for it. Often, U.S. private health insurance policies of full-time workers exclude mental health care or easily dismiss it as a preexisting condition that cannot be covered (Reno et al. 1997). Many of the users Jeremy helped at the clinic told me in their interviews that they could not work because they needed public mental health insurance so that they would have some coverage for their incredibly expensive psychiatric medications. The public mental health insurance, though, sounded less than ideal—very long waits to get an initial appointment (as one woman said, "you call in suicidal and they tell you they can see you in two weeks"), crowded waiting rooms, psychiatrists who were seeing 60 patients per day and often did not speak English, problems getting the best medications because of limited prescription coverage and high co-pays, and so forth.

In contrast, Jeremy described his treatment as "very positive. I mean, I was feeling terribly lousy, but I got a lot of support." But Jeremy had the advocacy and knowledge of his upper-middle-class family, his excellent health insurance, and his access to excellent mental health care because he lived in a wealthy urban area of the United States. Jeremy underwent psychoanalysis, a psychotherapy technique that psychiatrists use to help a person reintegrate conflicting elements of their personality. He explained during our interview:

It really established me as a person in the best sense. I really gained a great deal from it, both from the time that I spent processing and the groups and the individual therapy and the insights that occurred.... [A]s far as I was concerned, they put my personality back together.

Jeremy strongly believed that his experiences helped him to be a better therapist, even if he did not necessarily share them with his clients during sessions, in order to maintain a clinical boundary. As he explained, "In every step of the way, there is growth and development. It grows from inside. It comes from acceptance of yourself more. I just think that a peer can lend that whole experience—deliver it better—to an individual who is going through what the peer therapist has gone through." Smiling, he added, "I know people get well. And I bring that to my sessions and to my coaching."

Jeremy also advocates for his clients to take medication, and he feels he can do so more effectively because he understands the side effects. "A lot of people are very resistant to medication, and you know medication is the first line of defense as far as I'm concerned. It cuts to the chase, you know, it does resolve things like delusions, it does elevate your mood, improve your perceptions, how you organize your life, even internally, how you organize your life, ... how you think about outside ... helps with anxiety."

Jeremy added, "There are side effects from some of them." Indeed, from other ethnographic work I have conducted in clinics, and the work of other anthropologists (Estroff et al. 1991; Jenkins et al. 2005; Luhrmann 2008), I know Jeremy's mention of side effects is a fundamental issue for many people suffering from psychosis. For example, many people who first start taking psychiatric medications gain a lot of weight. Others have serious sexual side effects—namely, an inability to experience pleasure.

Jeremy has his own approach to this problem, though. "I try to help them think intelligently about it, to maybe accept it, as a tool. It's not forever." This is in line with some recovery-oriented peer programs like Wellness Recovery Action Planning (Copeland 2008), which has been shown to have some positive effects on the mental health of program participants (Cook et al. 2012; Fukui et al. 2011).

I asked Jeremy if he was enjoying working as a peer. "I enjoy it. I enjoy the work I do. It's like, peers, you're with peers, with people you understand, know and love. You know, from your old days."

However, I noted significant differences between Jeremy and his clients. They were predominantly African-American men under 40, and Jeremy is a Euro-American man over the age of 60. Jeremy disagreed with me: "Humans are humans, and their problems are universal. At least as far as I know, in the United States, because of our culture, what we get hit with when we get sick, I mean it's all the same."

I pushed harder. I wanted to know if a peer had to be the same age or ethnicity as the client, which is an issue under debate. How can a person be a peer if there is a 40-year difference in age? Jeremy explained:

> I don't think age is a factor necessarily, it could be an advantage if you're older; a 16-year-old who has psychiatric involvement, like major mental illness, you can assume that they are looking for someone to help them, you know because they must be very terrified. I think a peer at any age, of any race, I don't think it has to be matched exactly. That's exactly the type of naiveté that blocks these kinds of things ... you know when you go into a normal psychiatric floor and the doctor, the nurse, or the therapist, this definition of what's good and what's not good rather than this feeling about relating to someone, shared humanity.

When I asked Jeremy what he thought was most important about peers, he told me: "I think growth is very important. Desire to grow, the understanding that you can grow, that you can grow your way out of the system. And caring. I think caring is a very big motive. . . . You know, both ways."

I asked Jeremy how he thought this would translate into participants' everyday lives, and he said that he really thought it came down to "belief in themselves, more hope, more trust, more training. . . . [I]f they understand themselves, a little better if not a lot better, and they know that they are not so different, and not so bad, then I think that will be very helpful to them, and if they leave with that then they are leaving with a lot."

## IMPLICATIONS FOR GLOBAL MENTAL HEALTH

In low- and middle-income countries (LMICs), including most in sub-Saharan Africa, neuropsychiatric disorders represent upward of 5% of the global burden of disease (Collins et al. 2011; WHO 2011). Jeremy's story illuminates some ways in which nonspecialist peer-care provider models proven successful in the United States may be particularly useful for providing mental health care in other contexts, including LMICs. Attempts to export U.S. mental health care practices to the rest of the world must acknowledge that (1) sociocultural conditions can affect schizophrenia outcomes; (2) schizophrenia outcomes are already better in the developing world than in the United States; and (3) much of what leads to "better" outcomes in LMICs may rely on the availability of locally relevant techniques to address stress (Myers 2010).

Peer services, including those provided by people like Jeremy, may help fulfill the need for more nonspecialists capable of providing mental health care in LMICs. Reliance on nonspecialists can provide critical mental health care in contexts with few specialists. Innovative service delivery models are critical in LMIC contexts, where more than 75% of people with serious psychiatric disabilities such as psychosis do not receive any mental health treatment (Becker and Kleinman 2013).

This is, in part, because there are not enough mental health care providers in LMICs. For example, in Tanzania, where I recently collected ethnographic data, there is one psychiatric hospital and five psychiatric units in general hospitals, three of which are tertiary care. Across the relatively large geographic space of Tanzania, there are only an estimated 20 psychiatrists for over 47 million people (WHO 2011). The dearth of psychiatrists in Tanzania underscores the need for alternative models for mental health care among people suffering from psychosis and other forms of severe mental illness.

Using the peer model may provide an ideal avenue for integrating mental health services into primary care. Current research indicates that primary care providers in East Africa often have no training in specialty mental health (WHO 2011) and may maintain stigmatizing attitudes toward people with mental illness (Ndetei et al. 2011). Many people initially visit community-based traditional healers (Ngoma et al. 2003), arguably the first and only portal for people seeking mental health care when primary care services are scarce. The WHO estimates that more than 80% of Africans use traditional healers, and that 40% to 60% of the people using traditional healers have some kind of mental illness (WHO 2002). For example, in Tanzania, the rate of mental health concerns of people using traditional healers was twice that of people visiting primary care clinics (Ngoma et al. 2003). Reasons cited in one study are trustworthiness of traditional healers, easy access to them as opposed to primary care, belief in a supernatural model, and less stigma than visiting a hospital (Chadda et al. 2001).

Because of the important role of traditional healers in many cultures and communities, integrating their services into a peer model may be important—for instance, in identifying someone with mental illness and matching that person with a "peer." Some researchers have been impressed with the traditional healers' mental health care in Tanzania (Rappaport and Dent 1979). But, using a traditional healer also led to delayed treatment more than five times more often than has biomedical care, and in some cases early biomedical intervention may promote recovery (Burns et al. 2011). However, because of the already established role of traditional healers in socio-spiritual healing, it is important to recognize their importance and utility in mental health service delivery.

There is thus a huge gap between what is needed and the help available, which is critical to tackling the social and disease burdens of psychosis. This may be why, when I asked people in rural Tanzania how they handled someone who heard voices or believed something no one else thought was true, my informants said such people were tied up in the house or outside to a tree and left to the mercy of nature, or denied food. While this is inhumane treatment, when people know of no other options, such as antipsychotic medications that can stop the most disruptive symptoms of psychosis, or when they cannot access care, then their choices are very limited.

Peer providers like Jeremy, trained as community mental health workers, or even working alongside primary care physicians or traditional healers to enhance their mental health expertise, may help to fill in the knowledge gap about mental illnesses when specialists are limited. There are a number of treatment models, including randomized controlled trials, wherein lay health workers are key service providers for persons living with psychotic disorders. In these models, nonspecialist health workers help local people learn local ways to manage mental health symptoms while also connecting them with clinicians to provide medications to manage their most distressing symptoms (Balaji et al. 2012; Chatterjee et al. 2011; Rajaraman et al. 2012).

Peers are a special group of nonspecialist providers because they have lived through experiences in the same condition as the person they are trying to help. Peer nonspecialist providers like Jeremy can model their own ability to thrive and then become role models to others who struggle with similar symptoms and trajectories (Boykin 1997; Dixon et al. 1994). When peers recognize that they can contribute to the well-being of others, they themselves may be imbued with a sense of hope and purpose to help others in the future once they can help themselves, in a process known as mutual self-help (Corrigan et al. 2002; Davidson et al. 1999). Peer care providers also focus on building a trusting relationship with their clients to help make sense of illness experiences in the context of everyday life rather than focusing on pathology (Mead and Hilton 2003).

Moreover, peer care providers embedded in the community may share local explanatory models of mental health concerns, including cultural and spiritual explanations, while also directing them to the treatment they need to mitigate symptoms. People who access treatment quickly have less time to damage relationships with family, friends, and employers as a result of their untreated illness and have less disability in the long run (Lloyd-Evans et al. 2011; Marshall et al. 2005). Nonspecialist peer care providers may connect people with treatment options more quickly, thereby reducing stigma, encouraging help-seeking, and helping protect a person's social life (Lloyd-Evans et al. 2011). Although several peer models exist, and innovative new models are being created all the time, more research is needed to build the evidence base around this exciting new direction in mental health care (Clay et al. 2005; Fuhr et al. 2014; Pitt et al. 2013). Such innovation is needed in LMICs in particular (Pitt et al. 2013).

Peer models for psychosis care may work well in LMICs, where mental health services often are community-based, designed locally, use local explanations of symptoms and treatment, and use nonspecialist providers such as peer care providers. Indeed, further research on peer care providers in LMICs may benefit people in countries like the United States, where innovative approaches to reduce stigma and improve social integration are needed. And, in turn, peer care provider models may translate well into LMICs when appropriate translational approaches are heeded (Myers 2010), as nonspecialist approaches to mental health promotion are gaining traction as an integral part of mental health care in low-resource settings. "Reforming mental health care," Vikram Patel (2013) has written, "requires a fundamental review of our ideas of who, and how, such care should be provided to communities." He notes that the "champions" of tireless innovation, like peer-led care, may be an excellent place to start anew and reverse a trend that renders mental health care too heavily professionalized for the majority.

## References

Balaji, M., Chatterjee, S., Koschorke, M., Rangaswamy, T., Chavan, A., Dabholkar, H., Dakshin, L., Kumar, P., John, S., and Thornicroft, G. (2012). The development of a lay health worker delivered collaborative community based intervention for people with schizophrenia in India. *BMC Health Services Research*, 12 (1): 42.

Becker, A. E., and Kleinman, A. (2013). Mental health and the global agenda. *New England Journal of Medicine*, 369 (1): 66–73.

Bellack, A. S. (2006). Scientific and consumer models of recovery in schizophrenia: concordance, contrasts, and implications. *Schizophrenia Bulletin*, 32 (3): 432–442.

Boykin, C. D (1997). The consumer provider as role model. In C. T. Mowbray, C. A. Jasper, and L. S. Howell (eds.), *Consumers as Providers in Psychiatric Rehabilitation*, pp. 374–386. Columbia, Maryland: International Association of Psychosocial Rehabilitation Services.

Burns, J. K., Jhazbhay, K., Kidd, M., and Emsley, R. A. (2011). Causal attributions, pathway to care and clinical features of first-episode psychosis: a South African perspective. *International Journal of Social Psychiatry*, 57 (5): 538–545.

Chadda, R. K., Agarwal, V., Singh, M. C., and Raheja, D. (2001). Help seeking behaviour of psychiatric patients before seeking care at a mental hospital. *International Journal of Social Psychiatry*, 47 (4): 71–78.

Chatterjee, S., Morven, L., Koschorke, M., McCrone, P., Naik, S., John, S., Dabholkar, H., Goldsmith, K., Balaji, M., and Varghese, M. (2011). Collaborative community based care for people and their families living with schizophrenia in India: protocol for a randomised controlled trial. *Trials*, 12 (1): 12.

Chinman, M., Rosenheck, R., Lam, J., and Davidson, L. (2000). Comparing consumer and nonconsumer provided case management services for homeless persons with serious mental illness. *Journal of Nervous and Mental Disease*, 188 (7): 446–453.

Clay, S., Schell, B., and Corrigan, P. W. (2005). *On Our Own, Together: Peer Programs for People with Mental Illness*. Nashville, Tennessee: Vanderbilt University Press.

Collins, P. Y., Patel, V., Joestl, S., March, D., Insel, T. R., and Darr, A. S. (2011). Grand challenges in global mental health. *Nature*, 475 (7 July 2011).

Compton, M. T., Kelley, M., Ramsay, C., Pringle, M., Goulding, S., Esterberg, S., Stewart, T., and Walker, E. (2009). Association of pre-onset cannabis, alcohol, and tobacco use with age at onset of prodrome and age at onset of psychosis in first-episode patients. *American Journal of Psychiatry*, 166 (11): 1251–1257.

Cook, J. A., Copeland, M. E., Jonikas, J. A., Hamilton, M. M., Razzano, L. A., Grey, D. D., Floyd, C. B., Hudson, W. B., Macfarlane, R. T., and Carter, T. M. (2012). Results of a randomized controlled trial of mental illness self-management using Wellness Recovery Action Planning. *Schizophrenia Bulletin*, 38 (4): 881–891.

Copeland, M. E. (2008). *WRAP: Wellness Recovery Action Plan: WRAPPIn' Virginia in Recovery*. Richmond: Virginia Department of Mental Health, Mental Retardation, and Substance Abuse Services.

Corrigan, P., Calabrese, J., Diwan, S., Keogh, C., Keck, L., and Mussey, C. (2002). Some recovery processes in mutual-help groups for persons with mental illness, I: Qualitative analysis of program materials and testimonies. *Community Mental Health Journal*, 38 (4): 287–302.

Davidson, L., Chinman, M., Kloos, B., Weingarten, R., Stayner, D., and Tebes, J. K. (1999). Peer support among individuals with severe mental illness: a review of the evidence. *Clinical Psychology: Science and Practice*, 6: 165–187.

Dixon, L., Krauss, N., and Lehman, A. (1994). Consumers as service providers: the promise and challenge. *Community Mental Health Journal*, 30 (6): 615–625.

Estroff, S. E. (1993). Identity, disability, and schizophrenia: the problem of chronicity. In S. Lindenbaum and M. Lock (eds.), *Knowledge, Power and Practice: The Anthropology of Medicine in Everyday Life*, pp. 247–286. Los Angeles: University of California Press.

Estroff, S. E., Lachicotte, W. S., Illingworth, L. C., and Johnston, A. (1991). Everybody's got a little mental illness: accounts of illness and self among people with severe, persistent mental illnesses. *Medical Anthropology Quarterly*, 5 (4): 331–369.

Fuhr, D. C., Salisbury, T. T., De Silva, M. J., Atif, N., van Ginneken, N., Rahman, A., and Patel, V. (2014). Effectiveness of peer-delivered interventions for severe mental illness and depression on clinical and psychosocial outcomes: a systematic review and meta-analysis. *Social Psychiatry and Psychiatric Epidemiology*, 49: 1691–1702.

Fukui, S., Starnino, V. R., Susana, M., Davidson, L. J., Cook, K., Rapp, C. A., and Gowdy, E. A. (2011). Effect of Wellness Recovery Action Plan (WRAP) participation on psychiatric symptoms, sense of hope, and recovery. *Psychiatric Rehabilitation Journal*, 34 (3): 214–222.

Harding, C. M., Zubin, J., and Strauss, J. S. (1987). Chronicity in schizophrenia: fact, partial fact or artifact? *Schizophrenia Bulletin*, 38 (5): 477–486.

Hopper, K. (2002). Returning to the community—again. *Psychiatric Services*, 53 (11): 1355.

International Association of Peer Supporters (iNAPS) (2013). Draft of Peer Support National Standards. *E-News Bulletin.* http://inaops.org/national-standards/.

Jenkins, J. H., Strauss, M. E., Carpenter, E. A., Miller, D., Floersch, J., and Sajatovic, M. (2005). Subjective experience of recovery from schizophrenia-related disorders and atypical antipsychotics. *International Journal of Social Psychiatry*, 51 (3): 211–227.

Kristensen, K., and Cadenhead, K. S. (2007). Cannabis abuse and risk for psychosis in a prodromal sample. *Psychiatry Research*, 151 (1): 151–154.

Lloyd-Evans, B., Crosby, M., Stockton, S., Piling, S., Hobbs, L., Hinton, M., and Johnson, S. (2011). Initiatives to shorten duration of untreated psychosis: systematic review. *British Journal of Psychiatry*, 198 (4): 256–263.

Luhrmann, T. M. (2008). "The street will drive you crazy": why homeless psychotic women in the institutional circuit in the United States say no to offers of help. *American Journal of Psychiatry*, 165 (1): 15–20.

——. (2010). What counts as data. In J. Davies and D. Spencer (eds.), *Emotions in the Field: The Psychology and Anthropology of Fieldwork Experience*, pp. 212–238. Palo Alto, California: Stanford University Press.

Marshall, M., Lewis, S., Lockwood, A., Drake, R., Jones, P., and Croudace, T. (2005). Association between duration of untreated psychosis and outcome in cohorts of first-episode patients: a systematic review. *Archives of General Psychiatry*, 62 (9): 975.

Mattingly, C. (2010). *The Paradox of Hope: Journeys through a Clinical Borderland.* Berkeley: University of California Press.

Mead, S., and Hilton, D. (2003). Crisis and connection. *Psychiatric Rehabilitation Journal*, 27 (1): 87–94.

Mueser, K. T., Bennett, M., and Kushner, M. G. (1995). Epidemiology of substance use disorders among persons with chronic mental illnesses. In A. Lehman and L. Dixon (eds.), *Double Jeopardy: Chronic Mental Illness and Substance Use Disorders.* Newark, New Jersey: Harwood Academic.

Ndetei, D. M., Khasakhala, L. I., Mutiso, V., and Mbwayo, A. W. (2011). Knowledge, attitude and practice *(kap)* of mental illness among staff in general medical facilities in Kenya: practice and policy implications. *African Journal of Psychiatry*, 14 (3): 225–235.

Ngoma, M. C., Prince, M., and Mann, A. (2003). Common mental disorders among those attending primary health clinics and traditional healers in urban Tanzania. *British Journal of Psychiatry*, 183 (4): 349–355.

Patel, V. (2013). Rethinking mental health care: what the developed world can learn from the developing. ThInk, electronic document from Wellcome Trust, March 19, 2013. http://thinkneuroscience.wordpress.com/2013/03/19/rethinking-mental-health-care/.

Pitt, V. J., Lowe, D., Prictor, M., Hetrick, S., Ryan, R., Berends, L., and Hill, S. (2013). A systematic review of consumer-providers' effects on client outcomes in statutory mental health services: the evidence and the path beyond. *Journal of the Society for Social Work and Research*, 4 (4): 333–356.

Rajaraman, D., Travasso, S., Chatterjee, A., Bhat, B., Andrew, G., Parab, S., and Patel, V. (2012). The acceptability, feasibility and impact of a lay health counsellor delivered health promoting schools programme in India: a case study evaluation. *BMC Health Services Research*, 12 (1): 127.

Rappaport, H., and Dent, P. L. (1979). An analysis of contemporary East African folk psychotherapy. *British Journal of Medical Psychology*, 52: 49–54.

Regier, D. A., Farmer, M. E., and Rae, D. S. (1990). Comorbidity of mental disorders with alcohol and other drug abuse. *JAMA*, 264: 2511–2518.

Reno, V., Jerry, P., Mashaw, L., and Gradison, B. (1997). *Disability: Challenges for Social Insurance, Health Care Financing and Labor Market Policy*. Washington, DC: National Academy of Social Insurance.

Ridgway, P., McDiarmid, D., Davidson, L., Bayes, J., and Ratzlaff, S. (2002). *Pathways to Recovery: A Strengths Recovery Self-Help Workbook*. Auburn Hills, Michigan: Data Production Corporation.

Schutt, R. K., and Rogers, E. S. (2009). Empowerment and peer support: structure and process of self-help in a consumer-run center for individuals with mental illness. *Journal of Community Psychology*, 37 (6): 697–710.

Shergill, S. S., Murray, R. M., and McGuire, P. K. (1998). Auditory hallucinations: a review of psychological treatments. *Schizophrenia Research*, 32: 137–150.

Torgalsboen, A. (2005). What is recovery in schizophrenia? In L. Davidson, C. Harding, and L. Spaniol (eds.), *Recovery from Severe Mental Illness: Research Evidence and Implications for Practice*, pp. 302–315, Vol. 1. Boston: Center for Psychiatric Rehabilitation, Sargent College of Health and Rehabilitation Sciences, Boston University.

West, C. (2011). Powerful choices: peer support and individualized medication self-determination. *Schizophrenia Bulletin*, 37 (3): 445.

World Health Organization (WHO) (No. 2, May 2002). WHO policy perspectives on medicines: growing needs and potentials. Geneva: World Health Organization. http://whqlibdoc.who.int/hq/2002/WHO_EDM_2002.4.pdf.

——. (2011). *Mental Health Atlas 2011*. Geneva: World Health Organization.

Conclusion

# A Road Map for Anthropology and Global Mental Health

Brandon A. Kohrt, Emily Mendenhall, and Peter J. Brown

THE PAST DECADE HAS SEEN RAPID growth in research, intervention, and funding for global mental health. Researchers and practitioners have demanded that political leaders of national and international institutions provide commensurate financial and human resources to reduce the burden of mental health problems in resource-constrained settings. These advocacy efforts have produced results as measured by the emergence of scholarship, pilot programs, and policies dedicated to elevating mental health care.

There is still a tremendous amount of work needed to address the inequity in mental health research and interventions in both high- and low-income settings. There continues to be a shocking disparity between the burden of disease related to mental disorders and the proportion of funding available compared with other health conditions. The challenge of scaling up and sustaining mental health interventions and related services is a critical issue for achieving the goals of the global mental health movement, as described in the introduction to this volume. Anthropological research has enormous potential to contribute to these challenges by exploring cultural feasibility and acceptability of interventions, understanding the impact of health services on the daily lives of providers and patients, and uncovering institutional processes that lead to inadequate and disproportionate commitment to mental health.

During the next decade, anthropologists will need to overcome disciplinary practices that have impeded their productive engagement with the field of global mental health. Barriers to increased anthropological contributions to global mental health include the mechanisms of funding for anthropological research; the historical tendency for anthropologists to work as solitary researchers rather than as part of multidisciplinary teams; an academic value system biased toward critical analysis of problems and devaluing applications of anthropology toward public health and clinical medicine; and the marginality of medical anthropology within

*Global Mental Health: Anthropological Perspectives*, edited by Brandon A. Kohrt and Emily Mendenhall, 341–361. © 2015 Left Coast Press, Inc. All rights reserved.

the field of anthropology itself. Nevertheless, this volume demonstrates through 17 ethnographic narrative chapters how anthropological perspectives can push global mental health research and agendas further. Examples have ranged from the study of social and economic determinants of mental health to innovative approaches to the delivery of mental health care.

In this conclusion, we build upon the research described in this volume and discuss future directions for anthropology in global mental health research. Our goal is to consider key issues where anthropological research may have an important role in alleviating human suffering in an equitable and ethical manner around the globe. To achieve this, we have identified eight priorities for future anthropological research in global mental health.

1.  *Medical anthropology researchers and methods should become a standard part of public health and clinical intervention research.*

Presently, there is limited engagement of anthropologists in clinical and intervention research. This often results from expectations within anthropology itself of its practitioners' independence and isolationism. To overcome this disciplinary obstacle, anthropology programs should prepare students for work with interdisciplinary teams that are "problem-based"; this method of graduate training is increasingly central to public health and clinical training. This should be done while maintaining anthropology's traditional strengths that encourage a focus on the particularities of geographic and cultural context as well as a well-developed theoretical orientation.

This approach can enhance public health and clinical intervention research in three fundamental ways. First, ethnographic methods can be utilized in the exploration of the historical, social, cultural, and political issues entwined in multilevel causes of mental health problems. Second, the addition of an anthropological perspective can uncover the cultural rules and idioms used to recognize and communicate suffering. Third, the anthropological approach, which is often "patient centered," is relevant to the design, piloting, and implementation of mental health programs, as it will reveal how task-sharing and other initiatives are experienced from patients' and families' perspectives.

Across disciplines, it is widely accepted that intervention programs must fit the local condition and be culturally acceptable; as such, anthropologists should be useful consultants as area experts. The full integration of anthropology requires an expansion beyond the qualitative approaches of public health that are often applied in a superficial manner without attention to power dynamics and social desirability expectations—that is, participants provide limited novel insight because the research methods elicit only what participants think that researchers want to hear. Understanding the complexities of the lived experiences of local people is a challenging task, but it is also the goal of true ethnography. There is increasing use of qualitative and mixed-methods research in public health, health services, and global mental health research (Bolton, Tol, and Bass 2009; Pereira et al. 2011; Robins et al. 2008). But it is important to recognize that qualitative research is not synonymous with ethnography (Bernard 1995; LeCompte and Schensul 1999). This point is clearly demonstrated in Chapter 2, the methods section of this volume. In order to employ expert ethnographers to inform public health programming, it is crucial to develop better communication about who can serve in this role and how to find, fund, and prioritize ethnographer-consultants in the planning and pilot stages of mental health interventions.

To do this, anthropologists need to be multilingual across research approaches and domains leading to mixed-method interdisciplinary and multidisciplinary studies. By being conversant in cultural studies, linguistics, ethnography, statistics, biological studies, and clinical studies, anthropologists can communicate with a range of audiences and participate in interdisciplinary teams. Medical anthropological studies like those that led to new understandings of *kuru* (Lindenbaum 1979), menopause (Lock 1993a, 1993b), and autism (Grinker 2008) can help guide both new discoveries and interventions, as well as highlight potential harmful effects of exclusively cultural or exclusively biomedical interpretations. In other words, local knowledge about healing and healing systems can transform how mental health interventions are organized and orchestrated in order to ensure acceptability and feasibility of mental health services at the community level and among health workers. Medical anthropologists, therefore, can serve as "cultural brokers" across scholarly disciplines as well as among researchers, policy makers, practitioners, patients, and local communities.

2. *Anthropologists should address the broad scope of mental health problems, from common mental disorders such as depression and anxiety to severe psychoses, substance abuse, neurological problems, and suicide.*

A warranted critique of medical anthropologists' contributions to global mental health research is the overwhelming focus on common mental disorders (CMD), such as unipolar depression, anxiety disorders, and trauma-related disorders, as opposed to severe mental disorders such as bipolar disorder and schizophrenia. This volume generally reflects this reality. This emphasis is not surprising given the burden of CMD on overall populations as measured in DALYs. It is also expectable because anthropologists have strong interest in the social determinants of health, and these interconnections may—on the surface—appear more salient when studying anxiety, depression, and PTSD, but it is important that anthropologists do not fall prey to the fallacious assumption that common mental disorders are more affected by culture than are severe ones (e.g., Summerfield 2008).

Culture is as important in regard to the manifestation, prognosis, and treatment responses in severe mental illness as in common ones (Jenkins 1991, 1997; Jenkins et al. 2005; Karno and Jenkins 1993; Kleinman 1988; Martin 2007). Therefore, anthropological research is needed on the broad spectrum of mental and neurological disorders in diverse cultural contexts. In particular, as noted below, there needs to be more research on schizophrenia, substance abuse, and suicide.

*Schizophrenia and Bipolar Disorder.* A focus on schizophrenia and other psychotic disorders is important because the controversy regarding better outcomes for schizophrenia in LMICs versus high-income countries (HIC) has yet to be resolved. This is largely the result of methodological problems in the studies that have been conducted (Cohen 1992; Cohen et al. 2008; Edgerton and Cohen 1994; Patel et al. 2006). Expanded ethnographic work that focuses on understanding how sociocultural context influences schizophrenia outcomes will not only build clearer comprehension of the problem but also will support better study design, implementation, and analysis. For example, medical anthropological studies conducted by Ugandan researchers have shown significant treatment effects of traditional healing practices on serious mental illness (Abbo et al. 2012; Abbo et al. 2008). In this volume (Chapter 19), Neely Myers discusses the role that persons with psychotic disorders can play as treatment providers when they have access to training, as illustrated by peer helpers in the United States. The chapter by Brandon Kohrt and Rev. Bill Jallah (Chapter 15) illustrates that in Liberia, there is a lack of locally appropriate labels and treatment options for bipolar disorder, thus requiring the development of culturally appropriate training and treatment guidelines.

*Substance Abuse.* Substance abuse is an area that requires continued attention by anthropologists in global mental health, particularly in LMICs. In Chapter 5 of this volume, Daniel Mains demonstrates the complexity of khat use in Ethiopia. Based on Mains's ethnography (cf. Mains 2012; Mains, Hadley, and Tessema 2013), it is evident that a purely disease-focused model of khat use is inadequate. The questions of who uses khat and what motivates this drug use must be understood in the context of educational and economic environments. Daniel Lende's extensive anthropological work on substance use in Colombia (Lende 2005, 2008; Lende et al. 2007; Lende and Downey 2012) also demonstrates the complex interplay between sociocultural context and cognitive processes, as described in his and Sarah Fishleder's Chapter 8—a domain they refer to as "neuroanthropology."

*Mental Health in the Elderly and Children.* Although some progress has been made, the mental health problems of the young and elderly are also in need of additional anthropological attention. Child mental health is of growing interest to anthropologists, including critiques of attention deficit hyperactivity disorder (Folmar and Palmes 2009). In addition, biocultural anthropology studies have demonstrated commonalities in disruptive behavioral disorders among children across populations (Hruschka, Kohrt, and Worthman 2005; Kohrt et al. 2014). Further anthropological research into autism is crucial for learning how to identify the disorder cross-culturally and how to design interventions, and for understanding how cross-cultural parenting practices may influence the disorder. With the aging of the world's population, dementia increasingly will present a health and social challenge to all cultural groups. Understanding social responses to aging, behavior, and cognition is vital for the improvement of mental health care. This is especially the case as the elderly become increasingly institutionalized in the context of social and economic changes, even in LMICs (Cohen 1998).

*Suicide.* Suicidal behavior is the other vital domain for anthropologists to further explore. Growing awareness of the high rates of suicide in South and East Asia have demonstrated the existence of cultural biases of Western models of suicide risk, vulnerable groups, and prevention. Anthropologists have taken up the call to help reframe biased psychiatric understandings of self-harm and suicide (Billaud 2012; Chua 2012; Das 2011; Imberton 2012; Ji, Kleinman, and Becker 2001; Kral 2012; Niehaus 2012; Ozawa-de Silva 2008; Staples and Widger 2012; Zhang et al. 2011). Analysis of suicide and life-threatening behavior has an important role in anthropology and public health, not only because it is a marker of mental health mortality, but also because it is a cultural marker of distress. For example, elevated suicide among rural Indian farmers has demonstrated a sociocultural response to financial insecurity, government apathy, and a changing environment (Chowdhury et al. 2007; Dongre and Deshmukh 2012). Although psychiatric intervention may make an important impact for Indian farmers suffering from mental health problems, community-level programs may be more effective in addressing underlying causes and vulnerability factors. More ethnography around the topic of suicide is needed that can inform social policy and community-level prevention programs in countries undergoing rapid political and economic change.

3.   *Anthropological research should move toward more community-based and social ecological interventions, which can help to address the social determinants of health.*

There is both a tension and complementarity between public health and clinical medicine. Whereas most resources are devoted to individual clinical treatments, the greatest advances in health have come through public health efforts and overall socioeconomic transformations (McKeown 1976, 2014; Worthman and Kohrt 2005). The story of John Snow and the removal of the handle of the Broad Street Pump in London in 1854 to curb the spread of cholera is a model for the field of public health. Community changes can have widespread impacts for individual health (Smith 2002). In the field of global mental health, we must ask ourselves,

"What is the mental health equivalent of clean drinking water?" and "What are the Broad Street Pumps of the mind that can be targets of community interventions and may result in widespread mental health benefit?" (Kohrt 2013a).

Anthropologists can make important contributions toward addressing this question through ethnographic research on social determinants of mental health. Ethnographic insights from Part I of this book exemplify how social and structural factors determine the distribution and character of mental illness within specific populations. These cases range from the struggle for water in Bolivia, to policies that restrict immigrant survival strategies in Egypt, to links between poverty and substance use/abuse in Ethiopia and Colombia, to gendered and sexual survival strategies in Belize, and to how international labor migration shapes social and psychological suffering in Nicaragua. Such in-depth studies uncover processes of structural and everyday violence and provide important insights for interventionists and others concerned with community health.

Critical approaches to understanding the social organization around health and healing, such as social ecology theory, can provide constructive programmatic ideas. This is possible because ecological approaches explore the interactions of different levels of social reality, which shape individuals' experiences with their world (Baer, Singer, and Susser 2003; Bronfenbrenner 1979, 1994; Singer 1989, 1995). These different levels range from direct interactions with family, peers, and community, to larger social processes mediated by government policies, economic systems, religion, and other cultural practices. For example, the role of social action through festive fighting and forgiving in rural India highlights the power of social relationships and communal acts, as illustrated by Jeffrey Snodgrass in Chapter 10 of this volume. Also, studies from humanitarian settings where society is affected by war and related trauma illustrate how social realities can shape mental illness and related suffering (Argenti-Pillen 2003; Green 1999).

Despite acknowledging the importance of social ecology and social support, most global mental health intervention research focuses on individual treatments (Kohrt 2013b). For example, the majority of intervention research in humanitarian contexts examines individually based PTSD treatments (Tol et al. 2011). Even in treatments identified as social or family-focused, individually based assessments are the norm (Galovski and Lyons 2004). Overcoming the limited focus on individual-level outcomes requires researchers to move beyond patient self-reports or clinician ratings as the sole outcome of intervention research. This may be addressed by employing quantitative and detailed qualitative research to evaluate ripple effects in a social ecological system that may support or undermine sustained intervention effects. It is also necessary for identifying unintended consequences of such interventions (Kleinman 2010). Similarly, more research is needed to attend to community-wide social and economic changes that can transform individual, family, and community mental health (Earls 1982; Earls and Carlson 2001; Earls, Raviola, and Carlson 2008; Richters 1993).

Investigating a person's ability to contribute to the well-being of others—rather than focusing on specific psychiatric symptoms—may be especially salient from a cross-cultural perspective. The social and relational aspects of trauma and stress can be more distressing to the individual than the actual traumatic event. For example, in Nepal, one-third of the symptoms developed locally to measure traumatic distress were significantly related to impaired ability to improve the well-being of others (Karki, Kohrt, and Jordans 2009). Moreover, social and cultural resources may function as sources of healing, recovery, and resilience at the community level. This is demonstrated by anthropologist Sara Lewis (2013) who argues that the low prevalence of PTSD among Tibetan refugees in India may be the result of cultural practices and religious values like compassion, forgiveness, and meditation—as well as humor—irrespective of the fact that the trauma was a result of political violence and social marginalization.

From an anthropological perspective, the next steps for global mental health research should be to explore multiple social ecological levels, including families, communities, and political regions. Alongside epidemiological research grounded in social ecology, evaluation of social ecology–based interventions is essential. When theory is reflected in practice, ethnographic research focusing on social ecology has significant potential for informing mental health interventions not only for the afflicted but also for their families and communities more broadly.

4.  *Anthropological research about health systems is required to understand and inform treatment processes in mental health.*

Understanding health systems has been the project of notable and powerful ethnographies (cf. Closser 2010; Justice 1989; Pfeiffer 2003). A small number of medical anthropologists (including some in this volume) have conducted ethnographies related to task-shifting/task-sharing and the implications within the health system (see Part III in this volume). Task-shifting is usually defined by the rational redistribution of tasks among health workers. However, anthropological critics argue that task-shifting HIV/AIDS care to community health workers (CHWs) unveils inequalities in the global health system and places undue burden on people working at the community level (cf. Maes and Kalofonos 2013; Maes, Kohrt, and Closser 2010). The idea of task-shifting and utilization of CHWs in general often depends on unpaid labor—"volunteerism." Recognizing the political, economic, social, and cultural factors that shape health systems—and people's roles and rights within them—is an anthropological question underrepresented in research on health systems and policy. However, it is not only health delivery that is underrepresented but also issues of governance, financing, technologies, and innovations that require consideration by medical anthropologists.

As social and economic systems involve both resources and power, health systems should fall within the bailiwick of anthropology. In the tradition of critical medical anthropology (e.g., Baer et al. 2003; Singer 1989, 1995), anthropologists need to study the organization and mechanisms of health systems themselves, which should complement patient-centered studies which currently dominate the field. Patients—because they are often in the position of the least power and because many anthropologists are committed to understanding the plight of the most marginalized of society—are the typical subjects of research studies by anthropologists. Anthropologists have less frequently studied elites in positions of corporate and government power. This was a gap identified in 1972 by Laura Nader, who called for "studying up." Studying up refers to studying people in power such as policy makers, NGO leaders, clinicians, and employers. This contrasts with the dominant thrust of anthropological research, in which patients, persons living in poverty, and marginalized groups are the primary research participants. Svea Closser (2010) demonstrated such an approach in her study of the many levels of the international polio campaign in Pakistan, where she conducted ethnography and in-depth interviews with multiple stakeholders, from those developing the vaccine at the Centers for Disease Control and Prevention to those administering it in rural Pakistan, to those with power for local on-the-ground administration of the program from the WHO and Ministry of Health. Indeed, health systems, like many aspects of development, are also the locus of corruption (or "slippage") and therefore represent a challenge to improvements in global mental health programs.

In addition, in studying the culture of global health institutions, anthropologists should broaden their methodological strategy to include interpretive analysis of health system data as cultural artifacts. This work should focus on the entire chain of health systems, from policy makers to those implementing services; it should include both NGOs and government institutions. For example, medical anthropologists have used data-tracing methods to follow chains of medications (for tuberculosis, depression, and inducing childbirth) from their production and distribution to their use (Brhlikova et al. 2011; Ecks and Harper 2013; Harper 2006, 2014; Harper and Parker 2014). Along this chain, they have observed and conducted ethnographic interviews with distributors, wholesalers, pharmacists, prescribing clinicians, and patients. Such an analysis of the flow of biomedical commodities can provide important information and reveal the different assumptions—and cultural models—that health workers employ at different levels of the system. For example, what counts as a "case," "evidence-based practice," "treatment resistance," or "remission" varies significantly, depending on the bureaucratic level at which the health provider operates. New studies using ethnography plus data tracing to understand suicide within health systems are beginning in

Asia. Similar anthropological research is needed across national and local health systems.

5.  *Anthropological research into diagnostic labels, idioms of distress, and ethnopsychology should be employed and incorporated into mental health interventions.*

A great deal of attention has been paid to the issue of the applicability of diagnostic labels of mental illness across cultures. Anthropologists working in health systems and with individuals and families can learn more about how diagnostic labels are used and understood. Clinician application of a label, family use of that same label, and self-labeling are all different processes requiring study. The impact of introducing new, local labels or idioms of distress into health delivery systems should be studied for potential unintended consequences. For example, use of local idioms for stress and general psychological complaints has been proven beneficial to promote participation in psychological treatments (Patel et al. 2011). In contrast, in Liberia, introduction of a local idiom of distress ("open mole") into biomedical mental health diagnoses has led toward a trend of reinterpreting a heterogeneous idiom as a psychotic condition requiring medication, resulting in potentially inappropriate and harmful use of antipsychotic medications (Abramowitz 2010). Studying the use of idioms is especially important in primary care centers serving people with chronic illness; such patients may communicate their mental illness through a local idiom of distress (rather than a biomedical term) when they talk about their chronic illness (Mendenhall et al. 2010).

Future anthropological studies should move past studying single idioms of distress as well as psychiatric labels in isolation. It is important to explore how cultural idioms and emic labels are interconnected in order to reveal underlying cultural assumptions about well-being, normality, and pathology. This approach, captured in the field of ethnopsychology, suggests that idioms and labels are conceptualized as systematic worldviews rather than just laundry lists of terms (Kohrt and Hruschka 2010; White 1992). Studying single cultural concepts of distress does not address the range of forms and meanings for experiences of mental and physical suffering. Grounding studies in ethnopsychology, in contrast, can allow us to catalog a range of experiences of distress, with greater likelihood of encompassing forms of distress that are more mundane as opposed to culturally exotic (Fox 2003; Keys et al. 2012; Kohrt and Harper 2008; Kohrt and Hruschka 2010; Patel 1995). Within ethnopsychology, attention is directed more to basic emotions and symptoms of common mental disorders, and less to such cultural exotica as penis retraction, semen loss, arctic cannibal compulsions, and puppy pregnancies, which have sometimes become fetishes of cross-cultural psychiatry (Cheng 1996;

Chowdhury et al. 2003; Marano 1982; Sumathipala, Siribaddana, and Bhugra 2004).

Ethnopsychology is not limited to cataloging terms for different categories of mental illness in isolation. Instead, it provides a framework to group different types of distress associated with varied categories of experience, such as the range of "head/brain" and "heart" idioms observed in sub-Saharan Africa studies (Betancourt et al. 2009; Fox 2003; Patel 1995), the Caribbean and Central America (England, Mysyk, and Gallegos 2007; Keys et al. 2012; Quinlan 2010; Salgado de Snyder, de Jesus Diaz-Perez, and Ojeda 2000), and South Asia (Dolma et al. 2006; Kohrt and Harper 2008; Kohrt and Hruschka 2010; Parish 2004). Ethnopsychology also gives us models for predicting connections among symptoms, including changes with worsening severity (Hinton et al. 2012; Hinton and Otto 2006; Hinton, Pich, et al. 2010; Lewis-Fernández et al. 2002). The ethnopsychological approach emphasizes linkages among social, spiritual, and physical experiences and distress, thus spotlighting which experiences trigger mental distress and suggesting strategies for therapeutic resolution. This offers a potential frame for integration, rather than only a list of symptoms that may or may not cohere. Cultural processes in which negative meanings (also called "catastrophic cognitions" in cognitive therapy literature) are given to certain somatic symptoms can lead to worsening of psycho-biological symptoms (a process referred to as "biolooping" by cultural psychiatrists) (Hinton et al. 2006; Hinton et al. 2008; Hinton and Hinton 2002; Hinton, Hofman, et al. 2010; Kirmayer 2006). Studying ethnopsychology sheds light upon which meanings, cognitions, and somatic sensations are most relevant to these psycho-biological pathways. Understanding such downward spirals can suggest ways to intervene that can interrupt and mitigate symptoms.

Anthropologists should work with clinical trial researchers to include more culturally appropriate outcome measures, such as tracking clients' endorsement and understanding of cultural concepts of distress as they go through intervention programs (Kohrt et al. 2014). One major missed opportunity in the cultural psychiatry and global mental health literature to date is failing to assess local labels and idioms of distress in intervention studies. The few studies that have evaluated cultural concepts of distress outcomes during treatment have shown that depression may improve even when the client's sense of distress, as labeled with the cultural idiom, is not resolved, suggesting that social and cultural experiences of distress can persist in the absence of standard psychiatric symptoms (Kleinman 1982; Makanjuola 1987). Conversely, other studies have shown that distress labeled with a cultural idiom can be improved even while psychiatric symptoms resolve to a lesser degree (Hinton et al. 2009; Hinton et al. 2011; Hinton et al. 2012). This information is crucial because alleviation of cultural concepts of distress may represent the most meaningful outcome of a community mental health intervention. De Jong and Ries

(2010) argue that alleviation of the suffering associated with cultural concepts of distress is most effective when the response to the cultural construct addresses the perceived cause, rather than the symptoms of distress. For example, addressing underlying social tensions, social marginalization, and other vulnerabilities leads to alleviation of emic concepts of mental suffering and may therefore be more important than a therapeutic focus on symptoms and their management.

We also need more research into cultural concepts of recovery that can be used to recognize when distress is resolving. In Iran, there are both cultural constructs for distressed relationships and labels for the recovery and reconciliation process (Behzadi 1994). Ultimately, interventions need to be culturally and personally meaningful rather than only demonstrate symptom changes (Kleinman 1988). More research by anthropologists on the use of labels, idioms, and other terminology in experiencing suffering—and especially in terms of healing and health systems to foster recovery—is needed.

6.  *Ethnographic research needs to be conducted to understand how psychiatric medications are integrated into daily life and how they affect the daily experience of patients.*

Although there is a great deal of debate about the role of psychopharmaceuticals and pharmaceutical companies, in reality little is known about how medications affect the day-to-day life of persons and families. There are serious concerns about the medicalization of experience and the pathologizing of individuals, yet there are very few examples of whether or not this happens. Global mental health interventions suggest positive outcomes—and few negative outcomes—in most trials of psychopharmaceuticals conducted to date. Anthropologists may serve as research consultants to investigate how psychiatric drugs are prescribed and administered to evaluate the role of pharmaceutical companies and distributors in global mental health care delivery. We should resist an automatic ideological reaction against the use of medications, just as we should avoid the romanticization of traditional shamanistic therapies.

The days of anthropologists taking antipsychotic medication as part of participant observation fieldwork (Estroff 1981) are likely no longer possible, as biomedical standards of research ethics have changed. However, it is crucial that anthropologists employ the tools of ethnography to understand how taking (or not taking) medication is experienced on a phenomenological, interpersonal, and sociopolitical level (cf. Biehl 2013). Psychiatric assessment scores and clinical diagnoses provide only one aspect of evaluating a patient's experience with medication. Such measures do not capture the complex subjective experience of taking psychiatric medication with regard to changing cognition and emotions. It is important to understand how (or if) medications change patients' views of themselves, how others view the patient, and how the "self" is defined. Anthropological research on subjectivity, embodiment, and phenomenology should continue to be employed as tools to address this research gap (Adams 1998; Desjarlais 2003; Hinton, Hinton, and Hinton 2011; James 2004; Lock 1993a; Ozawa-de Silva 2008). The anthropologist and psychoanalyst Douglas Hollan (2014) has developed approaches to studying the "selfscape" as a way of understanding trauma, and the same model could be used for studying experiences in global mental health pharmacological and non-pharmacological intervention programs.

7.   *There is a need for an expanded role of medical anthropologists from LMICs.*

This book illustrates the need for training medical anthropologists who can conduct engaged and theoretically grounded research on mental health issues in their own countries. Currently—as demonstrated in this volume, where all contributors are from and trained in high-income countries—research on mental health remains dominated by high-income-country researchers. Focusing on the next generation of medical anthropologists from LMICs requires that current investigators embed capacity building for PhD-level medical anthropologists into their research and teaching programs. In this way, scholars from both high-income and low- and middle-income countries can learn alongside one another, drawing skills and knowledge from work in all settings. This means that investigators should incorporate PhD training programs that match funding and training for graduate students from all backgrounds to learn with and from one another.

8.   *Anthropologists working on global mental health must continue to emphasize the centrality of local cultural context—both to understand the causal chain of psychological suffering and to optimize the effectiveness of interventions.*

A major challenge going forward in global mental health is the conceptualization and operationalization of "global–local" exchanges (Bemme and D'Souza 2014). Medical interventions tend to offer "one size fits all" approaches, often assuming that pilot projects can be scaled up with little concern for the idiosyncrasies of local contexts. Perhaps this is because policy makers and program designers presume that making programmatic adaptations to local conditions is too difficult or may only have a marginal benefit. In future research, anthropologists need to demonstrate precisely *how* programs can be shaped to fit local contexts. This can be as simple as "ruling out" a claim that there is a cultural obstacle causing a program to falter. Local adaptation might be as modest as utilizing local vocabulary, idioms, symbols, and ethnopsychological categories. Understanding local contexts must be broader than the simplistic concept of "cultural competence," as it must take account of local social tensions such as politics.

   This final recommendation is meant to underscore that anthropologists must stay on message about the importance of context. The valuable examples nestled in the three parts of this volume need to be multiplied. But anthropologists should also try to go beyond describing the local context to showing *how* to make it work in a local context. This is an area where it is critically important to include local people—both researchers and community members—as real partners so that projects can be adapted rather than just implemented. As cultural brokers and engaged scholars, then, anthropologists have a critical role to play not only in understanding local problems but also in helping teams to design, implement, and scale up local solutions for mental health service delivery.

The past century has witnessed a dramatic transformation in our understandings of mental illness, the types of treatments for mental illness, our ability to travel and communicate across the globe, and the financial landscape of health care. The current diagnostic categories—let alone the medications to treat them—did not exist when anthropologists of the early 20th century conducted their first cross-cultural research. Yet, the basic anthropological questions and research challenges about mental health in different societies have changed little. Anthropologists still struggle to understand how labels are used to identify people with psychological suffering and how that labeling impacts daily experience and social relations. The fundamental processes of healing are still strongly tied to the interpersonal relationships of patients, healers, and families—regardless of the specific technologies of the interaction. Therefore, we believe that the future of global mental health needs to remain strongly connected with anthropologists and anthropological concepts and methods in order to strengthen how mental health treatment is designed and implemented to improve mental health for all people, everywhere.

## References

Abbo, C., Okello, E. S., Ekblad, S., Waako, P., and Musisi, S. (2008). Lay concepts of psychosis in Busoga, eastern Uganda: a pilot study. *World Cultural Psychiatry Research Reviews*, 3 (3): 132–145.

Abbo, C., Okello, E. S., Musisi, S., Waako, P., and Ekblad, S. (2012). Naturalistic outcome of treatment of psychosis by traditional healers in Jinja and Iganga districts, eastern Uganda—a 3- and 6 months follow up. *International Journal of Mental Health Systems*, 6 (1): 13.

Abramowitz, S. A. (2010). Trauma and humanitarian translation in Liberia: the tale of open mole. *Culture, Medicine, and Psychiatry*, 34 (2): 353–379.

Adams, V. (1998). Suffering the winds of Lhasa: politicized bodies, human rights, cultural difference, and humanism in Tibet. *Medical Anthropology Quarterly*, 12 (1): 74–102.

Argenti-Pillen, A. (2003). *Masking Terror: How Women Contain Violence in Southern Sri Lanka*. Philadelphia: University of Pennsylvania Press.

Baer, H. A., Singer, M., and Susser, I. (2003). *Medical Anthropology and the World System*. 2nd ed. Westport, Connecticut: Praeger.

Behzadi, K. G. (1994). Interpersonal conflict and emotions in an Iranian cultural practice: qahr and ashti. *Culture, Medicine, and Psychiatry*, 18 (3): 321–359.

Bemme, D., and D'Souza, N. A. (2014). Global mental health and its discontents: an inquiry into the making of global and local scale. *Transcultural Psychiatry*, 51 (6): 850–874.

Bernard, H. R. (1995). *Research Methods in Anthropology: Qualitative and Quantitative Approaches*. 2nd ed. Thousand Oaks, California: Sage Publications.

Betancourt, T. S., Bass, J., Borisova, I., Neugebauer, R., Speelman, L., Onyango, G., and Bolton, P. (2009). Assessing local instrument reliability and validity: a field-based example from northern Uganda. *Social Psychiatry and Psychiatric Epidemiology*, 44 (8): 685–692.

Biehl, J. (2013). *Vita: Life in a Zone of Social Abandonment*. Berkeley: University of California Press.

Billaud, J. (2012). Suicidal performances: voicing discontent in a girls' dormitory in Kabul. *Culture, Medicine, and Psychiatry*, 36 (2): 264–285.

Bolton, P., Tol, W. A., and Bass, J. (2009). Combining qualitative and quantitative research methods to support psychosocial and mental health programmes in complex emergencies. *Intervention*, 7 (3): 181–186.

Brhlikova, P., Harper, I., Jeffery, R., Rawal, N., Subedi, M., and Santhosh, M. R. (2011). Trust and the regulation of pharmaceuticals: South Asia in a globalised world. *Globalization and Health*, 7: 10.

Bronfenbrenner, U. (1979). *The Ecology of Human Development: Experiments by Nature and Design*. Cambridge, Massachusetts: Harvard University Press.

——. (1994). Ecological models of human development. In *International Encyclopedia of Education*, Vol. 3, 2nd ed., pp. 37–43. Oxford: Elsevier.

Cheng, S. T. (1996). A critical review of Chinese Koro. *Culture, Medicine, and Psychiatry*, 20 (1): 67–82.

Chowdhury, A. N., Banerjee, S., Brahma, A, and Weiss, M. G. (2007). Pesticide practices and suicide among farmers of the Sundarban region in India. *Food and Nutrition Bulletin*, 28 (2 Suppl): S381–391.

Chowdhury, A. N., Mukherjee, H., Ghosh, K. K., and Chowdhury, S. (2003). Puppy pregnancy in humans: a culture-bound disorder in rural West Bengal, India. *International Journal of Social Psychiatry*, 49 (1): 35–42.

Chua, J. L. (2012). Tales of decline: reading social pathology into individual suicide in South India. *Culture, Medicine, and Psychiatry*, 36 (2): 204–224.

Closser, S. (2010). *Chasing Polio in Pakistan: Why the World's Largest Public Health Initiative May Fail*. Nashville, Tennessee: Vanderbilt University Press.

Cohen, A. (1992). Prognosis for schizophrenia in the Third World: a reevaluation of cross-cultural research. *Culture, Medicine, and Psychiatry*, 16 (1): 53–75.

Cohen, A., Patel, V., Thara, R., and Gureje, O. (2008). Questioning an axiom: better prognosis for schizophrenia in the developing world? *Schizophrenia Bulletin*, 34 (2): 229–244.

Cohen, L. (1998). *No Aging in India: Alzheimer's, the Bad Family, and Other Modern Things*. Berkeley: University of California Press.

Das, A. (2011). Farmers' suicide in India: implications for public mental health. *International Journal of Social Psychiatry*, 57 (1): 21–29.

de Jong, J. T., and Reis, R. (2010). *Kiyang-yang*, a West-African postwar idiom of distress. *Culture, Medicine, and Psychiatry*, 34 (2): 301–321.

Desjarlais, R. R. (2003). *Sensory Biographies: Lives and Deaths among Nepal's Yolmo Buddhists*, Vol. 2. Berkeley: University of California Press.

Dolma, S., Singh, S., Lohfeld, L., Orbinski, J. J., and Mills, E. J. (2006). Dangerous journey: documenting the experience of Tibetan refugees. *American Journal of Public Health*, 96 (11): 2061–2064.

Dongre, A. R., and Deshmukh, P. R. (2012). Farmers' suicides in the Vidarbha region of Maharashtra, India: a qualitative exploration of their causes. *Journal of Injury and Violence Research*, 4 (1): 2–6.

Earls, F. (1982). Cultural and national differences in the epidemiology of behavior problems of preschool children. *Culture, Medicine, and Psychiatry*, 6: 45–56.

Earls, F., and Carlson, M. (2001). The social-ecology of child health and wellbeing. *Annual Review of Public Health*, 22: 143–166.

Earls, F., Raviola, G. J., and Carlson, M. (2008). Promoting child and adolescent mental health in the context of the HIV/AIDS pandemic with a focus on sub-Saharan Africa. *Journal of Child Psychology and Psychiatry and Allied Disciplines*, 49 (3): 295–312.

Ecks, S., and Harper, I. (2013). Public-private mixes: the market for anti-tuberculosis drugs in India. In J. Biehl and A. Petryna (eds.), *When People Come First: Critical Studies in Global Health*, pp. 252–276. Princeton, New Jersey: Princeton University Press.

Edgerton, R. B., and Cohen, A. (1994). Culture and schizophrenia: the DOSMD challenge. *British Journal of Psychiatry*, 164 (2): 222–231.

England, M., Mysyk, A., and Gallegos, J. A. (2007). An examination of *nervios* among Mexican seasonal farm workers. *Nursing Inquiry*, 14 (3): 189–201.

Estroff, S. E. (1981). *Making It Crazy: An Ethnography of Psychiatric Clients in an American Community*. Berkeley: University of California Press.

Folmar, S., and Palmes, G. K. (2009). Cross-cultural psychiatry in the field: collaborating with anthropology. *Journal of the American Academy of Child and Adolescent Psychiatry*, 48 (9): 873–876.

Fox, S. H. (2003). The Mandinka nosological system in the context of post-trauma syndromes. *Transcultural Psychiatry*, 40 (4): 488–506.

Galovski, T., and Lyons, J. A. (2004). Psychological sequelae of combat violence: a review of the impact of PTSD on the veteran's family and possible interventions. *Aggression and Violent Behavior*, 9 (5): 477–501.

Green, L. (1999). *Fear as a Way of Life: Mayan Widows in Rural Guatemala*. New York: Columbia University Press.

Grinker, R. R. (2008). *Unstrange Minds: Remapping the World of Autism*. New York: Basic Books.

Harper, I. (2006). Anthropology, dots and understanding tuberculosis control in Nepal. *Journal of Biosocial Science*, 38 (1): 57–67.

——. (2014). *Development and Public Health in the Himalaya: Reflections on Healing in Contemporary Nepal*. London: Routledge.

Harper, I., and Parker, M. (2014). The politics and anti-politics of infectious disease control. *Medical Anthropology*, 33 (3): 198–205.

Hinton, D., and Hinton, S. (2002). Panic disorder, somatization, and the new cross-cultural psychiatry: the seven bodies of a medical anthropology of panic. *Culture, Medicine, and Psychiatry*, 26 (2): 155–178.

Hinton, D. E., and Otto, M. W. (2006). Symptom presentation and symptom meaning among traumatized Cambodian refugees: relevance to a somatically focused cognitive-behavior therapy. *Cognitive and Behavioral Practice*, 13 (4): 249–260.

Hinton, L., Hinton, D., and Hinton, A. (2011). Panel: "*Unus mundus*": transcendent truth or comforting fiction? Overwhelm and the search for meaning in a fragmented world. *Journal of Analytical Psychology*, 56 (3): 375–380.

Hinton, D. E., Chhean, D., Pich, V., Um, K., Fama, J. M., and Pollack, M. H. (2006). Neck-focused panic attacks among Cambodian refugees: a logistic and linear regression analysis. *Journal of Anxiety Disorders*, 20 (2): 119–138.

Hinton, D. E., Hinton, A. L., Eng, K. T., and Choung, S. (2012). PTSD and key somatic complaints and cultural syndromes among rural Cambodians: the results of a needs assessment survey. *Medical Anthropology Quarterly*, 26 (3): 383–407.

Hinton, D. E., Hofmann, S. G., Orr, S. P., Pitman, R. K., Pollack, M. H., and Pole, N. (2010). A psychobiocultural model of orthostatic panic among Cambodian refugees: flashbacks, catastrophic cognitions, and reduced orthostatic blood-pressure response. *Psychological Trauma-Theory Research Practice and Policy*, 2 (1): 63–70.

Hinton, D. E., Hofmann, S. G., Pitman, R. K., Pollack, M. H., and Barlow, D. H. (2008). The panic attack–posttraumatic stress disorder model: applicability to orthostatic panic among Cambodian refugees. *Cognitive Behaviour Therapy*, 37 (2): 101–116.

Hinton, D. E., Hofmann, S. G., Pollack, M. H., and Otto, M. W. (2009). Mechanisms of efficacy of CBT for Cambodian refugees with PTSD: improvement in emotion regulation and orthostatic blood pressure response. *CNS Neuroscience and Therapeutics*, 15 (3): 255–263.

Hinton, D. E., Hofmann, S. G., Rivera, E., Otto, M. W., and Pollack, M. H. (2011). Culturally adapted CBT (CA-CBT) for Latino women with treatment-resistant PTSD: a pilot study comparing CA-CBT to applied muscle relaxation. *Behaviour Research and Therapy*, 49 (4): 275–280.

Hinton, D. E., Kredlow, M. A., Bui, E., Pollack, M. H., and Hofmann, S. G. (2012). Treatment change of somatic symptoms and cultural syndromes among Cambodian refugees with PTSD. *Depression and Anxiety*, 29 (2): 147–154.

Hinton, D. E., Pich, V., Marques, L., Nickerson, A., and Pollack, M. H. (2010). Khyal attacks: a key idiom of distress among traumatized Cambodian refugees. *Culture, Medicine, and Psychiatry*, 34 (2): 244–278.

Hollan, Douglas. (2014). From ghosts to ancestors (and back again): on the cultural and psychodynamic mediation of selfscapes. *Ethos*, 42 (2): 175–197.

Hruschka, D. J., Kohrt, B. A., and Worthman, C. M. (2005). Estimating between- and within-individual variation in cortisol levels using multilevel models. *Psychoneuroendocrinology*, 30 (7): 698–714.

Imberton, G. (2012). Chol understandings of suicide and human agency. *Culture, Medicine, and Psychiatry*, 36 (2): 245–263.

James, E. C. (2004). The political economy of "trauma" in Haiti in the democratic era of insecurity. *Culture, Medicine, and Psychiatry*, 28 (2): 127–149, 211–220.

Jenkins, J. H. (1991). Anthropology, expressed emotion, and schizophrenia. *Ethos*, 19 (4): 387–431.

——. (1997). Subjective experience of persistent schizophrenia and depression among US Latinos and Euro-Americans. *British Journal of Psychiatry*, 171: 20–25.

Jenkins, J. H., Strauss, M. E., Carpenter, E. A., Miller, D., Floersch, J., and Sajatovic, M. (2005). Subjective experience of recovery from schizophrenia-related disorders and atypical antipsychotics. *International Journal of Social Psychiatry*, 51 (3): 211–227.

Ji, J. L., Kleinman, A., and Becker, A. E. (2001). Suicide in contemporary China: a review of China's distinctive suicide demographics in their sociocultural context. *Harvard Review of Psychiatry*, 9 (1): 1–12.

Justice, J. (1989). *Policies, Plans, and People: Foreign Aid and Health Development*. Berkeley: University of California Press.

Karki, R., Kohrt, B. A., and Jordans, M. J. D. (2009). Child led indicators: pilot testing a child participation tool for psychosocial support programmes for former child soldiers in Nepal. *Intervention: International Journal of Mental Health, Psychosocial Work and Counselling in Areas of Armed Conflict*, 7 (2): 92–109.

Karno, M., and Jenkins, J. H. (1993). Cross-cultural issues in the course and treatment of schizophrenia. *Psychiatric Clinics of North America*, 16 (2): 339–350.

Keys, H. M., Kaiser, B. N., Kohrt, B. A., Khoury, N. M., and Brewster, A. R. (2012). Idioms of distress, ethnopsychology, and the clinical encounter in Haiti's Central Plateau. *Social Science and Medicine*, 75 (3): 555–564.

Kirmayer, L. J. (2006). Beyond the new cross-cultural psychiatry: cultural biology, discursive psychology and the ironies of globalization. *Transcultural Psychiatry*, 43 (1): 126–144.

Kleinman, A. (1982). Neurasthenia and depression: a study of somatization and culture in China. *Culture, Medicine, and Psychiatry*, 6 (2): 117–190.

——. (1988). *Rethinking Psychiatry: From Cultural Category to Personal Experience*. New York: Free Press and Collier Macmillan.

——. (2010). Four social theories for global health. *The Lancet*, 375 (9725): 1518–1519.

Kohrt, B. (2013a). Broad Street Pumps of the mind: human biology in the advancement of global mental health. *American Journal of Human Biology*, 25 (2): 263-263.

——. (2013b). Social ecology interventions for post-traumatic stress disorder: what can we learn from child soldiers? *British Journal of Psychiatry*, 203: 165–167.

Kohrt, B. A., and Harper, I. (20008). Navigating diagnoses: understanding mind–body relations, mental health, and stigma in Nepal. *Culture, Medicine, and Psychiatry*, 32 (4): 462–491.

Kohrt, B. A., and Hruschka, D. J. (2010). Nepali concepts of psychological trauma: the role of idioms of distress, ethnopsychology and ethnophysiology in alleviating suffering and preventing stigma. *Culture, Medicine, and Psychiatry*, 34 (2): 322–352.

Kohrt, B. A., Hruschka, D. J., Kohrt, H. E., Carrion, V. G., Waldman, I. D., and Worthman, C. M. (2014). Child abuse, disruptive behavior disorders, depression, and salivary cortisol levels among institutionalized and community-residing boys in Mongolia. *Asia-Pacific Psychiatry*. doi:10.1111/appy.12141 (Epub ahead of print).

Kohrt, B. A., Rasmussen, A., Kaiser, B. N., Haroz, E. E., Maharjan, S. M., Mutamba, B. B., and Hinton, D. E. (2014). Cultural concepts of distress and psychiatric disorders: literature review and research recommendations for global mental health epidemiology. *International Journal of Epidemiology*, 43 (2): 365–406.

Kral, M. J. (2012). Postcolonial suicide among Inuit in Arctic Canada. *Culture, Medicine, and Psychiatry*, 36 (2): 306–325.

LeCompte, M. D., and Schensul, J. J. (1999). *Designing and Conducting Ethnographic Research*. Walnut Creek, California: AltaMira Press.

Lende, D. H. (2005). Wanting and drug use: a biocultural approach to the analysis of addiction. *Ethos*, 33 (1): 100–124.

——. (2008). Addiction: more than innate rationality. *Behavioral and Brain Sciences*, 31 (4): 453–454.

Lende, D. H., Leonard, T., Sterk, C. E., and Elifson, K. (2007). Functional methamphetamine use: the insider's perspective. *Addiction Research and Theory*, 15 (5): 465–477.

Lende, D. H., and Downey, G. (eds.). (2012). *The Encultured Brain: An Introduction to Neuroanthropology*. Cambridge, Massachusetts: MIT Press.

Lewis, S. E. (2013). Trauma and the making of flexible minds in the Tibetan exile community. *Ethos*, 41 (3): 313–336.

Lewis-Fernández, R., Guarnaccia, P. J., Martinez, I. E., Salman, E., Schmidt, A., and Liebowitz, M. (2002). Comparative phenomenology of *ataques de nervios*, panic attacks, and panic disorder. *Culture, Medicine, and Psychiatry*, 26 (2): 199–223.

Lindenbaum, S. (1979). *Kuru Sorcery: Disease and Danger in the New Guinea Highlands*. Mountain View, California: Mayfield.

Lock, M. (1993a). Cultivating the body: anthropology and epistemologies of bodily practice and knowledge. *Annual Review of Anthropology*, 22: 133–155.

——. (1993b). *Encounters with Aging: Mythologies of Menopause in Japan and North America*. Berkeley: University of California Press.

Maes, K., and Kalofonos, I. (2013). Becoming and remaining community health workers: perspectives from Ethiopia and Mozambique. *Social Science and Medicine*, 87: 52–59.

Maes, K. C., Kohrt, B. A., and Closser, S. (2010). Culture, status and context in community health worker pay: pitfalls and opportunities for policy research. A commentary on Glenton et al. (2010). *Social Science and Medicine*, 71 (8): 1375–1378, 1379–1380.

Mains, D. (2012). *Hope is Cut: Youth, Unemployment, and the Future in Urban Ethiopia*: Philadelphia: Temple University Press.

Mains, D., Hadley, C., and Tessema, F. (2013). Chewing over the future: khat consumption, anxiety, depression, and time among young men in Jimma, Ethiopia. *Culture, Medicine, and Psychiatry*, 37 (1): 111–130.

Makanjuola, R. O. (1987). "Ode Ori": a culture-bound disorder with prominent somatic features in Yoruba Nigerian patients. *Acta Psychiatrica Scandinavica*, 75 (3): 231–236.

Marano, L. (1982). Windigo psychosis: the anatomy of an emic–etic confusion. *Current Anthropology*, 23 (4): 385–412.

Martin, E. (2007). *Bipolar Expeditions: Mania and Depression in American Culture*. Princeton, New Jersey: Princeton University Press.

McKeown, T. (1976). *The Modern Rise of Population*. London: Edward Arnold Publishers, Ltd.

McKeown, T. (2014). *The Role of Medicine: Dream, Mirage, or Nemesis?* Princeton, New Jersey: Princeton University Press.

Mendenhall, E., Seligman, R. A., Fernandez, A., and Jacobs, E. A. (2010). Speaking through diabetes: rethinking the significance of lay discourses on diabetes. *Medical Anthropology Quarterly*, 24 (2): 220–239.

Nader, L. (1972). Up the anthropologist: perspectives gained from studying up. In D. Hymes (ed.), *Reinventing Anthropology*. New York: Pantheon Press.

Niehaus, I. (2012). Gendered endings: narratives of male and female suicides in the South African Lowveld. *Culture, Medicine, and Psychiatry*, 36 (2): 327–347.

Okello, E. S., and Neema, S. (2007). Explanatory models and help-seeking behavior: pathways to psychiatric care among patients admitted for depression in Mulago Hospital, Kampala, Uganda. *Qualitative Health Research*, 17 (1): 14–25.

Ozawa-de Silva, C. (2008). Too lonely to die alone: Internet suicide pacts and existential suffering in Japan. *Culture, Medicine, and Psychiatry*, 32 (4): 516–551.

Parish, Steven M. (2004). The sacred mind: Newar cultural representations of mental life and the production of moral consciousness. In J. Corrigan (ed.), *Religion and Emotion: Approaches and Interpretations*, pp. 149–184. Oxford: Oxford University Press.

Patel, V. (1995). Explanatory models of mental illness in sub-Saharan Africa. *Social Science and Medicine*, 40 (9): 1291–1298.

Patel, V., Chowdhary, N., Rahman, A., and Verdeli, H. (2011). Improving access to psychological treatments: lessons from developing countries. *Behaviour Research and Therapy*, 49: 523–528.

Patel, V., Cohen, A., Thara, R., and Gureje, O. (2006). Is the outcome of schizophrenia really better in developing countries? *Revista brasileira de psiquiatria*, 28 (2): 149–152.

Pereira, B., Andrew, G., Pednekar, S., Kirkwood, B. R., and Patel, V. (2011). The integration of the treatment for common mental disorders in primary care: experiences of health care providers in the MANAS trial in Goa, India. *International Journal of Mental Health Systems*, 5 (1): 6.

Pfeiffer, J. (2003). International NGOs and primary health care in Mozambique: the need for a new model of collaboration. *Social Science and Medicine*, 56 (4): 725–738.

Quinlan, M. B. (2010). Ethnomedicine and ethnobotany of fright, a Caribbean culture-bound psychiatric syndrome. *Journal of Ethnobiology and Ethnomedicine*, 6: 9.

Richters, J. E. (1993). Community violence and children's development: toward a research agenda for the 1990s. *Psychiatry*, 56 (1): 3–6.

Robins, C. S., Ware, N. C., dosReis, S., Willging, C. E., Chung, J. Y., and Lewis-Fernández, R. (2008). Dialogues on mixed-methods and mental health services research: anticipating challenges, building solutions. *Psychiatric Services*, 59 (7): 727–731.

Salgado de Snyder, V., Nelly, V., Diaz-Perez, M. J., and Ojeda, V. D. (2000). The prevalence of *nervios* and associated symptomatology among inhabitants of Mexican rural communities. *Culture, Medicine, and Psychiatry*, 24 (4): 453–470.

Singer, M. (1989). The coming of age in critical medical anthropology. *Social Science and Medicine*, 28: 1193–1203.

——. (1995). Beyond the ivory tower: critical praxis in medical anthropology. *Medical Anthropology Quarterly*, 9: 80–106.

Smith, G. D. (2002). Commentary: behind the Broad Street Pump: aetiology, epidemiology and prevention of cholera in mid-19th century Britain. *International Journal of Epidemiology*, 31: 920–932.

Staples, J., and Widger, T. (2012). Situating suicide as an anthropological problem: ethnographic approaches to understanding self-harm and self-inflicted death. *Culture, Medicine, and Psychiatry*, 36 (2): 183–203.

Sumathipala, A., Siribaddana, S. H., and Bhugra, D. (2004). Culture-bound syndromes: the story of dhat syndrome. *British Journal of Psychiatry*, 184: 200–209.

Summerfield, D. (2008). How scientifically valid is the knowledge base of global mental health? *British Medical Journal*, 336 (7651): 992–994.

Tol, W. A., Barbui, C., Galappatti, A., Silove, D., Betancourt, T. S., Souza, R., and Van Ommeren, M. (2011). Mental health and psychosocial support in humanitarian settings: linking practice and research. *The Lancet*, 378 (9802): 1581–1591.

White, G. M. (1992). Ethnopsychology. In C. Lutz, G. M. White and T. Schwartz (eds.), *New Directions in Psychological Anthropology*, pp. 21–46. New York: Cambridge University Press.

Widger, T. (2012). Suffering, frustration, and anger: class, gender and history in Sri Lankan suicide stories. *Culture, Medicine, and Psychiatry*, 36 (2): 225–244.

Worthman, C. M., and Kohrt, B. (2005). Receding horizons of health: biocultural approaches to public health paradoxes. *Social Science and Medicine*, 61: 861–878.

Zhang, J., Wieczorek, W. F., Conwell, Y., and Tu, X.M. (2011). Psychological strains and youth suicide in rural China. *Social Science and Medicine*, 72 (12): 2003–2010.

# Index

Note: Italicized page numbers indicate illustrations.

# Contributors

## Eileen Anderson-Fye, EdD

Eileen Anderson-Fye is a psychological and medical anthropologist. She is the Robson Associate Professor of Anthropology at Case Western Reserve University, adjunct associate professor of psychiatry at Case School of Medicine, and assistant research anthropologist at the University of California at Los Angeles. Trained in a multidisciplinary program of human development and anthropology at Harvard, Anderson-Fye conducts research on adolescent well-being in contexts of rapid cultural change. She has worked in Belize for 19 years, conducting longitudinal studies on the region's first cohort of secondary-educated young women. This research examines the roles of gender, education, globalization, and subjective meaning-making on outcomes related to personal well-being and societal change. Anderson-Fye also leads a cross-cultural comparative multi-method project on Global Obesity Stigma among youth in seven countries. In addition, she has authored a forthcoming book regarding a longitudinal study of college student psychiatric medication usage in North America. Her work has received funding from the National Science Foundation, National Institutes of Health, Spencer Foundation, Woodrow Wilson Foundation, Social Science Research Council, Rockefeller Center for Latin American Studies, and the Foundation for Psychocultural Research, among others. She has published widely in anthropology, psychiatry, psychology, social work, and education. She also has won her university's highest awards for teaching and mentoring, and frequently consults with schools and foundations to design, implement, and assess adolescent mental health interventions. Anderson-Fye serves on the boards of the Foundation for Applied Psychiatric Anthropology and the national Center for Research on Girls. She is also a consulting editor for *Culture, Medicine, and Psychiatry*.

## Alexandra Brewis, PhD

Alexandra Brewis is a President's Professor at Arizona State University. Trained in medical anthropology, human biology, and demography, she received her PhD from the University of Arizona in 1992. Her broad program of research explores how culture shapes the human body in the contexts of such massive, uncertain, and dynamic processes as climate change, growing social inequalities, urbanization, and globalization, and she has conducted long-term field-based projects in Micronesia, Polynesia, Mexico, and the United States. Currently she is doing comparative research in a number of countries on topics that can help illuminate how unfairness—social inequities, discrimination, and stigma—create ill health for millions around the globe. Her recent publications include *Obesity: Cultural and Biocultural Perspectives* (Rutgers University Press).

## Peter J. Brown, PhD

Peter J. Brown, a medical anthropologist, has been a professor of anthropology and global health at Emory University since 1978. Brown's long-standing research interest is in culture and health—particularly with the infectious disease malaria and chronic diseases related to obesity. Actively involved in the university's strategic planning in global health, he serves as senior academic adviser for the Emory Global Health Institute. Past positions include editor-in-chief of the journal *Medical Anthropology*, president of the General Division of the American Anthropological Association, and director of the Center for Health, Culture, and Society at Emory. Brown's passion is teaching and he has edited or coedited three textbooks: two for introductory courses (*Applying Anthropology* and *Applying Cultural Anthropology*) and the most commonly used reader in medical anthropology (*Understanding and Applying Medical Anthropology*). Over the years, he has won several teaching awards at Emory as well as from the American Anthropological Association and Society for Medical Anthropology. Brown is extremely proud of the two dozen doctoral students he has worked with and who have completed the PhD program since 1989; he is currently working with a dozen graduate students. In 2007, he designed and became director of an undergraduate minor program: Global Health, Culture and Society at Emory College.

## Jose B. Rosales Chavez, PhD/MPH candidate

Jose B. Rosales Chavez is a Gates Millennium, Leadership Alliance and McNair Scholar graduate student working on his PhD in global health at Arizona State University and an MPH in nutrition from the University of Minnesota. His area of interest is nutrition, food access, obesity, and health disparities. He would like to develop community-based participatory research studies that help address disparities in health using a social justice approach. Upon completion of his graduate degrees, he would like to work for the federal or state government's department of health and continue to do research and implement effective interventions.

## Nadia El-Shaarawi, PhD, MPH

Nadia El-Shaarawi is the Global Migration Postdoctoral Fellow at the Kenan Institute for Ethics at Duke University. Her research interests in medical and psychological anthropology focus on forced migration, mental health, and humanitarian intervention in North Africa and the Middle East. She received her PhD in anthropology from Case Western Reserve University in 2012 and her MPH with a concentration in international health in 2009. Her dissertation research was a study of mental health, urban displacement, and the process of resettlement among Iraqi refugees in Cairo, Egypt.

## Erin P. Finley, PhD, MPH

Erin P. Finley is a research investigator with the South Texas Veterans Health Care System and assistant professor in the Division of Hospital Medicine, Department of Medicine, and the Department of Psychiatry at the South Texas Veterans Health Care System; she is also an adjunct assistant professor with the Division of Clinical Epidemiology, Department of Medicine, at the University of Texas Health Science Center at San Antonio. Finley is a medical anthropologist who has worked extensively in clinical and public health settings. Her research has explored the impact of stress and violence on physical and mental health in the United States and abroad. In 2011, she published *Fields of Combat: Understanding PTSD among Veterans of Iraq and Afghanistan* (Cornell University Press); it garnered the Margaret Mead Award in 2012. Her research interests include PTSD and related comorbidities, access to care, and the implementation of evidence-based treatments in inpatient and outpatient health care settings.

## Sarah Fishleder, MA, MPH, CPH

Sarah Fishleder is pursuing her PhD in anthropology at the University of South Florida, having already completed her MA in applied biocultural medical anthropology and an MPH in epidemiology. Her master's research focused on drug use, adolescents, and Colombia. She has worked as the project manager on a health assessment of older adults in The Villages, a community of about 90,000 older adults in South Florida. The research project at The Villages constitutes the largest single comprehensive health assessment of older adults ever undertaken at one time.

## Jack R. Friedman, PhD

Jack R. Friedman received his PhD in cultural anthropology from Duke University. His doctoral research—conducted during 34 months of fieldwork—examined anxiety and political economy among an increasingly downwardly mobile population of coal miners in Romania's Jiu Valley. Following the completion of his PhD, he received two NIMH-funded postdoctoral fellowships. He was an NIMH "Culture and Mental Health" Fellow in the University of Chicago's Department of Comparative Human Development, where he received training and conducted research on mental illness in Chicago. This fellowship led to a further 14 months of fieldwork in Romania, exploring the changing face of psychiatric care and the changing meanings—personal and public—of mental illness in post-socialist Romania. His second postdoctoral fellowship was in the Department of Psychiatry at the University of California, Los Angeles, where he was the lead anthropological researcher on an NIMH-funded, R01 project examining the implementation of the Recovery Model of Care in public mental health clinics in southern California. Friedman is currently a research scientist in the Center for Applied Social Research at the University of Oklahoma, Norman, where he has conducted research on rural mental health care in primary care settings in Oklahoma. In addition to his continuing research in Romania, Friedman's most recent research examines (1) the experience of cancer among Native Americans in Oklahoma and (2) the development of useful psychiatric and psycho-cultural tools for accounting for the stress associated with climate change and severe weather and drought conditions in communities throughout rural and urban Oklahoma.

## Charu L. Jaiswal

Charu Jaiswal recently completed her undergraduate degree in biology at York University in Canada. She is also a filmmaker, having produced a documentary web series for National Geographic and the Fulbright Foundation about the importance of subsistence hunting and gathering for the food security and culture of indigenous Alaskans. She has won awards for her leadership and entrepreneurship, including being selected to shadow the CEO of GE Canada.

## Reverend Bill Jallah

Reverend Bill Jallah is a social entrepreneur and advocate for persons living with mental illness, and supports youth affected by poverty and armed conflict. He earned his bachelor's degree in biblical studies in 1989 from the African Bible College in Nimba County, Liberia. He previously worked for Save the Children Liberia. Reverend Jallah worked as a broadcast journalist at Radio ELWA from 1981 to 1985, the only Christian Radio at the time in Liberia. He established the Living Faith Academy in Bentol City, Liberia, and the Paynesville Christian Academy, now named the Hunger Pillar Mission Academy. He is a specialist in poultry management and has worked with 4H-Liberia. He has been an advisor and trainer with The Carter Center Liberia Mental Health Initiative.

### Bonnie N. Kaiser, PhD, MPH

Bonnie N. Kaiser completed her PhD in anthropology and MPH in epidemiology at Emory University. Her dissertation explores experiences of mental health and illness in Haiti's Central Plateau, with a focus on resilience and coping. In particular, she investigates how perceptions and experiences of the social and spirit worlds affect mental health. Her previous publications from her work in Haiti have focused on idioms of distress and mental health communication, development and testing of transcultural screening tools, development of training programs, and treatment resources and decision making. Previously, she worked in coastal Kenya, exploring the impact of food insecurity on treatment decision-making among people living with HIV.

### Ippolytos Kalofonos, MD, PhD, MPH

Ippolytos Kalofonos is a medical anthropologist and a psychiatrist. He has conducted an ethnography on the implementation of global AIDS treatment interventions in Central Mozambique. His book manuscript, entitled "'All I Eat is ARVs': Therapeutic Congregations and the AIDS Economy in Central Mozambique," looks at how these interventions framed care as a biological intervention, bracketing out "social" problems and exacerbating local dynamics of exclusion and inequality. He has also worked in northeastern Brazil on leptospirosis epidemics, on the U.S.–Mexico border on access to prenatal care, and in Alaska looking at a peer-based, phenomenological approach to treating psychosis. He is currently a Robert Wood Johnson Foundation Clinical Scholar at the University of California, Los Angeles. He was a Minority Leadership Fellow with the American Psychiatric Association from 2012 to 2014. His research has been honored by the Virchow prize from the Critical Anthropology of Global Health Caucus and the Charles Hughes Prize from the Society for Medical Anthropology, and has appeared in *Medical Anthropology Quarterly, Social Science and Medicine, Global Public Health,* and *American Journal of Public Health.*

### Hunter Keys, MSN, MPH

Hunter Keys completed a master's in nursing (MSN) and master's in public health (MPH) at Emory University, with specializations as an emergency nurse practitioner and in global environmental health. As a graduate student, he undertook fieldwork in both Haiti and the Dominican Republic, where he examined mental health and forms of stigma and discrimination. He currently works as an emergency nurse practitioner in rural Georgia.

## Anne Kohler

Anne Kohler is a doctoral student in medical anthropology at the University of Connecticut. Her research explores how categories of "ability" and "disability" are cast as political identities or medical problems. She is particularly interested in adoption and Down syndrome, with a focus on religious families in the United States who adopt children with Down syndrome and other disabilities from institutional care settings. Her other research interests include visual narratives of disability and the anthropology of genetic difference.

## Brandon A. Kohrt, MD, PhD

Brandon Kohrt is a medical anthropologist and psychiatrist. He is assistant professor of global health and psychiatry at Duke University. He conducts global mental health research focusing on populations affected by war-related trauma and chronic stressors of poverty, discrimination, and lack of access to health care and education. He has worked in Nepal for 16 years using a biocultural developmental perspective integrating epidemiology, cultural anthropology, ethnopsychology, and neuroendocrinology. With Transcultural Psychosocial Organization (TPO) Nepal, he designed and evaluated psychosocial reintegration packages for child soldiers in Nepal. He currently works with The Carter Center Mental Health Liberia Program, developing anti-stigma campaigns and family psychoeducation programs. He was a Laughlin Fellow of the American College of Psychiatrists and a John Spiegel Fellow of the Society for the Study of Psychiatry and Culture (SSPC). Dr. Kohrt has contributed to numerous documentary films, including *Returned: Child Soldiers of Nepal's Maoist Army*.

## Daniel H. Lende, PhD

Daniel Lende is associate professor of anthropology at the University of South Florida. He has played a leading role in developing the new field of neuroanthropology. He co-runs the Public Library of Science Neuroanthropology blog, and was coeditor of the 2012 volume, *The Encultured Brain: An Introduction to Neuroanthropology* (MIT). He has published extensively on addiction, including articles in *Addiction*, *Addiction Research and Theory*, and *Ethos*. He has done mixed-methods research in both Colombia and the United States on alcohol and drug abuse.

## Kenneth Maes, PhD

Kenneth Maes is an assistant professor of anthropology at Oregon State University's School of Language, Culture and Society. He joined OSU in 2012 after receiving his PhD from Emory University and completing a postdoctoral fellowship at Brown University's Population Studies and Training Center. His research and advocacy centers on the roles of community health workers, with a focus on Ethiopia and Oregon. He has studied the interplay of unemployment, food insecurity, HIV/AIDS, and psychological distress in Ethiopia's capital; water insecurity and maternal and newborn survival in Ethiopia's agrarian highlands; and the eradication of polio in Ethiopia's southwestern borderlands. He has published research and commentaries in *Social Science and Medicine, The Bulletin of the World Health Organization, The American Journal of Public Health, Health Policy and Planning*, and *The Journal of Nutrition*.

### Daniel Mains, PhD

Daniel Mains is Wick Cary Assistant Professor of Honors at the University of Oklahoma. He holds a PhD in anthropology from Emory University. Mains's book, *Hope is Cut: Youth, Unemployment, and the Future in Urban Ethiopia* (2012, Temple University Press), examines young men's struggles to attain their aspirations in a context of extremely high rates of urban unemployment. Mains also has worked on a collaborative project examining the relationship between aspirations and mental health among youth in urban and rural Ethiopia. He was a Fulbright Fellow in Hawassa, Ethiopia (2013–2014), where he conducted research concerning the cultural and political dynamics of urban infrastructural development.

### Kristen E. McLean, MPH

Kristen McLean is a PhD student at Yale University studying medical anthropology and global health. She received her MPH from Emory University in 2012 with a concentration in mental health. Her research interests lie in the arena of global mental health, with a focus on post-conflict settings and the role of parenting in mediating stress responses in children. She is currently working on a study in rural Sierra Leone to understand how men raise their children in the aftermath of conflict, and the impact of father engagement on family dynamics and child well-being. Previously she has worked in Liberia, on mental health stigma, and in Haiti, on the development of a task-sharing mental health intervention.

### Emily Mendenhall, PhD, MPH

Emily Mendenhall is a medical anthropologist and assistant professor of global health in the Science, Technology, and International Affairs (STIA) Program at Georgetown University's School of Foreign Service. She has conducted cross-cultural research on the syndemics of poverty, depression, and diabetes in vulnerable populations residing in urban India, Kenya, South Africa, and the United States. This research culminated in a book entitled *Syndemic Suffering: Social Distress, Depression, and Diabetes among Mexican Immigrant Women* (2012) and several peer-reviewed journal articles. More recently, she was a visiting research fellow at the Center for Global Mental Health at the London School of Hygiene and Tropical Medicine. She also edited three volumes of stories about global health inequity as founding director of a nonprofit dedicated to developing global health education: *Global Health Narratives* (2009), *Environmental Health Narratives* (2012), and *Community Health Narratives* (2015).

### Neely Anne Laurenzo Myers, PhD

Neely Myers is an assistant professor of anthropology at Southern Methodist University (SMU). She is a sociocultural anthropologist working at the intersections of medical and psychiatric anthropology among underserved people in low-resource settings in the United States and in East Africa. Her current research investigates ethnographically decision-making for young people with early psychosis after an initial hospitalization. Her interests lie at the crossroads of culture, gender, global mental health, madness, trauma, neuroanthropology, health disparities, and social justice. Myers has taught courses at SMU, the University of Chicago, and the George Washington University. Her new book, tentatively titled *Recovery's Edge: An Ethnography of Mental Illness, Moral Agency and Mental Health Care*, is expected from Vanderbilt University Press in 2015. *Recovery's Edge* is based on three years of ethnographic research on people's efforts to achieve "recovery" from serious emotional distress as participants in America's public mental health care system. She has also published articles in *Culture, Medicine, and Psychiatry; Alternative Therapies in Clinical Practice; Psychiatry Research; Schizophrenia Research; Clinical Schizophrenia and Related Psychoses; Psychiatric Services; Annals of Anthropological Practice*; and *Current Psychiatry Reports*. Her work has been funded by the National Center for Complementary and Alternative Medicine, the National Institute of Mental Health, and the Elliott School of International Affairs' Institute of Global and International Studies at the George Washington University. She is an elected member (2013–2016) of the American Anthropological Association's Committee on Ethics. Myers is also part of the editorial board at Somatosphere (www.somatosphere.net) and the co-founder of the website www.globalpublicpsychiatry.net.

### Vikram Patel, MSc, MRCPsych, PhD, FMedSci

Vikram Patel is a psychiatrist with a primary interest in global mental health. Dr. Patel serves as joint director of the Centre for Global Mental Health, a partnership of the London School of Hygiee and Tropical Medicine with Kings Health Partners (www.centreforglobalmentalhealth.org), and joint director of the Centre for Chronic Conditions and Injuries at the Public Health Foundation of India. He has been funded by a Wellcome Trust–supported Senior Research Fellow in Clinical Medicine since 2005, and additionally has led projects supported by the

NIMH, Department for International Development (UK), Autism Speaks, and the Sir Jamsetji Tata Trust. He has lived and worked in Zimbabwe (1993–1995) and India (since 1996) building a program of research and capacity building, with the goal of improving mental health care in India and other low- and middle-income countries. His major accomplishments include (1) co-founding Sangath (www.sangath.com), an NGO in India that won the MacArthur Foundation's International Prize in 2008 and is a pioneer of task-sharing for mental health care to primary care and community-based workers; (2) serving as an editor of several influential journal series on global mental health (*The Lancet* 2007, 2011, and *PLoS Medicine* 2009, 2012) and editor of two recent Oxford University Press textbooks on global mental health; (3) being a founding member of the Movement for Global Mental Health (www.globalmentalhealth.org), a global coalition of professionals and civil society working together to improve the lives of people affected by mental illness; (4) leading efforts to identify research priorities in global mental health, most recently as the co-chair of the Grand Challenges in Global Mental Health (www.grandchallengesgmh.nimh.nih.gov); and (5) writing "Where There Is No Psychiatrist," a mental health care manual for nonspecialist health workers, which is widely used in developing countries. He has led the development of a number of capacity-building programs in global mental health, including the Leadership in Mental Health course in India and the Master's in Global Mental Health in the United Kingdom, and engages with policy makers at international (e.g., WHO) and national levels (notably with the Government of India).

## Jeffrey G. Snodgrass, PhD

Jeffrey Snodgrass is professor of anthropology at Colorado State University, and has published widely on caste, ritual performance, spirit possession, and religious healing in India. He is the recipient of grants from the American Institute of Indian Studies, the National Endowment for the Humanities, the Spencer Foundation, the National Geographic Society, and the National Science Foundation. He is currently examining how the health and healing practices of tribal communities in Madhya Pradesh are being impacted by environmental changes and new conservation initiatives. In addition to his work in India, Snodgrass is interested in better understanding the therapeutic and addictive dimensions of "virtual worlds." He hopes to use this online gaming research, combined with findings from his ongoing study of religion and health resilience in Indian indigenous contexts, to refine "biopsychocultural" accounts of the health dynamics of stress and relaxation.

## Sarah S. Willen, PhD, MPH

Sarah Willen is assistant professor of anthropology at the University of Connecticut, where she is also director of the Research Program on Global Health and Human Rights at the Human Rights Institute. A medical and sociocultural anthropologist, she has conducted ethnographic research on a range of topics, including the illegalization and criminalization of African and Asian migrant workers in Israel, Israeli health and human rights activism on behalf of illegalized migrants, invocations of health and human rights in the United States, and efforts to render cultural competence "teachable" and "learnable" in U.S. medical education. An alumna of Emory University and former NIMH postdoctoral fellow at Harvard Medical School, she has taught at Emory, Harvard, and Southern Methodist Universities, and at the University of Connecticut. Willen has authored over 25 articles and book chapters and edited or coedited seven volumes, including *Shattering Culture: American Medicine Responds to Cultural Diversity* (Russell Sage, 2010) and special issues of *Culture, Medicine, and Psychiatry* (2013), *Social Science and Medicine* (2012), *Ethos* (2012), and *International Migration* (2007). In 2010, she was elected to serve on the executive board of the Society for Medical Anthropology.

### Amber Wutich, PhD

Amber Wutich is an associate professor of anthropology at Arizona State University's School for Human Evolution and Social Change. She holds affiliate appointments at the Center for Global Health, Global Institute for Sustainability, and Center for the Study of Institutional Diversity at ASU. Wutich received her PhD from the University of Florida in cultural anthropology, with a specialization in tropical conservation and development. She was a postdoctoral scholar in the National Science Foundation's Long-Term Ecological Research Program in Central Arizona-Phoenix. Her research examines the limits of human adaptability to resource scarcity and insecurity, with a particular emphasis on water, in Bolivia, Paraguay, and the United States. She directs the Global Ethnohydrology Study, a multi-year, multi-site study designed to examine cross-cultural knowledge of water and climate in 10 countries. She has published in *Social Science and Medicine, American Journal of Public Health, American Journal of Human Biology,* and *Medical Anthropology Quarterly.* She also serves as associate editor of the journal *Field Methods* and teaches qualitative analysis as part of the National Science Foundation's programs in research methods for cultural anthropology.

### Kristin Yarris, PhD, MA, MPH

Kristin Yarris is assistant professor of international studies at the University of Oregon. A medical anthropologist, Yarris's research focuses on the social determinants and cultural meanings of health, mental health, mental illness, and emotional distress. She is currently completing a book manuscript based on her research with Nicaraguan transnational families titled "Caring across Generations:

Grandmothers and Nicaraguan Transnational Families." She is also a faculty mentor for the University of Southern California's Latino Mental Health Research and Training Program (MHIRT). Her work has appeared in *Ethos: The Journal of Psychological Anthropology*; *Culture, Medicine, and Psychiatry*; *International Migration*; and *The Journal of Latin American and Caribbean Anthropology*. She teaches courses in global health and development, migration and health, global reproductive health, and gender and transnational migration. She received her PhD in sociocultural anthropology (2011) and her MPH (community health sciences, 2004) and MA in Latin American studies (2004) from UCLA.